I0814746

THE SECOND MANASSAS CAMPAIGN

MILITARY CAMPAIGNS OF THE CIVIL WAR

Volumes in the Military Campaigns of the Civil War series feature insightful original essays by leading scholars and public historians. Taking advantage of recent scholarship and drawing on the full range of primary sources, contributors to the series reexamine common assumptions about pivotal campaigns, the experiences of major figures and common soldiers involved in the fighting, the connection between strategy and tactics on the ground, and the political and social ramifications of battles on the respective home fronts. The series offers an ideal introduction to key ideas and debates in Civil War history.

A complete list of books published in Military Campaigns of the Civil War is available at https://uncpress.org/series/military-campaigns-civil-war.

THE SECOND MANASSAS CAMPAIGN

EDITED BY

CAROLINE E. JANNEY

AND

KATHRYN J. SHIVELY

THE UNIVERSITY OF NORTH CAROLINA PRESS

Chapel Hill

Designed by Jamison Cockerham
Set in Arno, Irby, Cutright, and Scala Sans
by codeMantra

Cover art: Engraving of the Second Battle of Bull Run, August 1862. © IStock.

Manufactured in the United States of America

LIBRARY OF CONGRESS CATALOGING-IN-PUBLICATION DATA
Names: Shively, Kathryn J., editor | Janney, Caroline E., editor.
Title: The Second Manassas Campaign / edited by
Caroline E. Janney, Kathryn J. Shively.
Description: Chapel Hill : The University of North Carolina Press, [2025] |
Series: Military Campaigns of the Civil War |
Includes bibliographical references and index.
Identifiers: LCCN 2024047415 | ISBN 9781469685366 (cloth) |
ISBN 9781469683782 (epub) | ISBN 9781469687865 (pdf)
Subjects: LCSH: Bull Run, 2nd Battle of, Va., 1862. | Virginia—History—Civil War, 1861–1865. | Pope, John, 1822–1892—Military leadership. | Porter, Fitz-John, 1822–1901—Military leadership. | Lee, Robert E. (Robert Edward), 1807–1870—Military leadership. | BISAC: HISTORY / United States / Civil War Period (1850–1877) | HISTORY / Military / General
Classification: LCC E473.77 .S433 2025 | DDC 973.7/32—c23/eng/20241023
LC record available at https://lccn.loc.gov/2024047415

CONTENTS

List of Illustrations
vii

INTRODUCTION
Caroline E. Janney and Kathryn J. Shively
1

MANAGEMENT MOST WRETCHED: LOGISTICAL SELF-DESTRUCTION IN THE ARMY OF VIRGINIA
Kathryn J. Shively
14

THE ARMY OF VIRGINIA CONFRONTS THE "MORAL SPECTACLE" OF FREEDOM
John J. Hennessy
36

THE TIDE OF WAR HAS BEEN ROLLED BACK: SECOND MANASSAS IN CONFEDERATE PERSPECTIVE
Gary W. Gallagher
65

GENERAL POPE GOES TO WASHINGTON: RADICAL REPUBLICANS AND THE FAILED HOPE OF THE SECOND BULL RUN CAMPAIGN
Cecily Zander
97

SHAKE YANKEEDOM TO ITS CENTRE: ROBERT E. LEE AND THE MAKING OF CONFEDERATE STRATEGY IN THE SECOND MANASSAS CAMPAIGN
Peter C. Luebke
124

THE BATTLE FOR WHICH WE HAD SO LONG BEEN YEARNING: THE 6TH WISCONSIN AT BRAWNER FARM
James Marten
145

AS AMBITIOUS AS HE WAS BRAVE AND DARING: GENERAL JOHN BELL HOOD AT THE BATTLE OF SECOND MANASSAS
Keith S. Bohannon
168

A CARNIVAL OF HYPOCRISY: THE ORDEAL OF FITZ JOHN PORTER
William Marvel
190

A NATIONAL DISGRACE: THE BATTLE TO PROTECT THE BULL RUN MONUMENTS
Caroline E. Janney
218

Bibliographic Essay
243

Index
253

ILLUSTRATIONS

FIGURES

Starke's brigade of Louisianians
throwing rocks at Deep Cut
8

Retreat of Pope's army
24

Formerly enslaved people crossing the Rappahannock
57

Confederate reaction to Pope's orders
83

Maj. Gen. John Pope
99

Lee pushing Pope's army deep into Northern Virginia
138

The Battle of Gainesville, Va., Aug. 28, 1862
156

Brig. Gen. John Bell Hood
172

Maj. Gen. Fitz John Porter
192

Dedication of the Bull Run monument
on Henry Hill, June 11, 1865
221

MAPS

Strategic overview of Second Manassas campaign
x

Second Manassas campaign, August 26–28, 1862
154

Hood's attack at Second Manassas, August 30, 1862
176

THE SECOND MANASSAS CAMPAIGN

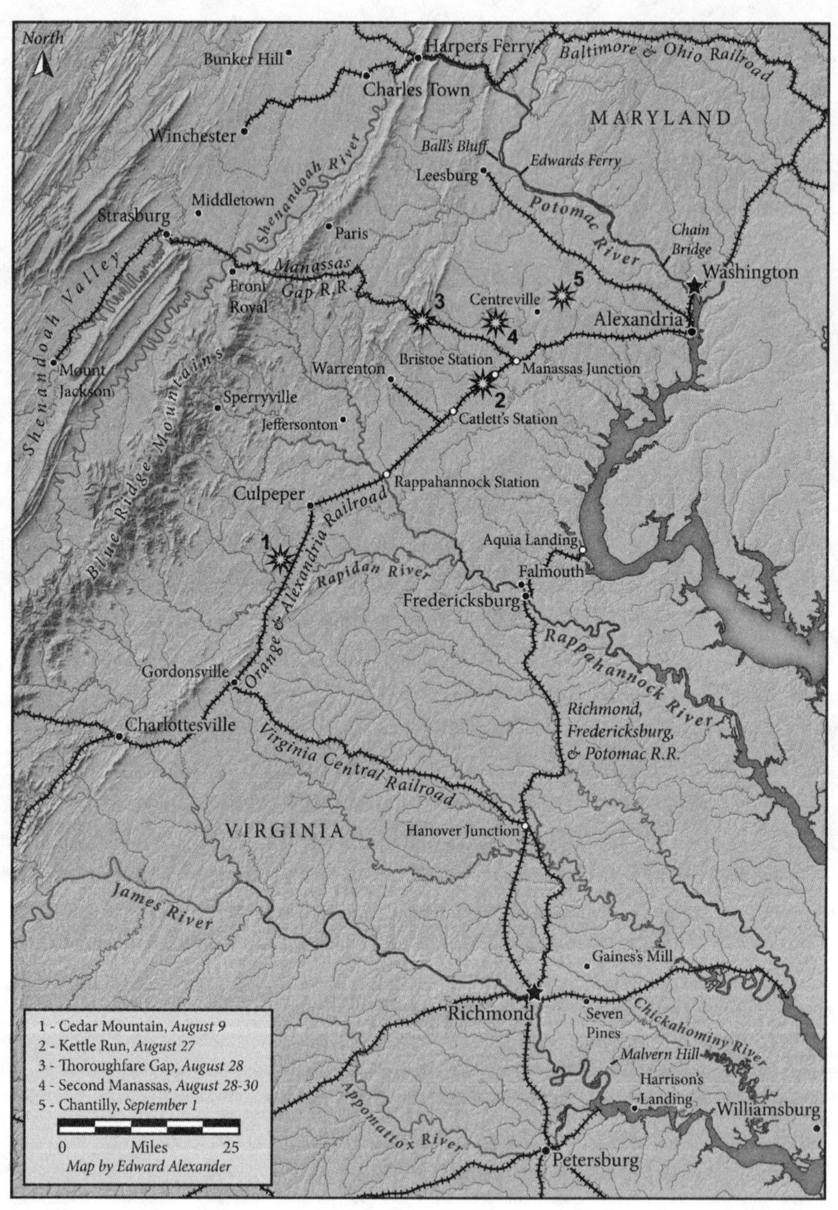

Strategic overview of Second Manassas campaign

INTRODUCTION

CAROLINE E. JANNEY AND KATHRYN J. SHIVELY

In 1863, editor of the *Richmond Examiner* Edward A. Pollard declared Second Manassas "the most decisive victory yet achieved" by Confederates in the Eastern Theater. Chronicling the war in his multivolume *Southern History of the War,* he observed "the rapid change in the fortunes of the Confederacy, and the sharp contrast between its last forlorn situation and what were now the brilliant promises of the future." Only three months had passed since the columns of a massive Union army had threatened the capital of Richmond—"since our armies were retreating weak and disorganized before the overwhelming force of the enemy." But Second Manassas had changed the tide. "Now," he marveled, "we were advancing with increased numbers, improved organization, renewed courage, and the prestige of victory, upon an enemy defeated and disheartened." In the campaign's aftermath, the Confederacy had proven "more invincible in spirit than ever."[1]

Even those writing in the immediate wake of the campaign charted the rapid transformation in the US Army's fortunes. Taking to her diary on August 31, 1862, the day after the climactic battle of Second Manassas, twenty-year-old Confederate Lucy Buck reflected on all that had changed in the past six months. In the early days of the summer, "we saw nothing but disaster and destruction before us," she recalled. Southern ports and cities had been occupied, ironclad boats swarmed the coast, and Richmond faced an exultant US Army flush with victory. "Our army seemed to have melted away or were within the coils of a mighty serpent that must soon crush them—oh it was all so disheartening enough! —and I have wondered how we ever struggled through such depths of gloom," she remembered. "But the day I trust has gone on our midnight."[2] Writing to his daughter a week later, Union brigadier general Alpheus S. Williams, whose division fought in portions of the Second Bull Run campaign, likewise lamented the changing course of events. "Instead of hopeful and confident feelings we are all depressed with losses and disasters," he confessed. "Instead of an offensive position the enemy is now in Maryland and we are on the defensive. What a change!" But for Williams and other Union loyalists, the second loss at Manassas proved more than a setback; it offered a dire warning: "If we fail now" he cautioned his daughter, "the North has no hope, no safety that I can see. We have thrown away our power and prestige. We may become the supplicant instead of the avenger."[3]

Both Unionists and Confederates pointed to the pivotal role that the battle, called Second Manassas in the Confederacy and Second Bull Run in the United States, and its larger campaign played in the momentum and morale of both sides. Though its parameters are debatable, the Second Manassas campaign reasonably began when Maj. Gen. John Pope took command of the newly created Army of Virginia on June 26, 1862, included the battle of Cedar Mountain on August 9, and concluded following the battle of Chantilly on September 1, when Gen. Robert E. Lee forded the Potomac River and marched into Maryland on September 5. The climactic battle of the campaign saw three days of fighting on the plains of Manassas between August 28 and 30, when some 63,000 Union troops collided with 54,000 Confederates, resulting in nearly 24,000 casualties, making it the largest battle in the Eastern Theater to that date and one of the ten largest of the war.[4]

Despite its significance in the summer of 1862, the campaign has been neglected. Compared with other major battles and campaigns, there are relatively few books on Second Manassas (for more on these titles, see the Bibliographic Essay). But why has the battle of Second Bull Run and its campaign received such scant attention from public and academic historians? Perhaps as John J. Hennessy has suggested, it is because Second Manassas was neither a beginning nor an end. Instead, it was stuck in the middle, between the well-studied Peninsula and Maryland campaigns.[5] While it garnered a great deal of attention in late August 1862, memories of its effect on morale and momentum faded. The Peninsula campaign afforded a narrative of Lee's rise to command, his christening of the Army of Northern Virginia, and the consequential Seven Days' battles (June 25–July 1), which pushed back Maj. Gen. George B. McClellan's mighty Army of the Potomac from the gates of Richmond to the banks of the James River, securing the Confederate capital and Lee's renown. The failure to capture Richmond prompted President Abraham Lincoln's new resolve to issue executive emancipation when the opportunity afforded. Antietam, alternatively, showcased Lee's failure to capitalize on his first invasion of the North. Combined with its legacy as the bloodiest single day of the war and Lincoln's subsequent issuance of the preliminary emancipation proclamation, Antietam took its place as one of the most noteworthy battles of the war. Second Manassas became merely a footnote within that trajectory.

But the Second Manassas campaign deserves its own serious scholarship. As the essays that follow collectively argue, the campaign proved one in which policy and politics critically intermixed with military operations. By pausing to concentrate on this campaign—without jumping ahead to Antietam—we can better understand this interplay. For example, we see how repeated Union battlefield defeats not only hurt morale within the ranks but also shaped the degree to which politicians would or could intervene. A deep dive into this crucial period reveals the motivations for Union policy toward rebel civilians and enslaved people and, ultimately, the timing of the preliminary emancipation proclamation. It highlights the internal discord among Union high command, why Lincoln struggled to secure suitable military leadership to combat Lee, and why Lincoln felt compelled to return to McClellan when the campaign failed. It also explains the timing of Lee's foray into the North during the Maryland campaign, as his army rode the rising tide of Confederate victories.

A few words on terminology are in order. First, we have elected to use both names of the battle: Second Bull Run (when discussing the US perspective) and Second Manassas (when providing the Confederate perspective). Second, we employ the phrase Second Manassas or Second Bull Run to describe both the campaign and the culminating battle within that campaign. Third, although James Marten's essay in this collection and some Union veterans described the fighting on August 28 alternatively as the battle of Gainesville, Brawner Farm, or Groveton, we define the battle of Second Manassas to include the fighting from August 28 to August 30.

The basic outline of this campaign is well-known to many students of the Civil War.

By late June 1862, Lincoln was growing increasingly frustrated with the war in the Eastern Theater and with his principal general, George B.

McClellan. Not only had McClellan's Army of the Potomac come within a few miles of capturing Richmond and then failed to do so, but from March to early June, an outnumbered Confederate force under Maj. Gen. Thomas "Stonewall" Jackson had defeated three separate Union commands in the Shenandoah Valley.

On June 26, Lincoln sought to address both problems by forming the Army of Virginia out of the fragmented forces in the Shenandoah Valley and Fredericksburg area. To lead this new force, Lincoln selected John Pope, a forty-year-old West Pointer who had demonstrated great skill with a series of victories in the Western Theater. Perhaps most importantly, unlike the Democrat McClellan, who reluctantly implemented the Republican program of confiscation, resisted emancipation, and was painfully secretive about his military plans, the Republican-leaning Pope could transfer his aggressive interpretation of confiscation and punishment of meddlesome Confederate civilians from West to East. Pope did exactly that with his famous general orders of July and August 1862, but he did not directly address African Americans and emancipation.

Pope's Army of Virginia was tasked with protecting Washington and operating northwest of Richmond, thereby taking pressure off McClellan's Army of the Potomac, which faced Lee's army outside of Richmond. While watching McClellan with Maj. Gen. James Longstreet's divisions of the Army of Northern Virginia, Lee sent Stonewall Jackson's wing across the Rapidan River on July 13 to counter Pope's movements in north-central Virginia and protect the railroad junction at Gordonsville. On August 9 at the battle of Cedar Mountain, nearly 17,000 Confederates under Jackson punished Maj. Gen. Nathaniel Banks's corps of 8,000 Federals. The armies remained in place until August 11, when Jackson strategically withdrew from the field, as Pope consolidated his troops at Culpeper.

Lee had been waiting for the right opportunity to shift the bulk of his force on the offensive and that moment had arrived, as the US troops stationed on the Peninsula reoriented away from Richmond to reinforce Pope. Maj. Gen. Ambrose Burnside's Ninth Corps disembarked in Fredericksburg beginning on August 3, and soon thereafter McClellan's Army of the Potomac began departing the Virginia Peninsula. On August 13 Lee sent Jackson around Pope's left with orders to disrupt US supply lines and cut off the Army of Virginia from its reinforcements. Lee then departed Richmond along with General Longstreet's wing with the hope of destroying Pope before Burnside's and McClellan's troops could add to his numbers. Yet before Lee could cross the Rapidan River and accordingly trap Pope in the triangle convergence of the Rapidan and Rappahannock Rivers, on August 18 Pope learned of Lee's advance via orders captured by the 1st Michigan Cavalry, who also nabbed Confederate cavalry commander Maj. Gen. J. E. B. Stuart's plumed hat. Pope withdrew behind the Rappahannock.

Stymied, Lee unsuccessfully probed Pope's flanks for several days, his attempted crossings inundated by torrential rains, until Stuart exacted his revenge by capturing crucial intelligence along with Pope's dress coat during a raid at Catlett's Station on August 22–23. Pope's purloined dispatch book revealed what Lee suspected, that McClellan would reinforce him and that Pope had been ordered to maintain his link to Aquia to receive these reinforcements, impairing his movement. Indeed, on August 22, Maj. Gen. Fitz John Porter's Fifth Corps of the Army of the Potomac began joining Pope's position, while on August 24, Maj. Gen. Samuel Heintzelman's Third Corps would arrive from Alexandria. Lee snatched his opportunity to break the stalemate before being outnumbered with a bold plan: he split his army, sending Jackson on a fifty-five-mile trek around Pope's right flank, cutting the US Army's main supply and communication line, the Orange & Alexandria Railroad, and then tracing the Manassas Gap Railroad through the Bull Run Mountains, on the easternmost front of the Blue Ridge Mountains, to strike at Pope's rear. Jackson's maneuver would be followed by Stuart's cavalry and then Longstreet's divisions, who would carefully supplant Jackson, providing the appearance of force along the Rappahannock. Unfortunately for Pope, he interpreted Jackson's sudden disappearance as a retreat to the Shenandoah Valley and remained in position with his men around Warrenton.

As reinforcements from the Army of the Potomac slowly made their way toward Pope under confused orders without proper guides, Jackson burst through Thoroughfare Gap, Gainesville, and Bristoe Station on August 26. At Bristoe Station, on the Orange & Alexandria Railroad, Confederate cavalry tore up track, cut telegraph wires, and ransacked three trains filled with supplies. A portion of Maj. Gen. Richard Ewell's division and Stuart's cavalry then progressed up the railroad to strike the Union supply depot at Manassas Junction, and on August 27, Jackson's main body enjoyed the fruits of the Union supply dump. As 21st Virginia Infantryman John Worsham remembered, the men had been hungry for three days. "Now here are vast storehouses filled with everything to eat . . . with all the delicacies, potted ham, lobster, tongue, candy, cakes, nuts, oranges, lemons, pickles, catsup, mustard." As his unit departed with orders to take four days' rations, one comrade "filled his haversack" with "nothing but French mustard."[6]

After this great feast and burning what supplies they had not consumed, the Confederates began trickling along various routes toward the village of Groveton near the old Manassas battlefield. Based on a rare consultation with his cavalry, Pope seized the moment. Believing Lee's divided army vulnerable, he abandoned his line along the Rappahannock on the morning of August 27 and ordered his 66,000 men toward Manassas Junction to "bag Jackson"—failing to account for the fact that Lee was moving northward with Longstreet's wing to reunite his army. Given Jackson's meandering route, Pope, now headquartered at Bristoe Station, haplessly debated the enemy's location and intentions, directing his troops to Gainesville, then Manassas, then Centreville. He failed to post troops at Gainesville and Thoroughfare Gap to block Longstreet's advance, though the Third Corps commander Maj. Gen. Irvin McDowell anticipated the threat and left his second division at Thoroughfare Gap under Brig. Gen. James B. Ricketts.[7]

On the evening of August 28, Jackson's troops, lying in wait in the woods along Warrenton Turnpike toward Centreville, caught Brig. Gen. Rufus King's division of McDowell's corps unaware and walloped King's men with artillery. King counterattacked at Brawner Farm, insensible to the fact that his single division faced Jackson's entire wing, but Jackson failed to rout the Union troops largely because of the stiff resistance of Brig. Gen. John Gibbon's brigade. Jackson also lost an important lieutenant when General Ewell was severely wounded in the leg, requiring amputation. Meanwhile, Ricketts's Second Division took a beating from Longstreet's advance at Thoroughfare Gap along both sides of the Manassas Gap Railroad and had to withdraw east. Neither McDowell nor Pope comprehended the importance of these engagements—that Jackson remained in force, now redeploying along the Manassas Gap Railroad, while Longstreet had an open path to join him—and redirected Ricketts to Bristoe Station and King to Manassas. Meanwhile, Pope ordered the First Corps commander, Maj. Gen. Franz Sigel, to the old Manassas battlefield to fix in place an allegedly retreating Jackson until the Army of Virginia could converge.

By the morning of August 29, Jackson had reorganized his troops behind an unfinished railroad cut on a front that ran nearly 3,000 yards defended by 20,000 Confederates. Pope, convinced he could destroy Jackson before Longstreet arrived, issued what would later be known as the joint order around 10:00 a.m. Based on the faulty premise that Jackson was retreating, Pope envisioned a plan by which the scattered corps of his army would simultaneously converge on Jackson in his front and along his vulnerable right flank, thereby cutting off an escape route via Thoroughfare Gap. Pope instructed McDowell and Porter, who accompanied McDowell with the Fifth Corps of the Army of the Potomac, to move toward Gainesville, where they would connect with the other commands and together roll up Jackson's right. But the joint order did not clearly convey Pope's intentions or directly order Porter and McDowell to attack. Instead, Pope's vague, qualifying language suggested that the corps commanders might use their best judgment and retreat if necessary. When McDowell and Porter learned that Longstreet was on his way and there would be no Confederate retreat, they used their own discretion, which proved to be utterly at odds with Pope's intentions. As William Marvel details in his essay, their decision would prove one of the most controversial of the campaign.

That morning only Sigel's corps managed to attack along Jackson's lines on the old Manassas battlefield, aided by meager reinforcements from Samuel Heintzelman's corps. Their efforts were ground to a halt when the vanguard of Longstreet's divisions arrived and began deploying artillery batteries along Jackson's right, astride the Warrenton Turnpike facing east. By noon, the line had been stretched three miles east and southeast, creating a pincer pointing directly at Pope's now exposed left flank. Lee, meeting with Longstreet and Jackson near Brawner Farm, wanted to strike immediately, but Longstreet advised caution. Reports from Stuart detailed a formidable Union force on the Gainesville-Manassas Road directly in front of Longstreet's line.[8]

Still convinced that Jackson's right flank remained exposed, Pope continued to confuse his subordinates, ordering Porter to attack on the right before changing his mind and recalling Porter to the main field. Pope arrived on the Manassas battlefield from Centreville around noon on August 29 and ordered a series of isolated attacks, first along the left and then along the entirety of Jackson's line, coming close to but failing to break the Confederates' position. By the end of the day Pope continued to ignore reports of Longstreet's presence (and by recalling Porter, ensured Longstreet's safe arrival). Once again, Pope interpreted Jackson's adjustments on his lines as evidence of an impending withdrawal.

The following day, August 30, brought a similar and even more dismaying scene for the Army of Virginia: Pope failed to press the Confederates in the morning and then ordered Porter to attack Jackson's right, despite Porter's warning that a large Confederate force (Longstreet's men) stood ready to flank him. Around 3:00 p.m. Porter reached the edge of the unfinished railroad cut and smashed into Jackson's line, rattling the Confederates, whose line threatened to buckle. With ammunition running low, Louisiana and Virginia soldiers picked up rocks and began hurling them at Federals on the

With ammunition running low, Brig. Gen. William A. Starke's brigade of Louisianians positioned along the Deep Cut picked up rocks and began lobbing them at the approaching Federals. (Robert Underwood Johnson and Clarence Clough Buel, *Battles and Leaders of the Civil War*, 4 vols. [New York: Century, 1884–88], 2:534)

east side of the railroad cut. Having borne the brunt of the battle for more than two days, Jackson's men were exhausted and struggling to keep up the fight. Longstreet stood ready to intervene and ordered a devastating artillery enfilade into the advancing Federals. As one New Yorker recalled, "Longstreet's batteries . . . were enfilading the approaching troops with solid shot, shell, and sections . . . which tore up the earth frightfully, and was death to any living thing that they might touch on their passage." Porter's men soon retreated, but Jackson's battered troops proved unable to mount a pursuit.[9]

Because Pope had ordered the majority of his troops off Chinn Ridge to support Porter, Lee and Longstreet concluded that now was the moment to launch what would prove one of the largest Confederate flanking attacks of the war: 28,000 men strong. Their goal was Henry Hill, the site that had earned Jackson his moniker of "Stonewall" in the previous year's battle. Control of this high ground might prevent a Federal retreat across Bull Run. With nearly two miles to cover and a terrain that included numerous small creeks, woods, and ridges, Longstreet recognized it was a formidable task and selected Brig. Gen. John Bell Hood's division to lead the assault. At 4:00 p.m., Hood's troops stepped off, smashing into the 10th and 5th New York, adorned in their Zouave uniforms on a wooded ridge. Battering the New Yorkers, Longstreet's men pressed forward. Pope had hastily ordered men back to Chinn Ridge, stalling Longstreet's columns long enough to establish a final line along Henry Hill. But by 5:00 p.m., the Confederates had swept the Federals off Chinn Ridge, allowing Longstreet's forces to surge forward toward the Manassas-Sudley Road. As night fell, the Confederate attack faltered. Just as McDowell had done little more than a year earlier, at 8:00 p.m. Pope ordered his army to retreat across Bull Run and reform at Centreville. After a brief, inconclusive aftershock at Chantilly on September 1, in which two Union generals, Brig. Gen. Isaac Stevens and Maj. Gen. Philip Kearny, were killed, Pope retreated to the defenses of Washington.[10] General McClellan assumed command of all Union forces around Washington on September 5, and the next day Pope was reassigned to Minnesota to suppress a Sioux uprising, virtually ending his Civil War career. Pope blamed Porter for defeat at Second Bull Run, and Porter was subsequently court-martialed and expelled from the army until an 1878 investigation exonerated him.

As with all previous volumes in the Military Campaigns of the Civil War series, *The Second Manassas Campaign* addresses disparate elements of the campaign. The volume does not provide a narrative of all the strategic and tactical action nor an analysis of all the important commanders. For detailed narratives of various parts of the fighting and biographies of leaders on both sides, readers should consult the bibliographical essay at the end of this book. These nine essays seek to illuminate specific aspects of the operations, highlight the interplay between military affairs and politics, explore army culture, and connect the battlefield with the home front. Some of the contributors bring new light to bear on familiar topics, while others explore less well-known aspects of the military picture in the summer of 1862. The essays do not purport to offer a single coherent argument or consensus on all aspects of the campaign; indeed, some of the essays come to different conclusions about similar topics. But together they help to explain why the campaign proved of crucial importance to both the Union and Confederate armies in 1862, even if that relevance has been largely forgotten.

The collection opens with Kathryn J. Shively's essay, which presents a major reason for US failure in the Second Bull Run campaign: logistical collapse. Neither the new commander of the Army of Virginia nor the new general-in-chief of the United States proved capable army administrators in the midst of the most complex logistical situation the Union had seen to date in the Eastern Theater. In contrast, and despite reproachable personal behavior during the campaign, McClellan's administrative skills shined, rendering him Lincoln's only suitable choice to repel Lee's subsequent invasion of Maryland. Shively also reinterprets Pope's famous general orders as less the harbinger of a unified Republican "hard war" policy and more the hapless commander's botched attempt to resolve logistical disorder, which Pope perceived as caused by his subordinates' lax discipline and Confederate civilian sabotage. Nevertheless, the political impacts of Pope's orders reverberated powerfully, as Pope's soldiers and Confederate leaders interpreted the edicts as license to plunder. More, not less, US logistical discord followed suit.

John J. Hennessy turns our attention to the attitudes and policies of the Union army toward enslaved people and emancipation while giving voice to enslaved people, who unflinchingly looked to the Army of Virginia for deliverance from bondage. Close interaction with civilian and enslaved populations sharpened Union soldiers' ideas about slavery, race, and the nature of the war. Indeed, the spring and summer of 1862 would prove pivotal in demonstrating to the men in Pope's army that the institution of slavery and Confederate resistance were intimately connected. Hennessy's essay is a reminder of how military history has (or at least ought to have) evolved in the last three decades. We simply cannot understand this campaign, or any other, without reckoning with the larger context of slavery, emancipation, and the experiences of civilians, white and Black, during the war.

Gary W. Gallagher's essay takes up the Confederate perspective, arguing that the Second Manassas campaign proved transformative for Lee, his army, and Confederate prosecution of the war for two reasons. First, it offered a testing ground for Lee and his new leadership style, which differed markedly from that of Joseph E. Johnston. By the time Lee crossed the Potomac into Maryland in early September, the Army of Northern Virginia had developed a culture of aggressiveness that would define the force for the remainder of the war. Second, Pope's orders, US policies about emancipation, and the actions of Union soldiers in Virginia convinced Confederates that, in their words, Federals had moved aggressively toward a more "brutal" and "savage" type of war. As Gallagher explains, "Any notion of brokering an end to the war that would restore the antebellum status quo largely disappeared in the summer of 1862."

The interplay between army leadership and war goals likewise played out on the Union side during the summer of 1862. Cecily Zander's essay returns to a discussion of Pope and his Army of Virginia, highlighting the deep ties between military and political dimensions of the war. A rare Republican among a sea of Democratic officers, Pope inspired high hopes among Republican congressional leaders. Testifying before Congress, Pope promised to fight an aggressive campaign, abandoning the culture of caution and conciliation fostered by the Democrat McClellan. But as Zander explains, in the end, Pope's bombastic boasting meant little. Unable to back up his threats with a battlefield victory, Lincoln removed him from command. Battlefield performance, not political loyalty, proved paramount.

Turning back to the Confederacy, Peter C. Luebke invites us to understand the Second Manassas campaign as the first true test of Lee's offensive strategy against the United States. Luebke begins with seldom-studied portions of Lee's field command in 1861 western Virginia and the winter of 1861–62 in the Department of South Carolina, Georgia, and East Florida. Through these experiences, Lee decided that "energetic marching and fighting" in the style of Frederick the Great would crush Northern morale. This, Lee posited, was the only way to defeat an enemy possessing superior manpower and matériel. The Second Manassas campaign, not the 1862 invasion of Maryland, was the culmination and debut of Lee's aggressive military strategy.

James Marten shifts the focus from an entire army to a single regiment: the 6th Wisconsin. Organized in the summer of 1861, the regiment had weathered a year in the ranks without seeing any action. While other units had found glory along Virginia's Peninsula, the 6th had endured countless hours of picket duty, drilling, and boredom. Frustration with army politics and command decisions swelled. But the fighting at Brawner Farm on August 28, 1862, would forever change the regiment and what would soon be known as the Iron Brigade. That day's trial by fire helped create a culture of confidence and determination that would play out in future battles. But as Marten explains, the story extends well beyond that of one regiment: the men of the 6th Wisconsin offer a microcosm of the experience of untested officers and soldiers in the Army of the Potomac.

Volumes in the Military Campaigns of the Civil War series always have featured one or two biographical essays, and Keith S. Bohannon's portrait of Confederate general John Bell Hood continues that tradition. Detailing Hood's actions on August 29 and 30, Bohannon argues that Hood's performance showed his mettle as a division commander and helped to ensure Confederate victory. But some of his decisions—namely, failing to designate a field officer to command his old brigade—proved problematic. Hood's division made a significant contribution but suffered high casualties. Bohannon concludes that the criticisms of Hood's command choices failed to detract from his rising reputation as a capable division leader.

Questions of leadership likewise dogged Union generals. Following the Army of Virginia's defeat, Lincoln had relieved Pope of command. But Pope was not one to suffer humiliation alone. In his estimation, Fitz John Porter, one of "McClellan's men," had deliberately disobeyed his orders on August 29 to attack Jackson's retreating troops. When Lincoln shared Porter's telegram mocking his commander, Pope had the evidence he needed to launch an investigation into Porter's behavior. Once more, politics and military decisions collided, as William Marvel's essay on Porter's military commission trial reveals. "Creating the impression that Porter had acted from treasonable motives—a common Radical Republican strategy for discrediting Democratic generals—would help discredit the conservative element generally," Marvel notes, "and signal the inauguration of a crackdown on officers critical of government policy."

Caroline E. Janney closes the volume with an examination of the place of both First and Second Manassas in memory. Although both battles had resulted in Union defeats, in the summer of 1865 the plains above Bull Run became the site of two of the earliest monuments to the Union cause, a funerary tribute to the men who had preserved the Union and ensured the death of slavery. Yet the importance of the memorials and battlefield would soon begin to recede from Union memory. Throughout the 1880s and into the early 1900s, Union veterans from every loyal state erected thousands of regimental and state monuments at Gettysburg, Antietam, Chickamauga, Vicksburg, and Shiloh, even as Congress worked to designate the sites as national battlefields. Second Manassas faded from importance in the pantheon of Union memory, and the stone memorials on the fields fell into disrepair. Ironically, the Lost Cause proved paramount in ensuring that the monuments to Union patriots would be protected for future generations. The monuments still stand today. But as Janney points out, the story of their placement and preservation is a timely reminder that Civil War memory was always—and remains—bound up in contemporary politics and culture.

We would like to thank each of the contributors to this collection. As with previous volumes, the authors include both public and academic historians. We appreciate their steadfast patience with us as we brought this volume into publication. Cartographer Edward Alexander distilled our complex requests into remarkably clear maps, and we are grateful for his flexibility and skill. We would also like to thank the National Park

Service employees at Second Manassas and other parks who have assisted us with research and advice, including Ray Brown, Jim Burgess, Hank Elliott, R. E. L. Krick, and Eric Mink.

Notes

1. Edward A. Pollard, *Southern History of the War: The Second Year of the War* (1863; repr., New York: Charles B. Richardson, 1865), 101, 120–22.

2. Lucy Buck, *Sad Earth, Sweet Heaven: The Diary of Lucy Rebecca Buck* (Birmingham: Buck, 1992), 137–38.

3. Alpheus S. Williams, *From the Cannon's Mouth: The Civil War Letters of General Alpheus S. Williams* (Lincoln: University of Nebraska Press, 1995), 111.

4. Figures are from "The Opposing Forces at Second Bull Run," in *Battles and Leaders of the Civil War*, ed. Robert Underwood Johnson and Clarence Clough Buel, 4 vols. (New York: Century, 1884–88), 2:497–500.

5. "The Battle of Second Manassas: Then & Now: An Interview with John Hennessey," American Battlefield Trust, accessed May 10, 2023, www.battlefields.org/learn/articles/battle-second-manassas-then-now.

6. John R. Worsham, *One of Jackson's Foot Cavalry: His Experience and What He Saw during the War, 1861–1865* (New York: Neale, 1912), 120–21.

7. John J. Hennessy, *Return to Bull Run: The Campaign and Battle of Second Manassas* (New York: Simon and Schuster, 1993), 6.

8. A. Wilson Greene, *The Second Battle of Manassas* (n.p.: Eastern National, 2016), 26.

9. Theron W. Haight, "Gainesville, Groveton, and Bull Run," in *War Papers Read before the Commandery of the State of Wisconsin, Military Order of the Loyal Legion of the United States*, vol. 2 (Milwaukee: Burdick, Armitage and Allen, 1896), 357–72; Greene, *Second Battle of Manassas*, 38.

10. Greene, *Second Battle of Manassas*, 39–45.

MANAGEMENT MOST WRETCHED

Logistical Self-Destruction in the Army of Virginia

KATHRYN J. SHIVELY

A cavalry "paralyzed" by deficient supply, men and beasts starving, intelligence leaks to the press, aimless reinforcements, broken and misused transportation, soldier absenteeism, plundering, officers voicing flagrant disrespect or failing to report at all: Maj. Gen. John Pope's Army of Virginia manifested a shocking level of logistical and communications dysfunction during the Second Bull Run campaign. It scarcely needed Confederate help to meet its end. The hapless Pope, accustomed to victory and renown in the West, tried various approaches to administrate his disjointed army, concluding that the root problems were poor discipline, subordinate incompetence, and Confederate sabotage. This myopic assessment prompted Pope to issue a string of general orders, which not only failed to resolve the army's disunity and stagnancy but also famously escalated US-Confederate retaliations in the summer of 1862. The outsize political ramifications of Pope's actions have long pulled scholarly attention away from the logistical problems of the campaign, which deserve attention as a central reason for US defeat. The sources of the Army of Virginia's disarray were, in fact, more complex than Pope could reasonably address on his own, involving the most intricate logistical puzzle the US military would face in the Eastern Theater until operations at City Point in 1864. Additionally, within his tortured job of army administration, Pope was plagued by politics in its broader sense: the power relations among army leadership within high command and with civilian government.[1]

While Cecily Zander's essay evaluates the partisan dimensions of Pope's leadership during the summer 1862, this essay adopts a different and, at times, slightly contrasting interpretation of Pope's motivations and actions, particularly regarding his famous set of general orders. While the orders' enforcement of congressional confiscation and stringency on Confederate civilians pleased many Republicans, I argue that, typical of West Pointers, Pope's primary motivation was practical army administration, with Republican politics a secondary concern. Conspicuous was his choice to ignore African Americans, whose status preoccupied Republicans of all stripes that summer. In hindsight, the political context appeared amplified because of the fallout from Pope's orders; Federals and Confederates alike assessed them as escalatory, even though they rearticulated congressional law and de facto policy Pope had employed in his previous assignment in 1861 Missouri. While I do not disregard the important political context, ably described by Zander, I trace less of a straight line from "conciliation" to "hard war" than scholars have come to depict.[2] Because the Second Bull Run campaign is so understudied, a bit of scholarly dissonance merely suggests how much we have left to explore.

The seeds of the Army of Virginia's ruin were sown before the army's creation and Pope's arrival in mid-June 1862. No single authority below that of President Abraham Lincoln and Secretary of War Edwin M. Stanton had unified the Federal troops occupying the Shenandoah Valley, western mountains, and northern reaches of Virginia. Instead, the region was fragmented into disjointed military departments. The primary function of these commands had been occupation duty, interrupted by a spectacularly calamitous spring campaign against Confederate major generals Thomas "Stonewall" Jackson and Richard Ewell. The Federals' tenuous continuing presence, from Fredericksburg to western Virginia, invited sabotage from local civilians (especially to railways and telegraphs), dismal logistical coordination (leaving troops bereft of supplies and transport), and disciplinary problems (namely Federal plundering, but in Fredericksburg even alleged sexual violence against civilians).[3] In contrast, the troops who would soon serve as reinforcements to Northern Virginia—Maj. Gen. George B. McClellan's Army of the Potomac and Maj. Gen. Ambrose E. Burnside's newly formed Ninth Corps—had enjoyed a taste of successful offensive campaigning and, in McClellan's case, tight administrative control over the ranks. Sewing together such a patchwork of men with varied experiences and discipline would require herculean effort.

In the absence of a general-in-chief, Stanton and Lincoln had failed to foster a sense of responsibility or unity.[4] By mid-June it was apparent that Stanton had lost any sense of where the scattered troops were, let alone their strength and their activities. Vexation emanated from a barrage of rapid-fire-question telegrams to the various commands, yet Stanton offered no directives.[5] When a commander made the mistake of responding to the secretary of war, that general only received an instant missive with more questions, precipitating avoidance and mistrust. If Stanton's communications wafted prickly desperation, this betrayed a larger tension distracting him and the president. McClellan appeared poised to pluck Richmond if only he would act, but the Army of the Potomac commander continued to offer excuses and demand unreasonable numbers of reinforcements. Instead, Confederate opponent Gen. Robert E. Lee initiated what became the Seven Days' battles on June 26, as Jackson's Shenandoah Valley conquerors moved to join him by rail and foot. This would only lead to more disappointment in McClellan's performance, a series of tactical wins but strategic retreat.

Administrators in Washington concluded that a new army with a new commander could curb the aimlessness of the fragmented Virginia troops and, possibly, reverse McClellan's perceived noncompliance. Stanton favored John Pope, whose impressive Western Theater military record included successes at New Madrid, Missouri; Island Number Ten on the Kentucky-Tennessee border; and Corinth, Mississippi. Additionally, Pope boasted a record in Missouri as a stern disciplinarian of Confederate civilians without overstepping Republican Party edicts, as his superior Maj. Gen. John C. Frémont had done by issuing a premature emancipation proclamation. Pope's measured disciplinarianism appealed to an administration limping from a spring of political disputes over Confederate bushwhacking in Virginia.[6] On June 24, Pope arrived in Washington.

In his memoirs, Pope recalled his first June 26 private meeting with Stanton as distinctly uncomfortable. Stanton detailed the failed Shenandoah campaign, which Pope scorned as "a campaign conducted from Washington by the President and the Secretary of War, in which the generals played no part except to obey orders." Based on his Missouri experiences, Pope was well-versed in civilian meddling in military affairs and, typical of West Pointers, had little stomach for it. Additionally, Pope recalled that Stanton baldly related "the lame results accomplished by the great army under McClellan's command and . . . McClellan's [unsatisfactory] personal and official conduct toward the authorities." While Pope balked at heading an army that was clearly in a sorry state of organization, discipline, and equipage and at taking command over generals senior in rank to him—all the while coordinating with a second army whose commander the Lincoln administration manifestly resented—he had little choice but to accept.[7]

For its part, the Lincoln administration had little choice but Pope, as he was one of few winning generals with sufficient rank to head an army.[8] Stanton and Secretary of the Treasury Salmon P. Chase envisioned Pope as a politically appealing choice who would serve the Republican Party better than the Democrat McClellan. Chase, however, grew mildly disappointed in Pope's moderate party-line responses to promptings about advances in Republican policy that summer; while Pope was "in favor of using every instrument which could be brought to bear against the enemy . . . he did not speak in favor . . . of arming the slaves as soldiers." Chase concluded that Pope did not wish to "impair . . . the general tone of the service."[9] Lincoln likely had the true measure of Pope—that the general would serve his ego over any party mandate—thanks to encounters they had shared in 1861; however, Lincoln credited Pope's battlefield victories and had managed previously to disarm Pope's characteristic bluster by inviting him into the fold. While Pope dutifully courted cabinet and congressional Republicans during a month of being stationed in Washington, as Zander details in this volume, Pope's memoirs would later note his distaste for the "moral odor of sewer gas in the air" of Washington. Compounding Pope's displeasure with his removal from his preferred command out west, his infant daughter would sicken and die in St. Louis over the course of July, severely clouding his mood and judgment once in the field.[10]

Pope's official June 26 orders placed him over the new Army of Virginia, to be composed of Maj. Gen. John C. Frémont's First Corps (from the Mountain Department), Maj. Gen. Nathaniel P. Banks's Second Corps (from the Shenandoah Department), and Maj. Gen. Irvin McDowell's Third Corps (from the Department of the Rappahannock), with Brig. Gen. Samuel P. Sturgis's Washington-area troops in reserve. The new army was to protect

"Western Virginia and the national capital[,] . . . attack and overcome the rebel forces under Jackson and Ewell, threaten the enemy in the direction of Charlottesville, and render the most effective aid to relieve General McClellan and capture Richmond."[11] By the time Pope received his instructions, however, Jackson and Ewell had rejoined Lee's army, and when Pope wrote to McClellan, it was evident that the Army of the Potomac commander would not cooperate. Over time, in fact, McClellan would actively champion Pope's failure. Thus, Pope requested that McClellan be replaced or, as former general-in-chief Winfield Scott recommended, that Maj. Gen. Henry Halleck, who commanded the Western Theater, be brought east to help coordinate the two armies. Without any chance of working together with McClellan, Pope, headquartered in DC, used the telegraph to scatter his troops from Sperryville to Washington, while threatening the railroad and depot at Gordonsville to divert Confederates from Richmond. Surely, for a man of Pope's egoism, who had just been snatched from an army that celebrated him to a miserable assignment in which he was rebuffed, his ensuing decisions also reflected a desire to attract attention and renown to his new position. Thanks to a dim view of his subordinates and soldiers, whom he later demeaned as grossly unamalgamated, "never having served together and having also been subjected to every different kind of service and very diverse modes of discipline," Pope began firing off his own badgering set of telegrams to learn basic information about his command. After all, the president and War Department, thanks to their poor management all spring, could offer few insights on his far-flung troops.[12]

One of the first signs of trouble for Pope within his army came from a former superior and nemesis: Frémont. The two officers had suffered bad blood from their pre–Civil War days exploring for the old army, as well as a more recent power struggle during the 1861 pacification of Missouri. Being senior to Pope, Frémont refused to submit to the new order of rank and reveled in throwing his former unit into organizational chaos upon his resignation by absconding with all his papers. Second Corps brigadier general George H. Gordon mused in his memoirs that "Fremont retired, carrying with him everything but our regrets." But the situation in the First Corps was far from humorous, especially for next-in-line Brig. Gen. Robert C. Schenck, who staggered to temporary command so uninformed that he failed to realize he was part of a new army. Unsympathetically, Pope mocked Schenck's ignorance and grilled him on matters impossible to answer without Frémont's paperwork. To compound insult, Schenck learned erroneously from the newspapers that he was to turn over his command to Brig. Gen. Rufus King, a division commander presently under McDowell in the Department of the Rappahannock, when Lincoln supplanted Schenck with Maj. Gen. Franz Sigel. Hardly pleased by his advancement, Sigel lamented, "My transfer from a division which I had just succeeded in organizing, equipping, and making effective to the command of the First Army Corps, which I found to be in a very bad condition . . . has imposed severe labor upon me." As Schenck before him, Sigel was "greatly inconvenienced by the removal of all papers and documents by General Fremont," gaining information only by "direct inquiries and inspections." Pope and the First Corps would be grappling with Frémont's mess for weeks to come. Sigel, in turn, would face a punishing and humiliating campaign, constantly arriving late to the field with exhausted and underfed men, enduring verbal shellackings from Pope that almost led to Sigel's resignation, bearing the brunt of Jackson's fury at Groveton, and then leaking his grim report of the battle, featuring an open critique of Pope, to the press. The crushing discord within the high ranks of the Army of Virginia is a reminder that McClellan's Army of the Potomac generals did not monopolize bickering, nor did inter-army political strife result primarily from partisan differences. Afterall, Pope, Frémont, and Sigel shared ties to the Republican Party.[13]

If Frémont had managed to demoralize the command of the First Corps at its very inception, Pope soon extended the pall over the full range of subordinates by manifesting poor administrative skills. His impatience, arrogance, and propensity to muddle orders quickly compounded a preexisting culture of noncooperation, mistrust, and incompetence, instilled in Pope's generals from their experiences under civilian leadership earlier that year. Here, the Second Corps commander, Banks, was a standout, manifesting an exceptionally bleak relationship with Pope. It began with bungled orders on troop placement telegraphed by Pope's chief of staff, Col. George D. Ruggles. After a brief written scuffle over Banks's inability to follow the orders, Ruggles admitted responsibility, citing the rapid, haphazard organization of his office. That incident could be attributed to poor staff work, which was indeed one tangle in the knot of incompetence ensnaring Pope throughout the campaign. But Banks—problematic even before the reorganization—performed ever more pitifully as Pope's stinging reprimands piled up in response to the Second Corps' continual tardiness, wanton burning of bridges, and absurdly excessive field baggage. Banks attracted particular infamy that summer when he unwittingly precipitated a major battle at Cedar Mountain, on August 9, in which his old Shenandoah rival, Jackson, punished Banks with a Confederate force twice the size of the US Second Corps. Banks's corps remained so demoralized thereafter that only its cavalry participated in the climactic battle of Second Bull Run.[14]

A pattern emerged in which Pope viewed his subordinates' lack of immediate compliance with orders as cowardice, which hardly motivated improvement among the admittedly insipid Shenandoah-area generals. Brig. Gen. Abram S. Piatt, who initially commanded a brigade detached from the First Corps near Winchester and later served under Sturgis, endured a humiliating tirade when Pope alleged that the newspapers reported "a force advancing against Winchester and . . . your force retreating toward Harper's Ferry. . . . It is better to lose your whole force than to make a hasty or discreditable retreat." Piatt objected, "The tone of your dispatch would intimate that I had in some way given you to believe that we would not hold this place." Similarly, the long-suffering Schenck, who delayed moving the First Corps to Sperryville in part because he labored to protect his trains, received the alarming rebuke from Pope, "I regret to see that there is so great a tendency in your command to unnecessary alarms and 'stampedes.' You had best send [less-intimidated] officers to Middletown to conduct your trains . . . who will think less of 'rescue and retreat' and more of advance." Single-minded in his determination to get his army on the move, Pope demanded "immediate compliance" from all corps, division, and brigade commanders to rid themselves of surplus baggage and prepare to march with two days' rations at an hour's notice. "No excuse will be listened to for any failure," Pope spat.[15]

After a string of individual chastisements to subordinates failed to produce results, Pope opted for a shaming public rebuke on July 14, which he hoped would finally goad the army toward improved discipline and performance. His infamous address berated the entire Army of Virginia for over-attending to their "lines of retreat" and "bases of supplies," words that hang heavy in hindsight, considering that Pope's failure to attend to these very things precipitated defeat. He further needled, "Success and glory are in the advance, disaster and shame lurk in the rear." Schenck, who had the least to lose of the disgruntled officers since he had already lost a command he had never wanted, explained that cowardice was not the root problem; the troops were bogged down by mercurial weather, insufficient transportation, and lack of forage and subsistence, all the while "trying to protect public property" from bushwhackers and locate "hospital accommodations" for the sick and wounded.[16]

Schenck's analysis of the numerous logistical difficulties facing the Army of Virginia, especially in his sector, is duly reflected in the historical record. As Virginia heated up for summer, making foot travel wearying in the mountainous Shenandoah Valley, food and supplies for humans and horses became an increasing problem that intersected with growing deficiencies in transportation and communication. Medical care and supplies had long been erratic, making it difficult to treat the sickness and, later, casualties of active campaigning. Even for the Third Corps, which initially enjoyed better supply lines, thanks to civilian oversight of the railroad and the robust seaboard depot at Aquia Landing, logistics would strain. Indeed, Pope himself contributed to the supply problem as his orders to get the army on the move came to fruition. On July 10 he had ordered every unit, from brigade to corps, to dispense with all excess supplies and send the "surplus baggage, subsistence, quartermaster's and ordnance stores, and also medical supplies" to "the depot at Alexandria," provoking a situation in which the soldiers had no food or ammunition reserves, while the trains and roads were tied up with a backflow of Union supplies.[17]

The elevation of General Halleck to US general-in-chief that summer had the potential to arrest the momentum of logistic collapse, but Halleck gradually worsened matters. When, on July 23, 1862, he arrived in Washington, finally freeing up Pope to travel into the field on July 29, Pope and the Lincoln administration had reason to anticipate improvements. While the president hoped Halleck would use liberal leeway to coordinate the two armies (and even to remove McClellan, if necessary), instead Halleck began by allowing McClellan to stay his course. When McClellan again requested impossible numbers of reinforcements, Halleck made one big decision, not to fire McClellan but, against Pope's wishes, to retract the Army of the Potomac to Aquia Landing to support Pope and protect Washington. Burnside, whose troops would have constituted McClellan's chief reinforcements, was ordered to precede McClellan to Aquia.[18] The removal of more than 120,000 troops from the James River to the Fredericksburg area would consume the attention of Quartermaster General Montgomery Meigs and fluster Halleck over the next month. Now Halleck, McClellan, and Burnside would need to coordinate with Pope to provide reinforcements and receive supply, and the delicate situation with the Army of Virginia's logistics would further devolve. Pope would receive little sympathy or understanding from his superiors, who faced a level of logistical complexity not yet matched in the Eastern Theater.[19]

The Army of Virginia's intensifying logistical problems revolved chiefly around lines of supply and communication and the human decisions that affected their use or disuse. A brief tour of logistical malfunction should rightly begin with the wagons. Historian Earl Hess calculates that "Pope allowed his wagon supply to balloon" to "fifteen wagons per regiment," as opposed to the usual six. The reasons for this bloat were manifold and extremely challenging to correct. Topping the list were the legacy of poor coordination in the isolating Shenandoah geography, the reassignment of baggage when the independent commands were consolidated, and quartermaster mismanagement. But when Pope stared down the preposterous fact that even his cavalry attempted raids and reconnaissance with lengthy baggage trains in tow, he learned that discipline lacked among the officers who might have checked such impracticality. Pope initially attempted to reduce the baggage burden by consolidating depots and ordering commanders to whittle down their ammunition and ration supplies, but the result was clogged roads, poor supply flow, and sluggish campaigning.[20]

Equally problematic were the railroads. The rails (particularly the US-controlled segments of the Orange & Alexandria, the Manassas Gap Railroad, and the Richmond, Fredericksburg & Potomac Railroad) critically supplied the Union's Northern Virginia troops; but as Irvin McDowell and Secretary Stanton had learned over the spring, an unconventional civilian arrangement kept the eastern tracks operating better than the military ever achieved. Stanton had elevated railroad executive Daniel McCallum to overall management in Washington and assigned former West-Pointer-turned-civilian-engineer Herman Haupt (with the nominal rank of colonel) to oversee trains in the field. At the time when Pope took command, Haupt supported McDowell in the Department of the Rappahannock, along with a permanent detail of civilian workers rather than soldiers, having recognized that the constant turnover inherent to unskilled military details hampered work. The partnership was highly effective until Pope, typical of western commanders, felt the military should command the rails and dismissed Haupt, who went home to Massachusetts to conduct his private business. As complaints piled up of soldiers and beasts starving while self-serving generals monopolized tracks for their own needs, Pope soon realized his mistake and recalled Haupt, who would return in early August. Even then it took Haupt weeks to reestablish authority over military commanders, repair tracks, and get the trains moving—that is, for a brief time, until Jackson got behind the Army of Virginia and tore up track. On August 14 Pope complained that "the management of the railroad from Washington to Culpeper is most wretched and inefficient," as his men had received neither mail nor supplies in weeks. What is more, they could not expediently receive the reinforcements Halleck attempted to provide from Aquia Landing; so slowly had Maj. Gen. Jesse L. Reno's 1st Division of Burnside's Ninth Corps reached Pope that he felt Reno's men could have walked in half the time. In an attempt to arrest the haphazard manner in which his subordinates had been dominating individual cars and tracks, Pope decreed that he alone could command the railroads with Haupt executing.[21]

But the rail supervision Pope promised never came. Throughout the major campaign actions in late August, Haupt could scarcely get hold of Pope, let alone efficiently move reinforcements, food, and forage to where they were needed. On August 22 and 23, while recently promoted Maj. Gen. J. E. B. Stuart's troops ravaged the Orange & Alexandria at Catlett's Station and Pope's headquarters, Haupt desperately tried to comply with Pope's orders to stage Sturgis's, Maj. Gen. Samuel P. Heintzelman's, and Brig. Gen. Jacob Cox's reinforcements near Warrenton but found no available cars; they either hadn't been returned by General Sturgis or were filled with the sick. When Haupt tried to warn Pope, the commander did not respond, so Haupt cast around for supervision from the secretary of war, Halleck, and even McClellan. Once the reinforcements moved, horse feed became the next pressing problem. Pope's horses were starving, and Haupt had grain at the Alexandria depot; however, the railroad cars were too heavy for the nearby bridges, so no forage could advance. By August 28 Haupt had received no clear orders on supply and sent his own reconnaissance party of 200 sharpshooters by rail with operators to repair the telegraph and report observations on the tracks. They discovered the track cut fourteen miles from Alexandria. Two days later, to his utter exasperation, Haupt learned the army was completely out of forage and food and had lost the major battle of Second Bull Run.[22]

While moving men and supplies southwesterly proved challenging, the transportation route southward from Washington to Fredericksburg, which involved roads, steamships on the Potomac, and a fourteen-mile line of track from Aquia Landing to Fredericksburg, also posed a unique challenge for McDowell and the arriving troops under Burnside and McClellan—in large part because of an influx of civilian needs. In late July, Pope found his time unexpectedly consumed responding to the movement of goods to market in this important economic corridor. While he continued to allow "tobacco or wheat" to be shipped "north from Fredericksburg," he halted all nonmilitary supplies moving south to improve military supply. Pope's chief of staff, Colonel Ruggles, explained to railroad manager McCallum that "nothing but public property, private stores for officers and soldiers, and ice . . . for hospitals" should be transmitted on railroad cars, steamboats, "or other [military] conveyance . . . within limits of this command." Moreover, as the summer wore on, streams of loyal civilians, including Black refugees, flooded the roads to Alexandria. Haupt recognized the Black refugees as a vital source of

Rufus Fairchild Zogbaum illustrated the August 30, 1862, retreat of John Pope's Army of Virginia in logistical collapse. (Johnson and Buel, *Battles and Leaders*, 2:488)

intelligence on the Rebel pursuit and the status of the telegraph lines, and yet the sheer amount of human movement in the area magnified the logistical congestion.[23]

The results of the transportation logjam were staggering: a medical crisis erupted, while horses and men starved. Pope's medical director, Thomas A. McParlin, assigned June 30, 1862, immediately confronted a multitude of ongoing mistakes on invoices; supplies and instruments that arrived damaged, destroyed, or not at all; and a lack of the most basic necessities in caring for the sick, including tents, washing equipment, and food. In his report on the campaign, he described a circus of retreat as he attempted to stage the sick and wounded at Warrenton, then Culpeper, then Bristoe Station, and then Alexandria, while Lee's army marched behind the Army of Virginia, cutting rails and destroying bridges. Journeys on the stony or corduroyed roads extracted "groans and outcries" from the wounded, while the wagons that arrived to help transport the patients were of the wrong type or wholly lacking in brakes. The sick, many suffering from endemic typhoid, went without food, which Pope tried to alleviate by ordering the infantry commissaries to issue rations to hospitals "no matter to what . . . command . . . [you] belong." McParlin proclaimed the horses tasked with pulling the ambulances "poor and weak" because, again, they had no access to forage. In response, Pope, characteristic of command in 1862, vocally declared soldier malingering to be the major problem. He ordered his officers to tighten the reins on their men or face disciplinary consequences, further degrading morale and trust.[24]

But the standout story of logistical collapse was the horses. From the beginning of the campaign, Pope complained that his horses were in a deplorable state and his cavalry urgently needed forage, shoes, and replacement animals. He begged new horses and feed from Halleck, who groused that McClellan's arriving troops also needed forage; there was hardly enough to go round. Pope again sought a simple answer to a complex problem, this time blaming the Quartermaster Department, which he thought operated with the "grossest possible carelessness." His own chief quartermaster, Col. Robert E. Clary, was "too old and too easy." Clary's "whole management of that department is inefficient." As Pope explained to Montgomery Meigs, the quartermaster general, "Although only 70 or 80 miles from Alexandria, I cannot get forage for my cavalry"; "this arm of service is paralyzed by the neglect of some quartermaster." Meigs, who had his hands full retracting the Army of the Potomac, was unmoved by Pope's assessment. The chief quartermaster told Halleck that the horses were breaking down because of "inexperienced" soldiers who "destroy their horses" in the summer heat "by hard and unnecessary riding." Moreover, Meigs decried Pope's insistence on twenty carloads of grain per day and his refusal to use corn and the "large quantities of uncut timothy hay and unthreshed wheat" reported to be in Culpeper. In other words, Meigs, who viewed Pope's baggage as "unnecessarily large," saw an untapped opportunity to confiscate Rebel forage, which Pope appeared to ignore. High command never sorted out the problem, and by the end of the battle of Second Bull Run, Pope had received not a single fresh horse. "We have no cavalry—not a horse that can possibly perform service," he said, and "there are not five horses to a company that can raise a trot." As a result, throughout the campaign, Pope's cavalry seldom provided intelligence on enemy movements.[25]

Interrelated was telegraph communication, which often ran along the same transportation routes as supplies. Frequent telegraph interruptions from enemy combatants and civilians were challenging enough in July, but as multiple bodies of troops began arriving at Aquia Landing over the month of August—all needing directions on where to go, means of maneuvering, and access to supplies—communications devolved entirely. Halleck was clearly overwhelmed by the prospect of coordinating so many communications, something he had never attempted at this volume before, nor had any other commander. He testily snapped at Pope on August 26, "Just think of the immense amount of telegraphing I have to do, and then say whether I can be expected to give you any details as to movements of others, even when I know them." Moreover, in the most critical phase of the campaign, from August 23 to 30, Halleck had virtually no telegraph communication at all with Pope, because Confederates had cut the telegraph lines at Kettle Run. During this period when Pope most needed reinforcements from McClellan and Burnside, Halleck could only guess at Pope's whereabouts and often learned what he could of Pope's activities through Maj. Gen. Fitz John Porter's tainted communications to Burnside, all of which oozed contempt for the commander of the Army of Virginia.[26]

In addition to enemy attacks and periodic civilian sabotage on telegraph wires, much of the communications problem could be traced to poor army administration and a lack of cooperation among generals. Halleck grew increasingly frustrated with Pope, who at first asked much, then ceased all communication. McClellan actively countermanded Halleck's orders and openly advocated for Pope's failure.[27] Internally in the Army of Virginia, Pope profoundly mistrusted even credible intelligence, because he doubted his subordinates.[28] The corps and division commanders generated their own messes. Schenck monopolized the telegraph to request massive numbers of leaves of absence for officers. Sigel and Banks withheld reports because they loathed their overbearing commander. McDowell failed to report on critical (and, for this campaign, rare) cavalry intelligence on Maj. Gen. James Longstreet's approach through Thoroughfare Gap. This omission contributed to Pope issuing his most wretched orders of the whole campaign on August 29 and 30, which placed Porter in the impossible situation that ended his military career.[29]

Then there was the fact that nearly every move Pope made was instantly reported on by Confederate civilians to the enemy, which Pope initially tried to correct by denying traveling passes to all but the most trusted Unionists. Halleck claimed the betrayal went deeper still: "I think your staff is decidedly leaky," the general-in-chief warned, noting that official telegrams seemed to materialize immediately in the newspapers. Thus, he ordered Pope to "remove from your army all newspaper reporters." Pope rejected the idea that his staff was undermining operations, instead implicating Banks's inner circle: "I observe newspaper reports from the senior aide de camp of Banks that never reach me." Pope underscored discipline as the main problem: "The several corps composing this army have until recently acted quite independently, and it is difficult to put a stop to practices which have prevailed hitherto." He did try to halt all "dispatches to the Associated Press," but to no avail. In the end,

Sigel and cohort officers leaked damning reports to the papers both during and in the immediate aftermath of the campaign.[30]

The interpersonal and logistical challenges rippled outward in ever-widening circles. Pope's task, to create a sleek, offensive army from disparate parts, proved beyond his capabilities—perhaps beyond any commander's capabilities. This is the context necessary to understanding Pope's attempts to administrate the army via general orders, as each order correlated quite specifically to the discrete, unfolding problems described above. Scholars have overlooked this central aspect of Pope's orders by emphasizing only their political context, but this not altogether surprising given the orders' outsize political results. Sadly for Pope, the orders likely worsened his army's ability to cohere.

A brief tour of Pope's edicts reveals their primary origins in army administration. The July 17 General Orders No. 3 aimed to keep the army together, on the move, and under tighter officer control by limiting passes, thus addressing the First and Second Corps' munificence with leaves that tied up the telegraph wire, eroded officer control over the troops, and encouraged absenteeism. The more famous General Orders No. 5, issued the next day, addressed the army's cumbersome baggage problem and deficient supply: "Hereafter, as far as practicable, the troops of this command will subsist upon the country in which their operations are carried on." "In all cases" the relevant department officers were to oversee the resource extraction and present vouchers to the "loyal" owners of confiscated goods to be repaid after the war. Pope's reasoning for his stern employment of the congressional confiscation policy was that "the use of trains for carrying subsistence will be dispensed with as far as possible." Also dated July 18, General Orders No. 6 addressed excess baggage in the cavalry; no longer were cavalry to use "supply or baggage trains of any description," but they were to subsist as General Orders No. 5 had stipulated.[31]

Additional edicts punished bushwhacking, which Pope deemed a major cause of disruption to the "railroad and telegraph." General Orders No. 7, mistakenly dated July 10 in the *Official Records* but presumably dated July 18 based on newspaper reports, decreed that the civilians "throughout the region of operations of this army" would be "held responsible for any injury done to the track, line, or road, or for any attacks upon trains or straggling soldiers by bands of guerrillas in their neighborhood." Ununiformed civilians who carried out enemy operations, including "molest[ing] trains of supplies" and "destroy[ing] railroads, telegraph lines, and bridges," or those who fired on US soldiers would be subject to military law and potentially shot. Similarly,

General Orders No. 11, with a delayed issue on July 23 because Pope waited to solicit Lincoln's approval, ordered army officers to arrest "all disloyal male citizens within their lines." Those who took an oath could remain in their homes, but those who refused would be "considered spies" and subjected to military law; if one took the oath and then "violated it, he shall be shot."[32] A final pair of orders, No. 15 and No. 18, in early August stated that "no officer . . . shall have any communication . . . except through the proper military channels," aiming to end leaks to the press, and additionally sought to curb straggling.[33]

To Pope, these orders, imperious though they were in tone, directly addressed the integrity of supply and communication lines. They also fell within the limits of congressional confiscation and the anti-guerrilla policy that Pope and colleagues had tested, under Lincoln's watch, in Missouri. Nevertheless, they detonated like a bomb in the Eastern Theater. Many of Pope's soldiers and officers increased their already notorious marauding or, alternately, resented what they perceived as a mandate to plunder. McClellan, who had bristled at but largely obeyed congressional confiscation, fumed all the more at his miserable colleague's emphasis on it, particularly Pope's charge that "no guards will be placed over private houses or property." McClellan perceived this statement as an open attack on his own army administration, which, in comparison with Pope, must be described as highly competent, even if Republican leadership viewed McClellan as recalcitrant. Halleck, who had carefully navigated the jagged edges of just war out west, found some of Pope's orders "very injudicious." And Confederates, chief among them Lee, deemed Pope's decrees as distinctly escalatory. As Lee wrote to Jackson on July 27, "The course indicated in his orders if the newspapers report them correctly cannot be permitted and will lead to retaliation on our part." Pope had, in short, likely attracted more political sewer gas than he intended, though some good did come of it: Lee abandoned the Peninsula to chase Pope.[34]

Pope, for his part, did seem surprised—chiefly at the fact that his orders, which had meant to tighten discipline and reverse logistical disaster, instead led to an avalanche of plundering. McClellan had avoided the plundering side effect of confiscation by posting guards over private property, highlighting that while his practices read conservative, they also promoted army discipline and coherence. The fact that Lincoln returned to the politically detested McClellan as commander of eastern forces after the failure of Pope demonstrates that Lincoln perceived McClellan's administrative worth. Pope, however, did not reflect on McClellan's practices but expressed shock and disappointment at his soldiers' flagrant violation of orderly confiscation in General Orders

No. 19, dated August 14. With "great dissatisfaction" he chastised that Orders No. 5 "has either been entirely misinterpreted or grossly abused by many of the officers and soldiers of this command." His evident disgust with his soldiers' looting and "molest[ing]" of citizens is oddly minimized in the modern scholarship, as if the results redefined his intent. But Pope was distinctly unsettled, as this was not the first time his orders had been misinterpreted; he had experienced similar outrage against what he believed were reasonable edicts in Missouri.[35]

It is just as important to point out what Pope's orders did not address: African Americans. This omission speaks volumes to whether or not Pope's orders should be understood as mere tools of the Republican Party, whose Washington elite was expressly concerned with confiscation's relationship to emancipation that summer. There were plenty of Black southerners populating Northern Virginia and Black refugees flooding the roads toward Washington to beg Pope's consideration. He ignored them to focus on internal army administration.[36]

The forced withdrawal of Pope's army to the Washington area at the end of the Second Bull Run campaign had drastic logistical consequences across Northern Virginia for those loyal to the United States who had benefited from Federal occupation. Scenes of the evacuation of Fredericksburg, McDowell's former sector, presented a calamitous end to the logistical nightmare of the campaign. Railroads and roads were reclaimed by Confederate soldiers and civilians, and the massive supply depot at Aquia, which had received over 100,000 men in the month of August, had to be abandoned. Military engineer and railroad superintendent W. W. Wright described with wonderment to Haupt the scene of destruction and evacuation that followed: "On the 28th of August General Burnside telegraphed me" to move "all Government property and stores from Fredericksburg and Falmouth Depot." By August 30 they had removed "all troops, baggage, and stores . . . together with all railroad property" to Aquia. By September 4 they engaged in the arduous task of loading locomotives onto ships, sinking a steamer in the process. Anything they couldn't take they burned, including fifty-seven railroad cars, along with the pier and railroad bridges over the Rappahannock, Potomac Run, and Accokeek Creek. A "number of white families, with such of their goods as could be readily moved," fled before the burning, and "during the last two days" of evacuation followed a "continuous black line of [African American] men, women, and children moving north along the road, carrying all their worldly goods on their heads." Tucked away in all that logistical self-destruction were the refugees from slavery, whom Pope had studiously ignored.[37]

Notes

1. US War Department, *The War of the Rebellion: A Compilation of the Official Records of the Union and Confederate Armies*, 128 vols., index and atlas (Washington, DC: Government Printing Office, 1880–1901), ser. 1, 12(3): 571, 577 (hereafter cited as *OR*, with all citations from series 1 unless otherwise noted). The primary story that the official US miliary documents related to the Second Bull Run campaign tell is one of logistical collapse; these records mainly appear in National Archives Record Group 393.8, Records of Armies, 1832–65, Army of Virginia, 1862, and *OR*, vol. 12, pts. 2 and 3. For the purposes of this essay, I tie together logistics and army communications, which typically ran along telegraph wires, linked to the same roads and rails as supplies and, therefore, subject to the same human decisions and enemy interference. For research assistance I extend my gratitude to Trevor Plante, Jim Burgess, and Hank Elliott; for editorial assistance I thank Peter Luebke, Caroline Janney, Andrew Lang, and Wayne Hsieh.

2. Modern scholarship has seemingly closed ranks around depicting Pope's general orders as heralding a political shift toward "hard war" in the Eastern Theater. The best-known book to present a phased US approach toward Confederate civilians, from conciliation to pragmatism to hard war, is Mark Grimsley, *The Hard Hand of War: Union Military Policy toward Southern Civilians, 1861–1865* (New York: Cambridge University Press, 1995), though Russell Weigley and Daniel E. Sutherland had previously described Pope's orders as a political move away from conciliation and, according to Sutherland, toward "total war"; see Weigley, *The American Way of War: A History of United States Military Strategy and Policy* (Bloomington: Indiana University Press, 1973), 137–38; and Sutherland, "Abraham Lincoln, John Pope, and the Origins of Total War," *Journal of Military History* 56, no. 4 (October 1992): 567–86. While Grimsley famously explained that Pope issued a "series of draconian orders" that signaled "an end to the kid gloves," it is important to remember that even Grimsley depicted Pope's phase as transitional (85). Since then, scholars have emphasized Pope's alleged hard war ever more stridently. See, for example, Peter Cozzens, *General John Pope: A Life for the Nation* (Urbana: University of Illinois Press, 2000); John H. Matsui, *The First Republican Army: The Army of Virginia and the Radicalization of the Civil War* (Charlottesville: University of Virginia Press, 2016); John H. Matsui, "War in Earnest: The Army of Virginia and the Radicalization of the Union War Effort, 1862," *Civil War History* 58, no. 2 (June 2012): 180–223; John H. Matsui, "Second Bull Run/Manassas: A Clash of Partisan Armies," in *The Oxford Handbook of the American Civil War*, ed. Lorien Foote and Earl J. Hess (Oxford University Press, 2021), 286–99; and Lorien Foote, *Rites of Retaliation: Civilization, Soldiers, and Campaigns in the American Civil War* (Chapel Hill: University of North Carolina Press, 2021). Joan Cashin, however, reclaims a sense of the material need behind the orders, as well as the fact that in the Northern Virginia area Federals had already engaged in intense foraging before Pope came on the scene; see *War Stuff: The Struggle for Human and Environmental Resources in the Civil War* (New York: Cambridge University Press, 2018), 70–74. Clay Mountcastle, *Punitive War: Confederate Guerrillas and Union Reprisals* (Lawrence: University Press of Kansas, 2009), 108, sees Pope's general orders as a slightly more stringent implementation of his policies out West. Similar to my argument in this essay, D. H. Dilbeck, who focused mainly on Pope in Missouri, saw a balance of destruction and restraint in Pope's actions; Dilbeck,

A More Civil War: How the Union Waged a Just War (Chapel Hill: University of North Carolina Press, 2016), 16–21.

3. For Confederate guerrilla activities, see Sigel to Pope, June 30, 1862, *OR* 12(3): 447; and Daniel E. Sutherland, *A Savage Conflict: The Decisive Role of Guerrillas in the American Civil War* (Chapel Hill: University of North Carolina Press, 2009), 87–95. For Union depredations, see General Orders No. 12, *OR* 12(1): 52–53; and Schurz to Lincoln, *OR* 12(3): 379–80. Sigel had warned Pope of Confederate guerrilla activity in the Shenandoah before he arrived; see Mountcastle, *Punitive War*, 108.

4. Lincoln's shaky performance as commander in chief in 1862 reveals that the president learned hard lessons in military leadership through numerous mistakes and missteps, a far cry from the portrayal of Lincoln by T. Harry Williams, who famously wrote, "With no knowledge of the theory of war, no experience in war, and no technical training, Lincoln, by the power of his mind, became a fine strategist" in *Lincoln and His Generals* (1952; repr., New York: Knopf Doubleday Publishing Group, 2011), 7. For another laudatory take on Lincoln's military prowess, see James M. McPherson, *Tried by War: Abraham Lincoln as Commander in Chief* (Baltimore: Penguin, 2008).

5. *OR* 12(3): 432; more examples follow through 435, and see Pope to Cox, July 29, 1862, Letters and Telegrams Sent, Army of Virginia, 1862, Records of Armies, 1832–65, Record Group 393.8, National Archives and Records Administration, Washington, DC (hereafter LTS, Army of Virginia, RG 393.8, NARA).

6. John Pope, *The Military Memoirs of General John Pope*, ed. Peter Cozzens and Robert I. Girardi (Chapel Hill: University of North Carolina Press, 1998), 22–24; Mark E. Neely Jr., *The Fate of Liberty: Abraham Lincoln and Civil Liberties* (New York: Oxford University Press, 1991), 34. For the dispute over Confederate guerrillas in Virginia, see Sutherland, *Savage Conflict*, 93.

7. Pope, *Military Memoirs*, 119; Cozzens, *General John Pope*, 73–74.

8. The other clear choice was Burnside, but Lincoln hoped Burnside would replace McClellan over the more important Army of the Potomac; August Woodbury, *Major General Ambrose E. Burnside and the Ninth Army Corps: A Narrative of Campaigns in North Carolina, Maryland, Virginia, Ohio, Kentucky, Mississippi and Tennessee, during the War for the Preservation of the Republic* (Providence: Sidney S. Rider and Brother, 1867), 104. It should be noted that Burnside was a Democrat; therefore, Lincoln's choice of officers was less about partisan affiliation and more about potential for victory. All military commanders had to obey and enforce the law, including congressional confiscation.

9. Salmon P. Chase, *Diary and Correspondence of Salmon P. Chase*, vol. 2 (Washington, DC: Government Printing Office, 1903), 46–47; Pope, *Military Memoirs*, 118. Lt. Col. David H. Strother, a member of Pope's staff, affirmed Pope's more conservative approach to emancipation, which seemed to harmonize with Strother's own views. After a conversation with Pope, Strother wrote, "Wherever the Union armies move, the old system of master and slave falls. The disorganization that follows can never be cured. The Negro becomes free absolutely or worthless and dangerous property. Pope's ideas are clear and strong. He thinks they ought to be taken and used remorselessly whenever needed. The arming of them in organized regiments is only doubtful as a matter of policy. They will not make soldiers but as laborers they might be extensively used. Congress should let the matter alone. Let the

commanders in the field use Negroes as circumstances require and never interfere to return them to slavery which they voluntarily renounce. Damn Congress." David Hunter Strother, *A Virginia Yankee in the Civil War: The Diaries of David Hunter Strother*, ed. Cecil D. Eby Jr. (Chapel Hill: University of North Carolina Press, 1961), 67. For a different interpretation of Chase on Pope, see Cecily Zander's essay in this collection.

10. According to foremost biographer of Pope, Peter Cozzens, in early 1861 Pope wrote a seven-page letter to president-elect Lincoln, providing a flurry of unbidden advice, and jockeyed, unsuccessfully, to secure high rank in the regular army. Though Pope begrudged Lincoln, the president graciously maneuvered their relationship, even inviting Pope to accompany him on the inaugural journey to Washington; Cozzens, *General John Pope*, 28, 33–34, 52, 83, 90.

11. *OR* 12(3): 435. Maj. Gen. John C. Frémont headed the Mountain Department with a reported 11,500 to 12,000 men at Strasburg, Maj. Gen. Nathaniel P. Banks oversaw the Shenandoah Department with 12,050 to 14,500 at Middletown (but only 8,000 effectives), and Maj. Gen. Irvin McDowell commanded the Department of the Rappahannock with approximately 18,000 to 18,500 troops dispersed from Manassas to Fredericksburg; see *OR* 12(3): 433–34 and 603; John C. Ropes, *The Army under Pope* (New York: Charles Scribner's Sons, 1881), 3–4; and George H. Gordon, *Brook Farm to Cedar Mountain: In the War of the Great Rebellion, 1861–62* (Boston: James R. Osgood, 1883), 264. The estimates of McDowell's numbers include both Brig. Gen. Rufus King's and Brig. Gen. James B. Ricketts's troops, who were stationed in the Fredericksburg and Manassas areas, respectively. Thus, early troop totals, before reinforcements, were 37,500 effectives on the low end and 45,000 on the upper.

12. Pope, *Military Memoirs*, 119. As Cozzens points out, Pope and McClellan also disliked each other previous to this assignment. While McClellan initially kept his feelings to his inner circle, Pope had publicly defamed McClellan for overexaggerating enemy numbers; Cozzens, *General John Pope*, 78–79. For Pope's telegrams and responses, see *OR* 12(3): 439–45.

13. Gordon, *Brook Farm*, 264; *OR* 12(3): 455. For more information on the Pope-Frémont relationship, see Cozzens, *General John Pope*, 20, 40–46. For more on Schenck and Pope that July, see *OR* 12(3): 438, 440–41. For the change in command of the First Corps, see Ruggles to Sigel, June 29, 1862, LTS, Army of Virginia, RG 393.8, NARA; *OR* 12(3): 444–47; and Pope, *Military Memoirs*, 128. As Pope described in his memoirs, Frémont published a letter to the *New York Tribune* denying that his men were in poor condition. The use of newspapers to air disputes among command became a staple of the summer campaign in the Army of Virginia. For an account of Sigel's mishaps and treachery to the *New York Tribune*, see Cozzens, *General John Pope*, 92, 105, 126, 185.

14. For the Ruggles-Banks scuffle, see *OR* 12(3): 467–68, 470; and Ruggles to Banks, July 13, 1862, LTS, Army of Virginia, RG 393.8, NARA. For highlights in the breakdown of Banks and Pope's relationship, see *OR* 12(3): 465, 472–73; and Pope to Banks, July 14 and July 25, 1862, LTS, Army of Virginia, RG 393.8, NARA.

15. *OR* 12(3): 483; Pope to Schenck, July 10, 1862, LTS, Army of Virginia, RG 393.8, NARA (and also see Pope to Schenck, July 9, 1862); *OR* 12(3): 464–65, 473–74.

16. *OR* 12(3): 466. Scholarly examinations of Pope's famous address to his troops tend to focus on Pope's lack of self-examination and its poor reception in the ranks (Cozzens, *General John Pope*, 84) or its function as a mouthpiece of the Lincoln administration to denounce McClellan; see John J. Hennessy, *Return to Bull Run: The Campaign and Battle of*

Second Manassas (1993; repr., Norman: University of Oklahoma Press, 1999), 12–13. While the address did prompt outrage, particularly in McClellan, it came on the heels of Pope sending nearly verbatim individual chastisements to his subordinates because of operational failures he perceived as their personal responsibilities. Thus, a valid interpretation of the main reason for the address is that Pope *intended* to provoke his troops in the hopes of goading them toward improvement.

17. *OR* 12(3): 465; Pope, *Military Memoirs*, 128.

18. Pope, *Military Memoirs*, 124, 131; *OR* 12(2): 5; William Marvel, *Burnside* (Chapel Hill: University of North Carolina Press, 1991), 97–102; John F. Marszalek, *Commander of All Lincoln's Armies: A Life of General Henry W. Halleck* (Cambridge, MA: Harvard University Press, 2004), 12–17, 127–33.

19. The problems with relocating Burnside's and McClellan's troops separately immediately manifested. Halleck urged McClellan to hasten to Aquia to unify the forces, because they risked "being attacked and defeated in detail"; Burnside "is without cavalry and artillery, and in that condition an attack on him would be disastrous" (*OR* 11[3]: 360).

20. Earl J. Hess, *Civil War Supply and Strategy: Feeding Men and Moving Armies* (Baton Rouge: Louisiana State University Press, 2020), 303; *OR* 12(3): 440, 444; Ruggles to McDowell, June 29, 1862; Ruggles to Sturgis, July 29, 1862; Ruggles to Sigel, June 30, 1862; Ruggles to Quartermaster at New Creek, VA, July 3, 1862; Pope to Wool, July 1, 1862, Ruggles to McDowell, July 4, 1862; Ruggles to Banks, July 5, 1862; and Ruggles to McDowell, July 5, 1862, LTS, Army of Virginia, RG 393.8, NARA. For the baggage dispute with the cavalry, see *OR* 12(2): 499.

21. *OR* 12(3): 571; Hess, *Civil War Supply*, 297–300, 303; Herman Haupt, *Reminiscences of General Herman Haupt* (Milwaukee: Wright and Joys, 1901), 63–67, 69–70; *OR* 12(3): 637.

22. *OR* 12(2): 59–60, 63; *OR* 12(3): 623, 636, 659, 66–63, 719, 736. Porter's Fifth Corps of the Army of the Potomac began arriving at Pope's position on August 22, and Samuel Heintzelman's Third Corps followed on August 24. Both became entangled in the railroad snafu and were demoralized by Pope's unclear orders about exactly where to go.

23. Ruggles to King, July 19, 1862; and Ruggles to McCallum, July 21, 1862, LTS, Army of Virginia, RG 393.8, NARA; *OR* 12(3): 718–19. For an understanding of the experiences of refugees, see Yael Sternhell, *Routes of War: The World of Movement in the Confederate South* (Cambridge, MA: Harvard University Press, 2012); and Thavolia Glymph, *The Women's Fight: The Civil War's Battles for Home, Freedom, and Nation* (Chapel Hill: University of North Carolina Press, 2020).

24. US Surgeon General's Office, *The Medical and Surgical History of the War of the Rebellion*, 6 vols. (Washington, DC: Government Printing Office, 1870–88), vol. 1, pt. 1, 117, 108–10, 111–12, 114; A. C. Baslow, Medical Purveyor, Army of Virginia, in the field, to J. B. S. Baxter, Medical Purveyor, Alexandria, Virginia, August 15, 1862, and McParlin to Baxter, July 26, 1862, Medical Purveyor of Army of Virginia, RG 393.8, NARA. In May through August 1862 there were virtually no tents available or arriving in which to place the sick and wounded, and the hospitals were full to capacity; see Lucius P. Woods to Brig. Gen. Buford, August 5, 1862, and Dr. Thomas Antisell to Baxter, July 22, 1862, Medical Purveyor of Army of Virginia, RG 393.8, NARA, for examples. Medical director McParlin painted a scene of logistical crisis wherever the Medical Department attempted to load trains or wagons with "vagrant" soldiers trying to board along with those in need and swarms of surgeons being

detailed to stay behind with those too incapacitated to move (US Surgeon General's Office, *Medical and Surgical History*, 1:111–12).

25. *OR* 12(3): 576–78, 596; *OR* 12(2): 81–83; for more discussion of the horses being incapacitated and needing forage, see also *OR* 12(2): 12–17; *OR* 12(3): 439, 490–500, 514, 581, 588, 628, 677. For more on the importance of military horses in the Civil War, see David J. Gerleman, "As Much a Military Supply as a Barrel of Gunpowder: Horses and Mules as Nineteenth-Century Engines of War," in *Animal Histories of the Civil War Era*, ed. Earl J. Hess (Baton Rouge: Louisiana State University Press, 2022), 45–68.

26. Pope, *Military Memoirs*, 134; *OR* 12(3): 666. Among the manifold problems with the telegraph, Wool complained that in his sector, near the Baltimore & Ohio Railroad, the telegraph operator was a Confederate spy, reflecting the mixed loyalties of the region (*OR* 12[3]: 477). For more examples of interruptions, see Pope to Brig. Gen. James Wadsworth, July 19, 1862, and Ruggles to Ricketts, July 10 and 11, 1862, LTS, Army of Virginia, RG 393.8, NARA. For examples of Haupt's attempts to observe and protect the telegraph, see *OR* 12(3): 718–20, 762. For the lack of communication between Halleck and Pope, see *OR* 12(3): 646; and *OR* 12(2): 6. For examples of Porter's communications to Burnside, see *OR* 12(3): 661–62, 699, 733.

27. Marszalek, *Commander of All Lincoln's Armies*, 145. McClellan famously told Lincoln to "leave Pope to get out of his scrape" on August 29; Pope, *Military Memoirs*, 163.

28. *OR* 12(2): 24; *OR* 12(3): 499, 514. Cozzens thoroughly discusses the difficulties with the Army of Virginia cavalry and Pope's poor decisions in response to a lack of what he considered believable intelligence; see Cozzens, *General John Pope*, 69–70, 104, 122, 145.

29. *OR* 12(2): 75–76; Cozzens, *General John Pope*, 137–39, 150. Pope had set up a signal station at Thoroughfare Gap, as Pope himself noted (*Military Memoirs*, 134), while McDowell's cavalry also observed Longstreet's advance (*OR* 12[2]: 338).

30. *OR* 12(3): 602, 608; Pope to All Telegraph Operators and Employees, July 18, 1862, LTS, Army of Virginia, RG 393.8, NARA. For Pope's attempts to improve discipline surrounding communications, see Ruggles to Schenck, June 29, 1862, and Pope to Banks, July 23, 1862, LTS, Army of Virginia, RG 393.8, NARA. The *New York Tribune* received the majority of the leaked information; see *OR* 12(3): 608–9; and Cozzens, *General John Pope*, 185. Lt. Col. David Strother on Pope's staff admitted to chatting with Mr. Smalley of the *New York Tribune*; Strother, *Virginia Yankee in the Civil War*, 72.

31. *OR* 12(3): 479, 498–99; *OR* 12(2): 50.

32. *OR* 12(2): 51–52. To Lincoln, Pope explained that General Orders No. 11 meant to address communications: "I find it impossible to make any movement . . . without having it immediately communicated to the enemy. Constant correspondence, verbally and by letter, between the enemy's forces and the so-called peaceful citizens in the rear of this army, is carried on, which can in no other way be interrupted" (*OR* 12[3]: 500–501). All the orders on confiscation and guerrillas, save No. 11, appeared in the *New York Times* on July 19 and therefore must have been issued July 18; "Gen. Pope's General Orders," *New York Times*, July 19, 1862.

33. *OR* 12(3): 525; *OR* 12(2): 52–53.

34. *OR* 12(3): 509; *OR* 11(3): 349; George C. Bradley and Richard L Dahlen, *From Conciliation to Conquest: The Sack of Athens and the Court-Martial of Colonel John B. Turchin* (Tuscaloosa: University of Alabama Press, 2006), 217; *The Wartime Papers of R. E. Lee*, ed.

Clifford Dowdey and Louis H. Manarin (Boston: Little, Brown, 1961), 245. For McClellan's implementation of confiscation, see Glenn David Brasher, *The Peninsula Campaign and the Necessity of Emancipation: African Americans and the Fight for Freedom* (Chapel Hill: University of North Carolina Press, 2012). For congressional confiscation and 1861 Missouri policy against Confederate civilians, see *An Act to Suppress Insurrection, to Punish Treason and Rebellion, to Seize and Confiscate the Property of Rebels, and for Other Purposes*, Public Law 195, *US Statutes at Large* 12 (1863): 589–92; Pope, *Military Memoirs*, 24; and Neely, *Fate of Liberty*, 33–35, especially for Lincoln's tacit approval of Missouri confiscation by Ulysses S. Grant and policies against civilians by Pope and Frémont. For discussion of the marauding effects of Pope's orders, see Marsena Rudolph Patrick, *Inside Lincoln's Army: The Diary of Marsena Rudolph Patrick, Provost Marshal General, Army of the Potomac*, ed. David S. Sparks (New York: Thomas Yoseloff, 1964), 120; Matsui, *First Republican Army*, 48–50; Grimsley, *Hard Hand of War*, 106; Foote, *Rites of Retaliation*, 29; and Benjamin P. Thomas and Harold M. Hyman, *Stanton: The Life and Times of Lincoln's Secretary of War* (New York: Alfred A. Knopf), 218.

35. *OR* 12(3): 573; *OR* ser. 3, 2:397. In his memoirs Pope lamented about how his General Orders No. 3 in 1861 Missouri, which sought to employ peaceful civilians in counteracting guerrilla activity against transportation and supply, was misinterpreted; Pope, *Military Memoirs*, 22–23, and for the full text of the order, see *OR* 3: 417–18.

36. Thus, this interpretation of Pope and his army contrasts with Matsui, *First Republican Army*. There is some question of whether or not Secretary Stanton oversaw or even wrote some of Pope's orders; see Grimsley, *Hard Hand of War*, 106; Thomas and Hyman, *Stanton*, 217; and Walter Stahr, *Stanton: Lincoln's War Secretary* (New York: Simon and Schuster, 2017), 222. The sole piece of evidence upon which this rests is a postwar account: Jacob D. Cox, *Military Reminiscences of the Civil War*, 2 vols. (New York: C. Scribner's Sons, 1900), 1:223–24. As Cox wrote, "Pope has himself told me that [his much-ridiculed manifesto to the army], as well as the other orders issued at that time and which were much criticized, were drafted under the dictation, in substance, of Mr. Stanton. . . . He admitted that some things in them were not quite in good taste; but the feeling was that it was desirable to infuse vigor into the army" and "condemn McClellan's policy of over-caution in military matters." Surely, this postwar statement must be read in light of the calamitous outcome of Pope's orders, rather than as a factual account of their origins.

37. *OR* 12(3): 814–18.

THE ARMY OF VIRGINIA CONFRONTS THE "MORAL SPECTACLE" OF FREEDOM

JOHN J. HENNESSY

In the spring of 1862—months before John Pope arrived to take command—the men who would become his Army of Virginia poured into Virginia across a seventy-five-mile front, from the lower Shenandoah Valley across the Blue Ridge to Fredericksburg on the Rappahannock River. All volunteers, they marched with a near-universal commitment to restoring the fractured Union but with varied views on almost everything else associated with this war, especially race and slavery. Some were spectacularly racist, hardly less sympathetic to enslaved people than enslavers themselves. Others felt a commitment to emancipation, though that commitment often existed seamlessly with paternalistic, racist views toward enslaved people. Many, however, thought as Albert Young of the 6th Wisconsin did. "I had not given [slavery] much thought or attention," he wrote years later. "[I] had looked upon it as a thing with which I had nothing intimately to do. I had never thought I had entered the army in the interest of the slave."[1]

Ambivalence would not survive the summer of 1862.

The Union war effort had stalled. Defeat at Bull Run in 1861 and the slog of a campaign on the Peninsula were trial enough. But even successes in the West at Fort Donelson, Shiloh, and Corinth in 1862 had done little to nudge the needle toward a restored Union. And so, during that spring and summer, Abraham Lincoln, Congress, the cabinet, and the nation at large pondered new measures that would escalate the war and speed victory. Most measures were obvious—common to all wars. More troops: on July 1, 1862, Lincoln called on the states for 300,000 more. Expanded operations: across the South, US armies and the navy became more active across a vastly broader front. New technologies: improved weapons and tools, like the telegraph, found their way to the front lines.

But two issues closely enmeshed spoke to the complexities of *this* civil war and carried immense political implications. First, should the Federals continue their policy of conciliation toward disloyal Southern civilians—often, slave owners—in areas where Union armies operated? Present policy toward civilians had Union officers placing men to protect the houses, farmyards, and larders from unauthorized confiscation by the army. Would not waging a "harder war" diminish both the will and the ability of Southerners to support the rebellion? More personally, soldiers in the field wondered, did not these civilians deserve to have their lives disrupted by war as completely as the soldiers' lives had been? "They ask our kindness and then laugh at us for giving it," grumbled Capt. Andrew Jackson Glover of the 76th New York.[2]

Second, and most significant, should the war—and by extension US armies—be a tool for extinguishing slavery where it could be reached? In other words, should the war for the Union also be a war for freedom? This question rode two rails, becoming increasingly parallel (and thus functional) as 1862 progressed. The first: reality on the ground. As the Federal armies moved, enslaved people fled into Union lines. With their feet and a good deal of courage, they challenged the attitudes of enlisted men and officers and forced thousands to consider the place of freedom in the Union war effort. As a practical matter, evidence clearly shows that most soldiers—even those reluctant to embrace policies that would brand this a war for abolition—over time accepted freedom as an inevitable result of their presence in the field. The acts of enslaved refugees added urgency to the government's consideration of the role emancipation would play in the Union war effort. As historian James Oakes has argued, questions of evolving Federal policies "vested the often-solitary act of running away with tremendous political significance."[3]

Those policies constituted the second rail. Questions of official policies that would escalate the war—and inevitably redefine its political and social purpose—not only tested Union leaders but also divided the nation. The choices involved in setting "war policy" and aims of the war became the guideposts for fierce public debate in congressional and gubernatorial elections in 1862 and 1863 (and even in the presidential election of 1864). The men in the armies that would ultimately be called on to implement these policies debated them closely. In turn, soldiers became powerful voices on these topics, expressed often and widely in letters to newspapers and firesides in the North. Over time, while many in the Army of Virginia and the Army of the Potomac maintained a fierce loyalty to their first commander, primo conciliator George B. McClellan, they departed from him on the question of conciliation. By 1863, the army produced dozens of public proclamations equating support for the war with support for the Lincoln administration's policies, including emancipation.[4]

Maj. Gen. John Pope's tenure as commander of the Army of Virginia is inevitably associated with this debate about Union policies toward civilians and slavery. Contrary to popular view, however, his appointment did not provoke the debate. Instead, his appointment culminated a conversation long since underway. Pope was a *tool* for implementing change—and therefore became a focus of both praise and criticism—but the changes were not his. Instead, they were the product of policies being implemented nationwide, initiated not by Pope but by Lincoln, driven by an increasingly aggressive Congress. And those polices were driven in important ways by the experiences of Union troops in the field and the enslaved people who flocked toward them. That spring and summer, no troops had more extensive contact with Virginia's civilians than the soldiers who would serve in Pope's army.

The men who would make up Pope's army took to the field under three separate commands in March and April 1862. Each command would, in June, become a corps in Pope's Army of Virginia (and later in the Army of the Potomac). Maj. Gen. John C. Frémont (an antislavery Republican candidate for president in 1856) and then Maj. Gen. Franz Sigel commanded what would be Pope's First Corps. Sigel, a German national possessed of a military pedigree, was engaged by Lincoln because of his political influence among German immigrants, who made up a significant minority of his command. A notable Republican and a quiet, politic opponent of slavery, he encouraged "such means as will permanently introduce Liberty into the South." Ironically, the most stridently antislavery of Pope's eventual corps commanders would, until mid-July 1862, operate in the part of Virginia with the fewest enslaved people—the Shenandoah Valley and the mountains to the west.[5]

Former Massachusetts governor and Republican Speaker of the US House of Representatives Nathaniel Banks commanded what would become Pope's Second Corps. Like Frémont's and Sigel's, Major General Banks's men operated first in the Shenandoah Valley, where part of the command played foils to Maj. Gen. Stonewall Jackson's springtime successes. Banks opposed slavery, but always with the restraint of a political operator; he proselytized not at all to his men on the subject. Like Sigel, Banks moved his command wholly across the Blue Ridge to the Piedmont in July 1862.[6]

Maj. Gen. Irvin McDowell commanded the largest contingent of what would be Pope's army—the Third Corps. For much of the spring and summer of 1862, McDowell's men straddled the Piedmont and Tidewater at Fredericksburg, in a region deeply invested in the institution of slavery. There McDowell stood poised to advance on Richmond from the north, but Jackson's campaign in the Valley squashed those plans. Instead, much of McDowell's command experienced prolonged contact with local civilians and enslaved people. As much as any place in Virginia, circumstances near Fredericksburg tested Federal policies for the treatment of disloyal Southern civilians and the management of enslaved people entering Union lines.

McDowell, shadowed by the defeat at Bull Run, clung to the greased pole of command with intense loyalty to his nation, a politic demeanor, and the support of Treasury secretary Salmon P. Chase. Still, an uncharismatic persona and sometimes "arrogant manner" (as Pope put it) rendered him what one correspondent called "the most unpopular man in America." Like most officers of the regular army, McDowell never declared his politics publicly so far as we know. But his letters to his wife during that summer of 1862 confirm him to be a staunch advocate of conciliatory war, much in line with the Democrat (and future presidential candidate) Maj. Gen. George B. McClellan. Indeed, his solicitousness toward Southern civilians made many in his command question his loyalty, which in turn provoked McDowell to ask a court of inquiry to investigate and exonerate him (it did).[7]

In March and April 1862, the soldiers of McDowell's, Banks's, and Frémont's command marched to the interior of Virginia. That spring they would fight battles in the Shenandoah Valley, but until early August they mostly occupied or roamed across the landscape of central and Northern Virginia and the lower Shenandoah Valley. Close interaction with civilian and enslaved populations prompted many of these soldiers to ponder the great questions of war that confronted the nation that spring and summer. Their views about the nature of this war, race, and slavery would be tested and, often, sharpened.

Irvin McDowell's men marched toward Fredericksburg just days after Lincoln signed the bill providing compensated emancipation for enslaved people in the District of Columbia. Through fields green with winter wheat and peach orchards in bloom and farms untouched by armies, the men marched into a world dominated by bondage. They saw—often for the only time during the war—"practical slavery" in full, functioning form. If McDowell's soldiers held a wide range of opinions and a good deal of apathy about slavery and the war's purpose, they quickly discovered that enslaved people in Virginia saw the war and the Union army with hawkeyed clarity. For them, the approach of a column of Union troops meant one thing: deliverance.[8]

As the soldiers marched, slavery disintegrated before them. John Washington, an enslaved man in Fredericksburg and one of the few eventual refugees who wrote of his perceptions and experiences, explained that from the outset he saw the war as a mainspring for freedom. For him, the firing on Fort Sumter meant "the Death knell of slavery." He followed the war in local newspapers with intensity but conceded, "Little did I think that my deliverence was So near at hand."[9] When the Union army marched into Stafford County toward Fredericksburg that spring, the mechanism of freedom became instantly obvious to Washington and other enslaved people. Those people working in roadside fields or yards dropped their tools as the Union columns approached and, as an officer of the 14th Brooklyn wrote, "rushed to the sides of the road to meet us with wild demonstrations of joy." Another soldier told his hometown newspaper, "Some of them danced for joy, and all hailed us with delight as they looked upon us as their deliverers from bondage." A New Yorker wrote of a "venerable old man" who spoke with a profoundness made clear only by history: "We's mighty glad to see you gentlemen; been 'specting you long time; the more of you we sees, the gladder we is."[10]

Some enslaved people followed the Union columns for miles, tracking through adjacent fields. In a Pennsylvania regiment, soldiers broke ranks to shake hands with a group of enslaved women cheering from the roadside. The men received surprise kisses in return, which caused a quick retreat and some guffaws from the ranks. Elsewhere, a US sharpshooter wrote of his encounter with an enslaved woman. "[She] came up to me and said she had been waiting all her life time to see us come and she thanked the lord that we had come at last." An enslaved man asked a New York soldier what he ought to do next. "Well, do what you like, and go where you please," the soldier responded. "You dont belong to Massa any more than Massa belongs to you." A woman bid the soldiers on: "Our prayers are [with] you." One soldier called the appearance of the enslaved people a "moral spectacle."[11]

The reaction of enslaved people to the presence of the US soldiers exploded a myth that had long been propagated by Southerners: that the loyalty of enslaved people to their enslavers would prevent them from fleeing bondage. Some enslaved people certainly remained with their owners from a sense of loyalty or from fear of what running away (especially with children) might entail. But after watching thousands move through Union lines, a Pennsylvania soldier labeled the supposed affinity between master and slave "like the attachment between oil and water." Chaplain Cornelius Van Santvoord of the 20th New York State Militia blithely declared, "I haven't yet happened to see" evidence of the mythological attachment. Instead he saw hundreds heading north, "eager to turn their backs upon their masters forever, if they can only carry their families with them."[12]

In March in Charles Town (now West Virginia) in the lower Shenandoah Valley, Maj. Wilder Dwight of Banks's command watched "a large wagon full of negro men, women, and children, overrunning like the old woman's shoe," newly arrived from the farm of a "disloyal rebel." They were, Dwight wrote, symbolic of the "question typifying the status of the slave everywhere, as the army marches on." Dwight was no advocate of formal emancipation, but he rejoiced at the newfound freedom claimed by these people. "The leaven is working; there is no stopping it."[13]

Throughout the spring and early summer, the three commands of Pope's army-to-be established themselves at Winchester, Warrenton, Fredericksburg, and, in July, Culpeper, with a great deal of shuffling in between. Word of the Union army's presence traveled fast and wide among enslaved people, who soon embarked on life-changing journeys toward Union lines, some from nearly 100 miles away.[14]

In the Fredericksburg region, the enslaved population constituted about half of all those living in the town and adjacent Spotsylvania and Stafford Counties. The default story of the region's experience invariably describes the arrival of the hated Yankees at Fredericksburg in dire terms. But John Washington remembered Good Friday 1862 as a glorious day. Twenty-four years old, he had spent most of his life in Fredericksburg, enslaved by Catherine Taliaferro and her family, who both managed and lived in the Farmer's Bank on Princess Anne Street (the building still stands). In 1862, the family hired Washington out to the Shakespeare House Hotel, and on that April 18 morning, Washington served breakfast to a room full of boarders and Confederate soldiers. All was "unusually quiet," wrote Washington, until "every body was startled by several reports of cannon." McDowell's Yankee column had arrived.

The white customers bolted. "In less time than it takes me to write these lines, every White man was out of the house," Washington remembered in his 1872 memoir. While the white men fled, "every man servant was out on the house top looking over the river at the Yankees for their glistening bayonets could eaziely be seen." The sight stirred Washington: "I could not begin to express my new born hopes for I felt already like I Was certain of My freedom now."

Later that afternoon, Washington tripped upstream to Falmouth with two other men to, as he recalled, "get right oppisite the 'Union Camp,' and listen to the great number of Bands" playing patriotic songs. Once there, soldiers on the other shore spotted the men and yelled across, "Do any of you want to come over?" Washington yelled back, "Yes, I want to come over." The soldiers quickly appeared on the Fredericksburg shore with a boat, and John Washington was soon within Union lines, surrounded by curious soldiers full of questions. They informed him of the emancipation of enslaved people in Washington, DC. One of them asked, "Do you want to be free?" "By all means," Washington replied. He later explained, "I did not know what to say for I was dumb with joy and could only thank God and laugh. . . . *This was the First Night* of my freedom."[15]

Despite efforts by enslavers to stymie the flow of information, word of the Union army's advance spread widely, and so did hope. From Spotsylvania, Caroline, Orange, Madison, and counties farther south they came, not in a trickle, as in the early phase of the Peninsula campaign, but in such numbers that the Federals could hardly have resisted their advance had they wanted to.[16] Some fled because their owners threatened to move them south to "protect" them from the advancing Yankee hordes. Some came despite dire warnings from their exploiters that the Yankees would starve them, ship them to Cuba, cut off their legs, or simply sell them for a profit. A woman enslaved by former congressman Jeremiah Morton of Orange County told a relief worker that Morton said he would "put them in a barn and burn them all up" before he would let his people go free. That woman promptly bolted with her three children, without clothes or supplies. Another of Morton's bondwomen carried away six children—three of her own and three of her dead sister's. Along the way to Union lines, she fell twice, injuring the baby she carried so severely that it died after reaching Alexandria.[17]

Faced with the approach of the US Army, some white owners simply abandoned their farms or plantations, leaving the places to the care of presumably "loyal" enslaved people, who quickly disproved their enslavers' assumptions by heading north. Mostly they carried what they needed and little else in bundles on their backs or baskets on their heads. Some made off with their owner's horses, wagons, carts, and, occasionally, jewelry and other valuables. Three enslaved men coming through Confederate-controlled territory south of Fredericksburg "laid out" in the woods beyond Union lines for fully six weeks, "waiting for the chance to get within our lines," as a New Yorker reported. One couple traveled fourteen miles in the rain, riding into camp on two of their former owner's horses. They "sold them for five Dollars a piece," reported a soldier. "And nice horses they were too."[18]

Before leaving their places of bondage, some enslaved people took a measure of retribution. When a Union patrol reached the Somerville farm on the Rapidan in Culpeper County, the plantation's emboldened coachman marched into his owner's bedchamber, "dressed himself in his [owner's] best suit of clothes, put on his hat, watch and chain, [and] took his [riding] stick." The coachman proceeded to the parlor, where he informed his enslaver that he "might for the future drive his own coach." And then he left.[19]

The act of fleeing bondage was both a personal quest and a political act—indeed, perhaps the boldest, most courageous act of antislavery political action possible. Constant "Con" Hanks of the 20th New York State Militia seemed awed by the determination of enslaved people—and especially women—entering the lines of his regiment near Fredericksburg. He recounted a hot day when eighty "contrabands" (as the army termed enslaved refugees) arrived at his company's picket line: "Women, with little ones in their arms, eve[r]y one barefoot & bareheaded, some of the women were naked down to the waists." One woman "had her back all cut to pieces with the whip, for trying to run away once before, whipped till all raw then throw on brine." He especially recalled "an old grayheaded" woman "bent almost double with age" with a three-year-old girl in tow—both of them "barefooted and bareheaded" in the broiling sun. The woman explained that for three days they traveled at night and "hid in swamps" during the day until they reached Hanks's regiment. Though self-described as "rough-hewn," Hanks admitted her story brought him to tears. "The thought came rushing into my mind, [']Con, Suppose that was, your Mother, and little one[.']" Hanks worried for the refugees' future. He wrote, "It is the desire of my heart that the poor wretches may not be disapointed in the confidence they place in our flag but I fear, our government is still afraid of wounding the feelings of the Rebs."[20]

Enslaved people hailed the arrival of the amoeba-like army with their feet. The exodus was largest where enslaved people were most numerous—east of the Blue Ridge and, especially, near Fredericksburg, where the Tidewater met the Piedmont. Between the army's springtime arrival and August departure, the flow of refugees became a routine part of each day for the army. Across four months, more than 10,000 enslaved people entered McDowell's lines at Fredericksburg, with thousands more seeking refuge in Banks's and Sigel's commands in the Valley and the Piedmont.[21] The records we have of more than 2,400 individuals fleeing their owners between April and September in or adjacent to the counties where Pope's army operated tell us a good deal about the nature and pace of the exodus. Those able to flee were the core of the enslaved workforce in the region. About 70 percent were men. More than 60 percent were between the ages of eighteen and thirty-nine. Only 10 percent were over forty years old. That men outnumbered women by a two-to-one margin suggests the complexities of the choices enslaved women faced, as they considered the perils of carrying children and whole families through a dangerous landscape to freedom. Still, of those refugees who can be identified by age, 30 percent were under age eighteen—many of them teenagers.

The timing of their flight to Union lines seems to have had more to do with the proximity and direction of the Union army than emerging Federal policies. There is little empirical evidence to suggest that enslaved people reacted in numbers to political acts like the passage of the Second Confiscation Act or the appointment of John Pope to command. In the eleven counties affected by the presence of Pope's army, nearly 15 percent of those whose date of escape is known left in April and May; 21 percent fled in June, 24 percent in July, and 22 percent in August. These numbers reflect some dramatic local differences—differences invariably connected to the presence (or not) of part of the Union army. In Caroline County, just south of Fredericksburg, 85 percent of refugees whose date of departure is known left in June or July (McDowell's force left Fredericksburg in early August). In Orange County, August witnessed the peak of exodus, as Gen. Robert E. Lee's army arrived and Pope's army departed adjacent Culpeper County. In Shenandoah County—the heart of the Valley—more than 90 percent of reported escapees (admittedly a small sample) fled in April, when Banks's army arrived. When Banks's men reached Rockingham County and Harrisonburg in May, the county's commissioner of revenue, William Hamrick (who collected taxes on personal property, which included enslaved people), reported that the 60 enslaved people who had escaped in 1862 had done so in April (22 percent), May (50 percent), or June (28 percent). In the two months after the removal of Pope's army from Virginia, the seven counties in the region that reported more than 1,550 escapes from April through August reported just 15 in September and October 1862.[22]

The exodus astounded soldiers, sympathetic or not. Even a profoundly racist New Yorker who freely used tropes and slurs wrote of the spectacle of freedom: "It would astonish you if you should see the number of Negroes running around our and all the camps in this vacinity. I would hardly believe there could be the number in Slavery in all of Virginia."[23]

While in the Western Theater a few commanders actively worked to "confiscate" enslaved people—functionally freeing them—the armies in Virginia generally and simply *received* enslaved refugees entering Union lines. Still, a few worked to abet and protect enslaved people. Capt. E. P. Halsted on Brig. Gen. Abner Doubleday's staff was, wrote a fellow officer, "a thorough lover of the enslaved race." In April, he had ordered that "negroes coming into the lines . . . are to be treated as persons and not as chattels." In his own camp, Halsted went beyond that. He employed a Black man to go every day into the countryside to "bring in contrabands." Captain Halsted kept the escapees in a barn near his quarters and then, each morning, sent them on their way to Washington.[24]

Near Middletown in the Shenandoah Valley, a small group of soldiers from the 60th New York of Banks's command encountered an enslaved boy whose back bore the scars of the whip. They waited till night and then spirited the boy and his friend to freedom. One of the soldiers proclaimed, "If I never did it before, I am persuaded that I have now done God's service." Another soldier called their success "the proudest and happiest moment of my life."[25]

When an outraged enslaver entered camp to reclaim a man who had run away, soldiers of a New York regiment at Fredericksburg rose to the enslaved man's defense. They so roughed up the slave owner that the regiment's provost guard intervened to prevent his injury. Maj. Rufus R. Dawes of the 6th Wisconsin noted the moment: "Thus the great question of liberty is working for its own solution. The right must, and surely will, triumph in the end."[26] Soldiers also intervened when they saw Duff Green—one of the leading merchants in Falmouth, on the Rappahannock—"correcting" an enslaved woman with "great brutality." They stopped the beating, which prompted Green, a man accustomed to getting his own way, to complain to the provost marshal's office in Falmouth about their interference. The acting provost marshal told Green the soldiers had "acted perfectly right" and turned him away. The officer reported, "The woman is now under the care of one of my surgeons suffering severely from the beating she received."[27]

Soldiers also attempted to rile the local slavery-based economy by urging enslaved people to demand wages for their labor rather than simply leave—a strategy that undermined the institution while seeming to discourage the migration of African Americans to the North.[28] The stratagem outraged local slave owners like Jane Beale of Fredericksburg. In a haughty rant, she wrote that the idea of Northerners insisting Southerners pay wages was intended to "prevent the north from feeling the great evil of a useless, expensive and degraded population among them." Paying wages "cannot be submitted to," she wrote. The suggestion "strikes at the root of those principles and rights for which our Southern people are contending." She declared her "love" for her "servants" but then got to the crux: being forced to pay wages "fixes upon us the incubus of supporting a race, who were ordained of high Heaven to serve the white man."[29]

When local physician John Byrd Hall agreed to pay his enslaved people, the men of Fredericksburg called a hasty meeting and "wrote him a letter of remonstrance," as Betty Herndon Maury recorded in her diary. The letter declared the idea "a most dangerous precedent" and against the laws of Virginia—rendering the once-venerable Dr. Hall "a traitor to his state." "So," as Maury recorded, "the old man refused to hire them, and they all left him"—an outcome that likely fulfilled Hall's fears and explained his motivation for choosing to pay them in the first place.[30]

Across the river in Stafford County, the emboldened people owned by Unionist Dr. Hugh Morson of "Little Falls" refused to work without pay. A Union soldier unsympathetic to the laborers' cause asked Morson, "Why not tie them up and give them a sound thrashing?" Morson dared not; the prying eyes of too many Union troops were around, men who were "probably unaccustomed to such measures and would become prejudicial against him, that they might interfere and perhaps injure him or his property."[31]

Union soldiers and white Confederate civilians could agree on little, but they did agree on this: slavery functionally ended wherever the Union army went, and even beyond. Rufus Dawes of the 6th Wisconsin declared, "No system of abolition could have swept the system away more effectually than does the advance of our army. Behind us the slaves if they choose are free." Fredericksburg resident Jane Beale concurred, but with an angry lament: "The Federal army has abolished slavery wherever it has gone." She continued, "If their design was to punish us by subjecting us to every inconvenience and indignity" that the end of slavery would entail, "they have succeeded."[32]

Slavery indeed seemed to be crumbling, but questions remained—such as what to do with those who had fled? A man in the 60th Ohio mused at the crowds of Black refugees in Winchester. "I don't believe *any one* can solve this problem," he wrote. On the Rappahannock, a soldier marveled at the procession of refugees rafting their way across, "'comin,' as they say, 'to be free.'" But, he wondered, "who will take care of them and how will it be done? There seems as yet to be no provision made by the government for them, further than letting them enter our lines and look out for themselves."[33]

The army that would be Pope's came into the field with remarkably little formal guidance on how to manage this influx of enslaved people seeking freedom in Union lines. The First Confiscation Act, passed in the aftermath of Bull Run in August 1861, applied only to enslaved people working in direct support of the Confederate war effort. Few of the thousands of enslaved people who entered McDowell's, Banks's, or Frémont's/Sigel's lines in 1862 met that criterion. A March 1862 law prohibited anyone in the military from returning "fugitives from service or labor" to their owners. But for the first half of 1862, the legal status of most escaping refugees remained undetermined, and the army had in place no universal process for managing them.[34]

In the Western Theater, the influx of enslaved refugees required army commanders to transport and house them in "contraband camps," a logistically daunting undertaking. In the Army of Virginia's area of operations, troops occupied and vacated areas regularly, a condition far too unstable to allow for contraband camps near the front. Unlike their counterparts in the Western Theater, Banks, Sigel, and McDowell simply turned over those refugees not retained to work in the army to the Military District of Washington—which included the District of Columbia and Alexandria. Rather than contraband camps, visitors to the front witnessed the passage of thousands of people by steamboat from Aquia Landing or along the Orange & Alexandria Railroad toward Washington and Alexandria. In July, Chaplain Benjamin Tefft of the 1st Maine Cavalry watched a train bound for the District covered with "twelve hundred negroes; men, women and children." They were, he wrote, "piled up, very much as you see bees hanging to the limbs of a tree when swarming. In this style they are constantly getting out of Dixie, on every road of every description, every one with his bundle, and with his face set northward." It seemed to Tefft that "if the war continues three months Virginia will be a free State . . . there will be no negroes on the sacred soil."[35]

Still, thousands of newly freed people, mostly men, lingered with the army in the field. They soon assumed an essential place in its operations. The press delighted in reporting on the intelligence brought to Union lines by "contrabands." Though the information they provided rarely shaped the decisions of men like McDowell and Banks, they proved invaluable to local commanders. Railroad man Herman Haupt recalled that "friendly contrabands" alerted soldiers to the presence of explosives placed under the tracks at the depot in Fredericksburg. East of the Blue Ridge, rare was the Union scouting party that left camp without a local African American man acting as guide. Dabney Walker became something of a legend in the Union camps, leading repeated raids across the Rappahannock. "He seemed to me a sort of Daniel Webster in ebony," wrote an officer in the 76th New York, "a strong, clear-headed man, who had reached a true conception of the real issues in this war, and devoted himself, body and soul, on the right side." That spring, Alec Turner escaped from a farm in Caroline County, downstream from Fredericksburg. The next night, he helped lead a cavalry raid back to the farm. During the melee, he set off to hunt down his former overseer. He found him and killed him.[36]

Far less alluring to scribes—but probably more important—thousands of refugees from slavery took jobs as laborers with the army, often earning wages for the first time in their lives. Both Banks and McDowell issued orders that, as McDowell directed, the "colored fugitives" be "taken up for the public service, and . . . be enrolled and registered." In a foreshadowing of the later and popular corps badges issued in the Army of the Potomac, McDowell's Quartermaster Department issued "a uniform badge" to each man, assigning him to a work gang ranging in size from tens to hundreds of men. In both Banks's and McDowell's commands, the newly employed men worked at depots, on bridges and roads, and upon the railroads—the drudge work that would release uniformed soldiers from those duties. McDowell directed that the bondmen-cum-freedmen receive one ration and be paid between twenty-five and forty cents each day, depending on the job. Their duties expanded as the summer progressed. In the Shenandoah Valley, Chaplain Alonzo Quint from Massachusetts relished the idea of newly freed people working for the army: "We could make the South tremble by the statement, 'your slaves shall be free, and they shall help conquer you.'"[37]

Everywhere in Virginia that summer—even in the Army of the Potomac—the practical won out over the ideological. On July 22, the president issued an executive order that made the practices initiated by Banks, Sigel, McDowell, and McClellan universal.[38]

After entering Union lines at Fredericksburg or in the Piedmont or the Valley, thousands of "contrabands" swarmed into regimental camps, looking for unofficial work. Individual soldiers and officers hired them to tend to menial jobs—blacking boots, hauling water and wood, preparing food, and even carrying knapsacks on the march. Teamsters had them feed and clean their horses and trail their wagons. The 20th New York State Militia engaged "forty or fifty" Black men, and other regiments had like numbers.[39] John Washington, who had crossed to freedom on Good Friday, took charge of Brig. Gen. Rufus King's mess. King paid Washington eighteen dollars per month for his services. Remuneration was not always automatic. A soldier from Banks's command noted that the officers of his battery had engaged four men, then added, "and they are very cheap, as they pay them nothing."[40]

While some in the army lamented the flight of enslaved people that spring and summer, few resisted enslaved peoples' claim to freedom.[41] Throughout the army, men also soon recognized something essential: that the exodus of enslaved people diminished the Confederacy's ability to support armies in the field. By July 1862, nearly half of Fauquier County's 10,455 enslaved people had fled. The Spotsylvania court reported to Richmond that in 1862, "the public enemy have carried off two thirds of the available blacks labor of the county." In Caroline County, south of Fredericksburg, 75 percent of enslaved people had left by war's end. In the summer of 1862, the evidence of this exodus was all around in the form of abandoned farms and weed-choked fields. Writing from Warrenton, Chaplain Quint of the 2nd Massachusetts claimed, "Crops sufficient to feed all New England are to be lost for want of laborers." Quint also drew a direct connection between the status of slavery and the strength of the Confederate army: "Able-bodied [white] men can be spared to fight wherever the black laborers remain."[42]

Soldiers increasingly recognized that while slavery's collapse weakened the Confederate war effort, it also empowered Union armies. Pvt. Ira Slawson of McDowell's corps pointed out that the same soldiers who in the spring "felt like flogging [escaped refugees] and sending them back to their masters" had by July become "reconciled" to their freedom. Why? They discovered, Slawson wrote, "that a free negro can and will work and that they are making themselves useful" by doing work that would otherwise be done by "us soldiers." A Pennsylvania artilleryman put it plainly: "We can use the negro to as good advantage as they [the Confederates] can." The result: fewer soldiers working in rear areas and more remaining with their regiments.[43]

Few things had greater impact on the mind of the Army of Virginia's men than close, extended interaction with the institution of slavery and newly freed people. For some soldiers the often-deplorable condition of enslaved people reinforced racial stereotypes and the legitimacy of slavery as an American institution. A Union soldier from western Virginia declared in a letter to a Pittsburgh newspaper that anyone who "comes through Virginia and sees the institution, will say that the negro is far better conditioned as a slave." He posited, "They are contented and happy and what more is needed?" Another man from the 84th Pennsylvania—which later proclaimed itself the "Copperhead Regiment"—asserted that his regiment was "well satisfied with the negro" in their present condition and that the soldiers "are not willing to further serve a government or undergo any more privations than they have in order to free them." This view was by no means rare in 1862, but it is also clear (as we shall see) that the philosophical trend in the army was toward embracing freedom and eventually emancipation as an outcome of the war. Few who in 1862 expressed a determination to quit a cause associated with emancipation (including many officers, like Brig. Gen. John Gibbon) acted on their promise. By 1864, public expressions of this sort would be rare indeed.[44]

Far more soldiers found the reality of enslavement jarring and revelatory. Its pure ugliness sharpened opinions and helped push Pope's army toward a reckoning on the profound issues of war, property, and humanity. Again and again, the physical and living conditions of enslaved people astonished Union soldiers. When in July, the men of a New York battery arrived at "Ben Venue," the Fletcher home near Gaines Crossroads in Rappahannock County, they found the brick slave cabins "full of negroes of all colors, sizes and sexes," wrote one soldier. "The young ones were all dressed in tow frock, like a bag, with a string around their necks. It was a most wretched sight, and presented the worst features of the peculiar institution." An Ohio soldier near Catlett's Station looked upon a group of enslaved people and bid his hometown readers to "see the poor ignorant wretches living away their earthly time in an extensive and well-ordered hell." He called the overseer "the master's pimp of Hell." He advised his townspeople, "Judge harshly and well." Another soldier concluded, "[Slavery] hardens the heart and callouses all feelings of humanity."[45]

The lash was the universal symbol of terroristic control in the American South. A New York soldier on the road between Fredericksburg and Culpeper recalled a light-skinned boy of twelve who, when he arrived in camp, revealed his back. "I saw it," the soldier wrote, "and I could not have imagined such a sight." Hardly any unscarred skin remained. "Broad scars and thick, red and blue seams and ridges, standing out, some of them, as thick as the finger, covered his back, crossing and overlying each other in every direction." A soldier in the Valley described a similar sight. "My God!" he wrote. "We had all read of scarred backs, but this surpassed all description." A fellow soldier cursed "the monstrous fiend . . . who had occasioned this."[46]

Whippings surprised no one, but the sexual exploitation of enslaved women by white men astonished many. Few soldiers commented directly on this reality, but innumerable men noted the many shades of skin color within enslaved populations, and indeed within families, with all that they implied. Capt. Elijah Cavins of the 14th Indiana wrote more explicitly about the topic than most. On the main street of Warrenton, he watched several hundred freed refugees gather on a Sunday. "They were of all colors from a rosy cheeked, blue eyed octaroon [that is, one-eighth African blood], to a full blooded african." He noted especially one woman who "drew a great deal of attention and admiration on account of her beauty." "One could not tell by seeing her, that she had any negro blood," Cavins wrote, but "she was a slave, and probably destined for the southern market"—all to "gratify an unholy lust." For enslaved women, Cavins wrote, "beauty which is usually considered a blessing, proves a curse."

Cavins was no trailblazer on racial justice—he fantasized that he would love to live in a Virginia without Black people—but he saw slavery as an affront to the moral concepts that underpinned families and, by extension, American values. In Virginia, he wrote, brothers may be sons of the same father but destined for radically different paths. "One rises to honor and distinction—an educated and free man," while the other "by circumstances and birth descends to the level, legally speaking of the ox" and consequently "a miserable life." A white brother might sell his own sibling. "The masters blood often mingles with that of his slaves, and finally broils under the lash and hot sun." Cavins concluded, "The more I see of the institution, the more I, loat[h]e and dispise it."[47]

As the commands that would become Pope's army darted and sprawled across the Virginia landscape that spring and summer, questions of humanity, policy, and freedom hung in the background. Near Catlett's Station, a soldier opposed to a formal policy of emancipation watched newly freed people "dance for joy" and hail US soldiers "as their deliverers from bondage." He mused, "I felt sad to think how their expectations would be blighted." At Fredericksburg, Union chaplain Cornelius Van Santvoord from Schenectady, New York, looked upon a similar scene of people emerging from bondage, but he had a different response—one that would resonate in America for decades: "Is not the negro a man?"[48]

John Pope assumed command of the Army of Virginia on June 26, 1862, after the pieces and parts of the army had been in the field for months. He came to his new command charged with changing what

Lincoln, Secretary of War Edwin Stanton, and others on Capitol Hill saw as a too-timorous military and political culture in Virginia. Pope enthusiastically assumed the mantle of disruptor, wielding performative prose like a scimitar. But on the issues of slavery, freedom, and emancipation, Pope the disruptor disrupted not at all. During his command of the Army of Virginia, as the nation simmered over the place emancipation ought to play in the Union war effort, Pope made no public utterances and issued no orders or proclamations regarding the most contentious issue of the day. Though he possessed uncommon antislavery credentials for a professional soldier, he chose the path of quietude so common among his fellow officers.[49]

When Pope took command, Federal policy on slavery lagged behind what refugees from bondage needed to lay claim to a certain future. As the summer solstice passed, the public and Congress debated confiscation and emancipation, and (unknown to the public) Lincoln pondered a formal emancipation proclamation. On July 17, Congress passed and the president signed the Second Confiscation Act. This law set the terms for the taking of Confederate property, establishing the basis for Pope's decidedly non-conciliatory orders regarding the treatment of civilians. The act also declared enslaved people who entered Union lines to be free. It signaled the continued evolution of government policies regarding slavery and enslaved people, but the law was also retrospective, addressing circumstances on the front lines of every Union army. It answered the question posed by thousands of enslaved refugees: "What are you going to do with us now?" The act gave legitimacy to the long-standing reality on the front in Virginia—it gave legal status and certainty to men, women, and children entering Union lines. But for soldiers and officers, little changed. Refugees seeking freedom still came as they had been coming for months, and the army continued to employ them or pass them rearward, to Washington.[50]

By July and August, the debate in the army over slavery did not turn so much on the stark choices of freedom or bondage (to the army, freedom was already a reality) but on a finer distinction: Men and officers largely accepted "practical abolition" as an incidental *result* of the army's presence, but they often balked at the idea that freedom for Black persons should be the war's *purpose*—part of the army's mission. Months of occupying and crisscrossing Virginia, bearing witness to the constant stream of freedom-seekers, had crystallized the thoughts of many in the Army of Virginia. The burning issue swirled around campfires and home fires: How should the government integrate the unstoppable process of freedom into the war effort?

If nothing else, the spring and summer of 1862 demonstrated to the men in Pope's army that the institution of slavery and Confederate resistance were intimately connected. Lincoln used precisely that rationale to envision and justify emancipation as a "war measure."[51] While some of Pope's soldiers went at the issue of emancipation from a place of moral righteousness or unadulterated racial prejudice, far more viewed it as a question of "war policy." In that, they had a personal stake. What would be the speediest path to a victorious end—and home?

"If necessary to put down the rebellion, I say emancipate—obliterate, annihilate and exterminate, white and black traitors," wrote a Pennsylvania soldier in McDowell's corps. "I'm not willing to expose my throat for cutting, or my ears for clipping, unless I can have 'an eye for an eye, a tooth for a tooth.'" Charles Morse of Banks's command originally thought "no change would be produced" by a proclamation of emancipation, but by summer's end he had changed his mind. A proclamation would "set us straight with foreign nations," he wrote, and "gives us a decided policy. Though envisioned as "nothing but a war measure," a formal proclamation would be a "great reform and the first blow struck at the real, original cause of the war."[52]

But, Chaplain Quint of Banks's corps wrote, "there are differences of opinion in the army as to the slavery question." He enumerated them. "Some want emancipation proclaimed. Some, practical and effectual emancipation without proclamations. Some, to leave slavery as it was before the war." Quint asserted that most drifted toward the middle ground, "effectual emancipation without proclamation." As for his own views, the Congregationalist chaplain had never voted Republican and considered himself a "conservative patriot," but time in the field had modified his opinion: "The more I see, the more I believe in the feasibility of emancipation." But how to do it? He preferred a continuation of the spontaneous process of emancipation that had been ongoing since the Union armies took the field, a process driven not by the army but by enslaved people themselves. No proclamation needed.[53]

Lt. Charles Brockway of Matthews's Battery kept the people of Bloomsburg, Pennsylvania, alternately informed and provoked with a steady stream of letters to the local paper, the *Columbia Democrat*. A conservative Democrat, Brockway in July was "opposed now as I ever have been to freeing the slaves through a mawkish philanthropy." But, he offered, if freeing enslaved people "can weaken the enemy and strengthen ourselves by using them, it would be highly criminal not to do so." He made clear, "It is not against slavery as an institution that I would war, but against it as a source of strength to the enemy." He wanted it understood, he wrote, that emancipation "is not given to benefit the slave, but to benefit us." Like Chaplain Quint, Brockway accepted freedom claimed by enslaved people but opposed a formal proclamation as unconstitutional and unwise.[54]

While many *favored* freedom because it would degrade the South's ability to wage war, others *opposed* a proclamation of emancipation for precisely the opposite reason—because it would inspire Southerners to fight harder (it did). Lt. George Breck, an artilleryman who served first with Banks and then McDowell, kept a steady stream of conservative thought pouring into the columns of his hometown newspaper, the *Rochester Union and Advertiser*. In a private letter, he called slavery "a great evil, and a great blight to our nation," and then explained a common rationale for opposing a formal emancipation proclamation. It would be an "agitation," he wrote, and its introduction "would only aggravate the South and tend to prolong and inhumanize the war." He also predicted that a proclamation would "divide and distract the people of the North and destroy all unity of design and action in the prosecution of the war."[55]

On July 7, 1862, George McClellan warned Lincoln about the effect of issuing a proclamation of emancipation: "A *declaration* of radical views, especially upon slavery, will rapidly disintegrate our present armies" (italics added). The warning came after months of the armies' interaction with enslaved people, with thousands of them seizing freedom in Union lines. Incidental liberation—an "accident of war," as Ned Abbott of the 2nd Massachusetts put it—did not disturb McClellan, or indeed many others in either Pope's or McClellan's armies. But the idea of rebranding the war as an "abolition war" by declaring the end of slavery one of its goals was for many a step too far.[56]

To some men, the prospect of a proclamation by Lincoln seemed insufferable. Lieutenant Brockway of Matthews's Pennsylvania battery, who supported spontaneous freedom as a contribution to the war effort, saw the prospect of a formal emancipation as a betrayal. "I enlisted in this war to restore the Union *as it was*, and to see the Constitution literally carried out. So did thousands of my countrymen. When that ceases to be the object, I no longer wish to remain in an army procured by such fraud and perjury." Corp. James W. Price, who wrote under the pseudonym "Toodles" from one of the most conservative regiments in Pope's army, declared that in Ricketts's division, "nine-tenths of the soldiers . . . are not willing to further serve a government or undergo any more privations than they have in order to free" enslaved people. Capt. Ned Abbott of the 2nd Massachusetts asserted flatly, "To make the main object of the war emancipation cannot be allowed."[57]

While the high command of Pope's army included several known Republicans, it also included a core of Democrats and regular army officers—the latter customarily among the most conservative members of society.[58] General Gibbon, a classic conciliationist who commanded what would become known as the Iron Brigade, believed that a proclamation of emancipation was "calculated to prolong the war." Later, as the Emancipation Proclamation loomed, he wrote his wife, "If this contest is going to end in an abolition war I cannot remain in the service." In his disaffection, Gibbon had company at the highest levels. Both McClellan and Maj. Gen. Joseph Hooker expressed similar sentiments.[59]

It is tempting to dismiss sentiments like Gibbon's as blather. In fact, the divisions that beset the army also plagued the Northern body politic. Debate over the nature and purpose of the war would be the fissure that defined American politics though the presidential election of 1864. In 1862, these divisions seemed profound and irreconcilable. But ultimately, the army did not dissolve, as McClellan predicted it might. The men of Ricketts's division did not leave en masse. Gibbon and Hooker did not resign (only a few officers did). But the views and fears of these men represented those of a substantial portion of the American population. Debate raged on, its tone intensified by Pope's reverse at Second Manassas.

Defeat led to the dismantling of Pope's Army of Virginia after just seventy days of existence and thirty-six days under Pope's direct control in the field. Pope exited westward, while McClellan integrated the three corps into the Army of the Potomac. Sigel's corps became the Eleventh Corps (he retained command), Banks's corps the Twelfth Corps, and McDowell's corps became the Potomac army's First Corps, commanded by Joseph Hooker. Soon, the revamped army won victory on Maryland's Antietam Creek. Days later, Abraham Lincoln declared his intent to issue the most important executive order in American history, the Emancipation Proclamation.

The Army of Virginia was no monolith of Republicans, or Democrats, or antislavery activists, or anti-government or anti-war agitators. The men of the army could not be neatly categorized as either pro-slavery or antislavery. Their personal views on race and slavery sometimes seemed at odds with the policies their government chose to pursue, but over time the context within which these men deliberated those issues shifted away from the prewar consideration of politics, economics, race, and morality to one framed by the interests of the army and the nation. A year hence, most soldiers in the Army of the Potomac, including many who had despised Black people and threatened to quit the war effort if emancipation became reality, came to see the value of emancipation to the Union war effort—to *their* efforts in the field.

This evolution had a great deal to do with the soldiers' experiences in the field. Extended contact with Southern civilians certainly gave them a more rigorous education on the realities of slavery and the perils of being in an occupying army than their fellow citizens at home had. The experience of Pope's army in 1862 helped shape a mindset that became essential to Union victory. Richard Cary of the 2nd Massachusetts put it plainly: he desired only "to get the means to show the South our power to conquer them." To soldiers, that meant clearing away civilians meddling with military matters. That meant embracing (or at least tolerating) policies—like emancipation—that made the army's success more likely. That meant the fierce rejection of the growing number of voices that advocated peace with the Confederacy intact.[60]

The process begun in that momentous season of 1862 left an important legacy—a Union army in Virginia increasingly determined to justify its own sacrifices with victory, restoration of the Union, and, eventually, the extinction of slavery. As one of Pope's former soldiers lectured peaceniks in his hometown in early 1863, "You who are trying to put into the minds of the soldiers that they are not fighting for the Union, not fighting to maintain the Government, but for [n——]; you are cowards and traitors. . . . I am in the Union army, fighting to put down the rebellion, and if the President thinks that by setting the slaves free he will weaken their cause, I am with him." Thomas Lucas of the 1st Pennsylvania Cavalry put it in more political terms as he summed up the result of a half year in the field: "I believe there really is but one party among the soldiers, and that is the union party."[61]

Union would triumph, but defeat littered the road to victory. On August 19, 1862, Pope began his retreat from the Rapidan River, pursued by Lee, destined for a bloody twelve-day ordeal ending in defeat at Second Manassas. As the army moved, enslaved people in Culpeper and Fauquier Counties—fearing the return of the Confederates—followed, "willing to take their chances even with a retreating army," noted one man. While army wagons, soldiers, and cattle crossed the railroad bridge over the river at Rappahannock Station, enslaved people headed for Cow Ford, a few hundred yards below the bridge. Franklin Hough, a surgeon with the 97th New York, wrote that they came "singly, in pairs, in groups, by families and in squads of ten and twenty." Another man recalled "an old negro man, driving a yoke of oxen fastened to a rickety wagon, on which were piled women and children, bedding

In the summer of 1862, fugitive enslaved people crossed the Rappahannock River at Cow Ford, just below the bridge of the Orange & Alexandria Railroad, in modern Remington (then Rappahannock Station). The images taken by Timothy O'Sullivan that day may be the only photographs that show enslaved people on the move to freedom in Virginia during the war. (Library of Congress Prints and Photographs Division, reproduction number LC-DIG-cwpb-00218)

and boxes, in wonderful confusion." And still a third man described a group "with an ox-team drawing a wagon, filled with their worldly goods, and on top of these were three wenches, and a perfect swarm of ebony children." At some point, photographer Timothy O'Sullivan arrived at Cow Ford. He set up his equipment just south of the crossing and took at least two images—maybe of one of the groups described by these soldiers. The photos become iconic—perhaps the only images of enslaved people in the act of seizing freedom taken during the Civil War.[62]

The people in that image—some of them with their heads turned away from the camera, as if fearful—challenged a nation with a simple question that would have been easier to dodge if not for their insistence: Here we are. What will you do with us now? The men, women, and children at Cow Ford that day were but a handful of the thousands that summer who by dint of their own initiative, energy, and courage altered the course of their lives and—despite Union defeats—the war itself and in so doing helped force a nation onto a new path.[63]

Notes

1. For hostility toward emancipation and enslaved people, see "Army Correspondence," *Pittsburgh Daily Post*, July 21, 1862. For one who favored freedom but with racist tropes intact, see William E. Hughes, ed., *The Civil War Papers of Lt. Colonel Newton T. Colby, New York Infantry* (Jefferson, NC: McFarland, 2012), 118 (letter of May 1, 1862). For the Young passage, see Albert V. Young, "His Pilgrimage," *Milwaukee Sunday Telegraph*, July 1, 1888.

2. Capt. A. J. Glover, "From the 76th," *Gazette and Banner* (Cortland, NY), July 3, 1862.

3. James Oakes, *The Crooked Road to Abolition: Abraham Lincoln and the Anti-slavery Constitution* (New York: W. W. Norton, 2021), xxix.

4. See Timothy J. Orr, "'A Viler Enemy in Our Rear': Pennsylvania Soldiers Confront the North's Antiwar Movement," in *View from the Ground: Experiences of Civil War Soldiers*, ed. Aaron Sheehan-Dean (Lexington: University of Kentucky Press, 2007), 171–98; and John J. Hennessy, "Evangelizing for Union, 1863: The Army of the Potomac, Its Enemies at Home, and a New Solidarity," *Journal of the Civil War Era* 4, no. 4 (December 2014): 533–58.

5. "Letter from General Sigel," *Boston Daily Advertiser*, October 25, 1862. With Pope's appointment, Frémont resigned. For more on Sigel, see Stephen D. Engle, *Yankee Dutchman: The Life of Franz Sigel* (Baton Rouge: Louisiana State University Press, 1999).

6. For a biography of Banks, see Raymond H. Banks, *King of Louisiana, 1862–1865, and Other Government Work: A Biography of Major General Nathaniel Prentice Banks, Speaker of the U.S. House of Representatives* (privately printed, 2005). Digital copy accessible at https://sites.google.com/site/nathanielpbanksbiography/home.

7. George Alfred Townsend, *Rustics in Rebellion: A Yankee Reporter on the Road to Richmond, 1861–65* (Chapel Hill: University of North Carolina Press, 1950), 206; John Pope, *The Military Memoirs of General John Pope*, ed. Peter Cozzens and Robert L. Girardi (Chapel Hill: University of North Carolina Press, 1998), 214–15. For McDowell's conservative views, see his letter of August 14 to "Dear Nelly," in McDowell Letters, Fredericksburg and Spotsylvania National Military Park Bound Volume (hereafter FRSP BV) 542-04, and his testimony in the *Report on the Committee on the Conduct of the War—In Three Parts*, pt. 3 (Washington, DC: General Printing Office, 1863), 444–49.

8. Edward B. Fowler, "Colonel Fowler's Own Story," in *History of the Fighting Fourteenth*, by C. V. Tevis (New York: Brooklyn Eagle Press, 1911), 248. See also letter of "C" (Chaplain Cornelius Van Santvoord), 20th New York State Militia, *Kingston Argus*, April 30, 1862.

9. David W. Blight, ed., *A Slave No More: Two Men Who Escaped to Freedom* (New York: Harcourt, 2007), 186.

10. Fowler, "Colonel Fowler's Own Story," 248; letter of "Another Private," 30th New York, *Lansingburgh (NY) Gazette*, May 1, 1862; letter of "Bould Soger," quoted in *Chronicles of the Twenty-First Regiment New York State Volunteers*, by J. Harrison Mills (Buffalo: republished by the 21st Regiment Veteran Association of Buffalo, 1887), 160.

11. Letter of Edwin Aldritt, 2nd US Sharpshooters, April 23, 1862, in *Stephen S. Raab Autographs, Catalog 39* (December 2001), copy in FRSP BV 401-08, 71; letter of "Another Private," *Lansingburgh Gazette*, May 1, 1862; letter of "Bould Soger" in Mills, *Chronicles of the Twenty-First*, 160; Frederic Denison, *Sabres and Spurs: The First Regiment Rhode Island Cavalry in the Civil War, 1861–1865* (Central Falls, RI: E. L. Freeman, 1876), 64.

12. Letter from "Col. Crockett" (a pseudonym) of the 42nd Pennsylvania, *Tioga County Agitator* (Wellsboro, PA), May 14, 1862; letter of "C" (Chaplain Cornelius Van Santvoord), 20th New York State Militia, *Kingston Argus*, May 7, 1862. For the ability of family members to travel as decisive in the decision to flee, see Alonzo H. Quint, *The Potomac and the Rapidan: Army Notes, from the Failure at Winchester to the Reenforcement of Rosecrans, 1861–3* (Boston: Crosby and Nichols; New York: O. S. Felt, 1864), 133, 134.

13. Elizabeth Amelia Dwight, ed., *Life and Letters of Wilder Dwight, Lieut.-Col. Second Mass. Inf. Vols.* (Boston: Ticknor and Fields, 1868), 205–6. For Dwight's views on freedom and emancipation, see p. 169.

14. Henry R. Pyne, *History of the First New Jersey Cavalry* (Trenton: J. A. Beecher, Publisher, 1871), 31; letter of "Jean," 24th New York, *Oneida Weekly Herald* (Utica, NY), May 6, 1862. In August, an enslaved man told of his journey to Fredericksburg from Chesterfield County, south of Richmond; see "A Contraband's Story," *National Republican* (Washington, DC), September 22, 1862; see also Jonathan A. Noyalas, *Slavery and Freedom in the Shenandoah Valley in the Civil War Era* (Gainesville: University Press of Florida, 2021), 63.

15. Blight, *Slave No More*, 192–93, 195.

16. In his trailblazing work, Glenn Brasher points out that the initial slow flow of enslaved refugees on the Peninsula might have been turned away at the outset if the soldiers in the army had chosen to do so. By contrast, sudden and sustained influx at Fredericksburg and Winchester suggest turning them away would have been impossible. Glenn David Brasher, *The Peninsula Campaign and the Necessity of Emancipation: African Americans and the Fight for Freedom* (Chapel Hill: University of North Carolina Press, 2012), 145–46.

17. Thavolia Glymph, *The Women's Fight: The Civil War's Battles for Home, Freedom, and Nation* (Chapel Hill: University of North Carolina Press, 2020), 98–99; Luis Biskey, Diary, April 11, 1862, FRSP BV 256–01 (45th New York); letter of "Dixie," 75th Ohio, *Pomeroy (OH) Weekly Telegraph*, August 22, 1862; Dwight, *Letters of Wilder Dwight*, 239; Edward P. Tobie, *History of the First Maine Cavalry, 1861–1865* (Boston: Emery and Hughes, 1887), 66; Julia Wilbur, Diary, entry for November 6, 1862, Julia Wilbur Papers, Haverford College, Quaker and Special Collections, accessible at TriCollege Libraries Digital Collections, https://digitalcollections.tricolib.brynmawr.edu/collections/julia-wilbur-diaries.

18. "From Fredericksburg: What 'Contrabands Are Good For," *New York Daily Tribune*, May 28, 1862, 1; Daniel E. Sutherland, *Seasons of War: Ordeal of a Confederate Community* (New York: Free Press, 1995), 126; Rufus R. Dawes, *Service with the Sixth Wisconsin Volunteers* (Marietta, OH: E. R. Alderman and Sons, 1890), 40–41; "Army Correspondence," letter of "S. D.," 23rd New York, *Hornellsville (NY) Tribune*, May 8, 1862; Pyne, *First New Jersey Cavalry*, 31; "A. W. H." [Austin W. Holden], "Letter from the 22nd Regiment N.Y.S. Vol's," *Glens Falls Republican*, June 17, 1862; letter of Oliver McAllaster [McAllister], 35th NY, April 25, 1862, quoted in John Hennessy, "Emancipation and Freedom—the Difference," *Fredericksburg Remembered* (blog), February 11, 2011, https://fredericksburghistory.wordpress.com/2011/02/11/abolition-emancipation-and-freedom-1862-style/.

19. "Negro Insubordination and Insolence," *Richmond Enquirer*, August 8, 1862, quoted in part in Sutherland, *Seasons of War*, 126.

20. Glymph, *Women's Fight*, 96, 102–3; Constant C. Hanks to his "Madam Rose, Dear Moll," May 1, 1862, and Hanks to his mother, August 8, 1862, Constant C. Hanks Papers, David M. Rubenstein Rare Book and Manuscript Library, Duke University. Hanks's

encounter with only women was likely happenstance—most groups coming into Union lines appear to have been families. As was the case with Abraham and Hester Tuckson of Fall Hill near Fredericksburg, men sometimes chose to precede their families in a quest for freedom. Or enslaved spouses sometimes had little or no access to each other, leaving women to act on their own. Eric Mink, "Slaves of Fall Hill: Abraham and Hester Tuckson," *Mysteries and Conundrums* (blog), January 17, 2011, https://npsfrsp.wordpress.com/2011/01/17/slaves-at-fall-hill-abraham-and-hester-tuckson.

21. US War Department, *The War of the Rebellion: A Compilation of the Official Records of the Union and Confederate Armies*, 128 vols., index and atlas (Washington, DC: Government Printing Office, 1880–1901), ser. 1, 12(3): 816 (hereafter cited as *OR*); Noyalas, *Slavery and Freedom in the Shenandoah Valley*, 63, notes that at times several hundred per day arrived in Union lines near Winchester.

22. "Record of Slaves that have escaped to the enemy during the war [1861–1863]" for the counties of Caroline, Culpeper, Louisa, Orange, Greene, Page, Shenandoah, Albemarle (which includes several individuals from Orange and Culpeper), and Rockingham, Library of Virginia. These records are available through the Library of Virginia website. See, for example, Culpeper: http://rosetta.virginiamemory.com:1801/delivery/DeliveryManagerServlet?dps_pid=IE2564026. (Unfortunately, Culpeper's records, which include more than 600 names, do not include the dates of escape.) No such records exist for Fredericksburg, Spotsylvania, and Stafford, but I compiled a list of more than 200 individuals from an examination of "Confederate Papers Relating to Citizens or Business Firms, Compiled 1874–1899, Documenting the Period 1861–1865," RG 109, M36, NARA, accessed via Fold3.com. These have been incorporated into the analysis. It's worth noting that Northern Neck and Middle Peninsula counties downstream from Fredericksburg reported few enslaved people escaping during the Union army's presence near Fredericksburg.

23. Letter of Oliver McAllaster [McAllister], April 25, 1862, in Hennessy, "Emancipation and Freedom—the Difference."

24. Kristopher A. Teters, *Practical Liberators: Union Officers in the Western Theater during the Civil War* (Chapel Hill: University of North Carolina Press, 2018), 36–39; Tevis, *Fighting Fourteenth*, 252; Halsted to Colonel Shaul (46th New York), in *Free at Last: A Documentary History of Slavery, Freedom, and the Civil War*, ed. Ira Berlin (New York: New Press, 1992), 36.

25. Richard Eddy, *History of the Sixtieth Regiment New York State Volunteers* (Philadelphia: Crissy and Markley, Printers, 1864), 120–21. See also George H. Gordon, *Brook Farm to Cedar Mountain: In the War of the Great Rebellion, 1861–62* (Boston: James R. Osgood, 1883), 159.

26. Dawes, *Service with the Sixth Wisconsin*, 40–41.

27. H. E. Danes Jr. to Capt. R. Chandler, May 5, 1862, RG 393, entry 3580, NARA.

28. See, as examples, letter of Jeremiah G. Burdick, May 13, 1862, FRSP BV 037–13; and "Virginia," letter of Chaplain Benjamin F. Tefft, 1st ME Cavalry, *Delaware (OH) Gazette*, July 11, 1862.

29. Kerri S. Barile and Barbara P. Willis, eds., *A Woman in a War-Torn Town: The Journal of Jane Howison Beale* (Virginia Beach: Donning Company, 2011), 74.

30. Carolyn Carpenter, ed., "The Civil War Diary of Betty Herndon Maury," *Fredericksburg History and Biography* 9 (2010): 74–75.

31. Hughes, *Papers of Lt. Colonel Newton T. Colby*, 118.

32. Dawes, *Service with the Sixth Wisconsin,* 40–41; Barile and Willis, *Woman in a War-Torn Town,* 78.

33. Letter of "Jean," *Oneida Weekly Herald,* May 6, 1862; "Letter from the 60th Ohio," *Highland (OH) Weekly News,* September 4, 1862. For the lack of preparation for the exodus, see also Dawes, *Service with the Sixth Wisconsin,* 41.

34. United States, *The Statutes at Large, Treaties, and Proclamations of the United States of America,* vol. 12 (Boston: Little, Brown, 1863), 354; Chandra Manning, *Troubled Refuge: Struggling for Freedom in the Civil War* (New York: Alfred Knopf, 2016), 49, 192, 196–98.

35. Tefft, "Virginia," *Delaware Gazette,* July 11, 1862. Not all refugees opted for life in the North. According to the *New York Herald* ("From Washington," June 16, 1862, and "Our Fredericksburg Correspondence," July 25, 1862), nearly 1,000 refugees opted for colonization by boarding one of James Redpath's vessels at Aquia Landing that summer, bound for Haiti rather than freedom in America.

36. Herman Haupt, *Reminiscences of General Herman Haupt* (Milwaukee: Wright and Joys, 1901), 49; George F. Noyes, *Bivouac and Battlefield; or Campaign Sketches in Virginia and Maryland* (New York: Harper and Brothers, 1863), 46. For Alec Turner's story, see Jane C. Beck, *Daisy Turner's Kin: An African American Family's Saga* (Urbana: University of Illinois Press, 2015), 86–87. Division commander Rufus King labeled reports from "contrabands" as "so contradictory and seemingly unreliable that other means must be employed," *OR* 12(3): 503. It's worth pointing out that the mistrust of information from contrabands was by no means unique; unwillingness to accept the observations of civilian aeronauts also helped doom the Federal Balloon Corps in 1863.

37. For Banks's Special Orders No. 50, see Jonathan Berkey, "War in the Borderland: The Civilians' Civil War in Virginia's Lower Shenandoah Valley" (PhD diss., Pennsylvania State University, 2003), 189; and Noyalas, *Slavery and Freedom in the Shenandoah Valley,* 67. McDowell's policies, issued on May 10, were more explicit. *OR* 12(1): 53. For wages, see the testimony of Davis Tillson, *OR* 12(1): 80–81. For the expansion of duties assigned to contrabands, see Col. Edmund Schriver to Rufus King, August 5, 1862, "Telegrams Sent, March–September 1862, Department of the Rappahannock," in RG 393, part 2, entry 3577, NARA; and Quint, *Potomac and the Rapidan,* 175.

38. Acknowledging the value of labor provided by contrabands, McClellan, the ultimate conciliator, wrote on July 11, "The supply of these operatives has thus far been insufficient for our wants." See *The Civil War Papers of George B. McClellan: Selected Correspondence, 1860–1865,* ed. Stephen W. Sears (New York: Ticknor and Fields, 1989), 353. For Lincoln's executive order, see *OR* 11(3): 362–63; and Brasher, *Peninsula Campaign,* 225.

39. Letter of "Jean," *Oneida Weekly Herald,* May 6, 1862; "From Fredericksburg" (letter of "C"—Cornelius Van Santvoord), *Schenectady (NY) Evening Star and Times,* May 22, 1862.

40. Blight, *Slave No More,* 196; letter of M. H. M., "Battery L" (Reynolds's Battery), *Rochester Democrat and American,* July 22, 1862; Noyes, *Bivouac and Battlefield,* 45.

41. For examples of two who did, see "From King's Division," *Milwaukee Sentinel,* May 12, 1862. James T. Fritsch records in his *Untried Life: The 29th Ohio Volunteer Infantry in the Civil War* (Athens: Swallow Press/Ohio University Press, 2012), 172, that an officer of the 66th Ohio returned an enslaved person to his owner in March 1862. For confirmation of the general cooperation of officers with emerging Union policy elsewhere, see Teters, *Practical Liberators,* 45.

42. Charles Boyce, "History of the 28th Regiment New York State Volunteers," unpublished ms., 137, Library of Congress (this history differs from his published regimental history of the 28th); Quint, *Potomac and the Rapidan*, letter of July 16, 1862, 168; "The Slaves of Fauquier County," *Richmond Daily Dispatch*, July 24, 1862; Susanna M. Lee, "Central Virginia at War," 237, 314, 318. This is an unpublished study done for the National Park Service in 2008, on file at Richmond National Battlefield and Fredericksburg and Spotsylvania National Military Park. For the wide-scale impact of the exodus of labor in the South in 1862, see Armstead L. Robinson, *Bitter Fruits of Bondage: The Demise of Slavery and the Collapse of the Confederacy* (Charlottesville: University of Virginia Press, 2005), 121–27.

43. Ira Slawson, "Letter from a Soldier," *Yates County Chronicle*, July 17, 1862; letter of "Artillerist" [Charles B. Brockway], "Our Army Correspondence," *Columbia Democrat* (Bloomsburg, PA), August 2, 1862.

44. "Army Correspondence," *Pittsburgh Daily Post*, July 21, 1862; Toodles [James W. Price], "Our Army Correspondence," *Star of the North*, July 2, 1862. For the transformation of the army's view in 1864, see John J. Hennessy, "I Dread the Spring: The Army of the Potomac Prepares for the Overland Campaign," in *The Wilderness Campaign*, ed. Gary Gallagher (Chapel Hill: University of North Carolina Press, 1997), 71–72. See also Zachary Fry, *A Republic in the Ranks: Loyalty and Dissent in the Army of the Potomac* (Chapel Hill: University of North Carolina Press, 2020), 128–29.

45. Letter of M. H. M., "Battery L" (Reynolds's Battery), July 13, 1862, *Rochester Democrat and American*, July 22, 1862; Daniel A. Masters, ed., *Army Life According to Arbaw: Civil War Letters of William A. Brand of the 66th Ohio Infantry* (Perrysburg, OH: Columbian Arsenal Press, 2019), 64; letter of "Col. Crockett," *Tioga County Agitator*, May 14, 1862.

46. George C. Smithe, *Glimpses: Of Places, and People, and Things* (Ypsilanti, MI: Ypsilantian Press, 1887), 23; Eddy, *History of the Sixtieth Regiment*, 120.

47. Barbara A. Smith, ed., *The Civil War Letters of Col. Elijah H. C. Cavins, 14th Indiana* (Owensboro, KY: Cook-McDowell Publications, 1981), 81–82. See also Jerome Mushkat, ed., *A Citizen-Soldier's Civil War: The Letters of Major General Alvin C. Voris* (Dekalb, IL: Northern Illinois University Press, 2002), 54; and "Our Army Correspondence: A Letter from Battery D, Camp Opposite Fredericksburg," *Providence Evening Press*, May 8, 1862. Joshua D. Rothman, *Notorious in the Neighborhood: Sex and Families across the Color Line in Virginia* (Chapel Hill: University of North Carolina Press, 2003), 133–34, notes prewar observations that mirror Cavins's.

48. Letter of "Another Private," *Lansingburgh Gazette*, May 1, 1862; letter of "C" (Cornelius Van Santvoord), *Kingston Argus*, May 7, 1862.

49. While Pope is not known to have issued any orders directly addressing slavery and enslaved people, General Sigel did after the Second Confiscation Act passed. See journal entry of Carl Schurz, July 21, 1862, quoted in John H. Matsui, *The First Republican Army: The Army of Virginia and the Radicalization of the Civil War* (Charlottesville: University of Virginia Press, 2016), 106. Pope had ample opportunity to articulate his views on slavery. On June 25, he visited the floor of the House of Representatives; see "From Washington," *Pittsburgh Gazette*, June 26, 1862; and "Gen. Pope in Congress," *New York Tribune*, June 26, 1862, 4. And in July he testified before the congressional Joint Committee on the Conduct of the War; see Report of the Joint Committee on the Conduct of the War, part 1 (Washington, DC: Government Printing Office, 1863), 276–82. In neither instance did he express his views on slavery.

50. An Act to Suppress Insurrection, to Punish Treason and Rebellion, to Seize and Confiscate the Property of Rebels, and for Other Purposes, 37th Cong., 2nd Sess. (1862), chap. 195, pp. 589–92. For the impact of the act, see Manning, *Troubled Refuge*, 190–97.

51. Allen C. Guelzo, *Lincoln's Emancipation Proclamation: The End of Slavery in America* (New York: Simon and Schuster, 2004), 113–14, 120.

52. Letter of "H. U.," probably of the 95th Pennsylvania, *Beaver (PA) Argus*, June 18, 1862; Charles F. Morse, *Letters Written during the Civil War* (privately printed, 1898), 98–99.

53. Alonzo Quint, "Slaves within the Army Lines," *Portsmouth Journal of Literature and Politics*, May 10, 1862; Quint, *Potomac and the Rapidan*, letter of July 16, 1862, 168.

54. Letter of "Artillerist" [Charles B. Brockway], "Our Army Correspondence," *Columbia Democrat* (Bloomsburg, PA), August 2, 1862.

55. Blake McKelvey, ed., "George Breck's Civil War Letters from the 'Reynolds Battery,'" in *Rochester in the Civil War: The Rochester Historical Society Publications XXII*, ed. Blake McKelvey (Rochester: Rochester Historical Society, 1944), 119–20. For Breck's excellent letters to the *Rochester Union and Advertiser*, see New York State Military Museum and Veterans Research Center, https://museum.dmna.ny.gov/unit-history/artillery/1st-artillery-regiment-light/battery-l-1st-artillery-regiment-light/battery-l-1st-artillery-regiment-light-george-breck-columns-chapter-1.

56. *OR* 11(1): 74.

57. Letter of "Artillerist" [Charles B. Brockway], "Our Army Correspondence," *Columbia Democrat*, June 7, 1862; Toodles [James W. Price], "Our Army Correspondence," *Star of the North*, July 2, 1862; Edward Gardner Abbott to his father, May 20, 1862, Abbott Family Letters, Houghton Library, Harvard University.

58. See Matsui, *First Republican Army*, 51–67, for an analysis of the makeup of the subordinate command of the Army of Virginia.

59. John Gibbon to his wife, November 21, 1862, John Gibbon Papers, Historical Society of Pennsylvania, Philadelphia; Joseph Hooker to Senator James Nesmith, May 4, 1862, James Nesmith Papers, Oregon Historical Society, Portland. McClellan declared, "I cannot make up my mind to fight for such an accursed doctrine as that of a servile insurrection—it is too infamous" (*Civil War Papers of George B. McClellan*, 481).

60. Letter of "Phi," *Indianapolis Daily Journal*, May 6, 1862; Richard Cary to his wife, July 21, 1862, Richard Cary Letters, Massachusetts Historical Society, Boston, accessible online at Massachusetts Historical Society, https://www.masshist.org/collection-guides/view/fa0378.

61. Dona Bayard Sauerburger, ed., *I Seat Myself to Write You a Few Lines: Civil War and Homestead Letters from Thomas Lucas and Family* (Westminster, MD: Heritage Books, 2002), 103; Letter of "Union," "Camp Correspondence," *West Jersey Pioneer* (Bridgeton, NJ), April 18, 1863. See also Enoch T. Baker to his wife, July 27, 1862, Enoch T. Baker Papers, Historical Society of Pennsylvania.

62. Isaac Hall, *History of the Ninety-Seventh Regiment New York Volunteers ("Conkling Rifles") in the War for the Union* (Utica: Press of L. C. Childs and Sons, 1890), 59; Franklin B. Hough, *History of Duryee's Brigade during the Campaign in Virginia under Gen. Pope and in Maryland under Gen. McClellan, in the Summer and Autumn of 1862* (Albany: J. Munsell, 1864), 72; William H. Locke, *The Story of the Regiment* (Philadelphia: J. B. Lippincott and Co., 1868), 95; Theodore B. Gates, *The Ulster Guard and the War of the Rebellion* (New York:

Benj. Tyrrel, Printer, 1879), 241. For the photos, see the Library of Congress website, www.loc.gov/pictures/collection/cwp/item/2018671748/. A similar exodus took place at Fredericksburg; see "From Fredericksburgh: Exodus of the Slave Population," *New York Times*, September 7, 1862.

63. Yael A. Sternhell, "Bodies in Motion and the Making of Emancipation," in *Rethinking American Emancipation: Legacies of Slavery and the Quest for Black Freedom*, ed. William A. Link and James J. Broomall (Cambridge: Cambridge University Press, 2016), 16–23. During the campaign, Jackson's Confederates recaptured 200 refugees at Bristoe Station and Manassas Junction, returning them to slavery (*OR* 12[2]: 643).

THE TIDE OF WAR HAS BEEN ROLLED BACK

Second Manassas in Confederate Perspective

GARY W. GALLAGHER

The campaign of Second Manassas figured prominently in a transformative phase of the Confederacy's brief and violent history.[1] Pitting Gen. Robert E. Lee's Army of Northern Virginia against Maj. Gen. John Pope's Army of Virginia and part of Maj. Gen. George B. McClellan's Army of the Potomac, it should be framed as the second of three acts in a sprawling drama extending from June through September 1862. Second Manassas typically is relegated to a supporting role, garnering less attention than the more celebrated Seven Days, which saved Richmond and thrust Lee to the forefront of the war in the Eastern Theater, or Antietam, which ended Lee's first foray into the United States and allowed Abraham Lincoln to issue the preliminary emancipation proclamation. Because the campaign of Second Manassas commenced just two weeks after the Seven Days and ended a few days before Lee crossed the Potomac into Maryland, it somehow seems less important, a bridge, as it were, connecting two more noteworthy events. In fact, all three battles merit individual examination as crucial components of Lee's protracted offensive that reoriented the war in the Eastern Theater.[2]

Second Manassas shaped two defining elements of the Confederacy's bid for independence. First, it provided the initial testing ground for a new leadership style and command structure in the Army of Northern Virginia that would make Lee and his soldiers preeminent among Rebel military forces. As part of this development, Lee began his own ascent to replace Maj. Gen. Thomas J. "Stonewall" Jackson as the Confederacy's favorite military idol. Lee's army took the fight to the enemy during a six-week period in July and August, providing a striking contrast to earlier defensive maneuvering under Gen. Joseph E. Johnston. By the time the army entered Maryland in early September, the Confederate people saw that Lee had created a culture of command typified by the aggressiveness of Jackson, Maj. Gen. James Longstreet, and Maj. Gen. James Ewell Brown "Jeb" Stuart.

Confederates devoutly hoped that culture would inflict substantial pain on the Yankee enemy because of a second transformation that occurred while Lee and Pope faced off. Between July and September, Pope's general orders relating to guerrilla warfare and subsisting off the land, congressional and presidential policies about emancipation, and actions by Union officers and enlisted personnel in Virginia created an outpouring of anger from Confederate politicians, soldiers, and civilians. Pope's pronouncements triggered the most passionate invective, prompting Confederate demands for a more punishing kind of war to counter what they considered a "savage" and "uncivilized" foe. Fearful for the safety of their private property, the stability of their slavery-based social structure, and the status of civilians who might be charged with abetting irregular units, Confederates drew together with an enhanced sense of communal striving in pursuit of independence. Any notion of brokering an end to the war that would restore the antebellum status quo largely disappeared in the summer of 1862.[3]

This essay explores the transformative nature of the Second Manassas campaign in three sections. The first situates the confrontation between Lee and Pope within the larger framework of military activity from June to September 1862, drawing almost entirely on contemporary testimony from civilians, soldiers, politicians, and journalists. The second part examines Lee's restructuring of the Army of Northern Virginia and how his aggressive planning and execution affected the Confederate citizenry and bolstered his reputation. The final part draws on newspapers, governmental pronouncements, and civilian and military evidence to probe how Pope's statements and the actions of his army helped change Confederate conceptions about the nature of the war.

From the Banks of the James River to Those of the Potomac

The Confederate offensive in the Eastern Theater between June and September marked one of the war's great watersheds. It relocated the epicenter of action from five miles outside the Rebel capital at Richmond to the Potomac River frontier. Connections among the three phases of the campaign were apparent to Lee's soldiers and Confederates behind the lines. Many people took in the whole sweep of the summer's operations and assessed results from that vantage point. Welcome news from Lee's army boosted national morale, which had plunged by early June after Rebel defeats at Fort Donelson and Shiloh, Federal occupation of New Orleans and Nashville, and the Army of the Potomac's approach to the outskirts of Richmond. The end of the Confederate experiment had seemed likely as George B. McClellan prepared to invest the capital.

Quotations from two civilians illuminate how dramatically Lee's generalship altered the strategic situation. Judith McGuire, a refugee from Alexandria who ended up in Richmond, noted in mid-May how "a gentleman, high in position, panic-struck, was heard to exclaim, yesterday: 'Norfolk has fallen, Richmond will fall, Virginia is to be given up, and tomorrow I shall leave this city, an exile and a beggar.' Others are equally despondent." On the last day of that month, with the Army of the Potomac closing in on Richmond, she recorded, "The booming of cannon, at no distant point, thrills us with apprehension. We know that a battle is going on. God help us! Now let every heart be raised to the God of battles." From that moment of imminent peril, McGuire followed the progress of Lee's army until, on September 2, she observed, "The papers to-day give glorious news of a victory to our arms on the plains of Manassas, on the 28th, 29th, and 30th. . . . My heart is full." Ten days later a newspaper account told "of General Lee's being pleased with his reception in Maryland, and that our troops are foraging in Pennsylvania. I hope so; I like the idea of our army subsisting on the enemy; they certainly have subsisted on us enough to be willing that we should return the compliment."[4]

A Confederate bureaucrat's diary mirrored McGuire's observations. On May 19, John Beauchamp Jones described a grimly pessimistic mood in the capital: "We await the issue before Richmond. It is still believed by many that it is the intention of the government and the generals to evacuate the city."

Twelve days later the armies prepared to clash at the battle of Seven Pines or Fair Oaks, and Richmond's citizenry trembled "upon the tip-toe of expectation. It has been announced (in the streets!) that a battle would take place this day, and hundreds of men, women, and children repaired to the hills to listen, and possibly to see, the firing." The sea change in Confederate fortunes stood out in Jones's staccato recounting of welcome facts after Lee's victory at Second Manassas: September 1, "Official dispatches from Lee, announcing a 'signal victory,' by the blessing of God, 'over the combined forces of the enemy'"; September 2, "Winchester is evacuated! The enemy fled, and left enough ordnance stores for a campaign. It was one of their principal depots"; September 6, "We have authentic accounts of our army crossing the Potomac without opposition."[5]

Lee and other officers in the army linked the three phases of the summer's campaigning. "Since your great victories around Richmond," the commanding general assured his soldiers on October 2, "you have defeated the enemy at Cedar Mountain, expelled him from the Rappahannock, . . . utterly repulsed him on the plains of Manassas, and forced him to take shelter within the fortifications around his capital. Without halting for repose, you crossed the Potomac, stormed the heights of Harper's Ferry, . . . [and] on the field of Sharpsburg . . . repulsed every attack along his entire front of more than 4 miles in extent." Lee affirmed that "history records few examples of greater fortitude and endurance than this army has exhibited."[6]

Brig. Gen. John Bell Hood, who led a brigade and then a division during the summer, congratulated his men on September 28, 1862. "After having distinguished yourselves at the battle of Gaines' Farm, June 27th," proclaimed Hood while the army camped near Winchester, "your long and continued and tiresome march since leaving Richmond—dashing courage at the battle of Manassas Plains, August 30th, your truly veteran conduct at the battle of Sharpsburg, Md., September 17th, has won for you the merited praise and gratitude of the army and our country." During those three months, the soldiers "marched several hundred miles under trying circumstances, participated in several battles, and made yourselves the acknowledged heroes of three of the hardest fought battles that have occurred in the present war."[7]

Two of Stonewall Jackson's officers commented about the summer's action while camped at Bunker Hill, a village in the lower Shenandoah Valley midway between Winchester and Martinsburg. A member of the general's staff found time on October 12 to reflect on the army's extensive campaigning. "It has not been three months since I left home," related Elisha Franklin Paxton, who could "hardly realize that it has been so long, the time has passed so rapidly. During this period I have had the pleasure of participating in what history will record as the most astonishing expeditions of the war, for the severity of the battles fought and the hardships endured by our soldiers." Paxton hoped the protracted operation had come to an end. "We may have some more activity this fall," he conceded, "but I am inclined to think the campaign is over. It is too late now for either side to think of accomplishing much before winter sets in." Writing a few days before Paxton, Capt. Thomas Henry Carter, an artillerist, speculated that "there may be another great battle this fall but I doubt it. This summers campaign must be nearly closed."[8]

Views from the ranks often aligned with those of officers such as Paxton. Typical was James E. Keever, a member of the 34th North Carolina Infantry in Brig. Gen. William Dorsey Pender's brigade, who betrayed a casual approach to spelling in his summary of the campaign. "I am in the north corner of VA.," he informed his brother from near Winchester on October 2, and prepared "to give you a small sketch on my hardships since I rote to you before on the mountain." Keever had "been in ten battles and marched over one thousand miles," he claimed with exaggeration as to distance: "The first battle was at Cedar Run. The second at Manassas Junction, also three hard fightings on Bulls Run where the big fight was last year. The sixth battle was at Ox Hill, the seventh at Harpers Ferry and the eighth in Marriland." Neglecting to name the ninth and tenth battles, Keever mentioned casualties, Union prisoners, and material goods captured before abruptly switching gears: "I will now quit the fighting subject and tell you of the crops."[9]

Newspapers similarly conveyed a sense of one operation punctuated by a series of large battles. Charleston's *Daily Courier* posed a question on October 4: "Was not Southern prowess as splendidly illustrated at Sharpsburg as it was before Richmond or on the plains of Manassas?" The paper asserted that "our army . . . today is stronger in numbers, with courage as firm and spirits as high as when it drove the beleaguering host from the Chic[k]ahominy and put to flight his legions on the field of Manassas." The *Macon Journal and Messenger* in Georgia printed a letter from a correspondent in Winchester, dated September 23, 1862, that predicted the "heavy work of the campaign is probably at an end." Jackson's troops might remain in the Shenandoah Valley for a while, "but the greater portion of the Confederate army will, it is thought, take up its position behind the Rappahannock, preparatory to going into winter quarters; while the main body of the Federal army will return to Washington." Noting the suffering experienced by many of Lee's soldiers, this observer averred that "no army on this continent has ever accomplished as much or suffered as much, as the army of Northern Virginia within the last three months. At no time during the first Revolutionary war—not even at Valley Forge—did our forefathers in arms encounter greater hardships, or endure them more uncomplainingly."[10]

Richmond's *Dispatch*, which generally supported Jefferson Davis's administration, chose spacious chronological framing to counter grumblings about the retreat after Antietam. "Our people have been spoiled so thoroughly by the constant succession of victories that have marked the progress of our arms for the last four months," scolded the editors on September 23, "that they bear even the appearance of a reverse with less patience than we had a right to expect from the same men whose noble fortitude, at a time when our city was actually beleaguered by the enemy, made them the admiration of the world." In Maryland, "we did not gain a victory as decisive as those around Richmond and at Manassas." But the people "cannot expect such victories always. It should be recollected that the great object of the operations in Maryland was the capture of the Yankee army of the Valley. That object was triumphantly accomplished."[11]

Another Richmond paper, the *Daily Enquirer*, echoed the *Dispatch* one day later. It counseled patience to await definitive word from the Potomac front and reminded readers that Lee had outgeneraled McClellan on the Chickahominy, made a fool of Pope at Manassas, and then bested McClellan again by capturing Harpers Ferry. Too many Confederates worried too much about which side of the river Lee and his army occupied. The difference between the two positions, "in fact, is an hour's march" and no more.[12]

A number of women's diaries placed Second Manassas within a longer span of campaigning. Cornelia Peake McDonald, a resident of Winchester, welcomed liberation from Union occupation in the aftermath of Pope's retreat to Washington. "On the 3d of September our troops came in," she wrote. "Our army is nearly all marching north. On their entrance we first learned of the victories and steady march of Lee from the Peninsula, the flight of McClellan, the battles of Cedar Mountain and Second Manassas, the rout of the vaunted Pope and the crossing of our men into Maryland." From Fredericksburg, which like Winchester had been occupied by Federal troops, Betty Herndon Maury cheered news of Confederate progress in August and into September. After Second Manassas, she wrote, "God be praised. We have driven the Yankees out of Virginia except for a few in the 'Pan handle.'" Maury later noted that the military front remained in the far northern part of the state. "Our army is at Winchester," she stated, "and McClellan is on the south side of the Potomac near Harpers Ferry." A resident of Paris, in Fauquier County, applauded the seamless manner in which Confederates used success at Manassas to strike northward. "Jackson's wagons, about five hundred, are at Paris," she reported on September 5, "enroute for Maryland it is thought. . . . Oh! It does me so much good to see them coming up, and to gaze at the old secesh wagons in their encampment. The change has quite dispelled the blues."[13]

A young woman living near Front Royal celebrated news that Pope's whole army had been "repulsed at *Manassas* with great carnage." The prospect of Pope's withdrawal from central Virginia prompted a reflective passage from Lucy Rebecca Buck. "To think how it has all changed since six months ago," she mused on August 31. "Then, we saw nothing but disaster and destruction before us." Union armies had penetrated the Confederate hinterlands, "laying waste the land with fire and sword." Numerous cities fell under Federal control, the invaders drained areas of subsistence, and "our capital was menaced by a vast army of exultant and victory flushed foes. . . . Oh it was all disheartening enough!" Lee's victories meant that "the day I trust has gone on our midnight." "Surely God has been with us," wrote a hopeful Buck. "Tis He that arrested the tide of Union successes and nerved and inspired our men to such deeds of daring heroism."[14]

Four days after Buck recorded her thoughts, Jefferson Davis composed a tribute to Second Manassas as part of the summer's larger military action. The president addressed themes and employed verbiage similar to Buck's. "Once more upon the plains of Manassas have our armies been blessed by the Lord of Hosts with a triumph over our enemies," began the president's call for Confederates to observe September 18 as a day of prayer and thanksgiving: "A few months since, and our enemies poured forth their invading legions upon our soil. They laid waste our fields, polluted our altars, and violated the sanctity of our homes. Around our capital they gathered their forces, and with boastful threats claimed it as already their prize." The Army of Northern Virginia had defended the capital and then, by vanquishing Pope, "scattered our enemies and driven them back in dismay."[15]

Edward A. Pollard will have the last word about the sweep of military action from the aftermath of the Seven Days through Second Manassas and Antietam. An editor at the *Richmond Examiner* during the war, Pollard chronicled events in *Southern History of the War*, a quartet of thick volumes that appeared during and just after the conflict. In a single Faulkneresque sentence, Pollard summarized the Army of Northern Virginia's operations in the summer of 1862: "Leaving the banks of James river, it proceeded directly to the line of the Rappahannock, and moving out from that river, it fought its way to the Potomac, crossed that stream, and moved on to Fredericktown and

Hagerstown, had a heavy engagement at the mountain gaps below, fought the greatest pitched battle of the war at Sharpsburg, and then recrossed the Potomac back into Virginia." Pollard added that the "remarkable campaign . . . extending from the banks of the James river to those of the Potomac . . . set the whole of Europe ringing with praises of the heroism and fighting qualities of the Southern armies." To clinch this point, he quoted from *The Times* of London. "If the renown of brilliant courage, stern devotion to a cause, and military achievements almost without a parallel, can compensate men for the toil and privations of the hour," suggested *The Times*, "then the countrymen of Lee and Jackson may be consoled amid their sufferings."[16]

Our Gallant and Victorious Army Is Yet Driving the Enemy Before Them

During the summer of 1862, the Confederate people welcomed the Army of Northern Virginia's newly aggressive posture. Lee's bloody counterpunching during the Seven Days signaled the dawn of a new era, and operational and tactical decisions in July and August revealed the army commander's audacious tendencies. Before his wound at Seven Pines on May 31 cleared the way for Lee to take control of the army defending Richmond, Joseph E. Johnston's penchant for retreating had vexed many Confederates. "Our army has fallen back to the Rappahannock, thus giving up the splendid Valley and Piedmont country to the enemy," wrote Judith McGuire in Richmond: "This, I suppose, is right, but it almost breaks our hearts to think of it." A fifteen-year-old living in Bedford, Virginia, who avidly followed military events and would join the army in 1863 lamented, "The Battle of Yorktown will never come off for our army has fallen Back & Norfolk is left to the mercy of the enemy." Fearing that "Virginia will be overrun by the enemy," Joseph Graves detected "a want of management on our part" and hoped for "a gallant fight made before the capitol shall fall in their hands." Harsher words about Johnston's retreat up the Peninsula toward Richmond came from a junior officer serving in Savannah. "General Johnston, from whom we were led to expect so much, has done little else than *evacuate*," fumed Lt. Charles C. Jones Jr. in May, "until the very mention of the word sickens one." Johnston's "doctrine of evacuation on every occasion . . . discourages our troops and people generally," continued Jones, "and if persisted it must eventually contract our limits to an alarming extent."[17]

J. B. Jones seconded this reading of public sentiment, observing shortly before the Seven Days' battles that "our people are beginning to *fear* there will be no more fighting around Richmond until McClellan *digs* his way to it." Military passivity bred civilian discontent. "The moment fighting ceases," affirmed Jones, "our people have fits of gloom and despondency; but when they snuff battle in the breeze, they are animated with confidence." Confederates resented "that our armies have so seldom been led against the embattled hosts of the enemy."[18]

Lee's own reputation experienced a dramatic turnaround after he took the offensive against McClellan between June 26 and July 1. High public expectations at the war's outset had given way to widespread doubts after his deployments to western Virginia and the South Atlantic coast in late 1861 and early 1862. Upon hearing that he replaced Johnston on June 1, many Confederates doubted his capacity to save the capital. Edward Porter Alexander, a major on Lee's staff during the Richmond campaign in 1862, later recalled that "some of the newspapers—particularly the Richmond *Examiner*—pitched into him with extraordinary virulence," asserting that "henceforth our army would never be allowed to fight. It would only be allowed to dig, . . . spades & shovels being the only implements Gen. Lee knew anything about." Another staff officer pronounced the winter of 1861–62 a time when the "press and the public were clamorous" in opposing Lee. Typical of the disgruntled chorus was a North Carolinian who later became a great admirer of Lee's. "I do not much like him," confided Catherine Ann Devereux Edmondston to her diary on June 8; "he 'falls back' too much."[19]

The Seven Days changed everything. Recently very critical of Lee, the *Richmond Dispatch* published a flattering assessment just eight days after the battle of Malvern Hill, claiming that "the rise which this officer has suddenly taken in the public confidence is without precedent." Lee's repeated attacks on McClellan's positions left no doubt about his "great abilities." A diarist in South Carolina, whose "heart had been too anxious to write" while the armies maneuvered outside Richmond, termed the Seven Days a "glorious fight" and, with Lee in mind, thanked God: "Thou hast answered our prayers and given us one who is well able to guide us through this fearful time, and lead us on to freedom."[20]

Lee won at Richmond despite a cumbersome organizational structure and several problematic subordinates. Confederate law provided for no unit larger than a division and no grade between that of major general (two stars in modern parlance) and general (four stars), which limited the army commander's ability to exercise control over eleven major generals who possessed considerable authority. McClellan's Army of the Potomac still threatened Richmond from Harrison's Landing on the James River, and Pope's Army of Virginia soon would advance along the line of the Orange & Alexandria Railroad. With these dual threats in mind, Lee had three pressing concerns: first, to insert a level of responsibility between the division and army levels; second, to select his principal subordinates; and third, to rid the army of weak division commanders. Achieving those objectives would yield a more responsive, nimble army and prepare the way to focus on a fourth task—to inculcate in officers and the rank and file a devotion to, or at least an appreciation of, the military virtues of speed and boldness and a desire to inflict the greatest possible damage to an opponent. The campaign of Second Manassas would confirm Lee's success in dealing with these thorny issues and reveal why Edward Porter Alexander, the most astute of all former Confederates who wrote about the military side of the war, judged him "decidedly the most audacious commander who has lived since Napoleon."[21]

Lee envisioned three generals in a top level of subordinate command—two dividing responsibility for the army's infantry and one directing the cavalry. Congressional legislation creating infantry corps and the rank of lieutenant general (three stars) for the officers who led them lay four months in the future, but Lee applied the practical solution of simply assigning the army's divisions to James Longstreet and Stonewall Jackson. The commands would be known as Longstreet's Right Wing and Jackson's Left Wing—though Lee did not use that terminology at the outset—and eventually as the First Corps and the Second Corps. Jackson's command included the two divisions that had been in his little Army of the Valley—his own, under Brig. Gen. Charles S. Winder, and Maj. Gen. Richard S. Ewell's. Jeb Stuart remained at the head of the army's cavalry, organized as a division containing two brigades.[22]

Lee's choices perfectly suited his conception of an effective culture of command. Longstreet's performance during the Seven Days had impressed him greatly. The physically imposing "Old Pete," as Confederate soldiers called him, had handled his troops well in powerful assaults at Gaines's Mill and Glendale. On July 21, 1862, Thomas Jewett Goree of Longstreet's staff recounted a conversation between Lee and a person who offered congratulations for success against McClellan. Lee deflected the compliment by attributing victory to "the brave soldiers & officers under him. 'Longstreet,' he said, 'was the staff in my right hand.'" Goree proposed, with little or no exaggeration, that "Genl. Longstreet has undoubtedly acquired as much or more reputation than any other officer in this army." Stuart similarly had logged sound service in the fighting around Richmond. His daring "ride around McClellan," carried out on June 12–15, received considerable national attention as an example of aggressive success that lifted morale. Lee lauded the twenty-nine-year-old Virginian, who combined sound leadership and thirst for adulation in roughly equal measure. The army's chief took "great pleasure in expressing his admiration of the courage and skill so conspicuously exhibited throughout by the general and the officers and men under his command."[23]

Jackson presented a more complicated case. Lee knew the dour Virginian emerged from the Valley campaign as the Confederacy's leading martial hero, a hard-eyed warrior who had used deception, mobility, and a penchant for taking risks to win a series of small victories against seemingly befuddled Union opponents. A soldier in the 10th Alabama Infantry captured the depth of popular adulation on the eve of the Seven Days. "Jackson is the genius of this war," wrote an enthralled Elias Davis from near Richmond; "he can (like a strong man wielding a club) strike with his army a stunning blow and apply stroke after stroke until his foe is dead." But the Seven Days told a different story about the "hero of the Valley." Frequently late or strangely disengaged, Jackson utterly failed to live up to his reputation—though the Confederate citizenry heard little about his stumbling performance. "We of Gen. Lee's staff knew at the time that he was deeply, bitterly disappointed," noted Porter Alexander in his memoirs, "but he made no official report of it & glossed all over as much as possible in his own reports." Politically astute and always cognizant of civilian morale, Lee reasonably concluded that airing questions about his famous lieutenant would tarnish the triumph over McClellan. So he chose Jackson, whose ability to operate in a semi-independent fashion was beyond question, to share with Longstreet command of the army's infantry. Longstreet was, and always remained, Lee's senior lieutenant.[24]

These three officers would do far more than any others to help Lee transform the Army of Northern Virginia into the Confederacy's premier military instrument and, in time, its most important national institution.[25] That phenomenon began with the campaign of Second Manassas, during which Jackson's ability to maneuver apart from the rest of the army, Longstreet's gift for orchestrating tactical blows, and Stuart's skills at reconnaissance and screening left no doubt that Lee had made sound choices.

The process of restructuring also entailed easing several division commanders out of the army. Five senior major generals soon found themselves assigned elsewhere. Theophilus H. Holmes took charge of the Trans-Mississippi Department and John Bankhead Magruder the District of Texas, New Mexico, and Arizona. Gustavus Woodson Smith, who very briefly commanded the army after Johnston was wounded, took leave on June 2, declaring "himself utterly unable to endure the mental excitement incident to his actual presence with the army." Benjamin Huger traded division command for what must have been a humiliating post as "inspector of artillery and ordnance in the Army of the Confederate States," while W. H. C. Whiting, whose infantry had broken the Union line at Gaines's Mill, ventured south to the District of Cape Fear.[26]

Lee's operations against Pope tested an army that remained a work in progress. Thinking offensively, Lee pondered how best to strike the enemy before Pope and McClellan could concentrate against him. He devised a series of maneuvers that not only protected Richmond and its rail connections to the Shenandoah Valley but also cleared Federal forces from most of the state.[27]

The Confederate people followed Lee's movements with great interest and swelling approbation. He and his principal lieutenants delivered precisely what the anxious populace craved. Rather than waiting for the Federals to strike at the time and place of their choosing, Lee had taken the fight to Pope, putting him on his heels and controlling the action. Jackson carried out a famous flanking maneuver, Longstreet oversaw one of the most impressive tactical assaults of the war, and Stuart displayed energy and initiative. A dramatic and successful campaign closed with the satisfying images of Pope's humiliated army seeking shelter in Washington and Richmond, freed from immediate menace. The depth of public outrage directed against Pope and his army, which will be the focus of the next section of this essay, added to a sense of retributive justice among Confederates. More than 10,000 Confederate casualties at Cedar Mountain, Second Manassas, and Chantilly chastened people inside and outside Lee's army but did little to dampen overall enthusiasm about the triumph.[28]

The campaign illuminated a fundamental element of Lee's conception about how to wage the war. Well aware of the Federal preponderance of manpower and matériel, he saw offensive operations as the best way to prevent opponents from overwhelming Confederates who stood passively on the defensive. He sought always to maintain the initiative, keeping the enemy off balance and perhaps finding opportunities to win tactical successes that would depress civilian morale in the United States. As Jefferson Davis's principal military advisor in the spring of 1862, he had formulated the offensive that Stonewall Jackson executed to superb effect in the Shenandoah Valley. From that same desk in Richmond, he also had watched Johnston's retrograde movements with growing concern. Late in the war, Lee told the noted partisan John S. Mosby that "Joe Johnston ought not to have fallen back from the Rapidan to Richmond, and that he had written urging him to turn against Washington." Lee further observed that when "Johnston evacuated his lines at Yorktown, in May of that year, he should have given battle with his whole force on the isthmus at Williamsburg, instead of making a rear-guard fight." The less active the Confederate effort, reasoned Lee, the more likely operations could end in a siege that would inevitably favor the Union with its greater numbers.[29]

The brief interval between Chantilly and Lee's march into Maryland left a small window for Southern newspapers to react to Second Manassas. Within a few days, their emphasis shifted to operations north of the Potomac. Thus did one of the war's ten bloodiest battles became oddly marginalized by the press. The *Southern Illustrated News* published a long piece on September 20 that touched on points common in other press coverage. Pope's transgressions had converted the "whole Piedmont region, from the Rapidan to the Potomac . . . into a wilderness." Responding forcefully, "Gen. Lee determined to put a stop to these excesses, and to transfer the war to that portion of the country in which they were perpetrated." His efforts climaxed in "the brilliant achievements of our army on the 28th, 29th and 30th of August" and placed "Gen. Lee at the head of all living Captains." Unable to withstand "the fierce onset of our soldiers upon the plains of Manassas," the Yankees "fled before them, in the most utter confusion." The battle's verdict meant the "tide of war has been rolled back upon those who were so lately our invaders."[30]

Stonewall Jackson dominated much of the earlier newspaper reporting, a phenomenon explained by his victory at Cedar Mountain and widespread appeal tied to his successes in the Valley. Three examples convey the flavor of many others. Richmond's *Whig* labeled Jackson the greatest soldier of the age, to whose triumphs in the Valley had been added "the additional laurels of Cedar Run." Predicting that "General Pope, the braggart and bully," soon would be vanquished, the *Whig* anticipated "events about to occur in that region with unwavering confidence in the result, and a conviction that Stonewall Jackson, our great and noble leader there, will render still more glorious the name of Virginia and his own." In North Carolina, the *Wilmington Journal* took a similar, though less wordy, approach: "'Stonewall' Jackson has met Pope, the notorious Federal General, who had arrested a number of private citizens as hostages. Pope has been driven back, with a heavy loss." The *Richmond Daily Dispatch* relied on testimony from "one who actively participated" in the first day's fighting at Manassas to praise Jackson's performance at Groveton on the twenty-eighth, where he "determined to throw himself upon the enemy's flank" in "one of the most beautiful and masterly strategic movements of the war."[31]

Newspapers apportioned credit among various officers, though no others received as much notice as Lee and Jackson. The *Richmond Enquirer*'s coverage on September 2 acknowledged Lee's overall responsibility for the forces in the "sanguinary battle" but remarked that "Confederate troops were immediately under the command of Gen. 'Stonewall' Jackson." The same issue alluded to Jeb Stuart's "brilliant exploits," dedicating a short piece to "one of his peculiar dashes into the rear of the enemy's lines at Catlett's Station on the Orange and Alexandria Railroad" that netted prisoners and other booty. James Longstreet and division commanders Richard S. Ewell—wounded at Groveton—and Maj. Gen. A. P. Hill were among other generals singled out for mention by the press.[32]

Within the army, Lee had gained the respect but not yet the unqualified devotion of his troops. At the end of August, Jackson almost certainly remained the more famous and popular of the two. Artillerist Thomas H. Carter ruminated about this on September 7. Lee had earned "the entire confidence of the Army," Carter wrote his wife from near Frederick, "but there is no enthusiasm. Jackson on the contrary is idolized by the Army & people. All along the road he is inquired for." Still, as the army carried out "this daring movement" into Maryland, Carter affirmed that "we all trust in God & Lee." Another artillerist chose more fulsome language. "When by accident I at any time see Gen. Lee, or when I think of him," observed John Hampden Chamberlayne with the poet John Milton in mind, " . . . there looms up to me some king-of-men, superior by the head, a Gigantic figure, on whom rests the world, With Atlantean shoulder, fit to bear The weight of Empire." A Prussian cartographer in Jackson's entourage, in contrast, accorded Lee the most grudging of compliments, while also sourly conceding the general's popularity. "This person I believe to be exceedingly overrated by both troops and people," observed Lt. Oscar Hinrichs just prior to Second Manassas. "I cannot believe that he is the great General in the field. His talent appears to lie more in planning than in executing his plans when conceived. This appears to be Jackson's great forte."[33]

The degree to which the army had not yet fully become Lee's is evident in correspondence from late August and early September. Capt. Shepherd G. Pryor of the 12th Georgia Infantry, for example, sent his wife a long letter on September 2 that ignored Lee. Pryor mentioned Jackson's leadership in late August, the destruction of Pope's supply base at Manassas Junction, and how, while Stonewall maneuvered, "our army under Longstreet was advancing all the time, driving Pope before them." In another letter four days later, Pryor assured his wife, "Our success in the Manassas fights has added a great deal of confidence to our army. We have entire confidence in our leaders; they have proved themselves entirely worthy of the confidence of our nation." Surely Pryor counted Lee among those leaders, but the absence of any specific mention is striking—and would be impossible to imagine a few months hence.[34]

Jefferson Davis mentioned just one officer in his congratulatory statement to the Confederate Congress. "Too much praise," he wrote, "cannot be bestowed upon the skill and daring of the commanding General who conceived, or the valor and hardihood of the troops who executed, the brilliant movement whose result is now communicated." Davis also linked Second Manassas to the Seven Days. Under Lee's guidance, he emphasized, "our toil-worn troops" had "relieved from siege the city of Richmond" and then "advanced to meet another invading army."[35]

Whatever the relative fame of Lee and Jackson, soldiers in the army showed evidence of the aggressive spirit prized by both the army's commander and his celebrated lieutenant. A junior officer in the 2nd Virginia Infantry provides an example from early August. "We have been now for more than a week resting in camp; which is a most unusual thing for Genl Jacksons Army," he observed from near Gordonsville. "When he does start us again, he will work us all the harder for it; well, if he does it with the same or similar results as those attained heretofore, I shall not complain."[36]

Confederate civilians welcomed reports of victory at Second Manassas but, like the press, quickly cast their attention to events north of the Potomac River. Jackson loomed large in many of their reactions, again highlighting his status as the reigning military favorite in the Confederacy. That position as most favored would erode over the next few months, and by early 1863 Lee would surpass his able lieutenant in popularity and be synonymous with the Army of Northern Virginia.[37]

A pair of diarists in the Shenandoah Valley typified those who looked to Jackson as the key to success. Lucy Buck charted the progress of Confederate fortunes through references to him. On August 28, she noted, "Jackson is said to be at or near Manassas and to have completely surrounded the Feds." Ten days later she recorded news "brought directly from the army the night before." Jackson had crossed the Potomac, and "the old Genl. had outwitted the enemy most completely as he always does." Mary Greenhow Lee heard on September 5 that "Hill, Longstreet, & our General have crossed into Maryland, at Edward's Ferry; God be with them & protect them in danger." The next day she wrote again of "our General": "Jackson has crossed into

Maryland—jubilate. I almost envy the Marylanders." Julia Chase, a Unionist who lived in Winchester and kept an informative diary, expressed anxiety "as the 2 armies have been fighting for the past week." She also attested to Jackson's preeminence among her Confederate neighbors: "Secessionists today say that Jackson is whipping the Federal army at a great rate & that McClellan has been killed. . . . God grant that it may not be true."[38]

A clergyman in Georgia offered a revealing critique of Lee's effect on Confederate military fortunes in the summer of 1862. Triumphs at the Seven Days and Second Manassas had been so impactful that they warped perspectives. "Success began to intoxicate," stated Charles Colcock Jones, "and incline many to cry out for invasion of the enemy's territory. General Lee was induced to make the experiment in the most favorable moment." An opponent of projecting military power beyond the Confederacy, Jones thought nothing saved Lee and "his army from defeat and ruin but the blessing of God upon his skillful disposition of his forces, and the indomitable courage of his men—men to be annihilated but never defeated!" He welcomed the "invasion of Maryland and the return of our army to Virginia . . . *as a special providence in our behalf*" and hoped "this taste of invasion will be satisfactory—at least for the present." Misgivings aside, this Georgian's observations leave no doubt about how profoundly Lee's operations influenced attitudes and expectations.[39]

For most Confederates, the thrust into Maryland made sense as the final phase of Lee's radical reshaping of military affairs in the Eastern Theater. A civilian in Lynchburg aptly summed up such thinking. "Victory after victory has crowned our arms," wrote John W. Stone, "and our gallant and victorious army [is] yet driving the enemy before them and by the aid of a higher power than human, may we continue to drive them until not a vestige of that invading army tramp on that soil, ever again tread upon southern soil."[40]

An Unbridled License Has Prevailed among the Yankee Soldiery

The actions of John Pope and his "invading army" touched a profound chord among Confederates in and out of uniform. Lee's retooling of the Army of Northern Virginia occurred simultaneously with an escalating political and military debate about "civilized" warfare, the relationship between armies and civilians and their property, and justifiable retaliation. These controversial topics had arisen earlier in Missouri, where anti-Union depredations by irregular forces had prompted discussions between Maj. Gen. Henry W. Halleck and the German-born scholar Francis Lieber. Inspired by his exchanges with

Halleck, Lieber codified the rules of war in a document signed by President Lincoln and issued as General Orders No. 100 in April 1863. Controversy in Missouri, a military backwater, was one thing—controversy in Virginia, where the most famous armies campaigned in proximity to the rival capitals, was entirely different.[41]

George B. McClellan's precipitate retreat after the Seven Days exacerbated another source of tension between the warring nations. Convinced by McClellan's failure that the war would go on much longer and require more extreme measures, both Congress and Abraham Lincoln acted to place emancipation on the table. The Second Confiscation Act of July 17, 1862, freed all slaves held by Rebel owners, authorized seizure of property from several categories of individuals in the Confederacy, and empowered the president "to employ as many persons of African descent as he may deem necessary and proper for the suppression of this rebellion." Four days earlier, according to Secretary of the Navy Gideon Welles, the president "first mentioned to Mr. Seward and myself the subject of emancipating the slaves by Proclamation in case the rebels did not cease to persist in their war on the govt' and the Union, which he saw no evidence." Prior to this, continued Welles, Lincoln had believed emancipation to be a state issue: "But the reverses before Richmond, and the formidable power and dimensions of the insurrection which extended through all the Slave States . . . impelled the administration to adopt extraordinary measures to preserve the National existence." At cabinet meetings on July 21 and 22, Lincoln discussed emancipation and his intention to issue a proclamation.[42]

These policies contrasted starkly with McClellan's ideas. Less than a week after the battle of Malvern Hill, he gave the president a didactic letter about how to conduct the war. The United States should adhere to the "highest principles known to Christian Civilization," insisted McClellan. The conflict "should not be, at all, a War upon population; but against armed forces and political organizations. Neither confiscation of property, political executions of persons, territorial organization of states or forcible abolition of slavery should be contemplated for a moment." On August 1, while still ensconced at Harrison's Landing, McClellan wrote to Halleck, recently named general-in-chief of US armies. "I believe that together we can save this unhappy country and bring this war to a comparatively early termination," he stated with a smarmy edge; "the doubt in my mind is whether the selfish politicians will allow us to do so. I fear the results of the *civil* policy inaugurated by recent Acts of Congress and practically enunciated by General Pope in his series of orders to the Army of Virginia."[43]

Pope brought experience with Missouri's irregular warfare to his new post in Virginia, and three general orders issued between July 14 and 23 signaled an unequivocal departure from McClellan's conciliatory approach. The first, General Orders No. 5, instructed Union troops to "subsist upon the country in which their operations are carried on" without reimbursement to pro-Confederate owners. Next, General Orders No. 7 held "people in the Shenandoah Valley and throughout the area where the Army of Virginia campaigns" responsible for any damage to railroads, roads, and telegraph lines at the hands of "lawless bands of individuals not forming part of the organized forces of the enemy nor wearing the garb of soldiers." Anyone connected to "such outrages, either during the act or at any time afterward, shall be shot, without awaiting civil processes." Finally, General Orders No. 11 instructed Union officers "immediately to arrest all disloyal male citizens within their lines or within their reach in rear of their respective stations." Those who refused to take the oath of allegiance would be sent south beyond the pickets of the army and if subsequently found "within our lines or at any point in rear they will be considered spies, and subjected to the extreme rigor of military law." Anyone who took the oath and later violated it "shall be shot, and his property seized and applied to the public use."[44]

The Confederate government responded forcefully to Pope's orders. On July 22, the United States and the Confederacy agreed to a cartel stipulating "that all prisoners of war hereafter taken shall be discharged on parole till exchanged." Nine days later, an indignant Jefferson Davis wrote to Lee regarding the "general order issued by Major General Pope on the 23rd of July." Because of that directive, the Confederate government recognized "General Pope and his commissioned officers to be in the position which they have chosen for themselves, that of robbers and murderers, and not that of public enemies entitled if captured to be considered as prisoners of war." For the present, the Confederacy would forgo retaliation against Pope's enlisted soldiers and treat them as prisoners of war. Should the United States continue its "savage practices," however, "we shall reluctantly be forced to the last resort of accepting war on the terms chosen by our foes, until the outraged voice of a common humanity forces respect for the recognized rules of war."[45]

August 1 brought two crucial actions. Davis instructed Lee to seek details from the Union general-in-chief about "alleged murders committed on our citizens by officers of the U.S. Army"—including one in Missouri supposedly ordered by Pope. Lee had sent a similar request to George B. McClellan on July 6, closing with an assurance that the Confederacy hoped to avoid retaliations. Davis's letter of August 1 also mentioned newspaper accounts

"Scene, General Head-Quarters, Richmond" mocked Confederate reaction to John Pope's orders. The general remarks, "What! going to carry on the War in earnest! . . . Ride at once to Jackson, and order him to hang the Scoundrel Pope at once! Chop his Head off! Roast him on a slow Fire! Crucify him!" (*Harper's Weekly*, August 30, 1862, 560)

of activities by Maj. Gen. David Hunter and other Union commanders who "armed slaves for the murder of their masters" and sought "to inaugurate a servile war, which is worse than that of the savage." Lee should allow General Halleck fifteen days from receipt of the query to reply; failure to do so would prove "the alleged facts are true and are sanctioned by the government of the United States," thereby setting in motion "retributive or retaliatory measures which we shall adopt to put an end to the merciless atrocities which now characterize the war waged against us."[46]

The Confederate War Department also issued General Orders No. 54 on August 1. It quoted part of Pope's General Orders No. 11 and another authored by Brig. Gen. Adolph von Steinwehr on July 13 to show that the United States had "determined to violate all the rules and usages of war and to convert the hostilities hitherto waged against armed forces into a campaign of robbery and murder against unarmed citizens and peaceful tillers of the soil." If captured, Pope, Steinwehr, and their subalterns would not be treated as the recent cartel mandated but instead held in "close confinement so long as the orders aforesaid shall continue in force and unrepealed by the competent military authorities of the United States." If the Federals murdered any unarmed Confederate civilians under Pope's orders, whether with or without trial, an equal number of US officers held in custody would be hanged.[47]

Lee sent two letters to Halleck on August 2. One dealt with the alleged murders in Missouri and New Orleans and the practice of arming slaves "for the murder of their masters" and trying to "inaugurate a servile war." The other focused on Pope's general orders and Steinwehr's conduct. Those two men had driven the Confederacy "toward a practice which we abhor and which we are vainly struggling to avoid." The terms of the prisoner cartel would not apply to Pope and his officers, wrote Lee, though men in the Union ranks would retain the protection of that agreement.[48]

Halleck waved off Lee's letters as "exceedingly insulting to the Government of the United States," and on August 18 Davis sent a message to the Confederate Congress. It reprised the points the president had made to Lee, accusing the United States of "rapine and wanton destruction of private property, war upon noncombatants, murder of captives, bloody threats to avenge the death of an invading soldiery by the slaughter of unarmed citizens, [and] orders of banishment against peaceful farmers." Moreover, claimed the message, at least two Union generals, unrestrained by Lincoln's government, had engaged "in exciting servile insurrection, and in arming and training slaves for warfare against their masters, citizens of the Confederacy."[49]

The particulars of these orders, letters, and messages soon appeared in newspapers across the Confederacy, elevating Pope to a position alongside Maj. Gen. Benjamin F. Butler, the "beast" of New Orleans, as a universally reviled Yankee villain. Confederates also read Northern newspapers such as the *Chicago Tribune*, which supported "Gen. Pope and the way he falls to work in the Shenandoah. . . . His orders have the right tone, and are based on the right principles of conducting the war." The fact that Pope did not enforce his orders on a grand scale made little difference. Perception trumped reality, as is almost always the case, and Confederates reacted to the threats inherent in the orders and to specific instances of Federal arrests and confiscation with a spasm of obloquy. Meanwhile, the increased movement of enslaved refugees toward Pope's lines stoked visceral fears of the consequences of emancipation. Confederates coalesced with an outraged sense of purpose, determined to resist a foe who threatened every aspect of their social and economic structures.[50]

Newspapers engaged in a carnival of outrage that in turn instigated popular fury directed at Pope. On July 24, the *Richmond Daily Dispatch* printed Pope's three orders under the heading "GEN POPE'S ARMY / VIRGINIA TO BE LAID WASTE." In early August, this paper offered readers a biographical portrait, calling Pope "cruel by nature" and deprecating his "most infernal record" in Missouri. Lincoln appointed him to head the Army of Virginia because he "wanted a tiger to suck blood, and he got him." Pope's proclamations constituted "an open invitation to plunder" and "a premium for murder." The *Daily Dispatch* hoped "to see this execrable villain and his lieutenant[s] expiate their crimes on the gallows, in pursuance of the President's proclamation." The editors also expressed disappointment at Davis's decision to exempt the Federal rank and file from retaliation: "Why should the mongrel crew who march under the banners of Lincoln be exempted from punishment?" As August drew to a close, the paper excoriated Pope's soldiers for their conduct around Culpeper: "An unbridled license has prevailed among the Yankee soldiery, and the country is now almost a desert. Unoffending citizens have been impoverished in a single day, their negroes all carried off, their fencing destroyed, their sheep hogs and cattle butchered, their grain entirely consumed, their horses all stolen."[51]

Other Richmond newspapers matched the *Daily Dispatch* in stridency. The *Christian Advocate* approved of Davis's "system of retaliation" because of the "brutal and uncivilized warfare Gen'l Pope has initiated in Virginia." The Confederate response relayed to Halleck by Lee showed "how far our Government has determined now to go," and if the Lincoln administration continued its policies, "war under the 'black flag' will have to come, and our soldiers will wreak terrible vengeance upon the cowardly assassins who are subjecting private, unoffending citizens to such inhuman treatment." The *Examiner* gleefully reported that Brig. Gen. Henry Prince and twenty-nine other officers captured at Cedar Mountain "had arrived at Gordonsville *hand-cuffed*" and would be "held as hostages to answer for any enforcement of the murderous decrees lately issued by their unprincipled superiors." Some officers also donned privates' clothing, the *Examiner* smirked, so, if taken prisoner, they could "claim to belong to the file."[52]

Newspapers outside Virginia joined in the feeding frenzy. In North Carolina, Winston's *Western Sentinel* deprecated the brace of Yankee military figures most loathed in the Confederacy: "Gen. Pope, in the Valley of Virginia, is rivaling the atrocities of Butler the Beast in New Orleans. He has issued an execrable order which exposes all sexes and ages to the severest cruelties of ruffian Yankee troops." This editor further observed that only the fortunes of war had spared North Carolinians comparable travails. "If North Carolina has hitherto been exempt from the operations of these brutal military decrees," he warned, "it is only because the minions of Lincoln in this State have not had the force at command to enforce their execution." The Virginia correspondent for Atlanta's *Southern Confederacy* and Mobile's *Advertiser and Register* also tied Pope to Butler: "It would seem that he is envious of Gen. Butler, and not content with being the greatest economist of truth in the Federal dominions, that he now seeks to rival the monster in atrocity and inhumanity." Northern newspapers approved of Pope's "proceedings, and affect to discover in them evidence of a disposition to prosecute the war with earnestness and determination." In truth, stated Peter W. Alexander in a mocking tone, "the less successful their arms are, the more bloodthirsty do they become."[53]

Robert E. Lee joined countless Confederates who read the texts of Pope's orders in newspapers. Although not, as Lost Cause advocates later asserted, a habitually even-tempered man who referred to Federals only as "those people," Lee seldom unburdened himself as he did regarding Pope. Mimicking the language Unionists routinely deployed about putting down the rebellion, he told Stonewall Jackson in late July, "I want Pope to be suppressed. The course indicated in his orders if the newspapers report them correctly cannot be permitted and will lead to retaliation on our part." To his daughter Mildred, Lee related that her brother Rob was "off with Jackson & I hope will catch Pope & his cousin Louis Marshall. I could forgive the latter for fighting against us, if he had not have joined such a miscreant as Pope." Lee's use of the word "miscreant" bears close attention. Its mid-nineteenth-century meanings, according to the *Oxford English Dictionary*, included "a misbeliever, heretic; an unbeliever, infidel" and "a vile wretch; a villain, rascal." Lee repeated the word in a letter to Secretary of War George Wythe Randolph when he explained dispositions that would permit reinforcing "Jackson without hazard to Richmond, and thus enable him to drive if not destroy the miscreant Pope."[54]

Others in the Army of Northern Virginia also selected harsh epithets, as did officers who followed events along the Rappahannock sector from elsewhere. A Catholic priest with the 14th Louisiana Infantry deplored "Pope's abolition robbers," while a British-born soldier stated that "our men heartily hated him for his ruthless cruelty to the inhabitants of the country, and his extraordinary amount of vanity and bombast." Col. Josiah Gorgas, the

Confederate chief of ordnance, called Pope the "morally worthless" author of "infamous orders holding citizens responsible for the shooting of his men by guerillas, or rangers." In a contest between such an individual and Stonewall Jackson, the latter "a just & upright man," Gorgas believed "Providence will help the righteous man who puts his shoulder to the wheel."[55]

Civilians left ample testimony about the impact of Pope's orders, much of which alluded to what newspapers decried as the "uncivilized" and "savage" conduct of Union soldiers. Reaction came both from eyewitnesses and from people across the Confederacy. In Fredericksburg, Betty Herndon Maury recounted on July 30 how an uncle, frightened by General Orders No. 11, "prepared to run this morning with the larger portion of his negroes, horses and other valuables but has concluded to wait a few days and see if 'Stone Wall' Jackson will not whip Pope in that time." Three days later Maury's father, then in Richmond and "very uneasy about the rest of the family in Fredericksburg since Gen' Pope's order," wanted "to get them away from there." Virginia Soutter Knox, whose family also lived in Fredericksburg, wrote with anguish to her brothers about an "unexpected trial that has come upon us all as a family in the imprisonment of our precious Father." Thomas Fitzhugh Knox and several other men from Fredericksburg had been arrested and transported to Washington. "Did you ever read a more stringent order," she asked, "than Gen. Pope's? Oh! I do grieve in my soul (not only for ourselves) for every body we love in Fred'burg." She worried about "the fear and dread of what may come upon them at any moment, individually and collectively, under the rule of such a tyrant—& such lawless soldiers." Confined to Old Capitol Prison, her father vowed to his wife, if released, not to "go back to Fredbg to stay long unless Our Army moves in & takes back my home." No one knew how far the enemy would go in their measures or "what is to become of *you* & our dear children."[56]

For Lucy Buck, living near Front Royal, the reality of General Orders No. 11 exceeded her worst imaginings. "This is what I have all the time been dreading," she wrote on July 26, "and now it had come in a more hideous shape than I had ever anticipated." Neighbors agreed: "We met Mr. Hope and Mr. Hainie and the former had been weeping and seemed to be utterly bewildered by the shock. Oh how intensely I did hate the whole race of Yankees." Throughout late July and August, Buck recorded many unpleasant confrontations between civilians and Federal troops seeking to impress goods.[57]

Residents of occupied Winchester chronicled daily encounters with Pope's soldiers. On July 30, according to Laura Lee, a Union officer "arrested many persons today, and says the oath is to be administered to everybody tomorrow. The gentlemen are quaking." Initially buoyed by all the men's refusal to take the oath, "even down to the lowest and poorest," she later complained that "most of the prominent men here have agreed to compromise by taking a parole, which will exempt them from the regular oath, but still a great concession to the Yankees. It is shameful!!" She found it comforting that "many of the men bravely refuse to give *any* oath, parole, or promise to the Yankees." Mary Greenhow Lee commented about foodstuffs. "These miserable Yankees think we have been too quiet for some days," she stated in her diary on July 23, "so they have commenced searching the houses again under Pope's new order, that the army is to be subsisted amongst the inhabitants." The situation worsened on July 24: "Our Yankee rulers have been unusually hateful to-day. I heard they were searching for sugar & molasses &c. &c as I have quite large supply of groceries, just now, I am unwilling to lose them. . . . They searched a house at 2-o-clock in the night, last night."[58]

Two diarists from outside Virginia evinced the national interest in Pope and his orders. Kate Edmondston clipped the texts of General Orders No. 5 and No. 7 from a newspaper and pasted them in her journal. "Gen. Pope has issued an order . . . monstrous in its cruelty and contrary to the practices of all civilized warfare," she commented with obvious anger, "but this is not civilized warfare, nor do our enemies show either the genius of Christianity or the spirit of Civilization." A few days later she attributed to the Army of Virginia "the most horrible excesses in the Valley and about Fredericksburg. . . . True it is that no war is so savage as a civil one!" From Upcountry South Carolina, Emma Holmes detailed the provisions of Pope's orders and Davis's letter to Lee, which she gleaned from her evening newspaper on August 5. "I am delighted to see our government is at last trying to stop, most probably vainly," she wrote, "the frightful barbarities and enormities committed by the boasted 'most civilized nation on the earth,' deeds which would disgrace a savage."[59]

Concern about the Union army's disruption of the slaveholding regime prompted many positive comments about African American refugees coming back under Confederate control. Five examples reflect this theme in the testimony. Near Sudley Ford after the battle of Second Manassas, Father James Sheeran found "about 700 negroes of all ages and sexes; beside these were 300 officers of Pope's command and consequently not to be paroled." The priest spoke with the officers, who, he seemed pleased to note, "complained much of their condition, the scanty supply of food and of being dragged about with negroes." A surgeon with the 13th South Carolina Infantry, when near Manassas Junction just before the battle of Groveton, similarly reported seeing "many prisoners and negroes there, who were all sent away towards Groveton." At almost exactly the same time, Amanda Edmonds happily wrote, "Jackson has arrived at Gainesville and taken a quantity of stores and several hundred negroes and Yankees. May kind Heaven smile on him and make him successful." Further evidence on this topic comes from a woman living near Fincastle in the upper Shenandoah Valley. "We had good news from General Jackson—another victory," Lucy Breckinridge wrote with a shaky grasp of numbers at the end of August; "8,000 prisoners captured, and 2,000 negroes who had been stolen by Pope's army." In early October, Robert H. Couper, a soldier in the 60th Georgia Infantry, wrote to his mother from Winchester. Reluctant to narrate recent campaigning, he nonetheless decided to pass along information likely to "concern your happiness. . . . At Harpers Ferry we captured thirteen thousand and five hundred of the enemy and three thousand negroes."[60]

Edmund Ruffin unsurprisingly accorded extensive attention in his voluminous diary to Federal policies relating to emancipation and confiscation. Unsurpassed in crafting vituperative sectional barbs, the old ultra-secessionist insisted Yankee armies had behaved badly from the war's outset. Under McClellan, Federals had seized enslaved people on the Peninsula, and the Second Confiscation Act merely shone a bright light on an already existing policy. In like manner, Pope's general orders "openly declared" what other Federals had been doing anyway. Ruffin favored immediate and remorseless retaliation against the Yankees. He recommended "the sentencing to death & to be hung as felons whenever captured, the commanding officers who order, or authorise & permit these outrages." Ruffin celebrated Pope's orders in one regard. "I am heartily rejoiced for the enactment or proclamation of these tyrannical & most oppressive rules," he averred. "For, without being declared, they have been acted upon everywhere when profitable or expedient, & would be so still more hereafter." But with the policies "declared & made universal" by Pope, all Confederates would "know that the occupation of their property by the enemy's forces will be equivalent to its total loss as to all moveables—& that their final success will sweep the land itself into the great fund of plunder." In other words, Union victory would obliterate the foundation of the Confederacy's slavery-based society. The magnitude of that threat might boost morale and stiffen spines in a fight that now placed everything at risk.[61]

Ruffin thus put his finger on one notable aspect of the Second Manassas campaign. Pope's actions in July and August, together with congressional and presidential policies and statements, created an impression among

Confederates that they faced a dishonorable foe bent on waging uncivilized warfare. Everything they prized had become a target. The same period gave them the general who would serve as their best hope to stave off the Federal menace. In three months, Lee had reorganized his army, humbled Pope, and restored Virginia's military frontier to the Potomac River. The butcher's bill for these accomplishments gave some of his troops pause, and many soldiers and civilians still considered Jackson their most talented commander. But for untold thousands of Confederates, Lee's decisive leadership and victories had catapulted him to the top position among Confederate military figures.[62]

William Dorsey Pender and Col. Robert H. Jones offered opinions in the immediate aftermath of Second Manassas that indicated awareness of what had happened. A North Carolinian who led a brigade in A. P. Hill's division, Pender praised Lee's "brilliant and daring feats of Generalship" as well as "the boldness of the plan and the quickness and completeness of execution. . . . Lee has immortalized himself." Jones, a South Carolinian, declared simply, "Genl Lee stands now above all Genls in Modern History. Our men will follow him to the end." In another few months, Jones's opinion would be that of the large majority of the Confederate people.[63]

Notes

1. This essay uses "Second Manassas" rather than "Second Bull Run" because the sources consulted, predominantly Confederate, almost always used "Manassas." It would have been awkward to alternate between contrasting terms throughout the text.

2. This is not the place to survey titles devoted to the three major battles between June and September 1862. It is enough to say that far more scholarly work has been published on the Seven Days and, especially, on the Maryland campaign and Antietam than on Second Manassas. The best study of the climactic battle between Lee and Pope remains John J. Hennessy, *Return to Bull Run: The Campaign and Battle of Second Manassas* (New York: Simon and Schuster, 1993).

3. A large scholarly literature deals with the limits of violence during the Civil War. Important titles, which offer very different interpretations, include Mark Grimsley, *The Hard Hand of War: Union Military Policy toward Southern Civilians, 1861–1865* (New York: Cambridge University Press, 1995); Mark E. Neely Jr., *The Civil War and the Limits of Destruction* (Cambridge, MA: Harvard University Press, 2007); Daniel E. Sutherland, *A Savage Conflict: The Decisive Role of Guerrillas in the American Civil War* (Chapel Hill: University of North Carolina Press, 2009); D. H. Dilbeck, *A More Civil War: How the Union Waged a Just War* (Chapel Hill: University of North Carolina Press, 2016); Aaron Sheehan-Dean, *The Calculus of Violence: How Americans Fought the Civil War* (Cambridge, MA: Harvard University Press, 2018); and Lorien Foote, *Rites of Retaliation: Civilization, Soldiers, and Campaigns in the American Civil War* (Chapel Hill: University of North Carolina Press, 2021).

4. Judith W. McGuire, *Diary of a Southern Refugee during the War* (1867; repr., Lincoln: University of Nebraska Press, 1995), 113, 118, 150–52.

5. J. B. Jones, *A Rebel War Clerk's Diary at the Confederate States Capital*, 2 vols. (1866; repr., Alexandria, VA: Time-Life Books, 1982), 1:126, 129, 151–52.

6. R. E. Lee, "General Orders No. 116," October 2, 1862, in US War Department, *The War of the Rebellion: A Compilation of the Official Records of the Union and Confederate Armies*, 128 vols., index and atlas (Washington, DC: Government Printing Office, 1880–1901), ser. 1, vol. 19, pt. 2:644–45 (hereafter cited as *OR*, with all citations from series 1 unless otherwise noted).

7. Quoted in Donald E. Everett, ed., *Chaplain Davis and Hood's Texas Brigade* (1863; repr., Baton Rouge: Louisiana State University Press, 1999), 139. Nicholas A. Davis, chaplain in the 4th Texas Infantry, drew on firsthand experience from the Seven Days through Antietam. His account first appeared in a Richmond edition in 1863.

8. *The Civil War Letters of General Frank "Bull" Paxton, CSA: A Lieutenant of Lee and Jackson*, ed. John Gallatin Paxton (Hillsboro, TX: Hill Junior College Press, 1978), 58; *A Gunner in Lee's Army: The Civil War Letters of Thomas Henry Carter*, ed. Graham T. Dozier (Chapel Hill: University of North Carolina Press, 2014), 143 (Carter wrote on October 8).

9. Elsie Keever, ed., *Keever Civil War Letters* (Lincolnton, NC: by the editor, 1989), 9.

10. *Charleston Daily Courier*, October 4, 1862; *Macon (GA) Journal and Messenger*, October 8, 1862 (account written by Peter W. Alexander).

11. *Richmond Dispatch*, September 23, 1862.

12. *Richmond Daily Enquirer*, September 24, 1862.

13. Cornelia Peake McDonald, *A Woman's Civil War: A Diary, with Reminiscences of the War, from March 1862*, ed. Minrose C. Gwin (Madison: University of Wisconsin Press, 1992), 73 (entry for September 26; McDonald had neglected her diary for two months due to the death of a child and probably misdated this passage inasmuch as subsequent entries carry dates of September 21, 22, and 23); Betty Herndon Maury, "The Civil War Diary of Betty Herndon Maury," ed. Carolyn Carpenter, in *Fredericksburg History and Biography* 9 (2010): 90–91 (entries for September 18, October 8, 1862); *Journals of Amanda Virginia Edmonds, Lass of the Mosby Confederacy, 1859–1867*, ed. Nancy Chappelear Baird (Stephens City, VA: Commercial Press, 1984), 111.

14. Lucy Rebecca Buck, *Shadows of My Heart: The Civil War Diary of Lucy Rebecca Buck of Virginia*, ed. Elizabeth R. Baer (Athens: University of Georgia Press, 1997), 144–45.

15. Various newspapers in Richmond and elsewhere printed Davis's statement. The quotations in this paragraph are from the *Richmond Daily Dispatch*, September 6, 1862. Judith McGuire copied the entire proclamation, which was dated September 4, 1862, in her diary on September 14 (McGuire, *Diary*, 153–54).

16. Edward A. Pollard, *Southern History of the War: The Second Year of the War* (1863; repr., New York: Charles B. Richardson, 1865), 142–43.

17. McGuire, *Diary*, 102 (entry for March 15, 1862); Joseph A. Graves, Journal (entry for May 13, 1862), transcription in the possession of Margaret Ryther prepared by Mary Roy Edwards; Charles C. Jones Jr. to his father, May 12, 1862, in *The Children of Pride: A True Story of Georgia and the Civil War*, ed. Robert Manson Myers (New Haven: Yale University Press, 1972), 893.

18. Jones, *Rebel War Clerk's Diary*, 1:135 (entry for June 24, 1862).

19. Edward Porter Alexander, *Fighting for the Confederacy: The Personal Recollections of General Edward Porter Alexander*, ed. Gary W. Gallagher (Chapel Hill: University of North Carolina Press, 1989), 90; Armistead L. Long, *Memoirs of Robert E. Lee: His Military and Personal History Embracing a Large Amount of Information Hitherto Unpublished* (1886; repr., Secaucus, NJ: Blue and Grey Press, 1983), 130; Catherine Ann Devereux Edmondston, *"Journal of a Secesh Lady": The Diary of Catherine Ann Devereux Edmondston, 1860–1866*, ed. Beth Gilbert Crabtree and James W. Patton (Raleigh: North Carolina Division of Archives and History, 1979), 189.

20. *Richmond Dispatch*, July 9, 1862; Grace Brown Elmore, *Heritage of Woe: The Civil War Diary of Grace Brown Elmore, 1861–1868*, ed. Marli F. Weiner (Athens: University of Georgia Press, 1997), 35 (entry for July 25, 1862).

21. Alexander, *Fighting for the Confederacy*, 91–92. For detailed examinations of Lee's changes in the Army of Northern Virginia's high command in July 1862, see Douglas Southall Freeman, *R. E. Lee: A Biography*, 4 vols. (New York: Charles Scribner's Sons, 1934–35), vol. 2, chap. 18; and Freeman, *Lee's Lieutenants: A Study in Command*, 3 vols. (New York: Charles Scribner's Sons, 1942–44), vol. 1, chaps. 42–43.

22. For the legislation regarding corps and the rank of lieutenant general, see "General Orders, No. 93," Adjutant and Inspector General's Office, November 22, 1862, in *OR*, ser. 4, 2:198. In his telegram dated August 30, 1862, to Jefferson Davis announcing the victory at Second Manassas, Lee referred to "each wing under Genls Longstreet and Jackson" (*The Wartime Papers of R. E. Lee*, ed. Clifford Dowdey and Louis H. Manarin [Boston: Little, Brown, 1961], 268).

23. Thomas W. Cutrer, ed., *Longstreet's Aide: The Civil War Letters of Major Thomas J. Goree* (Charlottesville: University Press of Virginia, 1995), 98; "General Orders, No. 74," Hdqrs. Dept. of Northern Virginia, June 23, 1862, in *OR* 11(1): 1042. On Stuart's effect on morale in the army, see H. B. McClellan, *The Life and Campaigns of Major-General J. E. B. Stuart, Commander of the Cavalry of the Army of Northern Virginia* (Boston: Houghton, Mifflin and Company, 1885), 67. Gov. John Letcher of Virginia presented Stuart with a "handsome sabre," and "the influence of this expedition on the *morale* not only of the cavalry, but of the whole army, was most important" (66–67).

24. Elias Davis to his parents, June 13, 1862, Elias Davis Papers, collection no. 2496, Southern Historical Collection, University of North Carolina, Chapel Hill (transcription by Earl Massey); Alexander, *Fighting for the Confederacy*, 96. In a letter to Alexander dated August 26, 1902, Walter H. Taylor, Lee's assistant adjutant general, addressed Jackson's behavior during the Seven Days: "Nothing was said of it in a general way, although there was quiet talk of it at the time, because we were so elated at raising the siege & there was no disposition to find fault" (Alexander, *Fighting for the Confederacy*, 569n9). On Jackson's problems during the Seven Days, see Robert K. Krick, "Sleepless in the Saddle: Stonewall Jackson in the Seven Days," in *The Richmond Campaign of 1862: The Peninsula and the Seven Days*, ed. Gary W. Gallagher (Chapel Hill: University of North Carolina Press, 2000), 66–95.

25. On Lee and the Army of Northern Virginia as the Confederacy's major national rallying point, see Gary W. Gallagher, *The Confederate War* (Cambridge, MA: Harvard University Press, 1997), especially chap. 3. See also Joseph T. Glatthaar, *General Lee's Army: From Victory to Collapse* (New York: Free Press, 2008), xv, 471–72.

26. For the specific reassignments, see John H. Eicher and David J. Eicher, *Civil War High Commands* (Stanford: Stanford University Press, 2001), 302 (Holmes), 308 (Huger), 360 (Magruder), 495 (Smith), 566 (Whiting). Smith's statement is quoted in Jasper S. Whiting to R. E. Lee, June 2, 1862, in *OR* 11(3): 685–86. It is perhaps a measure of their perceived failures that Holmes, Huger, and Magruder were deployed to the Trans-Mississippi Theater.

27. The key documents regarding Lee's initial dispositions are in *OR* 12(3): 915 (Jackson's deployment) and 11(3): 675–76 (Longstreet's deployment); and Lee to Jefferson Davis, August 14, 1862, in *Lee's Dispatches: Unpublished Letters of General Robert E. Lee, C.S.A. to Jefferson Davis and the War Department of the Confederate States of America 1862–65*, new ed., ed. Douglas Southall Freeman and Grady McWhiney (New York: G. P. Putnam's Sons, 1957), 45–48. On the later phase of the campaign, see *OR*12(2): 553–59 (Lee's report, dated June 8, 1863), 642–48 (Jackson's report, dated April 27, 1863), and 563–58 (Longstreet's report, dated October 10, 1862).

28. As with all Civil War campaigns, it is difficult to establish precise figures for casualties during Second Manassas. For different numbers, see, for example, E. B. Long, *The Civil War Day by Day: An Almanac, 1861–1865* (Garden City, NY: Doubleday, 1971), 250, 258 (10,538 at Cedar Mountain and Second Manassas; no figure for Chantilly); Patricia L. Faust, ed., *Historical Times Illustrated Encyclopedia of the Civil War* (New York: Harper and Row, 1986), 93, 122, 130 (11,050 at Cedar Mountain, Second Manassas, and Chantilly); and Margaret E. Wagner, Gary W. Gallagher, and Paul Finkelman, eds., *The Library of Congress Civil War Desk Reference* (New York: Simon and Schuster, 2002), 264 (8,350 for the period August 9–September 1).

29. *The Memoirs of Colonel John S. Mosby*, ed. Charles Wells Russell (1917; repr., Bloomington: Indiana University Press, 1959), 375. For Lee's instructions to Jackson, see *OR* 12(3): 859–60, 865–66. For the tenor of his communications with Johnston, see Lee's letters dated April 21, 23, 25, 30, May 2, 8, 11, 17, 18, 21, and 22 in *Wartime Papers of R. E. Lee*, 152–55, 157–58, 161, 164, 166–67, 170, 175–77. For a discussion of Lee's strategic thinking, see Gary W. Gallagher, "An Old-Fashioned General in a Modern War? Robert E. Lee as Confederate General," *Civil War History* 45, no. 2 (December 1999): 295–321.

30. *Southern Illustrated News*, September 20, 1862, 4.

31. *Wytheville (VA) Dispatch*, August 22, 1862 (clipping the piece from the *Whig*); *Wilmington (NC) Journal*, August 14, 1862; *Richmond Daily Dispatch*, September 6, 1862.

32. *Richmond Enquirer*, September 2, 1862; *Richmond Whig*, September 3, 1862. See also the *Richmond Enquirer* on September 6 (Longstreet), the *Richmond Whig* on September 1 (Stuart), and the *Richmond Dispatch* on September 10 (Jackson).

33. Thomas H. Carter to Susan Roy Carter, September 7, 1862, in *Gunner in Lee's Army*, 137, 139; John Hampden Chamberlayne to his sister, in *Ham Chamberlayne—Virginian: Letters and Papers of an Artillery Officer in the War for Southern Independence, 1861–1865*, ed. C. G. Chamberlayne (Richmond: Dietz Printing Co., 1932), 125–26; *Stonewall's Prussian Mapmaker: The Journals of Captain Oscar Hinrichs*, ed. Richard Brady Williams (Chapel Hill: University of North Carolina Press, 2014), 68–69.

34. *A Post of Honor: The Pryor Letters, 1861–63, Letters from Capt. S. G. Pryor, Twelfth Georgia Regiment and His Wife, Penelope Tyson Pryor*, ed. Charles R. Adams Jr. (Fort Valley, GA: Garret Publications, 1989), 251–52, 256.

35. Jefferson Davis to the Senate and House of Representatives of the Confederate States, September 2, 1862, in *A Compilation of the Messages and Papers of the Confederacy, Including the*

Diplomatic Correspondence, 1861–1865, 2 vols., ed. James D. Richardson (Nashville: United States Publishing Company, 1905), 1:240–41. Davis enclosed two dispatches from Lee announcing the victory on August 29–30. The *Richmond Whig* printed Davis's message on September 3.

36. Samuel J. C. Moore to his wife, August 4, 1862, folder titled "Series I June–Aug 1862," Samuel J. C. Moore Papers, Southern Historical Collection, University of North Carolina, Chapel Hill (transcription provided by Keith S. Bohannon).

37. On Jackson's fame and Lee's becoming the most important Confederate figure, see chaps. 1 and 5 of Gary W. Gallagher, *Lee and His Generals in War and Memory* (Baton Rouge: Louisiana State University Press, 1998).

38. Buck, *Shadows of My Heart*, 143, 147 (entries for August 28, September 7, 1862); Mary Greenhow Lee, *The Civil War Journal of Mary Greenhow Lee (Mrs. Hugh Holmes Lee) of Winchester, Virginia*, ed. Eloise C. Strader (Winchester, Va.: Winchester-Frederick County Historical Society, 2011), 139 (entries for September 5, 6, 1862); Michael G. Mahon, ed., *Winchester Divided: The Civil War Diaries of Julia Chase and Laura Lee* (Mechanicsburg, PA: Stackpole Books, 2002), 54 (entry for Chase on September 1, 1862).

39. Rev. Charles Colcock Jones to his son, October 2, 1862, in Myers, *Children of Pride*, 972.

40. John W. Stone to Julia A. Wood, September 22, 1862, in *The Wood Family of Fluvanna County, Virginia, 1795–1969*, ed. Margaret Williams Bayne (Norfolk, VA: privately printed, 1984), 187–88.

41. On Halleck, Lieber, and the code, see chap. 3 of Dilbeck, *More Civil War*. For the text of the code, see "General Orders, No. 100," War Department, Adjutant General's Office, Washington, April 24, 1863, in *OR*, ser. 2, 5:671–82.

42. "The Second Confiscation Act," Freedmen and Southern Society Project, accessed March 4, 2023, http://www.freedmen.umd.edu/conact2.htm; *The Civil War Diary of Gideon Welles: Lincoln's Secretary of the Navy*, ed. William E. Gienapp and Erica L. Gienapp (Urbana: Knox College Lincoln Studies Center and University of Illinois Press, 2014), 4–5; *The Collected Works of Abraham Lincoln*, ed. Roy P. Basler, 9 vols. (New Brunswick, NJ: Rutgers University Press, 1953–55), 5:336–37. On the connection between the Seven Days' defeat and the Second Confiscation Act, see Sen. Charles Sumner to John Bright, August 5, 1862, in *The Selected Letters of Charles Sumner*, ed. Beverly Wilson Palmer, 2 vols. (Boston: Northeastern University Press, 1990), 2:122. "The Bill of Confiscation & Liberation," wrote Sumner, "which was at last passed, under pressure from our reverses at Richmond, is a practical Act of Emancipation."

43. George B. McClellan to Abraham Lincoln, July 7, 1862, and McClellan to Henry W. Halleck, August 1, 1862, in *The Civil War Papers of George B. McClellan: Selected Correspondence, 1860–1865*, ed. Stephen W. Sears (New York: Ticknor and Fields, 1989), 344–45, 380–81.

44. Pope's orders are in *OR* 12(2): 50 (No. 5, July 18, 1862), 51 (No. 7, July 10 [?], 1862), and 52 (No. 11, July 23, 1862). Pope asked for Lincoln's opinion about No. 11, explaining, "I find it impossible to make any movement, however insignificant the force, without having it immediately communicated to the enemy. . . . A thousand open enemies cannot inflict the injury upon our arms which can be done by one concealed enemy in our midst" (*OR* 12[3]: 500–501).

45. Jefferson Davis to R. E. Lee, July 31, 1862, in *Jefferson Davis, Constitutionalist: His Letters, Papers and Speeches*, ed. Dunbar Rowland, 10 vols. (Jackson: Mississippi Department of Archives and History, 1923), 5:306–7.

46. Davis to Lee, August 1, 1862, in *Jefferson Davis*, 5:308; R. E. Lee to George B. McClellan, July 6, 1862, in *Wartime Papers of R. E. Lee*, 134–35.

47. "General Orders, No. 54," War Department, Adjutant and Inspector General's Office, Richmond, August 1, 1862, in *OR*, ser. 2, 4:836–37.

48. R. E. Lee to Henry W. Halleck, August 1, 1862 (two letters), in *OR*, ser. 2, 4:328–30.

49. Halleck to Lee, August 9, 1862, in *OR*, ser. 2, 4:362; Jefferson Davis, "Message to the Confederate Congress," August 18, 1862, in *Jefferson Davis*, 5:321–22. "I must respectfully decline to receive them," Halleck wrote of Lee's letters. "They are returned herewith."

50. *Chicago Tribune*, July 22, 1862. The *Tribune* also printed the texts of all three orders. For other examples of praise for Pope's actions, see *New York Herald*, August 10, 1862; *New-York Daily Tribune*, August 4, 1862; and Davenport, Iowa's *Daily Democrat and News*, August 15, 1862. For an example of the argument that Pope did not follow through on his orders, see James M. McPherson and James K. Hogue, *Ordeal by Fire: The Civil War and Reconstruction*, 4th ed. (Boston: McGraw-Hill Higher Education, 2009), 274.

51. *Richmond Daily Dispatch*, July 24, August 9, 25, 1862.

52. *Richmond Christian Advocate*, August 6, 1862; *The Lancaster (SC) Ledger*, August 20, 1862, quoting from the *Richmond Examiner*.

53. *Western Sentinel* (Winston, NC), August 8, 1862; Peter Wellington Alexander dispatch dated July 29, 1862, in William B. Styple, ed., *Writing and Fighting the Civil War: The Letters of Peter Wellington Alexander, Confederate War Correspondent* (Kearny, NJ: Belle Grove, 2002), 90.

54. R. E. Lee to Thomas J. Jackson, July 27; Lee to Mildred Lee, July 28; and Lee to George W. Randolph, July 28, 1862, in *Wartime Papers of R. E. Lee*, 239–41; *The Compact Edition of the Oxford English Dictionary: Complete Text Produced Micrographically*, 2 vols. (New York: Oxford University Press, 1971), 1:1811.

55. *The Civil War Diary of Father James Sheeran: Confederate Chaplain and Redemptorist*, ed. Patrick J. Hayes (Washington, DC: Catholic University of America Press, 2017), 15; [An English Combatant], *Battle-Fields of the South, from Bull Run to Fredericksburgh; with Sketches of Confederate Commanders, and Gossip of the Camps* (1864; repr., New York: Time-Life Books, 1984), 430; *The Journals of Josiah Gorgas, 1857–1878*, ed. Sarah Woolfolk Wiggins (Tuscaloosa: University of Alabama Press, 1995), 50–51 (entries for August 3, 16, 1862).

56. Maury, "Civil War Diary," 85–86 (entries for July 30, August 2, 1862); Virginia Soutter Knox to Robert Taylor Knox and James Soutter Knox, July 30, 1862, and Thomas Fitzhugh Knox Jr. to Virginia Ann Soutter Knox, July 29, 1862, in *The Circle Unbroken: Civil War Letters of the Knox Family of Fredericksburg*, by Central Rappahannock Heritage Center and Historic Fredericksburg Foundation (Fredericksburg, VA: Central Rappahannock Heritage Center and Historic Fredericksburg Foundation, 2013), 79–81.

57. Buck, *Shadows of My Heart*, 130. For other comments about interactions between Federal soldiers and civilians, see Buck's diary entries for July 31, August 16, 25, 1862 (pp. 132–33, 137, 141–42).

58. Mahon, *Winchester Divided*, 50, 52–53 (entries for July 30, August 2, 22, 25, 1862); Lee, *Civil War Journal*, 115–16.

59. Edmondston, *"Journal of a Secesh Lady,"* 222, 224 (entries for July 25, 30, 1862); *The Diary of Miss Emma Holmes*, ed. John F. Marszalek (Baton Rouge: Louisiana State University Press, 1979), 187.

60. *Civil War Diary of Father James Sheeran*, 50 (entry for September 1, 1862); Spencer Glasgow Welch, *A Confederate Surgeon's Letters to His Wife* (1911; repr., Marietta, GA: Continental Book Company, 1954), 24 (letter dated September 3, 1862); *Journals of Amanda Virginia Edmonds*, 110 (entry for August 27, 1862); *Lucy Breckinridge of Grove Hill: The Journal of a Virginia Girl, 1862–1864*, ed. Mary D. Robertson (Kent: Kent State University Press, 1979), 35 (entry for August 30, 1862); Robert H. Couper to his mother, October 1, 1862, folder 102, box 10, Colonial Dames of America Collection, No. 965, Georgia Historical Society, Savannah (text of Couper letter provided by Keith S. Bohannon). It is impossible to pin down exactly how many African Americans came back under Confederate control during the campaign, but Breckinridge and Couper almost certainly overestimated the number.

61. *The Diary of Edmund Ruffin*, 3 vols., ed. William Kauffman Scarborough (Baton Rouge: Louisiana State University Press, 1972–89), 2:386–87, 389–90 (entries for July 24, 28, 1862).

62. For an example of concern about casualties, see Shepherd G. Pryor to Penelope Tyson Pryor, September 2, 1862, in *Post of Honor*, 253.

63. William Dorsey Pender to Fanny Pender, September 2, 1862, in *The General to His Lady: The Civil War Letters of William Dorsey Pender to Fanny Pender*, ed. William W. Hassler (Chapel Hill: University of North Carolina Press, 1965), 171; Robert Jones to My Dear Wife, September 5, 1862, in Dorothy Jones Morgan, comp., *A Very Personal Glimpse of the Civil War Era from 1849 to 1863* (N.p., 1990), n.p.; transcription provided by Keith S. Bohannon.

GENERAL POPE GOES TO WASHINGTON

Radical Republicans and the Failed Hope of the Second Bull Run Campaign

CECILY ZANDER

Though the sun shone brightly on the national capital in the waning days of June 1862, political storm clouds were gathering across Washington.[1] Politicians were tense. Maj. Gen. George B. McClellan was falling back on the Peninsula. There were fears for the safety of his army and rumors that Washington might be evacuated. Abraham Lincoln, his cabinet, and Republicans in Congress were sensitive to a rising tide of criticism. It was a midterm election year and a decisive test for the Republican Party. There were a few optimists who spoke of a favored general among the presidential advisors, recently arrived from campaigns in the West where he had "only seen the backs of his enemies."[2] In the early summer of 1862, Lincoln selected Maj. Gen. John Pope as the general most likely to instill an offensive spirit into the stalemated Eastern Theater of the Civil War. On June 26, 1862, the forty-year-old Kentucky-born general assumed command of the newly formed Army of Virginia.[3]

Pope had a significant task in front of him. He needed to unite the commands of three independent armies, check the depredations of Confederate major generals Richard S. Ewell and Thomas J. "Stonewall" Jackson in the Shenandoah Valley, protect the national capital, and aid McClellan by diverting the attention of Confederate troops from the defenses of Richmond. As a rare Republican in an officer corps overflowing with Democrats, Pope also appealed to a cohort of congressional Republicans who longed for an officer who would take a more aggressive tack against the Confederacy, after more than a year of conservative army leadership.[4] These Radicals did not represent the majority within the Republican Party, but they held considerable sway, with prominent members chairing the Ways and Means Committee in the House and the Military Affairs Committee in the Senate and holding the Speaker's gavel in the Thirty-Seventh Congress. They were, as historian Eric Foner put it, "an essential part of the Republican constituency."[5] And they wanted to play a part in deciding how the Civil War would be waged.

Pope arrived in the national capital at the exact moment that multiple conversations about the conduct of the Civil War were occurring in the halls of Congress and the meeting rooms of the White House. One conversation had to do with slavery and the degree to which army officers and soldiers could interfere with or confiscate civilian property while occupying Confederate territory—including property in slaves. Another had to do with a perceived lack of agreement between politicians and generals as to how the war ought to be conducted. Many of the army's highest-ranking officers, exemplified by McClellan, believed in a conservative and limited war that would bring about the restoration of the Union without interfering with the institution of slavery.[6] By 1862, this placed McClellan and similarly inclined Union commanders at odds with prominent Republicans who sought aggression from army leaders.

During the summer of 1862, Republican political leaders intended to validate their ideas about how the Civil War ought to be waged through Pope's anticipated success. In his history of the Second Bull Run campaign, historian John J. Hennessy claims that Pope came from the West to "change the nature of the war in Virginia."[7] In order to do so, Hennessy rightly concludes, Pope needed to back up his policy shifts with battlefield successes. Pope's tenure with the Army of Virginia illuminates the profound ties between the military and political dimensions of the Civil War and underscores the degree to

A rare Republican in an overwhelmingly Democratic office corps, Maj. Gen. John Pope inspired high hopes among Republican congressional leaders in the summer of 1862. (Library of Congress Prints and Photographs Division, reproduction number LC-DIG-cwpb-06342)

which battlefield performances trumped politics in determining whether an officer would be kept in command.

Pope faced a significant challenge in his quest to make good on the promises he offered the Radicals. No challenge was more pressing than having to unite three previously independent commands, and three opinionated commanders, under the banner of one army and one general. Pope's Army of Virginia was something of a Frankenstein's monster—constituted on June 26, 1862, from three existing military departments: Maj. Gen. John C. Frémont's Mountain Department, Maj. Gen. Irvin McDowell's Department of the Rappahannock, and Maj. Gen. Nathaniel P. Banks's Department of the Shenandoah. All three officers held commissions dated earlier than Pope's, meaning that they technically outranked the general who was now supposed to command them. Frémont could not bear such an affront and resigned from the army. He was replaced by German revolutionary (and critic of slavery) Maj. Gen. Franz Sigel.[8]

The Army of Virginia was created, in part, as a direct challenge to the Army of the Potomac. By the summer of 1862, as naval secretary Gideon Welles understood it, Secretary of War Edwin Stanton could no longer place his confidence in George McClellan. Stanton, along with Radical Salmon Chase, the Treasury secretary, decided that McClellan's authority needed to be checked after Little Mac had come within sight of Richmond and failed to take the Confederate capital. Stanton and Chase, Welles explained, maneuvered to bring Pope to command an army that would function as a counterweight to McClellan in Virginia and pulled Maj. Gen. Henry Wager Halleck from his western operations to oversee the Union war effort from Washington.[9] Welles concluded that it had been Stanton's "malignant feelings" toward McClellan that provided the basis for Lincoln to agree to try out Pope.[10]

Although Pope offered the Radicals the declarations of aggression that they demanded through the war's first two years, the Second Bull Run campaign's political advancements were rendered moot by the fact that their chosen general could not back up his bombastic claims with a battlefield victory. To historians, Pope has been viewed as little more than a failed commander who could not get along with his subordinates and did not understand how to win a battle.[11] To his contemporaries, Pope represented the Radical hope that a Republican general, rather than a Democrat, could deliver the Union's first major victory over the Army of Northern Virginia. Pope's great strides toward changing the political tenor of the war in Virginia pleased politicians longing for aggression but were important only if they also helped Union armies defeat Gen. Robert E. Lee and the Army of Northern Virginia. Pope lacked the capacity to be the officer who could be both a political and a military success.[12]

The Radical Republicans and the War in 1862

By the time Pope checked into his Washington quarters in June, Republican congressional leaders (most of the Radical disposition) had frequently, and freely, voiced their frustration with the Lincoln administration's management of the war. Their critique—that Lincoln was too moderate on issues such as confiscation and emancipation—led several prominent Republicans to advocate for more legislative oversight of Union military policies. Men such as Zachariah Chandler, Benjamin Wade, and Charles Sumner in the Senate, joined by Thaddeus Stevens in the House, had campaigned in 1860 on outright opposition to slavery (rather than only forbidding its extension into the nation's western territories). As it became increasingly clear that the country would go to war, the Radical camp declared that the conflict should be waged not only to save the Union but also to end slavery.

In the early months of the Civil War, the Radicals realized that they would need cooperation from Union armies to help consummate their antislavery goals.[13] They faced a thorny problem, however, that arose from the separation of powers outlined in the Constitution by the standing army–fearing founding generation: they did not have sole control over the national armies that would wage the Civil War.[14] While their branch of the federal government had the power to declare war and to appropriate the money that would fund the Union war effort, their moderate party leader in the White House, Abraham Lincoln, held the title of commander in chief. Divided authority produced divergent ideas about how the war should be conducted.[15]

In their effort to assert authority over national military affairs, Radicals in Congress agitated early and often for emancipation as a war aim. To their consternation, however, most of the armies' leading officers did not share their goals. With McClellan, Maj. Gen. John Adams Dix, Brig. Gen. Charles Stone, Maj. Gen. Don Carlos Buell, and other Democrats controlling the army through the summer of 1862, Radical leaders saw little chance of achieving emancipation. Rep. Martin F. Conway of Kansas charged that there was not "more than one sincere abolitionist or emancipationist among the military authorities."[16] Joseph Medill, the pro-Republican editor of the *Chicago Tribune*, warned Secretary of War Stanton that he would "discover scores of luke warm, half secession officers in command who can not bear to strike a vigorous blow lest it hurt their rebel friends or jeopardize the precious protectors of slavery."[17]

The Radicals also abhorred the fact that when officers sympathetic to emancipation did emerge from the army's ranks, the president contravened their military orders advancing abolition. When General Frémont promulgated an order establishing martial law and emancipating the slaves in Missouri on August 30, 1861, for example, Lincoln quickly ordered the general to rescind the proclamation, insisting that the officer (and onetime Republican presidential nominee) had exceeded his authority as a military commander.[18]

In the aftermath of the Frémont fracas, Radical legislators grew particularly concerned with Lincoln's exercise of presidential war powers. In a letter to Chandler, Wade wrote that Lincoln "has done more injury to the cause of the Union, by receding from the ground taken by Frémont, than McDowell did by retreating from Bull Run."[19] Lincoln defended his position, insisting that his job as president was to ensure that Union armies operated within the limits of domestic and international law.[20] "If the General needs [slaves] he can seize them, and use them; but when the need is past, it is not for him to fix their permanent future condition," Lincoln explained, saying "that must be settled according to laws made by lawmakers, and not by military proclamations."[21] The justification failed to satisfy the Radical camp.

Tempers boiled over by the war's first winter. Radical policymakers arrived in Washington for the December 1861 meeting of Congress with the intention of calling the president to account for his conduct of the war. McClellan's inactivity, the decision to overrule Frémont, the Ball's Bluff disaster, and Lincoln's reluctance to adopt an emancipation policy stoked Radical fury.[22] The mounting rage of the faction and members' determination to have a voice in the establishment of war policies evidenced itself in a wave of legislative action. In the Senate, Lyman Trumbull proposed what would become the First Confiscation Act, writing to an acquaintance, "Action, action is what we want and must have."[23] Trumbull was joined by Ohioan Samuel Shellabarger in the House, who offered a resolution directed at censoring generals who returned fugitive slaves rather than granted them refuge behind Union lines. All the while, Radical senators urged their colleagues in the House to reject the readoption of the Crittenden resolutions, which aimed to limit the war to the preservation of the Union.[24]

Republican leaders turned to legislation to advance their antislavery aims. The First Confiscation Act authorized military leaders to seize the property of any individual participating in the rebellion (including property in slaves) but did not define the subsequent legal status of that property. The Second Confiscation Act, passed in July 1862 after McClellan's failed campaign against Richmond, stated that any slaves owned by individuals who supported or participated in the rebellion and all slaves in rebel territory captured by Union armies would be "forever free of their servitude, and not again held as slaves."[25] The act exempted Unionist slaveholders from its threat of confiscation. The acts, though bold and legally creative, depended on military commanders who would enforce them to their fullest extent—and such officers were still a rare commodity in 1862.

The Radicals also established a committee to provide congressional oversight on the conduct of the war. Following a disastrous Union defeat at Ball's Bluff in October 1861, legislators convened the Joint Committee on the Conduct of the War. This body, they suggested, would investigate the campaigns undertaken by Union armies and make recommendations to President Lincoln and Secretary Stanton on how they could make Union military operations more successful. The committee could, as Horace Greeley's anti-administration *New York Herald* explained to readers, "send for persons and papers."[26] The reports produced by the body, accounting for the actions of those persons and the contents of those papers, had no legal force. But they were taken seriously, as evidenced by the number of officers who agreed to be interviewed by the committee and cooperated with its work. Radical leaders hoped to dislodge the conservative elements of the army's high command and to use the committee "to bend the war to the goal of abolition."[27] Republicans George W. Julian (Indiana), John Covode (Pennsylvania), and Daniel Gooch (Massachusetts) represented the House; Benjamin Wade of Ohio, the Senate. They were joined by Senate Democrats Andrew Johnson of Tennessee and Joseph Wright of Indiana and Moses Odell of New York from the House.[28] Sen. Zachariah Chandler of Michigan, with whom the idea of the committee had originated, would serve as its leading investigator. Wade, Chandler, Julian, and Covode could all fairly be classed as Radicals—meaning they made up half of the committee's membership.

The creation and maintenance of the committee indicated that the Radicals wanted to take an active role in directing national military affairs. Henry Wilson, chairman of the Senate's Military Affairs Committee, championed the idea of bringing professional soldiers to account—for it would be West Point–trained officers, rather than citizen-volunteers, upon whom the committee principally focused its ire. "I want military men to understand," Wilson explained before the Senate, "that they are not to stand upon technicalities for the preservation of the old Army."[29] For Wilson and his colleagues, the "Old Army" connoted conservatism and military ineptitude—the very failings the committee aimed to expose in its investigations. And no officer better exemplified these traits than George McClellan, for whom Pope would emerge as a Radical-backed foil. Speaking in front of the Senate in the summer of 1862, Chandler declared that through his conservatism McClellan and his subordinates had been "stabbing their country in the dark . . . under the pretended guise of patriotism."[30]

During their first official investigation, the committee's members revealed that playing politics mattered far more than accurately identifying the reasons for Union military failures. And they made a regular army officer their first target. Brig. Gen. Charles P. Stone was an 1845 graduate of West Point who eagerly volunteered his services to the Union war effort. Ordered by George McClellan to conduct a reconnaissance of a Confederate position near Leesburg, Virginia, on October 20, 1861, Stone did as commanded. When one of his junior officers mistook some trees for a small Confederate camp, Stone gave his men permission to launch an attack across the Potomac River the following morning. Col. Charles Devens arrived on the opposite bank to find a company of Mississippi infantry. A skirmish quickly turned into a debacle, when, without orders, Col. Edward Baker (also the senator from Oregon Territory) used four boats to reinforce Devens. The mistake cost Baker his life and added 1,000 Union casualties to the war's mounting toll.

The Joint Committee placed all the blame for the incident at Ball's Bluff on Stone. Blinded by their rage over losing their friend and former colleague, Baker, and unable to see that Baker's lack of experience led to the tragedy, members' final committee report suggested Stone be arrested. Not willing to put himself in the committee's line of fire (a place where he would nonetheless frequently find himself over the next two year), George McClellan approved the recommendation. Stone was held in a military prison without trial or formal charges for nearly six months. When word of the arrest reached Winfield Scott, he reportedly declared, "If he is a traitor, I am a traitor, and we are all traitors."[31] But the opinions of professional military officers, even those of Scott's stature, mattered little to the Radical partisans of the Joint Committee. Falling in line with the majority, the Democrats on the committee manifested interest in rebutting the conclusions reached by their colleagues.[32] Reflecting on the investigation in 1863, Julian emphasized that Stone was cut from the same political cloth as McClellan. They were conservative generals "whose sympathies with the rebels were well known throughout the country."[33]

Compared with the soldiers they interrogated, Radical legislators had little grasp of the detailed work required to succeed in winning on the battlefield. And battlefield results mattered for sustaining civilian morale, getting

Republicans reelected, and forestalling foreign intervention in favor of the Confederacy. As historian Mark E. Neely Jr. explains, Republicans grew increasingly agitated with the failure of Union armies to achieve decisive victories, and party members revolted against the "military science" advocated by professional soldiers like McClellan.[34] Republicans blamed West Point–taught "strategy" for the lack of offensive campaigning undertaken by Union armies.[35] The committee did not hesitate to charge Union officers with coddling Confederates or opposing emancipation.[36] Members of the committee "convinced themselves that the army was beset with apathy and defeatism, and that any officer known to be a Democrat was guilty of these sins until proved innocent."[37] The committee sought known Republican officers—as few in number as they were—to offer testimony on the failures of their Democratic colleagues. When he arrived in Washington in late June, John Pope fit the needs of the committee perfectly.

Pope and the Radicals

John Pope cut a unique figure among the cohort of West Point–trained officers who hoped to lead the Union to victory. He matched most of his army contemporaries in his educational background and antebellum military experiences (exploring, surveying, and doing little actual fighting), but he did not adopt the apolitical attitude that permeated the officer class of the Old Army. Pope was proud to be branded a Republican, especially in an army that seemed to be guided by conservative ideas regarding slavery's future. Pope's father, Nathaniel, had served as a district judge in Illinois and frequently heard the young lawyer Abraham Lincoln argue cases before his bench. Lincoln seemed to like Pope, asking the then army captain to serve as an escort on his journey from Springfield to Washington, DC, after his election to the presidency.

There remains some question as to whether Pope would have identified himself as a Republican or whether he merely adopted Republican attitudes to advance his Civil War career in a Democrat-dominated officer corps. Neither answer is entirely satisfactory, if Pope's own reminiscences offer any indication of his feelings. When Pope recalled the early years of the Civil War, he emphasized that his conviction had always been, should North and South come to blows over slavery, that the only way such a war could end would be with the destruction of slavery—or with Confederate independence.[38] In an essay on Abraham Lincoln, in which Pope described his antebellum connections to the president and his role in accompanying Lincoln to Washington, he never indicated that he voted to send Lincoln to the White House. And while Pope could be shrewd when it came to army politics, ascribing ulterior motives to his Republicanism is difficult. The most that could be said is that Pope benefited from having a personal view of the war that placed him in direct opposition to the prominent Democrats who had bungled the Union war effort well into the summer of 1862. That he was not hesitant to share that view is not necessarily evidence of Pope playing politics but rather an indication of his lack of understanding of how to get along with his fellow officers in Virginia, where the war was not run in the way he had become accustomed to in the West.

What Pope believed, above all else, was that Union armies needed to place slavery in their crosshairs if they hoped to defeat the Confederacy. As David Hunter Strother, a Virginian who served as a topographer with Pope in 1862, recorded in his wartime diary, Pope was convinced "that the war had necessarily given the death blow to slavery."[39] This opinion aligned Pope with the Republican Party, and particularly its Radical wing. When he arrived in Washington, Pope found he was the man of the moment, his rise through the ranks perfectly timed to coincide with increased Republican agitation over the failures of the conservative Democratic leadership of the principal Union army. He became a darling of the leading Radicals in the capital, who let their antislavery fervor run out ahead of Pope's potential to alter the course of the war, whether he himself sought their favor or not. Radical zeal for aggression was gratified by Pope's bombast, and Pope benefited immeasurably, albeit briefly, from their support.

Secretary of War Stanton nurtured high hopes for the newly arrived officer. Stanton supported Pope as the nation's best alternative to George McClellan, for whom Stanton nursed a powerful loathing. Factors beyond the battlefield may also have endeared Stanton and Pope to one another. Both men suffered the intense grief of the loss of a young child during the summer of 1862. On July 8, Stanton lost his eight-month-old son, James. Just two weeks later, on July 22, Pope received word of the death of his one-month-old daughter, Cara, the only child he would ever have. And less than five months earlier, in late February, President Lincoln had laid to rest his eleven-year-old son, Willie. The men charged with leading the Union war effort, it seemed, found death much closer to home than the battlefields of Virginia.

Pope spent much of June in Washington, meeting with prominent Republicans. He also frequented the War Department offices, where he and Stanton discussed their plans for defending Washington and consolidating the formerly independent Shenandoah Valley commands of Frémont (later Franz Sigel), Nathaniel Banks, and Irvin McDowell under the banner of the Army of Virginia. In his memoirs of the war, Maj. Gen. Jacob Dolson Cox suggested that Stanton and Pope worked together closely to craft a series of orders that would "infuse vigor into the army by stirring words."[40] Stanton and Pope agreed that McClellan's conservative style needed correcting. It was a stance that almost guaranteed the approval of the Radical Republicans, in both Congress and the cabinet.

Outside of the War Department offices, Pope received a similarly hearty reception from Washington's denizens—especially among the leading lights of the Radical faction. Secretary of the Treasury Salmon P. Chase showed himself an ardent supporter of Pope, contrasting the newly arrived general and McClellan in his diary. Writing about Pope's wining and dining campaign in the capital, Chase gave an account of a dinner he shared with the Army of Virginia's new commander, during which Pope condemned McClellan's campaign on the Peninsula:

> Genl. Pope expressed himself freely and decidedly in favor of the most rigorous measures in the prosecution of the war. He believed that, in consequence of the rebellion, Slavery must perish, and with him it was only a question of prudence as to the means to be employed to weaken it. He was in favor of using every instrument which could be brought to bear against the enemy; and while he did not speak in favor of a general arming of the slaves as soldiers, he advocated their use as laborers, in the defence of fortifications, and in any way in which their services could be made useful without impairing the general tone of the service.[41]

Chase's account underscored the Radical belief that Pope's campaign would have significant bearing on the fate of slavery. Behind the scenes of the campaign, as Radical pressure from Congress increased and Pope toured the capital, Lincoln and his cabinet were engaged in discussions about issuing an emancipation proclamation, with senior Union officials divided over the best course of action.

On June 25, just as the forces of McClellan and Confederate commander Joseph E. Johnston clashed at Oak Grove in the first of the Seven Days' battles, Pope spoke before the House of Representatives about the war to that point. He also previewed, in broad outline, his intentions for the upcoming campaign. The general spent considerable time celebrating his own achievements in the war's Western Theater, slipped in a criticism of McClellan's ongoing failure to capture Richmond, and concluded by declaring that emancipation had to become the focus of the Union war effort. The Republican-dominated legislative body was, according to the pro-Republican *New York Daily Tribune*, "struck with Pope's frankness and ability."[42]

Pope offered similar comments in testimony given before the Joint Committee on the Conduct of the War on July 8. The general spent the entire day giving answers to a series of questions on his plans for defending Washington and supporting McClellan. In addition, he offered his opinions on how the war ought to be conducted and provided his personal assessments of the generalship of his more conservative colleagues. Each answer perfectly reflected the Radical Republican desire to hear Union officers speak in favor of aggression against the Rebels and action against slavery. Pope's pronouncements rang through the Capitol Building and seemed to suggest the possibility of a major shift in Union war policy.

More than anything, Pope spoke the single word that mattered most to the Radical coalition as adherents articulated their view of the war: aggression. In testimony that ran to seven pages in the printed record, Pope faced forty-five questions from the examiners. Many were simple questions of fact. Who was Pope? Where was his army? What was the condition of his troops and of the men who staffed the defenses of Washington? In his answers to the questions posed to him, Pope made statements about activity, the offensive, or the need to take aggressive actions against the Confederacy nine times. More than 20 percent of Pope's statements, in other words, focused on the ideology espoused by the Radicals.

To set himself apart from McClellan, Pope relied on his hard-war bona fides. He derived his ideas from his experiences in northern Missouri in 1861, where he confronted staunch Confederate guerrilla fighting. On July 21, 1861, Pope issued an order that held civilians accountable for the destruction of the North Missouri Railroad—a critical aid to the Union occupation of the border state. He intended to punish disloyal civilians, not enemy combatants, for hampering Union operations, just as he would do in Virginia. This had been a step McClellan had been unwilling to take. As historian D. H. Dilbeck explains, Pope believed his policies "restored peace, security, and loyalty to the Union."[43]

Pope's testimony before the Joint Committee used the recent example of McClellan's retreat from Richmond as an example of everything that was wrong with the conduct of the war in Virginia. Pope insisted that "the best way to defend Washington is to attack Richmond" and expressed disappointment in McClellan's decision to fall back to Harrison's Landing. He asserted to the committee that he would "very gladly march upon Richmond."[44] He also questioned the overall propriety of McClellan's choice to attack Richmond from the east, saying that he believed the best option for attacking the Confederate capital was to begin in Washington and move Union forces south—a plan that sounded similar, in broad outline, to the operation Ulysses S. Grant would undertake in the spring of 1864. Pope clarified that he shared his views on attacking Richmond with the newly appointed general-in-chief, Henry Halleck.

Pope also suggested that successful military operations required cooperation among army commanders. The subtext of his comments was that officers needed to share not only military goals but also political ones. When asked how his troops would operate in concert with the Army of the Potomac, Pope demurred, saying that two armies working together "should be commanded by generals of the same character and manner of operations."[45] Pope then linked Union successes in the war's Western Theater to a high degree of cooperation among army commanders. "I think a portion of our successes in the west," he explained, "has been due to the fact that we have never had anything but entire harmony in our forces." Pope conveniently neglected to mention the skirmishing among Ulysses S. Grant, Henry Halleck, and Don Carlos Buell in the aftermath of the battle of Shiloh, as Union troops aimed to capture the vital Confederate railroad hub in Corinth, Mississippi. Western troops, Pope asserted, "pursued an aggressive policy from the beginning."[46] Throughout the interview, Pope consciously depicted himself as the opposite of McClellan.

Pope's statements stoked Radical resentment toward conservative Union officers. Horace Greeley's antislavery *New York Tribune* applauded Pope's declarations before the committee. Pope's arrival, the *Tribune* explained, rightly inspired "public confidence" in the Union war effort. "It is very much to be questioned," the editors wrote on July 23, "whether pro-Slavery generals can wage this war of ideas successfully." Greeley's newspaper reminded sympathetic readers that the "heart is quite as essential as head or hand" in such a conflict.[47] In other words, Pope's declarations were as much to his credit as his previous military successes in the war's Western Theater—or so the most pro-Radical newspaper in the nation proclaimed.

While Pope's pronouncements certainly gratified the Radical faction, they also reached the man who often found himself a target of the Joint Committee's ire. Despite strong Republican backing for his ideas, Pope could not successfully beat the Rebels without support from his Democratic adversary, George McClellan. And Little Mac knew it. McClellan described the new commander of the Army of Virginia as "a paltry young man" whom he expected "to be in full retreat or badly whipped" upon his first encounter with the Rebels.[48] Never mind the fact that Pope was four years McClellan's senior. Pope returned fire by speaking in a cabinet meeting about McClellan's "incompetency and indisposition to active movements."[49]

While the Radicals cheered their aggressive new general, his conservative predecessor gnashed his teeth in resentment. Whether Pope's barbs caused McClellan to deliberately withhold support from the Army of Virginia can never be recovered. What is evident in the historical record is that McClellan did not respond with alacrity to General Halleck's order directing him to withdraw his troops from Harrison's Landing to Alexandria, Virginia, and to send them to the aid of Pope's forces in early August. McClellan vehemently protested the withdrawal order, citing the demoralizing effect it would have on his army, the depression it would breed in the people of the North, and the doubts such an action would leave in foreign minds.[50] McClellan ignored Halleck's order for almost two weeks. Lincoln's personal secretary John Nicolay estimated that "fully eleven days of inestimable time were unnecessarily lost, and the army of Pope was thereby put in serious peril" because of McClellan's petulance.[51]

Word of change—from news of retreat to promises of aggression—impressed many observers in the loyal states. Republican newspapers resounded with approval for the new commander. Boston's *Daily Advertiser* proclaimed that "the appointment of such an officer to the command in Virginia will be received with universal joy." The author hoped that Pope could solve the "want of concerted action" that had plagued the war in Virginia.[52] Bangor, Maine's *Daily Whig and Courier* likewise approved of Lincoln's decision to promote Pope, assuring readers that "Gen. Pope avowed himself an unequivocal Union man at the opening of the rebellion."[53] "Gen. Pope is one of the stirring sort of men," observed the *New York Daily Tribune*, "and will not be likely to stand on the bank of the Potomac until all the water has run down before crossing."[54] The loyal Republican press quickly backed Pope's political vision for transforming the war.

Radical Policies in Action and in Defeat

The soldiers in Pope's newly created army cautiously embraced their leader's altered vision for the war. More than anything, their positive reception referred to a series of general orders that allowed Union troops to act much more stringently against Confederate civilians. Prior to Pope's arrival in

Virginia, Union soldiers were deployed to protect Confederate property. This exercise fit in with the conservative vision of the war, which held that the less Union soldiers did to disrupt the lives of Confederates, the easier it would be for the two sides to achieve reconciliation and reunion. Without battlefield victories, however, soldierly goodwill toward Pope and his policies proved short-lived. As Gideon Welles explained, relating the opinion of Hiram Barney—an abolitionist and close associate of leading Radical Salmon Chase—Pope had been set up for failure by the conservative leadership of the Army of the Potomac. In the end, the failure of McClellan to support Pope resulted in "the great demoralization of the soldiers."[55]

Even before the second battle at Bull Run, some of Pope's soldiers doubted whether Lincoln or the Radical faction had placed their confidence in the right officer. Lt. Robert Gould Shaw said in a letter to his father that he felt Pope—who now commanded Nathaniel Banks's corps, to which Shaw belonged—could "be successful in his campaign." The son of Boston Brahmin abolitionists, the Harvard-educated Shaw believed (more so than the average soldier in the ranks) that there was "no doubt that good will ultimately come of this war; that slavery will disappear, and the country be eventually united." But, when he considered what failure on the part of eager officers such as Pope might mean for that outcome, he doubted "whether we shall accomplish it by force of arms."[56] In other words, Shaw believed that if Pope failed to produce the victories that he had all but guaranteed in his introductory orders, the abolition cause might also suffer a significant setback.

At the same time as Pope's tour of Washington in late June and early July, Lincoln offered a preliminary draft of an emancipation proclamation to his secretary of state, William H. Seward, and naval secretary, Gideon Welles. McClellan's continued caution and failure on the Peninsula, as well as Congress's passage of the Second Confiscation Act on July 17, pushed Lincoln to make his most aggressive statement on emancipation. Still, Seward urged caution on the matter, suggesting a presidential proclamation would create anarchy in the Southern states and sway foreign intervention in favor of the Confederacy. When Lincoln presented his plan to the full cabinet, his advisors told the president to wait for a military victory over the Confederates before announcing his intention to free the slaves living in Union-occupied territory.[57]

When he finally joined his army in the field in mid-July, Pope worked quickly to show his new soldiers how his approach to the war would differ from his predecessors'. From July 18 to July 23, he signaled his intent to turn the Army of Virginia into a force of "practical liberators."[58] General Orders

No. 5 dictated that Pope's troops were to live off the land and pay only loyal citizens for goods requisitioned in support of the army. General Orders No. 6 directed soldiers to require the residents of any town or village through which Union forces moved to provide supplies to the Federals. General Orders No. 7 required that Virginians cooperate with Union troops to suppress guerrilla activity or be considered disloyal and subject to arrest. General Orders No. 11 ordered unit commanders in the Army of Virginia to arrest any disloyal male citizens within Union-occupied territory and require them to swear an oath of allegiance to the United States. Any civilian who violated the loyalty oath would be subject to property seizure and be shot by Union forces. General Orders No. 13 denied private citizens protection from Union troops, claiming that energy of Federal soldiers should not be wasted in protecting the property of "those most hostile to the Government."[59]

The soldiers under Pope's command expressed initial enthusiasm regarding the orders promulgated by their general. Outside of the Army of the Potomac and beyond the influence of George McClellan, two soldiers serving in the Shenandoah Valley attested that the new orders offered them reason for optimism. William Kindig of the 33rd Iowa Infantry told a correspondent that "the men have great belief in [Pope] and his energetic policy. . . . We all regard his late stringent orders as just the thing, and all are down on slow coach McLellan [*sic*], who marched his army into the swamps of the Chickahominy, and kept them intrenching and digging, while they were dying by the thousand, and all this time made no attempt on Richmond."[60] A New Yorker likewise contrasted Pope's orders to the previous policies of McClellan, declaring in a letter to his hometown newspaper, "Nothing is more galling to a patriot and Union loving man than to be compelled to guard the property of the enemies. We are glad this has been put a stop to. It is a very important step toward ending the war."[61]

The Army of Virginia's soldiers viewed the orders as a practical change that benefited the army, rather than as a political statement about the goals of the conflict.[62] This was clear in the letter one Ohio soldier sent back to his local newspaper. "General Pope's orders are much commented upon through all ranks of the army," he wrote; "I have yet to hear the first disapproving word." The soldier expected the orders would supply the foundation for a "rapid, triumphant" campaign against the Rebels.[63] Soldiers were pleased with Pope's call for action but commented little on the officer giving the orders. It was a change in policy, not leadership, that inspired a vigorous response in the ranks. And, because Pope was yet to fight a battle, soldiers had little to criticize about their new commander.

Pope's orders cut across partisan bias in the Union press, with loyal newspapers from across the political spectrum reacting to the general's plans with approval. Democrat and Republican sheets alike reported that the new orders were providing great benefit to the Union cause. "The late order of Gen. Pope . . . is already bearing fruit in Fredericksburg," Bloomsburg, Pennsylvania's *Star of the North*, self-described as a "thoroughly Democratic" sheet, reported on July 30, claiming that the requirement for an oath of allegiance "caused thirty of the leading Rebels of the town" to flee to Richmond.[64] A Vermont editor for a paper founded in support of the Free-Soil Party assured readers that Pope's orders had "alarmed" the Confederate government in Richmond. "Gen. Pope's orders . . . go deeper and strike harder blows at rebellion," the editors believed, "than any hitherto promulgated."[65] Editors seized on Pope's orders as suggestive of action in a theater that had produced disappointing military news during the previous months.

Newspapers also reported on the favorable effect of the orders on the soldiers in the ranks. "These bold movements and the recent orders of Gen. Pope," the soldier-produced *Memphis Union Appeal* declared, "seem to inspire something like admiration among the soldiers."[66] An antislavery editor in Bellows Falls, Vermont, hoped that other Union generals would follow Pope's example and make similar proclamations to motivate their troops to action: "If those orders are good enough for Gen. Pope, are they not equally good for any other general?"[67] The politically idiosyncratic *New York Herald* passed a final word of approval, suggesting Pope's order appealed across the political spectrum, saying the order "has infused new vigor into our soldiers and given them additional strength and courage."[68]

The reception to Pope's orders showed that the new general had made an impression on his troops in Virginia. Overall, this was a positive development for Union arms and soldier morale. To the south, at Harrison's Landing on the James River, however, one Union officer seethed over the direction the Lincoln government had adopted toward the war. Shortly after Pope issued the last of his orders, McClellan confided in Halleck that that he feared "the *civil* policy . . . enunciated by General Pope." As far as McClellan was concerned, Pope's directives were political actions, not military necessities. On August 1, McClellan informed Halleck that "I and the Army under my command are fighting to restore the Union," differentiating his force from that of Pope—whom he portrayed as fighting for "revenge." McClellan believed Pope's policy changes had turned the war into "a useless effusion of blood."[69]

The orders also made an impression on Confederates, both military and civilian. Jedidiah Hotchkiss, principal mapmaker for Stonewall Jackson, observed "the atrocity of Pope's army and the suffering of the people from the enforcement of his order to 'subsist his army on the country.'"[70] Robert E. Lee opted for harsh language, deeming Pope a "miscreant." He told Jackson, "I want Pope suppressed."[71] Jefferson Davis threatened to treat all of Pope's officers and men as criminals and not as lawful combatants under the rules of war, should they be captured in battle. Davis's strong response mirrored the orders that he would later issue regarding the treatment of white officers captured in command of United States Colored Troops regiments.

Confederate newspapers did little to conceal their outrage at the conditions Pope looked set to impose upon Virginia. "The orders of General Pope," the *Richmond Daily Intelligencer* cried, "surpass in barbarity anything ever yet proclaimed by the Federals in a Virginia latitude."[72] One newspaper in North Carolina simply stated that Pope's orders went beyond the "rights of civilized warfare" and deemed the Union general an "outlaw."[73] Winston, North Carolina's *Western Sentinel* warned citizens to avoid Pope's "murderous decrees."[74]

On the Virginia home front, many observed the immediate impact of the change in Union conduct toward civilians. During the days leading up to the fight at Cedar Mountain, Union troops destroyed fences, ransacked homes, and carried off Confederate property. Unlike the violence that Maj. Gen. Philip Sheridan's troops would visit upon the Shenandoah Valley two years later, however, "no civilians were killed, no private houses were burned . . . and the incidents almost exclusively involved moveable property."[75] All of the activity made an impression. Soldiers in the 5th Connecticut Infantry recalled civilians shouting that "Old Jack will give you all you want" as they carried off Confederate property, suggesting that no matter what Union troops did to civilians, they were still likely to be bested by Southern armies on the battlefield.[76]

Though comfortable issuing broad general orders governing a campaign, Pope proved less capable directing troops on the battlefield. When faced with an enemy that confounded his expectations for how an army ought to behave, Pope became erratic and ineffective. At Cedar Mountain, where a force under the command of Nathaniel P. Banks crashed into elements of Stonewall Jackson's command of the Army of Northern Virginia, Pope offered no clear instructions to his subordinate on whether he should fight a battle or whether there would be reinforcements available if Banks did encounter the enemy.[77] One Federal officer observed after the battle that "if we were not conforming to Pope's order to live on the country, we are doing the next best thing to it,—we were dying on it."[78] The barbed comment communicated the soldier's sense that Pope did not have the military capacity to match his grandiose predictions for success in the summer's signature campaign.

If Cedar Mountain suggested that Pope had significant limitations as an army commander, the battle of Second Bull Run thoroughly exposed them. Over two days of fighting on the plains of Manassas, Pope demonstrated very few leadership traits that would have convinced his soldiers and subordinates that he was a capable army commander. Most shocking was the fact that Pope, for most of the battle, could not be convinced that more than one half of the Confederate army, which he believed to be some distance from Manassas, was on the battlefield. The general who projected self-assuredness and made proclamations of aggression could not unscramble the scene in front of him as confused Union units slammed into the two wings of the Army of Northern Virginia, led by Jackson and Maj. Gen. James Longstreet.

As Pope's defeated troops streamed into the national capital, citizens and soldiers alike sought an explanation for the events of the preceding three months. More than anything, the responses revealed how quickly Pope's achievements in advancing ideas about hard war were forgotten without a battlefield victory to back them up. Still, many Republicans, and especially Radicals, defended Pope and looked to place the blame for the defeat elsewhere. The degree to which politics intertwined with army operations came through clearly in the assessments.

In early September, Pope made his way to Washington to speak with Lincoln, Stanton, Halleck, and the cabinet about the campaign. "Pope came over and talked with the President," Chase wrote, "who assured him of his entire satisfaction with his conduct; assured him that McClellan's command was only temporary; and gave him some reason to expect that another army of active operations would be organized at once, which he (Pope) would lead."[79] The following day Irvin McDowell visited Chase and concurred with Lincoln, Stanton, and Seward, "attributing our ill success to the conduct of McClellan in not urging forward reinforcements."[80] By September 11, Chase added his own considered opinion to the weight of judgment against McClellan: "Pope was defeated at Bull Run because the Administration persisted in keeping McClellan in command of the Army of the Potomac, after full warning that, under his lead and influence, that army would not cooperate effectively with Pope."[81]

The fact that John Pope never received any official censure for his failures during the battle of Second Bull Run is the strongest piece of evidence for the degree to which the Radicals sought to use the army to push their political agenda. Though historians have chronicled and corrected the record of the court-martial of Fitz John Porter, they have concluded that the trial of such a prominent officer was an attempt to discredit the McClellan faction of the Union high command, of which Porter was a prominent member. Porter's court-martial was also, however, an effort to obscure the degree to which a Republican officer—Pope—had proven himself to be incompetent. The fact that the charges were later dropped, in an investigation that revealed the degree of political manipulation that had occurred to place the blame on Porter, underscored Radicals' commitment to advancing their policies, regardless of whether those policies benefited the health and leadership of the army.[82]

Men in the ranks were less certain about whom to blame than were leaders in Washington—and deep-seated loyalties to McClellan dominated their judgments. Capt. Francis Adams Donaldson, a prolific diarist of the Army of the Potomac, lamented the events of Second Bull Run. "The poor old Army of the Potomac, how I pity it," he wrote to his brother; "what a dreadful mistake to give Genl. Pope the command of it."[83] Though he mistakenly asserted that Pope had been given command of the entire Army of the Potomac, rather than temporary authority over elements of the army's Third, Fifth, Sixth, and Ninth Corps, Donaldson felt bitterness toward Pope. Donaldson's point of view would not have been unique among many of the soldiers transferred from McClellan's army to Pope's. His vitriol toward Pope suggested the depth of admiration that soldiers in the Army of the Potomac had for George McClellan and his conservative style of warfare.

With Pope out of the picture, soldiers rejoiced in being returned to service under McClellan—an indication of the degree to which political proclamations could provide momentary spikes in morale but were not sustainable without battlefield results. Thomas T. Ellis wrote in his diary following McClellan's reappointment to command in early September that "many of the soldiers who fought under him in the hardest battles of the war, wept with joy at having again for their commander one upon whom they could place implicit reliance."[84] "General Pope made a grave blunder when he assailed the entrenched hero worship of General McClellan," Wisconsin soldier Rufus Dawes recalled in his memoir. "The force of this feeling can be little understood now, because conditions akin to those which affected us have passed away," he explained. Pope stood little chance, Dawes noted, when "such a feeling, as that for General McClellan, was never aroused for another leader in the war."[85]

Pope's experience in the summer of 1862 underscored a central theme that emerged over the course of the American Civil War: what happened on the battlefield mattered. Proclamations of change, whether military or political, rang hollow without battlefield success. There is no doubt that Pope's ideas about fighting a harder war against the Confederacy pleased his soldiers and irked Confederates. But without a victory to back up his bombast, no permanent political changes occurred as the result of his campaign. Pope's testimony before the Joint Committee on the Conduct of the War offered one vision for how the Union war could be waged, but his position as a leader in the war effort became untenable when he failed to produce a victory at Second Manassas.

Notes

1. Robert K. Krick, *Civil War Weather in Virginia* (Tuscaloosa: University of Alabama Press, 2007), 62.

2. US War Department, *The War of the Rebellion: A Compilation of the Official Records of the Union and Confederate Armies*, 128 vols., index and atlas (Washington, DC: Government Printing Office, 1880–1901), ser. 1, vol. 12, part 1, p. 474 (hereafter cited as *OR*).

3. Pope has been the subject of two biographies, each of which focuses almost exclusively on his Civil War career: Wallace J. Schutz and Walter N. Trenerry, *Abandoned by Lincoln: A Military Biography of General John Pope* (Urbana: University of Illinois Press, 1990); and Peter Cozzens, *General John Pope: A Life for the Nation* (Urbana: University of Illinois Press, 2000). Cozzens's workmanlike treatment of Pope attempts to find a middle ground in narrating the Second Bull Run campaign, concluding that Pope failed to interpret information and was unaware of the presence of James Longstreet but did not experience full cooperation from his subordinates. Schutz and Trenerry attempt to defend Pope's reputation, but their efforts to exculpate Pope are largely unsuccessful, as they rely on casting the blame elsewhere. Readers wanting to understand Pope as a military thinker are best served by Richard N. Ellis, *General Pope and U.S. Indian Policy* (Albuquerque: University of New Mexico Press, 1970), though Ellis examines Pope as a regular army officer in the postbellum Indian wars rather than during the Civil War.

4. Historians have varied in their assessments of the Radicals, with some viewing the faction as an impediment to the more measured policies advocated by Abraham Lincoln. See, for example, T. Harry Williams, *Lincoln and the Radicals* (1969; repr., Madison: University of Wisconsin Press, 1941). Others, such as Hans L. Trefousse, argued that the Radicals provided the "backbone" for Lincoln's eventual decision to pursue emancipation as a war aim. Hans L. Trefousse, *The Radical Republicans: Lincoln's Vanguard for Racial Justice* (New York: Alfred A. Knopf, 1969), 33.

5. Eric Foner, *Reconstruction: America's Unfinished Revolution, 1863–1887* (New York: Harper and Row, 1988), 238.

6. Ethan S. Rafuse, *McClellan's War: The Failure of Moderation in the Struggle for the Union* (Bloomington: Indiana University Press, 2005), explains that McClellan was a conservative, in that he sought to wage a limited war to preserve the Union that would not attack the institution of slavery while striving to uphold the principle of states' rights. Rafuse also

offers an important reminder to historians who would otherwise treat McClellan's conduct harshly. Like all the war's officers, McClellan sought to achieve a set of goals—above all else, reconciliation without politically, socially, or economically alienating the citizenry of the Confederacy.

7. John J. Hennessy, *Return to Bull Run: The Campaign and Battle of Second Manassas* (New York: Simon and Schuster, 1993), 469.

8. John H. Matsui noted that "of the thirty-eight army, corps, division, and brigade commanders in the three corps of the Army of Virginia in August 1862, no fewer than nine were publicly antislavery, including two of three corps commanders. The fifty commanders from the army through the brigade level in the contemporary Army of the Potomac's five corps included only two antislavery officers, both brigade commanders, the lowest rung of unit command above the regimental level." Matsui, "War in Earnest: The Army of Virginia and the Radicalization of the Union War Effort, 1862," *Civil War History* 58, no. 2 (June 2012): 185–86.

9. See *The Civil War Diary of Gideon Welles: Lincoln's Secretary of the Navy*, ed. William E. Gienapp and Erica L. Gienapp (Urbana: University of Illinois Press, 2014), entries for September 2 (27), but especially entry for September 7, in which Welles explains Stanton's role in bringing Pope and Halleck to Washington (32–33).

10. *Civil War Diary of Gideon Welles*, 32.

11. Williamson Murray and Wayne Wei-Siang Hsieh, *A Savage War: A Military History of the Civil War* (Princeton, NJ: Princeton University Press, 2016), write, for example, that Pope was the sole author of his own misfortunes. He was a general, Murray and Hsieh conclude, "who knows everything and so refuses all advice or intelligence that contradicts his assumptions," and they rate Pope's performance as "abysmal" (191, 204). Allan Nevins concluded that Pope "worsened the moral climate of the war," while J. G. Randall and David Donald sharply noted in their indispensable synthesis of the conflict that "virtually all military historians condemn Pope." Hennessy likewise notes Pope's "organizational deficiencies," "attitude problems," and an "obnoxious personality" and writes that Pope displayed "utter impotence" as an army commander. Nevins, *The War for the Union: War Becomes Revolution, 1861–62* (New York: Charles Scribner's Sons, 1960), 155; Randall and Donald, *The Civil War and Reconstruction* (Boston: D. C. Heath, 1961), 218n11; Hennessy, *Return to Bull Run*, 11, 16, 451.

12. Historians have conceded that Pope did succeed—to a point—in promulgating and carrying out a series of general orders that indicated a turn toward a new, harder war that placed civilians in the sites of Union occupiers. Mark Grimsley, *The Hard Hand of War: Union Military Policy toward Southern Civilians, 1861–1865* (New York: Cambridge University Press, 1995), finds that Pope issued "draconian orders" (85, 91) before being "outmaneuvered and thrashed" by Lee (92), while concluding that the primary importance of the general's brief appearance on the scene in Virginia signaled an end to the "kid glove policy" previously pursued by Union armies (85–92). See also D. H. Dilbeck, *A More Civil War: How the Union Waged a Just War* (Chapel Hill: University of North Carolina Press, 2016), which discusses Pope's early-war willingness to pursue harsh measures against guerrillas in Missouri; and Aaron Sheehan-Dean, *The Calculus of Violence: How Americans Fought the Civil War* (Cambridge, MA: Harvard University Press, 2018), 73, which discusses Pope as one of many Union officers who attempted to hold Confederate civilians responsible for suborning rebellion, in both Missouri in 1861 and Virginia in 1862. John H. Matsui, *The First Republican Army: The Army of Virginia and the Radicalization of the Civil War* (Charlottesville: University of Virginia

Press, 2016), makes the most explicit case for viewing Pope as a harbinger of total war in the war's Eastern Theater, though, for the most part, his conclusions align with Hennessy's in *Return to Bull Run*—Pope pursued Republican ideology, but lack of victories sundered his efforts to effect change in the war's conduct.

13. From almost the first moments of contact between Union armies and enslaved peoples in the Confederacy, it became clear to all observers that the war would significantly disrupt the institution of slavery. This fact should not have come as a surprise. Whether or not white Union soldiers supported the actions of enslaved Black Americans to seek their freedom, they could not escape confronting the mass movement of self-emancipation undergirded by the war. Politicians in Washington, likewise, sought solutions that would empower Union troops to take legal action against slavery in a way that would be defensible as part of the war effort—in other words, dismantling the instruments of war vital to the Confederacy, namely, a population of nearly 4 million enslaved people. See James M. McPherson, "Who Freed the Slaves?," *Proceedings of the American Philosophical Society* 139, no. 1 (March 1995): 1–10, for an overview of the scholarly debate on wartime emancipation. See also Edward L. Ayers, *The Thin Light of Freedom: The Civil War and Emancipation in the Heart of America* (New York: W. W. Norton, 2017); Joseph P. Reidy, *Illusions of Emancipation: The Pursuit of Freedom and Equality in the Twilight of Slavery* (Chapel Hill: University of North Carolina Press, 2019); and Chandra Manning, *What This Cruel War Was Over: Soldiers, Slavery, and the Civil War* (New York: Vintage, 2007).

14. Though few Americans today question the maintenance of the country's vast military bureaucracy, Americans in the eighteenth and nineteenth centuries projected a great deal of uneasiness toward the nation's military forces—because large armies were antithetical to democratic republics. As Richard H. Kohn explains, wariness of large bodies of armed men was "central to the Revolutionary tradition, deeply interwoven with the language of independence and the birth of the United States as a nation." Kohn, *Eagle and Sword: The Federalists and the Creation of the Military Establishment in America, 1783–1802* (New York: Macmillan, 1975), 6.

15. Historian T. Harry Williams judged the Radical response "a concomitant of American war-time history"; Williams mustered little affection for the Radicals in his work on the faction—referring to them frequently as "Jacobins" in his *Lincoln and the Radicals*; quotes are from Williams's unpublished PhD dissertation "The Committee on the Conduct of the War: A Study of Civil War Politics" (University of Wisconsin, 1937), 43.

16. *Congressional Globe*, 37th Cong., 2nd Sess., 83 (1861).

17. Joseph Medill to Edwin McMasters Stanton, January 21, 1862, Edwin McMasters Stanton Papers, 1818 to 1921, Correspondence, 1831–1870, folder Jan. 14–Feb. 2, 1862, Library of Congress, accessed via http://hdl.loc.gov/loc.mss/ms010150.mss41202.002.

18. Lincoln's reasoning for countermanding Frémont probably had more to do with the president's concern over alienating the border states of Missouri and Kentucky, where the federal government had to tread lightly so as not to provoke proslavery partisans to agitate for secession. See Lincoln's letter to Frémont in September 1861, which warned the general not to take any action that might "ruin our rather fair prospect for Kentucky." "Frémont Proclamation," August 30, 1861, *OR* 3:466–67; Lincoln to Fremont, September 2, 1861, in *The Collected Works of Abraham Lincoln*, ed. Roy P. Basler, 9 vols. (New Brunswick: Rutgers University Press, 1953–55), 4:506–7 (hereafter cited as *CWAL*).

19. Wade quoted in Bruce Tap, *Over Lincoln's Shoulder: The Committee on the Conduct of the War* (Lawrence: University of Kansas Press, 1998), 17.

20. As William A. Blair notes in *With Malice toward Some: Treason and Loyalty in the Civil War Era* (Chapel Hill: University of North Carolina Press, 2014), the precedents and guidance of international law provided essential direction for understanding how the Federal government could legally deal with Confederates and how they ought to define the conflict—whether as a war between two nations or as an act of domestic insurrection. Confiscation could be legal only if the United States insisted they were waging war on a foreign power. As Blair puts it, the government had to manage "running a war against a domestic traitor who acted like a belligerent foreigner" (80).

21. Letter from Abraham Lincoln to Orville H. Browning, September 22, 1861, *CWAL*, 4:532.

22. In his first message to Congress, Lincoln continued to promote colonization as the best possible outcome should emancipation become a widespread result of the war. Lincoln maintained a steady focus on the preservation of the Union as the war's paramount (and solitary) goal, saying he "thought it proper to keep the integrity of the Union prominent as the primary objective of the contest." *CWAL*, 5:49.

23. Horace White, *The Life of Lyman Trumbull* (New York: Houghton Mifflin Company, 1913), 171–72.

24. Williams, *Lincoln and the Radicals*, 60.

25. "The Second Confiscation Act," Freedmen and Southern Society Project, accessed August 9, 2024, www.freedmen.umd.edu/conact2.htm.

26. *New York Herald*, December 11, 1861.

27. William Marvel, *Radical Sacrifice: The Rise and Ruin of Fitz John Porter* (Chapel Hill: University of North Carolina Press, 2021), 96.

28. In January 1864 the Democratic membership of the committee changed to Benjamin Harding of Ohio, Charles Buckalew of Pennsylvania, and, from the House, "Unconditional Unionist" Benjamin F. Loan of Missouri. Wade and Chandler carefully designed the Joint Committee to ensure that its Democratic members would not impede their political objectives. The sole Democrat from the House, Odell, was an obscure first-term congressman who lacked a reputation that would have justified taking an outspoken role. Andrew Johnson, at the time of his appointment, was widely considered trustworthy by the Republican Party because of his strong denunciations of secession. The Democratic committee members, in other words, were less likely to frustrate Republicans than the Democrats leading Union armies.

29. *Congressional Globe*, 37th Cong., 2nd Sess., 33 (1861).

30. *Congressional Globe*, 37th Cong., 2nd Sess., 3392 (1862).

31. Scott quoted in Stephen W. Sears, *Lincoln's Lieutenants: The High Command of the Army of the Potomac* (New York: HarperCollins, 2017), 14.

32. Bruce Tap concludes that by placing obscure Democrats on important committees, the Republican majority ensured that their investigations would not be interfered with—or negated. See Tap, *Over Lincoln's Shoulder*, 32.

33. George Julian, *Speeches on Political Questions, 1850–1868* (New York: Hurd and Houghton, 1872), 202.

34. Mark E. Neely Jr., *The Union Divided: Party Conflict in the Civil War North* (Cambridge, MA: Harvard University Press, 2002), 71.

35. Gideon Welles wrote in his diary on August 17, 1862, that the Federal government had tried for too long to "adapt and reconcile the theory and instruction of West Point to the war that was being prosecuted." Welles, concurring with the judgments of the Joint Committee, observed that "our generals act on the defensive. It is not and has not been the policy of the country to be aggressive." *Civil War Diary of Gideon Welles*, 10.

36. The committee's investigation into George McClellan underscored members' impatience with generals who were not pursuing a "hard war" that targeted Confederate property—including property in slaves. Tap, *Over Lincoln's Shoulder*, 101–2. Mark Grimsley notes that some Republican generals openly courted the favor of the Joint Committee by emphasizing their hard-war bona fides. Grimsley, *Hard Hand of War*, 127.

37. Marcus Cunliffe, "Soldiers and Politicians in the American Civil War," *American Studies in Scandinavia* 2, no. 1 (March 1969): 10.

38. *The Military Memoirs of General John Pope*, ed. Peter Cozzens and Robert I. Girardi (Chapel Hill: University of North Carolina Press, 1998). See, for example, Pope's discussion of Washington in 1861 on pp. 96–98.

39. *A Virginia Yankee in the Civil War: The Diaries of David Hunter Strother*, ed. Cecil D. Eby Jr. (Chapel Hill: University of North Carolina Press, 1961), 67.

40. Jacob D. Cox, *Military Reminiscences of the Civil War*, 2 vols. (New York: Charles Scribner's Sons, 1900), 1:222.

41. Salmon P. Chase, *Inside Lincoln's Cabinet: The Civil War Diaries of Salmon P. Chase*, ed. David Donald (New York: Longmans, Green, 1954), 94–95 (July 21, 1862).

42. *New York Daily Tribune*, June 26, 1862.

43. Dilbeck, *More Civil War*, 19.

44. Senate, Joint Committee on the Conduct of the War, *Report of the Joint Committee on the Conduct of the War*, 37th Cong., 3rd Sess., Rep. Com. No. 106, 276, 277.

45. Senate, Joint Committee on the Conduct of the War, *Report of the Joint Committee on the Conduct of the War*, 279.

46. Senate, Joint Committee on the Conduct of the War, *Report of the Joint Committee on the Conduct of the War*, 282.

47. *New York Tribune*, July 23, 1862.

48. George B. McClellan to Mary Ellen McClellan, July 22, 1862, in *The Civil War Papers of George B. McClellan: Selected Correspondence, 1860–1865*, ed. Stephen W. Sears (New York: Ticknor and Fields, 1989), 368; on the same day, Mary Ellen informed her husband of a consultation between the Lincoln cabinet and "General officers & probably Pope" at which she felt "indignant" (*Civil War Papers of George B. McClellan*, 371).

49. Chase, *Inside Lincoln's Cabinet*, 97–98.

50. *Civil War Papers of George B. McClellan*, 458.

51. John G. Nicolay, *A Short Life of Abraham Lincoln: Condensed from Nicolay and Hay's "Abraham Lincoln: A History"* (New York: Century Company, 1902), 310.

52. *Boston Daily Advertiser*, June 28, 1862.

53. *Bangor Daily Whig and Courier*, July 1, 1862.

54. *The New York Tribune*, June 27, 1862.

55. *Civil War Diary of Gideon Welles*, 35.

56. Robert Gould Shaw to Dear Father, August 3, 1862, in *Blue-Eyed Child of Fortune: The Civil War Letters of Colonel Robert Gould Shaw*, ed. Russell Duncan (Athens: University of Georgia Press, 1992), 225.

57. Paul Finkelman argues that there were four preconditions for Lincoln to consider issuing an emancipation proclamation: first, a constitutional or legal framework for ending slavery; second, political support; third, the security of the border states—especially Kentucky; and fourth, a military victory that would convince both loyal Americans and foreign observers that the Union could win the war. Finkelman, "Lincoln and the Preconditions for Emancipation: The Moral Grandeur of a Bill of Lading," in *Lincoln's Proclamation: Emancipation Reconsidered*, ed. William A. Blair and Karen Fisher Younger (Chapel Hill: University of North Carolina Press, 2009), 13–44.

58. Kristopher A. Teters, *Practical Liberators: Union Officers in the Western Theater during the Civil War* (Chapel Hill: University of North Carolina Press, 2018), 20.

59. General Orders No. 5, *OR* 12(2): 50; General Orders No. 6, *OR* 12(2): 50; General Orders No. 7, *OR* 12(2): 51; General Orders No. 11, *OR* 12(2): 52; General Orders No. 13, *OR* 12(2): 52.

60. William Kindig to Henry A. Bitner, July 21, 1862, Valley of the Shadow: Two Communities in the American Civil War, University of Virginia Library, https://valley.lib.virginia.edu/papers/F0711.

61. William B. Styple, ed., *Writing and Fighting the Civil War: Soldier Correspondence to the "New York Sunday Mercury"* (Kearny, NJ: Belle Grove, 2000), 112.

62. This rhetoric aligns with the finding of Zachary Fry in *A Republic in the Ranks: Loyalty and Dissent in the Army of the Potomac* (Chapel Hill: University of North Carolina Press, 2020). Fry notes that enlisted soldiers did not enter Union armies as political advocates or with a great deal of investment in politics. Fry finds that it was not until 1864 that most Union soldiers voted in support of the Republican Party, due in large part to the lobbying of men at the ranks of captain, major, and colonel on behalf of Lincoln—not, necessarily, his party's radical wing.

63. *Wyandot Pioneer* (Upper Sandusky, OH), August 1, 1862.

64. *Star of the North* (Bloomsburg, PA), July 30, 1862.

65. *Daily Green Mountain Freeman* (Montpelier, VT), July 19, 24, 1862.

66. *Memphis Union Appeal*, July 24, 1862.

67. *Bellows Falls (VT) Times*, July 25, 1982.

68. *New York Herald*, July 20, 1862.

69. McClellan to Henry Wager Halleck, August 1, 1862, in *Civil War Papers of George B. McClellan*, 381.

70. Archie P. McDonald, ed., *Make Me a Map of the Valley* (Dallas: Southern Methodist University Press, 1973), 66.

71. *OR* 12(3): 916, 918–19.

72. *Richmond Daily Intelligencer*, July 30, 1862.

73. *Wilmington Journal*, August 7, 1862.

74. *Western Sentinel* (Winston, NC), August 29, 1862.

75. Robert K. Krick, *Stonewall Jackson at Cedar Mountain* (Chapel Hill: University of North Carolina Press, 1990), 22–23.

76. Edwin E. Marvin, *The Fifth Regiment, Connecticut Volunteers: A History Compiled from Diaries and Official Reports* (Hartford: Wiley, Waterman and Eaton, 1889), 151.

77. See Krick, *Stonewall Jackson at Cedar Mountain*, for the fullest treatment of the engagement and its aftermath.

78. George H. Gordon, *Brook Farm to Cedar Mountain: In the War of the Great Rebellion, 1861–62* (Cambridge, MA: Riverside Press, 1883), 277.

79. Chase, *Inside Lincoln's Cabinet*, 120.

80. Chase, *Inside Lincoln's Cabinet*, 121.

81. Chase, *Inside Lincoln's Cabinet*, 133.

82. See Marvel, Radical Sacrifice, for the most even-handed treatment of the Porter case.

83. J. Gregory Acken, ed., *Inside the Army of the Potomac: The Civil War Experience of Captain Francis Adams Donaldson* (Mechanicsburg, PA: Stackpole Books, 2017), 104.

84. Thomas T. Ellis, *Leaves from the Diary of an Army Surgeon: or, Incidents of Field, Camp, and Hospital Life* (New York: J. Bradburn, 1863), 201.

85. Rufus R. Dawes, *Service with the Sixth Wisconsin Volunteers* (Marietta, OH: E. R. Alderman and Sons, 1890), 73.

SHAKE YANKEEDOM TO ITS CENTRE

Robert E. Lee and the Making of Confederate Strategy in the Second Manassas Campaign

PETER C. LUEBKE

In February 1870, former Confederate staff officer William Allan met with then college president Robert E. Lee in his office to talk about the Civil War. Lee read aloud a letter from Union general Fitz John Porter, and the pair discussed the battle of Second Manassas. Porter, who had been court-martialed for his supposed failures during that encounter, had lately written Lee for information, hoping that his former foe could help him clear his name. Allan and Lee then embarked on a wider-ranging discussion. Allan's memoranda of the conversation noted that Lee mentioned, "Everything was risky in our war." According to Allan, Lee "knew oftentimes that he was playing a very bold game, but it was the only *possible* one."[1] Though talking more broadly about his strategy in the war, Lee's musings to Allan also pertained specifically to his strategy in the Second Manassas campaign.

On one hand, Lee's statements to Allan could appear as special pleading or an attempt to absolve himself from responsibility for his actions and Confederate defeat. If Lee followed the "only *possible*" course of action, then he bore no real responsibility for its outcome. He had had no choice in the matter. If, on the other hand, one takes Lee's statements sincerely (or at least the paraphrase of them written by Allan)—that, instead of being an ex post facto attempt to shirk responsibility for defeat, they represent an honest assessment of Lee's wartime thinking—then Lee's thinking on strategy during the Civil War and why he embarked on the Second Manassas campaign comes into focus. The Second Manassas campaign represented the culmination of Lee's strategic thought, which had taken shape and matured during 1861 and 1862.[2] What had led Lee to believe that the Second Manassas campaign was the best choice for him and his nation? What made him think that he had to play a "bold game" because it was "the only *possible* one"?

What emerges from Lee's wartime writings, fragmentary as they are, is a leader simultaneously clear-eyed and rational about the slim chances for Confederate success in the war. Put differently, the rational soldier in Lee knew that to stand still would ensure a loss against overwhelming Northern production and manpower, and thus "the only *possible*" action lay in unremitting aggression. And Lee was quite clear about the goal of that aggression—to shatter the morale of the Northern civilians. He held almost from the beginning of the war that no foreign aid or recognition would come and that the Confederacy would have to help itself. In those circumstances, "the only *possible*" action with any hope of success lay with bold risk-taking, hoping that energetic marching and fighting would convince the North that the war was more trouble than it was worth.

Historians have hotly debated the roots of Lee's strategic thought and that of Confederate leadership more generally.[3] For example, how much did the Confederate leader owe to his engagement with Swiss theoretician Antoine Henri Jomini? Jomini, in texts derived from the study of history, attempted to create a scientific system or set of laws to govern warfare. Many of the precepts Jomini identified—such as concentration of forces and using advantages like interior lines to gain benefit—seemed commonsensical.[4] Lee himself likely encountered the teachings of Jomini during his time at West Point as its superintendent but apparently spent little time on the theoretical aspects of war. More probably, Lee discovered the idea through his own professional military reading that one should concentrate forces to attain local superiority and use maneuver to avoid the enemy's strength and engage on more favorable terms. It is also possible that Lee grasped these essential principles during his service during the Mexican-American War.[5] Regardless of the source—either book learning from Jomini and West Point or experiential knowledge from the Mexican-American War—Lee had both theoretical and practical education that shaped his views on how to defeat the enemy.

Events much more proximate to the summer of 1862 also informed Lee's sense of strategy. Understanding Lee's strategy in Virginia during 1862 requires beginning with a period of Lee's career that most historians have neglected—his time as head of the military Department of South Carolina, Georgia, and East Florida in the winter of 1861–62.[6] Lee's conduct and writings during these months provide important insights into the Rebel commander's military strategy, which evolved as a way to find solutions to the frustrating problems he faced. First, Lee believed that seemingly near-impossible odds could be combated only by aggression when sufficient forces could be mustered.[7] Second, Lee took such great risks with his strategy in the Second Manassas campaign because they presented a better chance of success than remaining on the defensive. Third, Lee's strategy during the Second Manassas campaign prioritized attacking the morale of the Union population; Lee grasped that the defeat of a Union field army served as a means to the real goal, which was to hurt the will of the Northern population to fight.[8] Thus, Lee's experiences in 1861–62 helped chart his way forward.

The Confederate War Department's Special Orders No. 206 of November 5, 1861, created the Department of South Carolina, Georgia, and East Florida in order to facilitate defense against the encroaching Federal forces. It also placed Robert E. Lee in charge of the department. Lee arrived two days later and formally assumed command the day after.[9] Though brief in duration, Lee's sojourn in South Carolina and Georgia would help forge his aggressive tactics and strategy. In the Deep South, Lee would experience intense frustration and helplessness as the combined military and naval forces of the Union enjoyed nearly complete freedom of action. Against overwhelming numerical and technological superiority, Lee could do little. These frustrations only buttressed his instincts to be aggressive because he saw that waiting on the Union led only to defeat.

The bad news for Lee began even before he assumed his new command in the Deep South. En route, Lee learned that a Union fleet had passed Confederate batteries outside Charleston, rendering those positions untenable. Moreover, the presence of Union warships in Port Royal Sound threatened the critical cities of Charleston, South Carolina, and Savannah, Georgia.

Lee scrambled to ascertain the situation on the ground and move troops to protect both the cities and the Charleston & Savannah Railroad, a critical transportation route. Circumstances appeared less than auspicious. Lee told Confederate secretary of war Judah P. Benjamin that "the enemy, having complete possession of the water and inland navigation, commands all the islands on this coast, and threatens both Savannah and Charleston." Lee further lamented that "we have no guns that can resist their batteries, and have no resource but to prepare to meet them in field."[10] Confronted with superior Union firepower and mobility, Lee had no real rejoinder except to gather what troops he could to oppose any kind of landing.

Disillusion set in quickly for Lee; after only a week he understood that it would be impossible to defend the coast against Union incursions. Union naval superiority permitted Union forces to outmaneuver Confederate forces and land troops nearly at will along the coast. So long as Union forces moved carefully and avoided exposing themselves in the field, Lee could do little. To his daughter he described his new command as "another forlorn hope expedition," one even "worse than Western Virginia," comparing his new assignment to his previous one, which had ended in defeat.[11] Lee evidently repeated this statement to his other children, as son Robert E. Lee Jr. mentioned in correspondence with his sister that "I got a letter from Pa written from some place near Savannah; he says he is well, but that affairs are about as bad down there as Western Virginia, 'another forlorn hope' as he expresses it."[12] Lee grappled with large problems and had little means with which he could solve them.

The coast lent the Union an unparalleled opportunity to employ sea power against the Confederates. The capture of Port Royal gave the Union army and navy a base from which they could raid along the coast. Sea power enabled Federal mobility, while the heavy naval ordnance provided support for forays ashore. Lee could do little in the face of such opposition. He groused to his son Custis that the enemy "never went 400 yds from his steamers, not even to the extent of the range of his guns." Lee also observed that the Union force could "move with great facility & rapidity & land any where he can bring his steamers, & burn, pillage & destroy, & we cannot prevent him."[13] To his wife, Lee explained that "there are so many points of attack, & so little means to meet [the enemy] on water."[14] To his daughter Anne, Lee explained his strategy in South Carolina and Georgia. He opined, "Against ordinary numbers we are pretty strong, but against the hosts our enemies seem able to bring everywhere, there is no calculation. But if our men will stand to their work, we shall give them trouble & damage them yet."[15]

Faced with long stretches of coastline, much of it indefensible, Lee could do little but recommend concentration of his troops. Lee instructed his subordinate Brig. Gen. Roswell Ripley that occupying a large area of land would "expose them to be taken in detail" and suggested that "if all the force was concentrated at advantageous points, I think the defense of approaches would be more effective."[16] And herein lay the dilemma: given the geographic expanse of his department, the relative lack of men, and the overwhelming superiority of the Union navy, it proved nigh impossible to identify any "advantageous points" at which troops could be "concentrated." In a later letter to Ripley, Lee noted that "the only difficulty I see to the measure is the want of troops to insure successful resistance should the enemy land in force."[17] In another letter written even later, Lee observed, "I am in favor of abandoning all exposed points as far as possible within reach of the enemy's fleet of gunboats and of taking interior positions, where we can meet on more equal terms." In a nutshell, this sequence of letters exhibited the dilemma of Confederate strategy writ large. A cordon defense would almost certainly result in defeat in detail, while concentration at specific points against such a disadvantage would be difficult, if not impossible. Some other solution would be required to solve the problem. Lee could see none at hand, locally. But the experience helped him to understand the need to act when he could create or identify a situation that presented "more equal terms."[18]

Lee explained the difficulties of the strategic situation to South Carolina politicians. Thinking that, in some cases, the elected leaders placed the needs of their local constituents ahead of the new nation, Lee admonished the South Carolinians that "the Confederate States have now but one object in view, the successful issue of the war of independence. Everything worth possessing depends on that. Everything should yield to its accomplishment."[19] Seeking to make his points plain while clarifying that he sought cooperation with the South Carolinian leadership, Lee noted, "You must not understand that this is written in a complaining spirit. . . . Our enemy increases in strength faster than we do and is more enormous."[20] Lee understood that time favored the Union; with the North's greater population and resources, time would enable it to mobilize more and overwhelm the Confederacy. To Gov. Francis Pickens, Lee explained, "The strength of the enemy, as far as I am able to judge, exceeds the whole force that we have in the State. It can be thrown with great celerity against any point, and far outnumbers any force we can bring against it in the field."[21]

Lee also assumed that the Confederacy would have to win its independence on its own. Unlike many others, Lee held out little hope that foreign intervention would bring salvation. Upon hearing of the *Trent* Affair—a diplomatic incident where a Union vessel stopped a British ship in order to arrest Confederate officials, thereby arousing a hostile reaction from the British government—Lee advised his wife not to expect much aid from abroad. He told her, "You must not build your hopes on peace on account of the U.S. going into a war with England." He found it unlikely that the British would intervene. Instead, Lee suggested that "we must make up our minds to fight our battles & win our independence alone." He bluntly stated, "No one will help us."[22]

To Adj. Gen. Samuel Cooper, Lee gave a thorough explanation of the problems that faced him. He stated, "I am aware that we must fight against great odds, and I always trust that the spirit of our soldiers will be an overmatch to the numbers of our opponents." In the same communication, Lee again drew attention to the fact that "the forces of the enemy are accumulating, and apparently increase faster than ours. I have feared, if handled with proportionate ability with his means of speedy transportation and concentration, it would be impossible to gather troops necessarily posted over a long line in sufficient strength." Lee's lamentations continued: "Wherever his fleet can be brought no opposition to his landing can be made except within range of our fixed batteries."[23] Lee grasped the Confederate strategic dilemma in South Carolina and Georgia, where the Union enjoyed not only a numerical superiority but also heavier firepower combined with a greater ability to concentrate. Experience taught Lee that waiting for a Union advance only gave the enemy time to marshal more resources. It must have come as a great relief to Lee when Confederate president Jefferson Davis wrote from Richmond on March 2, 1862, "If circumstances will, in your judgment, warrant your leaving, I wish to see you here with the least delay."[24] Lee notified his successor, Maj. Gen. John C. Pemberton, twelve days later from Richmond of "being assigned to duty at the seat of government" and that his absence would be permanent.[25]

Despite neither fighting major battles nor winning great distinctions, Lee's time in South Carolina and Georgia imparted important strategic insight. Lee understood that the Confederate army represented a wasting asset; as he had observed time and again, giving the Union time only meant that their numbers grew even greater. The powerful presence of the Union navy also drove home the advantages in production and supply that the North enjoyed. Against these threats, Lee could only plead for more troops and recommend concentration at advantageous places where the Confederates might enjoy something approaching equality.[26] All in all, these experiences must have reinforced for Lee the importance of mobility and action.

Lee's experiences in 1861 and 1862 in South Carolina bore disproportionately on the determination of Confederate strategy in 1862 more broadly, because Robert E. Lee himself determined much of Confederate strategy during that time, especially after his return to Virginia. As the principal military advisor to Jefferson Davis, Lee had to please only Davis. The Confederate States War Department and the Confederate secretary of war possessed little influence in directing Confederate strategy, leaving matters in the hands of the president and his top military advisor. The first Confederate secretary of war, Leroy Pope Walker, proved ineffective and in September 1861 resigned under pressure after only several months in the office. Judah P. Benjamin, the attorney general, stepped into the position, but only as a temporary measure until a permanent appointee could be settled upon. Benjamin quickly waded into controversy, including a dispute that almost led to the resignation of Maj. Gen. Thomas J. "Stonewall" Jackson. One early twentieth-century historian observed, with a note of subtle acerbity, that Benjamin's replacement, Brig. Gen. George W. Randolph, "had little part in developing military plans. . . . The Secretary [Randolph], however, was present at meetings where plans were discussed." With such short tenures, the Confederate secretaries of war provided little intellectual counterweight to the plans of Davis and Lee.[27]

In Jefferson Davis, Lee faced a receptive audience for his plans and ideas. Davis's thinking on how the Confederacy might win the Civil War paralleled Lee's.[28] Davis understood that the Confederacy, in order to secure its independence, would have to win offensive victories early on, not for the purpose of enlarging Confederate territory at the expense of the Union but to convince the public in the North that continued fighting would be fruitless. The Confederate president informed his brother Joseph in the summer of 1861 that "I hope before long to be able to change from the defensive to an offensive attitude. It will be thus only that we can hope to check the progress of the war by teaching the enemy its evils and discouraging the sending out of their surplus population." Despite victory at Manassas in July 1861, the Confederates could not follow up with any other successes. Instead, the Confederate army remained in a defensive position. To Gen. Joseph E. Johnston, Davis lamented, "I have felt, and feel, that time brings many advantages to the enemy, and wish we could strike him in his present condition; but it has seemed to me involved in too much probability of failure to render the movement proper with our present means." Writing later to the other General Johnston—Albert Sidney—Davis observed that offensive action could offset the enemy's superior numbers, allowing the Confederate commander the chance to "break up his plan of campaign." Critically, Davis thought that the while "inferior in numbers," the Confederacy could overcome the Union advantage with "public confidence." The morale of the Confederate public would prevail, as victory would enlarge it while correspondingly diminishing that of the Northern public. The Confederate president grasped the strategic problem facing the Confederacy—how to defeat an enemy with superior resources—and also grasped the solution, which lay in offensive action.[29]

Much to his embarrassment, Davis could not act on any kind of aggressive impulse until the summer of 1862. Circumstances had forced Davis and the Confederacy into a defensive policy, one that evidently dissatisfied him. Davis chided Alabama lawyer William M. Brooks in the spring of 1862, "You seem to have fallen into the not uncommon mistake of supposing that I have chosen to carry on the war upon a 'purely defensive' system." The Confederate president explained that while opportunities for offensive action had been identified, "the means have been wanting." Davis acknowledged the material disadvantages facing the Confederacy, such as a lack of stockpiles, a nascent manufacturing base, and difficulties importing goods through a Federal blockade, but thought that these setbacks ultimately could be overcome. Davis, confident of success, speculated that future "military critics will not say to me, as you do, 'your experiment is a failure,' but rather wonder at the disproportion between the means and the results."[30] To Brooks, then, Davis recognized the disadvantages the Confederacy faced at the same time he argued that they could be overcome.

With the return of Lee from the Deep South to Richmond and the successes of Jackson in the Shenandoah Valley, Davis could feel the slightest sense of optimism amid setbacks across the Confederacy. Davis, as with Lee, understood that the Confederate armies would need to embark on a bold course of offensive action, bold because it would entail great risk. Davis explained his thinking to his wife in June 1862: "I will endeavor by movements which are not without great hazard to countervail the Enemys policy." Davis suspected that such movements would rob the Union of the initiative and thereby secure an advantage for the Confederacy. He predicted that "if we succeed in rendering his works useless to him and compel him to meet us on the field I have much confidence in our ability to give him a complete defeat, and then it may be possible to teach him the pains of invasion and to feed our army on his territory." In the letter, Davis gave clear indication of his strategic concept: the Union armies had to be defeated so that the North could suffer "the pains of invasion." The Union army had to be beaten so that the North's civilians would opt for peace.[31]

Davis repeated such sentiments outside of his immediate family. For instance, he returned to the theme in a letter to Alabama lawyer and politician John Forsyth. Davis noted that "my early declared purpose and continued hope was to feed upon the enemy and teach them the blessings of peace by making them feel in its most tangible form the evils of war." With this phrase, Davis implied that the main object of the Confederate armies lay in the Northern populace. The North could learn "blessings of peace" only after the Confederate army had visited upon it "the evils of war." Davis averred that this goal had been his own from the start, professing he had never "preferred defensive to offensive war, but rather pined for the day when our soil should be free from invasion." He had waited to declare this as his policy only because "with what propriety could I say 'we stand upon the defensive no more' and what value would the declaration have unless it was followed by an advance into the enemy's country[?]"[32] Davis evidently believed that announcing an offensive war would prove counterproductive unless the Confederacy could make good on that threat.

The summer of 1862, however, looked like it would provide that opportunity for the "advance into the enemy's country" and realize the Confederate president's wishes. And Lee stood ready to do just that. Lee's early campaigns during the Civil War heightened an already aggressive personality. Lee knew that waiting for favorable circumstances would mean almost certain defeat. His engagement along the coasts of South Carolina, Georgia, and Florida had convinced him that the Union army and navy as a whole could not be defeated directly. Lee, however, had identified a vulnerability in the Northern war effort: the population. If Lee could defeat Union armies, he could damage the morale of the population, which in turn might sue to end the war. Thus, as he arrived in Richmond, Lee knew the only hope for Confederate independence lay in defeating the Union host gathering on the Peninsula under Maj. Gen. George B. McClellan. To prevail would require unflinching aggression, hard marching, and even harder fighting.

When Lee returned to Virginia, he had determined to act. He knew that waiting would only allow the Union forces to grow. Amid a series of military setbacks across the Confederacy, Lee pushed for offensive action in order to protect Richmond. As military advisor to Davis, Lee did all he could to enable the success of Stonewall Jackson in the Shenandoah Valley. There, Jackson's hard marching befuddled numerous Union commanders, yielding morale benefits as well as operational successes. Following the May 31 battle of Seven Pines, when Confederate general Joseph E. Johnston fell injured while attacking the Union Army of the Potomac under McClellan, Lee received command of the major Confederate forces outside of Richmond.

As early as June 1862, Lee suggested using troops from Georgia, South Carolina, and Florida to bolster the Confederate forces in Virginia. As they served little purpose in the Deep South, Lee thought that they might be put to better use in Virginia. Lee believed, "If it was possible to reinforce Jackson strongly, it would change the character of the war." If Jackson could head north and invade Pennsylvania, that move might "call all the enemy from the South Coast & liberate those states." In all events, Lee wished to avoid the hazard of "a battle of Posts," meaning a situation with entrenched and static positions. Lee had ample experience with that sort of war from his own time along the coast and saw McClellan replicating that pattern. Lee noted to Davis that McClellan stayed close to his big guns, similar to how Federal troops along the coast had remained under the aegis of the Union gunboats.[33]

Over a series of battles from the end of June to the start of July, Lee pushed McClellan's men back from Richmond. Lee bought time and space for the Confederate capital at the expense of horrendous casualties.[34] Confederate losses left Lee's overall concept for strategy unchanged; to him the sacrifice of his soldiers had been a necessary cost. The campaigns and battles confirmed for Lee that his subordinates had to possess the ability to operate independently and aggressively against a major Union force. Stonewall Jackson and James Longstreet, Lee's chief lieutenants at the start of the Second Manassas campaign, possessed the necessary attributes, despite Longstreet's blunders at Seven Pines and Jackson's delays and missteps during the Seven Days. Overall, the battles of summer 1862 established that "Lee, Jackson, and Longstreet knew what they were about," as one Confederate chaplain commented in his journal.[35] Lee took the pause after the Seven Days' battles to purge his army of subordinates found wanting as the first step in creating a culture in his army where all—from lieutenant generals down to the lowliest of lieutenants—would instinctively attack. An exodus of officers, transferred from Lee's army to garrison duty across the South—from sleepy Southside, Virginia, to the far-flung outpost of Galveston, Texas—attested to the new concept of operations.[36]

As Lee streamlined his army and reorganized, he realized that he had to take the offensive. While McClellan lay quiescently at Harrison's Landing, other Union forces collected in Virginia. Ominously, Abraham Lincoln united the disorganized formations that Jackson had handily defeated in detail during the Valley campaign under Maj. Gen. John Pope. Moreover, it also seemed as if the Union command would recall Maj. Gen. Ambrose Burnside from coastal North Carolina. Burnside's expedition had been successful in effecting a lodgment in the Confederacy, but the troops could not push very far into the interior. Using the Union navy, Burnside and his men might soon arrive in Virginia. In such an eventuality, Lee's small army would face major threats from two, if not three, directions: a resurgent McClellan, who would advance up the Peninsula; the newly formed Army of Virginia under Pope, who could press south from central Virginia; and Burnside, who might join either of the other two generals or operate independently. The combination of seaborne mobility and overmatch in Virginia might have reminded Lee of South Carolina.

Given the threat facing the Confederacy, Lee acted. As he later told William Allan after the war, he had no choice. To remain idle allowed the Union to bring more troops and equipment into the theater. The only prospect of success lay in attack, with the end goal of hurting Northern morale. Lee's first actions in this opening phase of the campaign occurred at the start of July, when he sent Stonewall Jackson north from Richmond to the vicinity of Gordonsville, where Jackson could watch Pope and perhaps strike. As late as July 23, 1862, Lee was still undecided about what to do, uncertain of whether McClellan would remain inert. As Lee put it, he could "get no clew as to" Federal "intentions." Lee noted to Jackson, however, that should Pope stray "within striking distance," Lee might reinforce Jackson to make it possible for Jackson to engage Pope. But, in the absence of any firm information of where the Union troops might lurk, Lee had no choice but to await further developments. Stonewall Jackson forced the issue when he marched north at the start of August 1862 and collided with Maj. Gen. Nathaniel P. Banks at Cedar Mountain on August 9. A close-run affair, the battle ended as a Confederate victory and widened the possibility for further action against Pope.[37]

Lee took initial steps on August 13, when he ordered a shift of operations from around Richmond to Gordonsville. Receiving word that Burnside's men had arrived in Fredericksburg and would reinforce Pope, Lee acted to move the bulk of his army northeast, in the hopes that Pope could be defeated before the arrival of all Burnside's men. Jackson, as noted, had already collided with Banks. Now, Lee shifted Longstreet north, to concentrate at Gordonsville. Lee also ordered Brig. Gen. John Bell Hood—then commanding a division of two brigades in the vicinity of Hanover Junction—to march to join Longstreet's force. He also directed the bulk of Maj. Gen. Jeb Stuart's cavalry to concentrate in the same area, less the horsemen needed to guard the railroad. Word also went out from Lee's headquarters to the Confederate

War Department asking for additional men, suggesting that a division of troops in fortifications along the James River would no longer have to watch McClellan and might more profitably join in field operations.[38]

By mid-August 1862, the situation in Virginia had become critical for Lee, as Union forces concentrated in Virginia, threatening to overwhelm the Confederate defenders. Despite the setback at Cedar Mountain, the Union continued to gather strength. Lee knew that "the enemy is accumulating a large force in Culpeper." The odds lengthened, as deserters from the Federal army warned Lee that Burnside had reached Fredericksburg, Virginia, with upwards of 10,000 men. Lee requested Gen. Richard H. Anderson's division be sent forward to balance the strengths.[39] News worsened as Lee received intelligence that McClellan, too, would relocate to northern Virginia; intelligence also revealed that Fitz John Porter's Fifth Corps was on the move.[40]

Although unsure about the enemy's intentions, on August 14, Lee directed Longstreet to act. At the fore of Lee's mind lay the presumed intelligence that "Burnside had left Fredericksburg," which rendered it imperative for Lee to act. As Lee wrote, "It is all-important that our movement, in whatever direction it is determined, should be as quick as possible." He feared that "General Pope can be re-enforced quicker than ourselves." Having so informed Longstreet, Lee determined that he had best join Longstreet in person, not only because he wanted to consult with him but also because going forward meant the chance to meet with Jackson.[41] Confederate staff officer G. Moxley Sorrel put it succinctly in his postwar memoirs: "Lee collected then his outlying commands with great skill and started in earnest against his braggart opponent."[42]

Planning on shifting to join Longstreet in person, Lee left instructions for the Confederate forces around Richmond under Gen. Gustavus Woodson Smith to keep an eye on McClellan. Lee warned that should McClellan's troops be withdrawn, a reallocation of Confederate troops would also be necessary.[43] Even as Lee wrote to Smith to be ready for McClellan's relocation, he secured Jefferson Davis's assent to strip Anderson's division from Smith, and accordingly orders directed Anderson's men to Louisa Court House.[44] Soon, Woodson received orders to hurry his own division forward "with the least delay practicable to re-enforce General Lee at Gordonsville."[45] Lee's assistant adjutant general Robert H. Chilton observed that "the whole of our army has been ordered up to this frontier."[46] Overall, Lee planned to use maneuver to shift the Union armies away from Richmond. As he explained to Jefferson Davis after reaching Gordonsville, "It may be that this part of the country is to be the scene of operations. In that event the War will for a season at least be removed from Richmond."[47]

Lee had planned to move his army across the Rapidan River—the major geographical obstacle between his forces and the Union army—on August 18, but delays in supplying his men and moving them into position rendered that date impracticable. Lee also awaited the arrival of his cavalry, a necessity for scouting and masking his army as it operated in proximity to Pope, and thus pushed his start date back two days, to August 20. Unfortunately for Lee, Pope had gotten wind of the advance and pulled back behind the Rappahannock River, the next major barrier to movement. Thus, when Lee crossed the Rapidan on August 20, he found that his quarry had slipped the trap. On August 21, Lee decided to send Jackson to attempt to turn Pope's right flank, while Longstreet menaced the Federal right. To sow confusion, Stuart and the cavalry began to operate in Pope's rear.[48] After these movements had been accomplished, Lee provided Jefferson Davis with an explanation of benefits: "If we are able to change the theater of the war from James River to the north of the Rappahannock we shall be able to consume provisions and forage now being used in supporting the enemy." He also noted, "This will be some advantage and prevent so great a draft upon other parts of the country."[49]

Lee's operations against Pope benefited from an intelligence coup when Stuart and the cavalry captured Pope's chief quartermaster. From captured papers, Lee learned that Pope would be reinforced by McClellan's men, noting that elements of the Army of the Potomac under Fitz John Porter had already reached Falmouth, indicating a major redistribution of Union manpower. Now knowing for certain that Pope and McClellan meant to concentrate against him, Lee wrote that "the whole army, I think, should be united here as soon as possible." Lee had already ordered General Ripley up from Culpeper but also requested that troops from the Richmond defenses—now no longer needed to keep McClellan in check—be sent to operate with the Army of Northern Virginia.[50]

Once in the field, Lee's strategy shifted from drawing the enemy troops away from Richmond to the broader goal of clearing Northern Virginia of the enemy. When that had been completed, Lee intended to head farther north, thereby damaging the morale of the Union populace. Lee told Jefferson Davis that he wanted to "relieve the portion of the country" in the area of Northern Virginia. Lee's aide Charles Marshall recalled after the war that Lee's "object was to cause General Pope to retreat" and then "use the Shenandoah Valley to approach the Potomac and so cause apprehension in the Federal Government for the safety of their capital."[51] As former Confederate William Allan observed, Lee sought to draw Pope away from central Virginia and defeat him before turning north. In a history of the Army of Northern Virginia, Allan noted that "there was no aggressive course open to the Confederates that did not involve great risk, and Lee followed in the footsteps of great captains in selecting one, the very audacity of which contributed largely to its success."[52]

Lee made the critical decision to divide his army with the object of drawing Pope away, fighting a battle to defeat him if necessary, and then operate to menace the North. On August 24, the die was cast when Lee decided to send Jackson north of the Rappahannock River. Staff officer Henry Kyd Douglas noted that "in the vicinity of Jeffersonton . . . was held the council at which Jackson's movement across the Rappahannock was determined upon." There, Lee, Longstreet, Stuart, and Jackson met, sitting around "a plain table . . . in the middle of an open field" and contemplating a map.[53] Apparently, Lee and his lieutenants agreed on the plan Lee sketched out. Thus resolved, Lee sent Brig. Gen. William Nelson Pendleton by train to Richmond on the morning of August 25 to "communicate with the President about some move for us." That evening, Pendleton met with Davis and Gustavus Smith, "considering what was best to be done."[54]

On August 25 and 26, Confederate leadership determined wholeheartedly to support Lee's plans for a northern advance. Before that date, substantial forces had been held back around Richmond to cover the city in case the Federal troops advanced from the Peninsula again. On August 25, President Davis, General Smith, and General Pendleton discussed strategy until midnight but failed to achieve any resolution. The next day, after breakfast, Davis convened another conference, this time including the Confederate secretary of war. After several hours' discussion, "the decision reached was that all troops near the Junction and certain brigades near Richmond called for by General Lee should be sent him whatever risk might ensue." Davis then dispatched Pendleton to carry the message to Lee, a task Pendleton completed on August 30.[55] In one of these dispatches, Davis observed, with a hint of warning, that "confidence in you overcomes the view which would otherwise be taken of the exposed condition of Richmond, and the troops retained for the defense of the capital are surrendered to you on a renewed request."[56]

With his army across the river, Lee allowed his two forces to maneuver independently. Although incredibly risky because it exposed his force to defeat in detail, Lee thought this choice might give him an advantage. Lee's shrewd reorganization of the army following the Seven Days aided him in his purpose; two trusted lieutenants, Longstreet and Jackson, commanded the separate main wings. These aggressive leaders had been briefed on strategy

Confederate general Robert E. Lee pushed Maj. Gen. John Pope's army deep into Northern Virginia as part of Lee's new offensive strategy. Lee sought to defeat Union armies to demoralize the Northern populace and bring an end to the war. The strategy ran high risks but offered the nascent Confederate nation its best chance of success. (Library of Congress Prints and Photographs Division, reproduction number LC-DIG-ppmsca-20509)

and operations. Moreover, Lee knew he acted with the support of President Davis. Thus, Lee confronted Pope with a sharpened instrument with a singular purpose, aligned from the president down to the private. Pope, as other essays in this volume describe, found himself hampered by a meddling chief executive, unclear military leadership, quarrelsome subordinates, and troops with low morale. Lee could not have asked for a better opponent. Writing on the morning of August 30, the final day of the battle of Second Manassas, Lee informed Davis that his army had "so far advanced in safety and has succeeded in deceiving the enemy as to its object."[57] By that afternoon, Lee's army had shattered Pope's force, which retreated in disarray. Lee telegraphed Davis, "This Army achieved today on the plains of Manassas a signal victory over combined forces of Genls McCellan and Pope."[58] Pendleton, who had reached the field on August 30, wrote to his wife the day after. Identifying Lee's strategy, Pendleton crowed, "We are in a fair way to shake Yankeedom to its centre. God be praised!"[59] In a postwar letter, Lee's former aide-de-camp Charles Marshall echoed Pendleton's wartime point, writing, "I must say again that General Lee's policy was not to capture any portion of Federal territory, but to protract the war by breaking up the enemy's campaigns and so bringing about the pecuniary exhaustion of the North."[60] Lee had broken up Pope's campaign. The way north stood open for Lee, and opportunity beckoned.

Lee's—and by extension Confederate—strategy during the Second Manassas campaign appears consistent with his statement to Allan after the war. His general understanding of warfare, informed by personal experience of Union strengths and Confederate weaknesses in South Carolina, Georgia, and Florida, led him to believe that he had to use the Confederate army aggressively. He also understood that he would have to hurt the morale of the Northern population, either by threatening major cities or by defeating major field armies in operations. Lee's understanding that the Confederacy would only become weaker as the Union mobilized convinced him that a reactive stance would doom the nascent nation. Attack, although risky, held at least a chance of success. Lee's conception of Confederate strategy explains why he could never modulate his approach during the war—because he had considered and rejected alternatives.[61]

Finally, considering Lee's strategy in 1861 and 1862 reveals that even from the start of the war, Lee had understood the weight of numbers to be against him. His explanation for his defeat at Appomattox, embodied in General Orders No. 9, in which he announced the surrender of the Army of Northern Virginia, stands not only as the first shot of the Lost Cause but also as the last instance of Lee's wartime thought. In General Orders No. 9, Lee ascribed defeat solely to Union numbers, not military aptitude, stating, "The Army of Northern Virginia has been compelled to yield to overwhelming numbers and resources." Lee's entire strategy during the Second Manassas campaign, drawing from his lifelong career as a soldier and his frustrating campaigns in 1861 and 1862, had been aimed at circumventing the tyranny of "overwhelming numbers and resources."[62]

Notes

I appreciate the comments and guidance that volume editors Caroline E. Janney and Kathryn Shively offered to me on this chapter. The suggestions of the two anonymous readers strengthened my argument. Veronica Slaght, my wife, also deserves great credit for applying her keen editorial eye to this piece. The views and opinions expressed in this piece are mine alone and do not represent those of the US government.

1. William Allan, "Memoranda of Conversations with General Robert E. Lee," in *Lee the Soldier*, ed. Gary W. Gallagher (Lincoln: University of Nebraska Press, 1996), 17.

2. This chapter uses historian Joseph L. Harsh's definition of the term "strategy" given in *Confederate Tide Rising*: "the large-scale plan generals devise for the employment of the armed forces within the guidelines of the government's policy for achieving the country's war aims." Joseph L. Harsh, *Confederate Tide Rising: Robert E. Lee and the Making of Southern Strategy, 1861–1862* (Kent: Kent State University Press, 1998), 176.

3. For more on Confederate strategy, see Thomas Lawrence Connelly and Archer Jones, *The Politics of Command: Factions and Ideas in Confederate Strategy* (Baton Rouge: Louisiana State University Press, 1973); and Harsh, *Confederate Tide Rising.*

4. Historian Carol Reardon has noted that while many military officers in the United States had a passing familiarity with Jomini and his writings, little consensus existed at the time on how to apply any of those teachings to military strategy during the Civil War. Indeed, as Reardon also observed, American military strategy—in the North but also in the South—depended greatly upon the individual responsible for its formulation, rather than on a central staff or planning body that drew upon a coherent body of doctrine and professional military thought. Carol Reardon, *With a Sword in One Hand and Jomini in the Other: The Problem of Military Thought in the Civil War North* (Chapel Hill: University of North Carolina Press, 2012), 17–53.

5. As a cadet at West Point, Lee read political philosophy, histories of the Napoleonic Wars, and histories of his father, cavalry general Henry "Light-Horse Harry" Lee. He also received some secondhand exposure to Jomini. These readings gave Lee a theoretical experience in war, one that would be matched with practical campaign experience. Historian Richard B. McCaslin wrote of Lee's experiences during the Mexican-American War: "From his readings of Antoine Henri de Jomini and work on Napoleon, Lee understand that a smaller army could defeat a superior opponent through maneuver. He saw this done in Mexico." Lee's assignment to West Point as superintendent in 1852 also gave him opportunity to read and ponder military treatises on strategy. Richard B. McCaslin, *Lee in the Shadow of Washington* (Baton Rouge: Louisiana State University Press, 2001), 32–33, 49, 54–55. For more on what the US Army learned during the Mexican-American War, see Wayne Wei-Siang Hsieh, *West Pointers and the Civil War: The Old Army in War and Peace* (Chapel Hill: University of North Carolina Press, 2009), 54–75.

6. The best overviews of Lee in South Carolina and Georgia are Roger S. Durham, "Robert E. Lee's Lost Campaign," in *Confederate Generals in the Western Theater: Essays on America's Civil War*, 4 vols., ed. Lawrence Lee Hewitt and Thomas E. Schott (Knoxville: University of Tennessee Press, 2018), 4:33–53; and H. David Stone Jr., *Vital Rails: The Charleston and Savannah Railroad and the Civil War in Coastal South Carolina* (Columbia: University of South Carolina Press, 2008), 73–89. Durham observed that Lee's time in the Deep South "has generally been looked at as nothing more than a footnote," but "it was actually a significant period of time in his development and for that department. It was a turning point for Lee in several ways." Durham detailed Lee's efforts to shore up the defenses in the area but mentions little on how the experience might have affected Lee's overall thinking on the war and strategy. The turning points Durham alluded to in his introduction end up being identified as "a greater knowledge in dealing with difficult situations and people . . . a new persona, his signature white beard, and his mount, Traveller" (33, 51).

7. Many historians have attributed to Confederate apologists writing in the postwar era the view that the Confederacy lost because it was outnumbered. Indeed, former Confederates often held that their cause had been a righteous one doomed only by its smaller battalions. But these views began during the war itself. Historian Gary W. Gallagher has noted that Confederate concerns of poor odds began during the Civil War. "Introduction," in *The First Day at Gettysburg: Essays on Confederate and Union Leadership*, ed. Gary W. Gallagher (Kent: Kent State University Press, 1992), 6–7.

8. Lee's aide-de-camp Charles Marshall commented at length on Lee's strategy during the war. Marshall observed that, in general, Lee sought to "neutralize the enemy's great superiority." He also noted that Lee acted "upon the apprehensions of the enemy" because

he was "unwilling to incur the risks and losses of an aggressive war having for its object the destruction of the enemy." *An Aide-de-Camp of Lee: Being the Papers of Colonel Charles Marshall, Sometime Aide-de-Camp, Military Secretary, and Assistant Adjutant General on the Staff of Robert E. Lee, 1862–1865*, ed. Frederick Maurice (Boston: Little, Brown, 1927), 68, 73. For discussion of Marshall's veracity, see Harsh, *Confederate Tide Rising*, 185–90.

9. Special Orders No. 206, [Confederate] Adjutant and Inspector General's Office, November 5, 1861, in US War Department, *The War of the Rebellion: A Compilation of the Official Records of the Union and Confederate Armies*, 128 vols., index and atlas (Washington, DC: Government Printing Office, 1880–1901), ser. 1, 6:309 (hereafter cited as *OR*); General Orders No. 1, [Department of South Carolina, Georgia, and East Florida], November 8, 1861, in *OR* 6:312.

10. Robert E. Lee to Judah P. Benjamin, November 9, 1861, in *OR* 6:312.

11. Lee to Mildred Childe Lee, November 15, 1861, Lee Family Papers, Mss1 L51 c323, section 16, VHS. Transcribed by Colin Woodward and accessed online at https://leefamilyarchive.org.

12. Robert E. Lee Jr. to Anne Carter Lee, December 1, 1861, Lee Family Papers, Mss1 L51 c327, section 16, VHS. Transcribed by Colin Woodward and accessed online at https://leefamilyarchive.org.

13. Lee to George Washington Custis Lee, January 4, 1862, Robert E. Lee Papers, 1749–1975, David M. Rubenstein Rare Book and Manuscript Library, Duke University. Transcribed by Colin Woodward and accessed online at https://leefamilyarchive.org.

14. Lee to Mary Anna Randolph Custis Lee, January 28, 1862, Lee Family Papers, Mss1 L51 c340, section 17, VHS. Transcribed by Colin Woodward and accessed online at https://leefamilyarchive.org.

15. Lee to Anne Carter Lee, March 2, 1862, Lee Family Papers, Mss1 L51 c345, section 17, Virginia Museum of History and Culture, Richmond. Transcribed by Colin Woodward and accessed online at https://leefamilyarchive.org.

16. Lee to Roswell Ripley, December 4, 1861, in *OR* 6:335.

17. Lee to Ripley, December 7, 1861, in *OR* 6:339.

18. Lee to Ripley, February 19, 1862, in *OR* 6:394.

19. Lee to [Andrew] Magrath, December 24, 1861, in *OR* 6:350.

20. Lee to Magrath, December 24, 1861, in *OR* 6:351.

21. Lee to Francis W. Pickens, December 27, 1861, in *OR* 6:357.

22. Lee to Mary Anna Randolph Custis Lee, December 25, 1861, Lee Family Papers, Mss1 L51 c330, section 16, VHS. Transcribed by Colin Woodward and accessed online at https://leefamilyarchive.org.

23. Lee to Samuel Cooper, January 8, 1862, in *OR* 6:367.

24. Jefferson Davis to Lee, March 2, 1862, in *OR* 6:400.

25. Lee to John C. Pemberton, March 14, 1862, in *OR* 6:406.

26. Durham points out that Lee also brought some order to the department and fortified Savannah, so much so that Union forces declined to attack the port directly and instead settled into a blockade of it. Durham, "Robert E. Lee's Lost Campaign," 50–51.

27. Rembert W. Patrick, *Jefferson Davis and His Cabinet* (Baton Rouge: Louisiana State University Press, 1944), 103–30, 162–81; George C. Rable, *The Confederate Republic: A Revolution against Politics* (Chapel Hill: University of North Carolina Press, 1994), 128–31, 137–38.

28. For a differing view of Davis as far more cautious than Lee, see Steven E. Woodworth, *Davis and Lee at War* (Lawrence: University Press of Kansas, 1995), 157–61. Woodworth argued that "for Davis, the war could be won simply by not losing" and "for Lee . . . it could be lost simply by not winning." *Davis and Lee at War*, 157.

29. Jefferson Davis to Joseph E. Davis, June 18, 1861, in *The Papers of Jefferson Davis*, vol. 7, ed. Lynda Lasswell Crist and Mary Seaton Dix (Baton Rouge: Louisiana State University Press, 1992), 203; Davis to Joseph E. Johnston, September 8, 1861, in *Jefferson Davis, Constitutionalist: His Letters, Papers and Speeches*, vol. 5, ed. Dunbar Rowland (Jackson: Mississippi Department of Archives and History, 1925), 129; Davis to Albert Sidney Johnston, March 12, 1862, in *Jefferson Davis, Constitutionalist*, 5:216.

30. Davis to William M. Brooks, March 15, 1862, in *The Papers of Jefferson Davis*, vol. 8, ed. Lynda Lasswell Crist, Mary Seaton Dix, and Kenneth H. Williams (Baton Rouge: Louisiana State University Press, 1995), 100.

31. Davis to Varina Howell Davis, June 11, 1862, in *Papers of Jefferson Davis*, 8:236.

32. Davis to John Forsyth, June 12, 1862, in *Papers of Jefferson Davis*, 8:293–95.

33. Lee to Davis, June 5, 1862, in *Lee's Dispatches: Unpublished Letters of General Robert E. Lee, C.S.A. to Jefferson Davis and the War Department of the Confederate States of America, 1862–1865*, new ed., ed. Douglas Southall Freeman (New York: G. P. Putnam's Sons, 1957), 5–8.

34. Gary W. Gallagher, "A Civil War Watershed: The 1862 Richmond Campaign in Perspective," in *The Richmond Campaign of 1862: The Peninsula and the Seven Days*, ed. Gary W. Gallagher (Chapel Hill: University of North Carolina Press, 2000), 3–27; William J. Miller, "'The Siege of Richmond Was Raised': Lee's Intentions in the Seven Days Battles," in *Audacity Personified: The Generalship of Robert E. Lee*, ed. Peter S. Carmichael (Baton Rouge: Louisiana State University Press, 2004), 27–56.

35. Entry for August 18, 1862, in *The Civil War Diary of Father James Sheeran: Confederate Chaplain and Redemptorist*, ed. Patrick J. Hayes (Washington, DC: Catholic University of America Press, 2016), 23.

36. Lee's dissatisfaction with John Bankhead Magruder's performance—and general comportment—led to the reassignment of that officer following the Seven Days' battles. See Gary W. Gallagher, "The Undoing of an Early Confederate Hero: John Bankhead Magruder at the Seven Days," in *Lee and His Generals in War and Memory* (Baton Rouge: Louisiana State University Press, 1998), 118–38. See also the example of Daniel Harvey Hill, whom Lee attempted to shunt off to command the Department of North Carolina, which also bore responsibility for Southside Virginia. Hal Bridges, *Lee's Maverick General: Daniel Harvey Hill* (New York: McGraw-Hill, 1961), 86–89. Historian Robert E. L. Krick also noted the ways in which Lee attempted to improve the work of his staff officers in the wake of the Seven Days' battles; see Robert E. L. Krick, "'The Great Tycoon' Forges a Staff System," in Carmichael, *Audacity Personified*, 82–106.

37. Robert K. Krick, *Stonewall Jackson at Cedar Mountain* (Chapel Hill: University of North Carolina Press, 1990), 7–20, 355–61.

38. Lee to John B. Hood, August 13, 1862, in *OR* 12(3): 928; Special Orders No. 181, August 13, 1862, in *OR* 12(3): 928–29; Lee to George W. Randolph, August 14, 1862, in *OR* 12(3): 929.

39. Lee to Davis, August 14, 1862, in *Lee's Dispatches*, 46–47.

40. Lee to Davis, August 14, 1862, in *Lee's Dispatches*, 49.

41. Lee to James Longstreet, August 14, 1862, in *OR* 12(3): 929–30.

42. G. Moxley Sorrel, *Recollections of a Confederate Staff Officer* (New York: Neale Publishing, 1905), 95.

43. Lee to Gustavus Woodson Smith, August 14, 1862, in *OR* 12(3): 930.

44. Lee to R. H. Anderson, August 14, 1862, in *OR* 12(3): 931; Lee to Davis, August 15, 1862, in *OR* 12(3): 931; Special Orders No. 190, [Confederate] Adjutant and Inspector General's Office, August 15, 1862, in *OR* 12(3): 931.

45. Samuel Cooper to Gustavus W. Smith, August 17, 1862, in *OR* 12(3): 932.

46. R. H. Chilton to James L. Corley, August 17, 1862, in *OR* 12(3): 933.

47. Lee to Davis, August 16, 1862, in *Lee's Dispatches*, 51.

48. Lee to Davis, August 23, 1862, in *OR* 12(3): 940–41.

49. Lee to Davis, August 23, 1862, in *OR* 12(3): 941. Lee blamed a spy for alerting Pope to his movement, but Pope had received some of Lee's dispatches captured during a cavalry raid. John J. Hennessy, *Return to Bull Run: The Campaign and Battle of Second Manassas* (New York: Simon and Schuster, 1993), 48.

50. Lee to Davis, August 24, 1862, in *OR* 12(3): 942. For further discussion of this dispatch, see Harsh, *Confederate Tide Rising*, 202.

51. Marshall, *Aide-de-Camp of Lee*, 130, 130n–131n.

52. William Allan, *The Army of Northern Virginia in 1862* (Cambridge, MA: Riverside Press, 1892), 200.

53. Henry Kyd Douglas, *Philadelphia Weekly Times*, April 20, 1887, in *The New Annals of the Civil War*, ed. Peter Cozzens and Robert I. Girardi (Mechanicsburg, PA: Stackpole Books, 2004), 113. See also Henry Kyd Douglas, *I Rode with Stonewall: The War Experiences of the Youngest Member of Jackson's Staff* (Chapel Hill: University of North Carolina Press, 1940), 132. For a thorough discussion of this conference and why Henry Kyd Douglas can be trusted despite his overall tenuous relationship with the truth, see Christian B. Keller, *The Great Partnership: Robert E. Lee, Stonewall Jackson, and the Fate of the Confederacy* (New York: Pegasus Books, 2019), 49–53, 276–77n13.

54. Susan P. Lee, *Memoirs of William Nelson Pendleton, D.D.* (Philadelphia: J. B. Lippincott, 1893), 205.

55. S. Lee, *Memoirs of William Nelson Pendleton*, 205–6, 208–9. For more on Pendleton's trip to Richmond, see Joseph L. Harsh, *Taken at the Flood: Robert E. Lee and Confederate Strategy in the Maryland Campaign of 1862* (Kent: Kent State University Press, 1999), 35–36.

56. Davis to Lee, August 26, 1862, in *OR* 12(3): 945.

57. Lee to Davis, August 30, 1862, in *Lee's Dispatches*, 56.

58. Lee to Davis, August 30, 1862, in *Lee's Dispatches*, 59–60.

59. S. Lee, *Memoirs of William Nelson Pendleton*, 209.

60. Marshall, *Aide-de-Camp of Lee*, 145–46.

61. See, for instance, an essay by historian Peter S. Carmichael, wherein he argued that Lee's offensive tactics and strategy served the Confederacy well during the early years of the war, but Lee should have shifted to defensive tactics and strategy after 1864. Peter S. Carmichael, "Lee's Search for the Battle of Annihilation," in Carmichael, *Audacity Personified*, 1–26. The most trenchant of modern critiques of Lee's aggressive generalship remains Alan T. Nolan, *Lee Considered: General Robert E. Lee and Civil War History* (Chapel Hill: University of North Carolina Press, 1991), 59–111.

62. General Orders No. 9, April 10, 1865, in *The Wartime Papers of R. E. Lee*, ed. Clifford Dowdey and Louis H. Manarin (Boston: Little, Brown, 1961), 934–35. For more on Lee and the Lost Cause, see Nolan, *Lee Considered*, 112–33; and Gary W. Gallagher and Alan T. Nolan, eds., *The Myth of the Lost Cause and Civil War History* (Bloomington: Indiana University Press, 2000).

THE BATTLE FOR WHICH WE HAD SO LONG BEEN YEARNING

The 6th Wisconsin at Brawner Farm

JAMES MARTEN

James P. Sullivan, who survived several wounds while fighting with the 6th Wisconsin of the famed Iron Brigade, often wrote commemorative poems for the brigade's reunions. In 1902 he chronicled the sanguinary exploits of his regiment and brigade in the battles of Gainesville and Second Bull Run:

> In the battle of "Gainesville," that rude baptism of blood,
> Th'o greatly outnumbered at close quarters it stood.
> And fought two Divisions with very slight aid,
> The famous "Stonewall," and "Ewell's," the old "Iron Brigade."
> "'Twas fierce, close and bloody," Stonewall Jackson did say,

"And with obstinate bravery" them Yanks stood at bay.
And when finally order to fall back Gibbon said,
"We'll give three times three for the 'Iron Brigade.'"
At "Bull Run," it stood calmly, in that terrible hail,
Of shot, shell and shrapnel, and not once did quail.
When the foe was victorious, and could not be stayed,
"Gibbon will cover the rear" with the "Iron Brigade."[1]

Sullivan's piece was better history than art, but it captured the pride with which he and his comrades remembered those long-ago days in late summer 1862. Their performance on August 28 at Brawner Farm—a prequel to the Union defeat at Second Bull Run—was one of the more dramatic and successful debuts of a unit in the history of the Union army. Although the engagement was, in the end, of fairly minor strategic importance, it had far-reaching effects on the soon-to-be-called Iron Brigade and on the 6th Wisconsin, particularly in creating a spirit of confidence and steadfastness that would serve the 6th well on more famous battlefields. This is the story of how one regiment prepared for combat, but it is also the story of frustration with army politics and command decisions that kept the unit out of the war for so long. In many ways, the officers and men in this one regiment provide a microcosm of the experience of the amateur officers and men of the Army of the Potomac. Their supreme confidence helped them counter the mistakes and miscalculations of division, corps, and army commanders with anger rather than defeatism, pride rather than despair. Everything the men thought about the war they learned during those stifling hours at John Brawner's farm: their grim resignation at the cost of war, their pride in holding up against heavy odds, and their resentment at their treatment by generals and policymakers. They also learned that their officers, from Col. Lysander Cutler down through Lt. Col. Edward Bragg and Maj. Rufus Dawes and the regiment's company captains, were leaders worth following. Brawner Farm was simply the first engagement of many, but it offered a glimpse at the development of the kinds of citizen-officers described by Andrew Bledsoe. They shared their men's values and sacrifices, inspired courage with their own displays of steadiness in combat, and maintained just the right balance of firm discipline and flexibility to inspire trust.[2]

The 6th Wisconsin had assembled during the great rush to arms during the spring and summer of 1861. Mustered into Federal service at Camp Randall in Madison in mid-July, the regiment was composed of companies recruited largely from eight counties. There were lumbermen from the state's northwest frontier, a few miners from the southwest corner of the state, and companies from Milwaukee that grew out of prewar Irish and German militia units. Most of the men had migrated to Wisconsin from other states as adults or as children, and they most commonly worked as farmers or farm laborers. Their first colonel was a crusty frontier businessman in his fifties named Lysander Cutler; a core of lawyers and up-and-coming community leaders commanded most of the companies. Rufus Dawes, who would later write the most famous account of the regiment's exploits, was a young graduate of the University of Wisconsin who happened to be in the state working—reluctantly—with his sometimes-estranged father when the secession crisis broke out and the war began.

The companies drifted into Camp Randall during June and July and, once the regiment was fully formed, shipped out to Washington in August. They were eventually brigaded with the 2nd and 7th Wisconsin and 19th Indiana under the command of Brig. Gen. Rufus King, a West Pointer and former Milwaukee newspaperman. King was promoted to divisional command in the early summer of 1862 and was succeeded by a regular army officer, the artilleryman Brig. Gen. John Gibbon. It was Gibbon who hammered the 4th Brigade into shape—although the men of the 6th had considered themselves among the best regiments in the army long before Gibbon arrived. He also dressed them in their distinctive headgear (which accessorized their old-army frock coats). Gibbon would lead the men into their first battle, and when the sharp, bloody fight along the Warrenton Turnpike began, they responded with an enthusiasm forged by their year of waiting and months of hard drill and strict discipline, honed by a bitter disregard for most generals but faith in their own officers, and sharpened by their nearly arrogant confidence in themselves. They had not yet earned the moniker of the Iron Brigade, but they were often called the "Western Brigade" and, later, the "Black Hats."[3]

The men had expressed confidence in their abilities from the very beginning. Even before the 6th entered Federal service, one of its company captains and a future regimental and brigade commander, Edward Bragg, wrote a letter to his wife, Cornelia, full of the ambition, patriotism, and excitement that would sustain him through the next year. "I must not fail as an officer and it requires all my patience & attention to get along," he wrote, "but I am determined to succeed and I know that I can—the task looks almost insuperable, but shall be overcome." He assured her that "when this trouble shall cease, we shall be together again, and your husband will be a patriot soldier, as well as a lawyer." Like many of the men examined in Peter Carmichael's compelling study of Civil War soldiers, the officers of the 6th tried to convince their wives that they would survive. Although they usually expressed confidence in their own abilities and prospects, they sometimes sent mixed signals, betraying understandable concern and even fear. One of Bragg's lieutenants—Edwin Brown, who would lead Company E by August 1862—wrote with a tone of ambivalent confidence. "Ruth," he wrote, "be prepared for good news or bad news from me. War is an uncertain game & the enemy have a very foolish & unpleasant way of pointing their guns at our officers, and the Sixth Wis Regt is looked upon too highly to remain inactive, when there is work to be done."[4]

They had barely settled into their tents at Camp Kalorama near Washington in August 1861 when a seventeen-year-old private and future captain named Henry Matrau wrote that, despite the desertion of one of the men the previous night, "our regiment is in good spirits & confident that it won't be long before we have a chance at them." A few weeks later another private reported a skirmish on the far side of the Potomac River the previous night—likely while the regiment was on picket duty near the Chain Bridge a short distance northwest of Washington. The 6th had crossed over, "but we were about an hour too late to see the fun." He added, "We are confidant that we will come out of this war without being killed or even wounded but if we are mistakened we trust it is all for the love of country & liberty."[5]

Although in the fall of 1861 the men of the 6th were ready for a fight and perhaps irrationally confident, they had to satisfy their martial ardor with picket duty and a few strenuous raids into Virginia, along with the formal reviews they came to hate. Lieutenant Brown complained of the visit of the divisional commander, Brig. Gen. Irvin McDowell, with his staff and several members of the president's cabinet. "We have had to parade before them, although it is Sunday, and everyone felt tired of the past week's labor, and anxious to have a little leisure time to read and write to their friends, but no it is Review! Review! and no fight yet." Some of the men could see the ironic humor; one of Brown's boys said after a minor disaster befell Union forces, "Well Boys we might as well prepare for another Review."[6]

Brown's dissatisfaction with the leadership and the relative inactivity only increased over the next few months. "We are getting quite discontented," he complained in June 1862, "for two reasons. One is the severity of the discipline (tyranny) to which officers & men are subjected to. And the other is the hopelessness of our being permitted to do anything to put down this Rebellion." Despite his hatred of reviews and contempt for most generals, Brown took pride in his regiment: "I will say one thing however that no regiment yet to be raised in our State can be made to equal the 6th Wis., in nicety of drill, cleanliness of appearance, completeness of dress & equipment and that elastic tread & jaunty air that marks the 'Espirit du Corps.'"[7]

Scholars from Charles Royster to Andrew Lang have described the ways in which American volunteers have chafed at the necessity for drill and military discipline. They hated idleness, felt that their manhood was threatened by what they deemed arbitrary rules, believed that their patriotic fervor was being wasted, and worried that their hopes for martial distinction would fade in the miasma of camp or garrison life. They had signed up to fight for a cause or for glory, and any other duty seemed peripheral to their country's needs and their personal motivations. As citizen-soldiers, they were deeply invested in the principles for which they fought; and while that may have instilled a powerful motivation for fighting, it often ran counter to the complicated needs and objectives of an army engaged in a civil war.[8]

By late June 1862, the men of the 6th had been in the ranks for nearly a year. They had endured harsh discipline, draining picket duty, and the mind-numbing boredom of winter camp. They had marched countless miles on various expeditions, all while other units fought for glory on the Virginia Peninsula. They had freed a few dozen slaves, torn up a few miles of railroad tracks, and seen Confederates from a distance. And without firing more than a few shots in anger, they had lost 236 men since entering the service: 21 had died of disease and 1 had drowned; 16 had been transferred and 14 had resigned; 28 had allegedly deserted (although many would later be cleared). All the rest—156—had been discharged due to "disability." A correspondent with a hometown newspaper—probably Sgt. Howard Huntington of Company A—complained that, despite the lack of fighting, "the number of members in the company have greatly decreased, and their appearance has changed much within a year." Huntington believed that "had we been placed in more active service, where our movement[s] were of a character to animate a soldier, and inspire him with confidence in their propriety and the earnestness of leaders . . . the health of the whole army would have been much better."[9]

Although they were ultimately disappointed, it seemed that late in June 1862 the men would finally join the rest of the Army of the Potomac in the great battles raging near Richmond. Indeed, they were scheduled to embark for the Peninsula on more than one occasion. Yet despite a few fruitless maneuvers, during June and July they remained near their position at Fredericksburg.

That changed in August, as the 6th and the rest of the brigade searched endlessly for Maj. Gen. Stonewall Jackson's wing of the Army of Northern

Virginia. Poor leadership and indecisiveness from Maj. Gen. John Pope, commanding the Army of Virginia, down through corps commander McDowell and division commander King, forced their men into a series of hot, dusty, fruitless journeys. During these three weeks the Wisconsin men began to get a better idea of what it meant to be on the sharp end of war.[10]

The run-up to Second Bull Run began for men of the 6th Wisconsin and their comrades when they left their camp near Fredericksburg on August 8, the day before Jackson's men defeated a force under Maj. Gen. Nathaniel Banks at Cedar Mountain. Following a night crossing of the Rappahannock, they reached the Cedar Mountain battlefield after a forced march of forty-five miles. Rufus Dawes, who had been promoted from captain of Company K to major earlier in the summer, reported that "we were obliged to bury many of the rebel dead whose corpses, left half buried upon the field, were intolerable. This was our first contact with one of the real horrors of war." A Sauk County veteran recalled his disgust at seeing the tops of the shallow graves "moving like gentle waves with living corruption." They stayed on the broiling, stinking battlefield for a week, while Pope, believing Jackson was in retreat, pondered his next move. For some, this was a typical decision by an out-of-touch commander. One private complained many years later that among Pope's many mistakes was "compelling his army to remain encamped more than a week during the hottest part of the year, on the battle field, subject to the overpowering stench of decaying horses and half buried bodies, when fifteen minutes' march would have placed them in an adjoining grove of timber where they would have shelter from the sun and have plenty of good water."[11]

It soon became apparent that Jackson was not withdrawing and that Pope did not know where he was. Moreover, Confederate units from Richmond were flowing northward. Pope ordered his men to fall back toward Manassas Junction. The 6th and the rest of the brigade crossed back over the Rappahannock on August 20. During the next two days the realities of war continued to catch up with them. On the afternoon of the twentieth they saw Confederate cavalry across the Rappahannock River near the Orange & Alexandria Railroad bridge. The next day, a battery opened fire on them, "the first artillery we had ever heard in an actual battle," one veteran later remembered. As the regiment maneuvered in support of the Yankee battery that came up to challenge the enemy guns, the Confederates "turned their fire full upon the 6th Wisconsin. This was our initiation. The shells whizzed and burst over us and around us. The men marched steadily, keeping their places, and holding their heads high. Yet they soon learned that a discreet and respectful obeisance to a cannon ball is no indication of cowardice." Part of the regiment was thrown out as skirmishers. This was a new experience, and Company E and part of Company B—led by now-captain Edwin Brown—became the first members of the regiment to fire on an enemy, killing and wounding a few Confederate troopers and capturing an officer and two men. Thus, wrote Dawes, was "won the first glory for the 6th Wisconsin on the field of actual battle." A day or two later a few men from the 6th assigned to the brigade Headquarters Guard helped repulse a Confederate raid on a wagon train.[12]

The 6th became accustomed to occasional shelling over the next few days, but many men were no doubt more interested in the distant dust clouds indicating that the Rebels were also on the move. The Yankees were back on the road on the twenty-third, although still under frequent, if ineffective, artillery fire. As part of Pope's efforts to concentrate his forces—made more urgent by Jackson's raid on his headquarters train and his burning of mountains of Union supplies at Manassas Junction—on August 26 Pope ordered McDowell's corps to Manassas, with each division making its own way. King's division, made up of four brigades commanded by Gibbon and Brig. Gens. Abner Doubleday, John P. Hatch, and Marsena R. Patrick, were assigned the Warrenton Turnpike (now US Highway 29). August 28 was a start-and-stop kind of day, with hints of war all around them—artillery firing in the distance (or sometimes at them); sightings and alleged sightings of Confederate cavalry and even infantry; and Union cavalrymen and skirmishers all over the countryside. Confederate and Union foragers stumbled across one another in the same farmhouse; three dead bodies lay under bloodstained blankets in plain sight as the men marched by; an officer in the 6th Wisconsin remarked on seeing a group of Confederate prisoners trudging past. Yet virtually no one thought the day would end in bloodshed. "Up to this time," wrote one man years later, "we had been aching for a fight and were fearful we would never have the chance to meet the enemy in battle."[13]

Early in the evening they marched tiredly past a hardscrabble farm rented by one John Brawner. Gibbon's brigade stretched from the village of Groveton to a point a few miles east of Gainesville. Part of Hatch's brigade was deployed to deal with a pesky Confederate battery, Doubleday's brigade was a few hundred yards behind Gibbon, and Patrick's was another few hundred yards behind him, at the intersection of Pageland Lane and the Warrenton Turnpike. In the battle to come, although the other brigades were hardly beyond supporting distance, only two regiments from the other three brigades would fight at Brawner Farm: Hatch would be unable to get reformed in time to help (although he tried); Doubleday's regiments took cover in woods along the turnpike and proved difficult to redeploy; and, according to Gibbon, Patrick's brigade—part of which had panicked when the unit first came under fire—"remained immovable and did not fire a shot."[14]

The turnpike paralleled an unfinished railroad bed, concealed by a tree line running along a low ridge about half a mile north of the road; the ground rose gradually to an elevation of about 100 feet above the turnpike, interrupted by a slight depression about halfway up. Much of this was open ground, although there was an old orchard near the farm and a small woods—less than a quarter-mile wide—starting just east of the farm and extending down to the turnpike. About an hour earlier, skirmishers from Hatch's brigade had reconnoitered the area around the farm and a battery had lobbed shells toward the woods, but aside from a few mounted Confederates, who quickly retired, no Rebels were in view.

In fact, Stonewall Jackson's entire wing was concealed behind the embankment or not far to the rear, and Jackson now had a chance to begin to destroy a significant piece of Pope's army. As the Confederates prepared to attack, Gibbon's isolated brigade of less than 3,000 men faced a first line of more than 5,000 Confederates, with close support from another 6,300 and less immediate support from another six brigades. The Confederate line also included guns from several different batteries, with more on the way. Gibbon would later write that he had not received any intelligence about Confederates in the area and was unaware that his flanks were not being protected. "It will thus be seen that we were completely surprised . . . no precautions having apparently been taken to protect that flank."[15]

No one in the regiment or brigade had any notion that their year of training and frustration was about to take a very bloody turn. The regiment marched, recalled one veteran, "with arms at will, with no thought of battle." There was no singing, drumming, or bugles, although one soldier recalled the men "were . . . chatting, joking and laughing in their usual manner." The sounds of tramping feet and quiet conversation, the clanking and thudding of arms and other equipment, and the occasional horse trotting up and down the line must have obscured the sounds of thousands of Confederates stepping out of the tree line and deploying in the open fields around and north of the farm. Foliage and topography obscured their movements.[16]

As the regiment trudged along, Gus Kline of the 6th—who would receive a battlefield promotion a few hours later—remarked, "See here! We have been in the service over a year and except a few skirmishes, we have never been in a fight. I tell you this d——n war will be over and we will never get into a battle!" At that moment—or so remembered at least one comrade—the first shot from a Confederate battery screamed over their heads. A private recalled that "every head was down in an instant, till the missile struck the ground, when the heads were all up again and laughing at each other for dodgeing."[17]

While the men of the 6th scrambled for cover below the three-foot-high embankment running along the turnpike, at the other end of the brigade's line of march another battery opened up. Gibbon believed both were unsupported artillery and ordered Battery B of the 6th US Artillery—his old unit, which was attached to the brigade—to handle the first threat and, riding back to the 2nd Wisconsin, ordered it to take the second battery. The men of the 2nd moved forward—their right flank rested on the west edge of the woods—and advanced on the Confederate guns, only to be surprised by Confederate skirmishers firing on their right flank. They wheeled and drove back the thin line of rebels, but more Confederates appeared on their left, near the farm buildings. Gibbon pushed the 19th Indiana forward to meet that threat.

Far to the right, the men of the 6th could only hear, not see, the beginning of the onslaught, but they could no doubt detect with some alarm and much anticipation the escalating quantity of fire, as in a matter of a few minutes more men were poured into both firing lines. From his vantage point near the turnpike and on the left wing of the 6th, Rufus Dawes could see the Confederate line open up on the 2nd as it deployed. "No sooner had the 2nd showed itself in the open field," he wrote, "than there burst from the woods skirting the opposite side of the field a perfect flame of musketry, while from batteries planted for a mile along the woods, round shot, shell, shrapnel, grape flew over our heads as we lay under the friendly bank. The surprise was complete."[18]

By now Gibbon had begun to understand that he was outnumbered and outflanked. He issued a flurry of instructions, hurrying the 7th Wisconsin up to the right of the 2nd; ordering the 6th Wisconsin to move forward along the right, or eastern, edge of the woods; and sending for help from his divisional commander, King, and from the other brigade commanders. Only two of Doubleday's regiments would eventually join the fighting and King would never respond. Gibbon and his men were virtually on their own.

Back on the turnpike, a staff officer galloped up to Colonel Cutler and shouted, "Go over Colonel and help the 2nd. They are being cut to pieces." The fight they had been spoiling for—if ever a group of men personified that old cliché, it was the 6th Wisconsin in the gathering dusk on that late August day—was, according to officers on both sides, one of the hardest fought

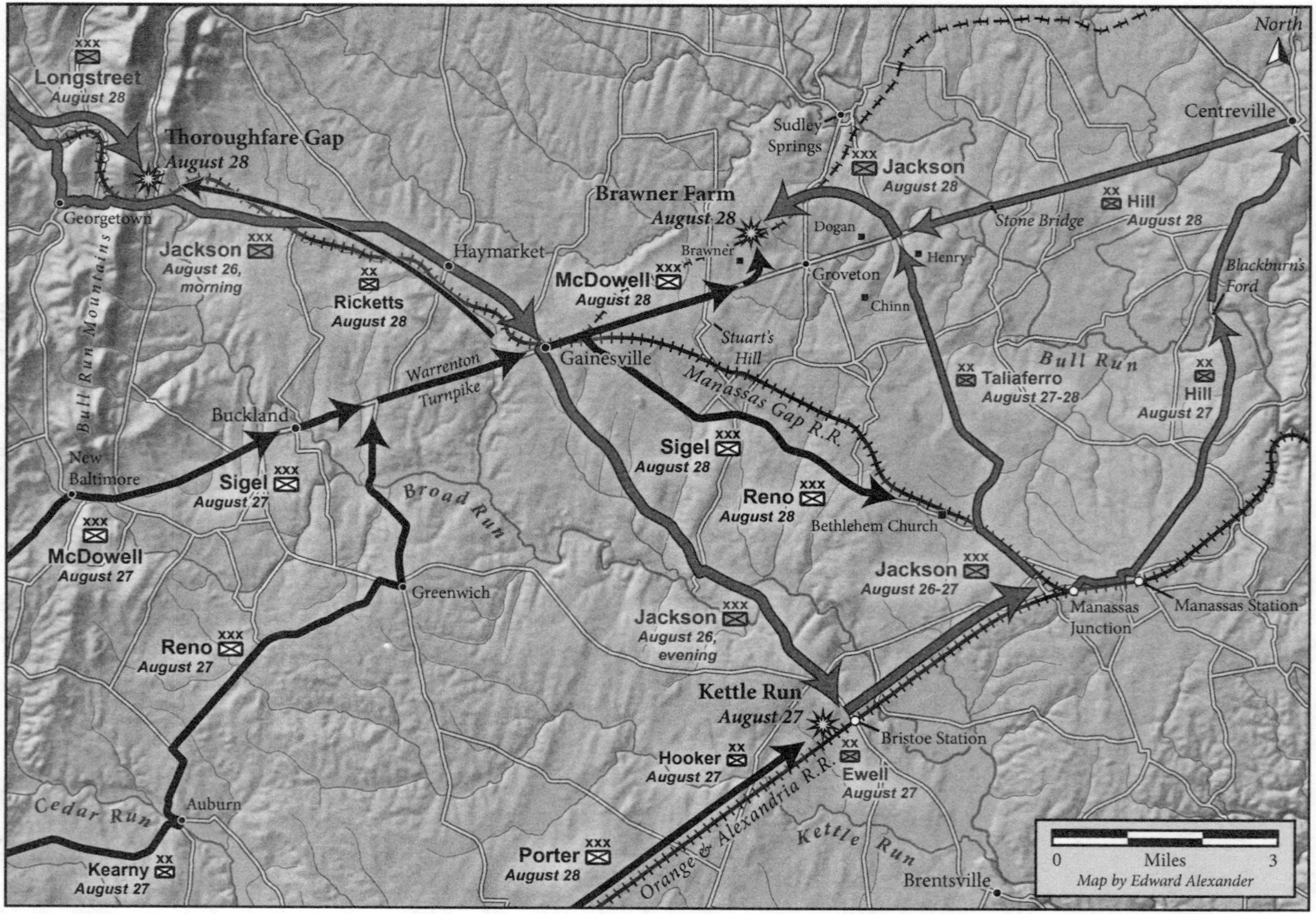

Second Manassas campaign, August 26–28, 1862

ninety minutes of the war. That statement should be taken with a grain of salt; soldiers often wrote their families that they had just been part of the hardest fighting of the war. But it was a difficult and bloody affair, and the men of the 6th went into it with gusto, leaving the relative safety of the embankment, tearing down the turnpike fence, and forming into a line of battle. "'Forward, Guide centre' was the command," Dawes recalled, "and every man scrambled up that bank and over the fence, in the face of shell shrapnel and Canister with just the same feeling of eagerness that one would hurry to save his dearest friend from great peril." Glancing again to his left, Dawes could see, to his horror, the 2nd Wisconsin "gallantly struggling and staggering under the fire of not less than six regiments of the enemy."[19]

The men in the ranks quickly responded to their orders, perhaps with the aplomb indicated by their postwar writings, but probably also with trepidation and doubt. One private admitted, "We had never been engaged at close quarters before, and the experience was new to all of us. I don't know how the others felt, but I am free to confess that I felt a queer choking sensation about the throat"—until the man behind him stepped on his heel, which started them "jawing and fussing" and broke the tension. The regiment held fire, made a half wheel to the left—"as accurately as if on the drill ground," according to Dawes—and moved quickly forward. Dawes described the "bloody red sun, sinking behind the hills," and most of the battle was fought in thickening gloaming and then darkness.[20]

A man from Company A remembered that "we heard a rip-rip, but did not fully realize" Confederates were shooting at them "until the boys began to fall." Another recalled that "it was now getting pretty dark and we were some time in getting into line in consequence of having several fences to cross. While we were arranging ourselves . . . we could see their line which looked like a black mass or ridge of ground thrown up and not more than fifty yards distant." Apparently thinking that the 6th was actually a Confederate regiment attacking the Federals' right flank, the Confederates hesitated until the 6th opened fire. Even then, because they were on slightly higher ground than the Wisconsin boys, the rebels tended to fire over their heads. This would keep the 6th's casualties down compared with the other Union regiments.[21]

By this time Jackson had committed another brigade; these units brought the total number of men engaged to 6,400 Confederate and 2,900 Union soldiers. Although Gibbon was flanked on both ends, the fight was largely stationary. Aside from a few temporary—and bloody—advances by individual units, the two lines stood fast, blasting away at each other for at least

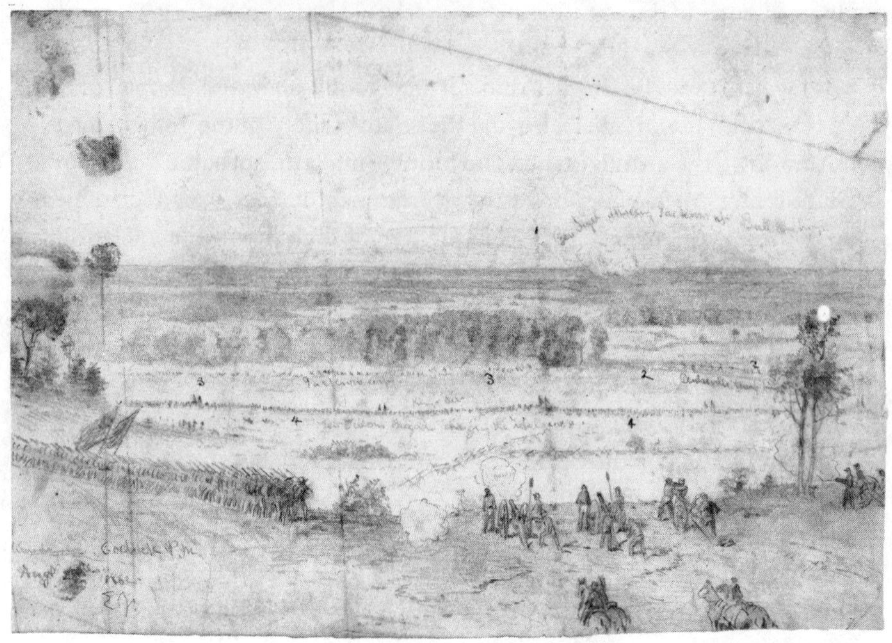

The Battle of Gainesville, Va., Aug. 28, 1862. Edwin Forbes's sketch featured the 6th Wisconsin marching into action on the far right of the Union line at Brawner Farm, with Battery B in the foreground. (Library of Congress Prints and Photographs Division, reproduction number LC-DIG-ppmsca-20510)

ninety minutes with no more than seventy-five yards separating them at any given place.

There was a brief lull in the firing as the 6th formed on the east edge of the woods. But soon, "the war that for a space did fail," wrote Dawes with a literary flourish from Sir Walter Scott's *Marmion*, "now trebly thundering swelled the gale." "The Rebels had rallied and there burst from that dark wood volley after volley. . . . Our line on the left was slowly being forced back. The Rebels were pushing up with their peculiar Whoop Whoop Whoop, a continuous shout." The young officer "galloped down the line crying Cheer! Boys!" Hoping to trick the Confederates into thinking help had arrived, he called for his men to "cheer as bad as you can 'hollar.' Call out 'Bully for Sigel' 'Three and a tiger for the reinforcements.'" Of course, Maj. Gen. Franz Sigel's corps was nowhere near the battlefield.[22]

About that time, Dawes rode up to his commander, Cutler, just as the old colonel, sitting calmly astride his house, was wounded; Dawes heard the sickening thud of the bullet striking his thigh. Cutler flinched, but calmly told Dawes to order Colonel Bragg to take over, and Bragg saw the regiment through the rest of the battle. In the gathering dusk, flashes from exploding artillery shells and rapid rifle fire cast terrifying shadows in the smoke that survivors remembered the rest of their lives. "During a few awful moments," wrote Dawes, "I could see . . . the whole of both lines," including the officers of the 2nd and 7th Wisconsin "working among and cheering up their men" at the other end of the Union line. He was struck by the image of a Confederate officer being shot off his horse. "We could see the enemy distinctly, as they could see us," a Sauk County soldier recalled.[23]

Doubleday finally got two of his regiments, the 56th Pennsylvania and the 76th New York, into the gap between the 6th and the rest of the brigade, steadying the line. The firing went on for a time, until the Union regiments on the left did, in fact, begin to fall back slowly. Darkness finally forced the Confederates to stop throwing reinforcements into the fight; otherwise, they would have eventually overwhelmed the outnumbered Federals. The sluggish effort by their senior officers—and high casualty rate among regimental and company commanders—had inhibited the Confederate effort throughout the fight. But the stern resistance of Gibbon's brigade and the darkness caused the fighting to peter out after one last failed rush on the 6th. Gibbon pulled his men back carefully, although he kept skirmishers on the field and was able to collect most of his wounded. Bragg ordered the 6th to conduct a firing retreat, loading and firing as they walked back down the hill. When they reached the turnpike, he called for "three cheers. No response of any kind was given by the enemy."[24]

The woods seemed to be filled with injured men, who had taken shelter there during the fighting. "They were now scattered about under its dark shadows," wrote Dawes, "suffering and groaning and some were dying. In the pitchy darkness we stumbled upon them. This was the battle for which we had so long been yearning." A young private reported that the men "had not felt any horror" during the actual fighting, but now that "everything had become still," the groans of the wounded "were the most pitiful sounds I ever heard. But we were weary and exhausted and soon fell asleep." The wounded who could walk or be moved were gathered up, and at midnight, tin cups and other equipment muffled, the brigade moved out for Manassas. Gibbon remembered it as "a sad, tedious march." George Fairfield wrote that, "ere sun was very high, we were 10 miles distant. I never saw men more in need of sleep. When we would halt for a few minutes one half would go to sleep, each man sitting or laying down upon the spot where he halted."[25]

All told, the brigade had lost about a third of its men: 133 killed, 539 wounded, and 79 missing. The 6th came off with the lightest casualties, a total of 72 out of the 504 who had gone into the battle. With their comrades, they had killed or wounded more than 30 percent of the Confederates engaged. The brief, bloody fight at Brawner Farm had pitted more than two brigades of Stonewall Jackson's veteran troops against a relatively untested Union brigade (only the 2nd Wisconsin had been in battle before, at First Bull Run). Yet the Yankees proved to be the best-led: the officers got their men where they needed to be and got the best out of them. On the Confederate side, no one did particularly well. Jackson was not clear in his instructions, and a number of his officers hesitated, delayed, or otherwise failed to bring their greater numbers to bear. Of course, many of the field officers and generals were wounded or killed, including Maj. Gen. Richard S. Ewell, commanding directly opposite the 6th Wisconsin, who lost a leg.[26]

Faced with the evidence that the Federal troops available late in the evening of August 28—King's division, including its two hard-used brigades—could not match Jackson's entrenched wing, and without orders from either corps or army commanders, the division marched east toward Manassas, away from Jackson and toward Pope, who had watched the muzzle flashes of the battle from a hill near Blackburn's Ford, a few miles to the east. Gibbon would regret the retreat later—it was more or less his idea and was made in the absence of a better idea—because it contributed to Gen. Robert E. Lee's ability to consolidate his army over the next two days.[27]

Jackson's troops still occupied the railroad embankment, but Pope determined that the Confederates were actually in the process of retreating to the west. Of course, quite the opposite was true; Jackson was still dug in, and Maj. Gen. James Longstreet and the rest of Lee's army was coming up to support Jackson. Nevertheless, Pope launched furious attacks against Jackson's position on the morning, in the late afternoon, and again in the evening of August 29, unaware that Longstreet had arrived on the field and south of the Warrenton Turnpike and wrongly believing that Maj. Gen. Fitz John Porter's Fifth Corps would soon fall on Jackson's right flank. The day's fighting was inconclusive but gave Pope, who clung to his belief that the Confederates were retreating, enough confidence to stay and fight.

Gibbon's battered brigade stayed out of the fighting on the twenty-ninth, but late in the afternoon of the thirtieth the men went into action, providing support for the other two brigades in their division as part of the attack Porter finally mounted against Jackson. Working through a thick wood along the Warrenton Turnpike, a little over a mile from the previous day's battlefield, the 6th Wisconsin and their comrades were out of sight of the forward battle lines. Confederate rifle and artillery fire decimated the New York regiments making up the first two brigades, eventually forcing them back in disorder. They eventually ran into Gibbon's line; the general angrily drew his revolver and ordered his men to shoot the stragglers if they refused to stop. Bragg directed the 6th to "kneel down! Captains, keep your men down! Let nobody tramp on them!" "It was a new experience," Dawes recalled, "but we were not swept away. Our men were down with the bayonets set, when the fugitives began to swarm upon them. All the officers were struggling to stop stragglers and force them to join our ranks. Many were held with us, but no Union troops were left in front of us."[28]

Gibbon's brigade provided cover when the Union lines devolved into an all-out retreat later that day. After the rest of the army had passed around or through their lines, Gibbon had his men build campfires to fool the Confederates into thinking they were still in position before beginning their own quiet departure. They made camp roughly four miles to the rear after working their way through the detritus of a defeated army. For the second time in three days, a nighttime withdrawal had followed a hard day of fighting.

The 6th Wisconsin and the other members of Gibbon's brigade had played a relatively minor role at Second Bull Run, suffering a total of only fifteen dead and eighty-seven wounded. Yet they could take pride in their steady performance in the face of devastating fire and had survived despite poor leadership and decision-making at the top. Their own commanders had proved to be brave, calm, and inspiring. Indeed, all three of the men who would lead the regiment through most of its great battles—Cutler, Bragg, and Dawes—had displayed extraordinary leadership at Brawner Farm and Second Bull Run, and Gibbon's decisiveness and obvious pride in the performance of his brigade endeared him to his men, who had chafed a bit under his strict discipline and old-fashioned ideas about uniforms.

The army and corps commanders, however, did not fare well in the eyes of the officers and men of the 6th. Dawes complained years later that "the best blood of Wisconsin and Indiana was poured out like water, and it was spilled for naught . . . against a dark background of blunders, imbecilities, jealousies and disasters." In a hurriedly written letter to his wife, Captain Brown assumed that "you are doubtless informed of the defeats of our Army which explains our being here. Three times has my life been in jeopardy. . . . You can say to your friends that your husband was no coward, when so many showed 'the white feather.'" Many of the other brigades had "behaved basely. The only troops, that . . . maintained for themselves a good name" were the westerners. He saw more experienced and more famous regiments break and run "almost at the first fire, loosing more retreating than fighting." As a result, "the Army is discouraged, having no confidence in any one." He asked her to show his letter to the rest of the family and to kiss their children "for their war worn father. Good Bye wife." He would be dead in a little over two weeks, shot through the mouth in the cornfield at Antietam.[29]

Brawner Farm—which men of the 6th would call Gainesville for the rest of their lives and would forever distinguish from the battle at Second Bull Run—was the first of four discrete actions the 6th fought between August 28 and September 17. Some of the Wisconsinites reflected at the time or years later on how their first battles had changed them. Dawes admitted that "our one night's experience at Brawner Farm had eradicated our yearning for a fight. In our future history we w[ould] always be found ready but never again anxious." The men had suddenly become veterans; no doubt some wondered how they could have been so naive as to have sought battle. One of the oldest men in the regiment, Lucius Murray of Company E, wrote to his daughter soon after Second Bull Run. He expressed sympathy for the recent loss of her eleven-month-old son, but, writing just over a week after his first battle, he could already say that "death in all forms here have become so familiar to us that we hardly look on it with dread."[30]

Despite his ambition to make a name for himself, Colonel Bragg was already looking forward to war's end, yearning to be a veteran surrounded by his proud family. "Kiss the children many times for me, and when I come home again around the fire will talk the battles over again when it is not quite so noisy & uncomfortable as it was on the 28th of August."[31]

Bragg would remain with the regiment and then the brigade for the rest of the war, while Dawes would go home to Ohio and get married when his enlistment expired in 1864; he would never be wounded despite fighting in dozens of large and small battles. But less than ten months after Second Bull Run, South Mountain, and Antietam, the 6th Wisconsin would be whittled down to about 300 officers and men. They would lose half of those men in their reckless but necessary charge led by Dawes on an unfinished railroad cut west of Gettysburg on the battle's first day, and the Iron Brigade would eventually be shattered beyond recognition and broken up.

For civilians back in Wisconsin, the battles of Gainesville and Second Bull Run, especially, and even South Mountain and Antietam just over a fortnight later, tended to blur together. Published casualty lists sometimes lumped together all of the killed and wounded. This is not surprising, as distance and technological limitations made timely and accurate reporting nearly impossible. The first notice of the Virginia fighting in the *Baraboo Republic*—the leading newspaper in the hometown of many members of

Company A—appeared a few days after Brawner Farm, although it did not mention the battle itself. Headlined "Gallant Conduct of Some Invalid Wisconsin Soldiers," the front-page article described the successful effort by a ragtag group of guards and men on the sick list to defend a wagon train from Confederate raiders. The editors seemed to know more, however; an inside page issued a call for ladies to come to the post office "at any hour during the week" to prepare bandages, lint, and other medical supplies to send to the army. A week later, the *Republic* had a better grip on what had happened and amplified its call for assistance. "Our brave boys of Co. A, in the 6th Regiment, were probably in the recent battles near Washington, and none who knew their mettle will doubt that the[y] would brave the hottest fire of the enemy. If a single life of that company could be saved by our utmost exertion, who would hesitate to make it?"[32]

The *Appleton Crescent*, the home newspaper of many men in Company E, made a brief, proud, and wildly inaccurate reference on September 6 to the battle: "Our Appleton boys in the 6th Wis. have seen and smelled powder, having been in some of those severe battles fought last week in Virginia. From what we can learn at the present writing none were hurt. Although our Wisconsin [regiments] . . . suffered severely yet they fought well. All honor to our brave Badgers." Not quite two weeks later, on the same day that the 6th suffered grievously when they crashed through the Cornfield at Antietam, Baraboo residents could finally read an eyewitness account of those first battles from Company A's Capt. D. K. Noyes. In two full columns, Noyes provided an update of the regiment's recent month of movement and "hardship." His account of Brawner Farm was accurate and dramatic. After the first three regiments went in,

> the 6th regiment soon formed on the right, just at dark, and proceeded to fire rebels a dose of pills in quick time. . . . Ewell's Division was opposed to us on that memorable evening, and the prisoners we took said that was the first time that Division ever turned their backs on their foe. . . . Col. Cutler of our regiment was wounded and had his horse shot under him. He went in as cool as an old veteran. When he left the field the command devolved on Col. Bragg, and no one who knows the little Col. doubts his fighting qualities—the boys like him. Major Daws was as cool as on dress parade. Co. "A." did nobly, all of them, not an exception in the ranks. . . . The boys all did their duty. . . . No Brigade stands better than Gibbons'; he is a perfect little Napoleon, and is loved by the whole brigade.

Unfortunately, the dead had to be left on the field: "It was terrible. The cries and groans of the dying and wounded, oh! The suffering." In the first of many casualty lists that would make their uncertain way back to Wisconsin, Noyes tried to give a truthful accounting of the company's wounded:

> John Starks, in leg, pretty bad; Philip Hoefer, in neck, bad; Peter Stackhouse, in leg, not bad; Harvey Clay, in arm, arm amputated at shoulder. I fear he may not survive as he was left at Manassas, as he could not be moved, and is cared for by the enemy, I presume. Dayton Hedges was there the last heard of, and he may be able to take care of Clay. Clay was a brave soldier.—Wm. L. Lively, wounded in lg, not bad; Phillip Nippert, wounded in hips, bad, and missing, probably a prisoner; Wm. Klyne, wounded in leg, slightly.

Newspapers would be filled with similar letters as soldiers tried to keep the home folks informed, and editors did their best to do the same. After a brief description of Second Bull Run, Noyes concluded that although some might think the army "jaded, worn out, *whipped*... we do not see it.... We will be all right when we are rested." He had to admit, however, that although the Confederates "are ragged and barefoot... they fight with a desperation worthy of a better cause. They fight as well as if they had on their new clothes."[33]

Even as the folks back home slowly learned more about the terrible fighting and were increasingly urged to support the troops materially and spiritually, a foreshadowing of the later debates over military service and conscription began to creep into Wisconsin newspapers. Less than two weeks after Brawner Farm, the *Manitowoc Herald* on September 11 only half-jokingly headlined the "Alarming Increase of Feeble Men," as recruiting ramped up again after a pause during the summer and Wisconsin prepared to conduct its first statewide draft. Apparently, the *Herald* sarcastically declared, men had been concealing serious conditions for years. "Your timid man has suddenly found out that his liver is effected. Our ranting friend has the rheumatism. Brain fever and spinal affection are alarmingly on the increase, kidneys are found to be weak, lungs are covered with tubercles, and the general anatomy suffers in common with everything else from the war." The *Baraboo Republic* also reported a certain reluctance among men to join their fellow Wisconsinites in the army: "Persons without front teeth have been held exempt from the draft on account of their not being able 'to bite the cartridge.'" In consequence of this a good many fellows, it is said, *have had their front teeth pulled*."[34]

Perhaps the news filtering back from the 6th and other regiments recruited from the area discouraged enlistments. In any event, the "momentous question" of "To Enlist or be Drafted" had already become "the almost exclusive topic of conversation" among the young men of Wisconsin before the bloody news from Virginia had arrived. "Not from craven fear of going into service and endangering your long stay on this mundane sphere, but from the higher motives of duty and your reputation as a Union loving citizen. . . . On the one hand, if you volunteer, you will receive ample bounty to leave your families well provided for, besides 160 acres of land [a common misperception at the time], your pay will be two dollars more per month, and you can choose your own company or reg't. . . . Drafted men will receive but $11 per month and no bounty." A month later, the *Crescent* declared with contempt that "we should like to be able to publish a list of all the applicants for exemption from the Draft. . . . They came with a perfect rush. Many of them without a scratch or blemish. Shame on their manhood."[35]

The fighting at Brawner Farm barely registered for most civilians, overshadowed by home front concerns and bigger battles, and even the reports of army, corps, and divisional commanders barely mentioned it. Yet it remained important to 6th Wisconsin survivors. Indeed, more than a year after the battle, Gibbon felt compelled to submit a second report correcting mistakes in Pope's published report. Rather than "being 'supported handsomely by Doubleday's brigade,'" he fumed, "but two regiments of that brigade came to our assistance, and then only when the brigade commander had been repeatedly urged to send them by my staff officers, and the late Major-General Reynolds, who came upon the ground during the fight." He also corrected the notion that his brigade was in the lead, which was how Pope explained their heavy losses: "The reason why it lost so heavily was that it was put into action and the other brigades were not." Twenty years later, at the Iron Brigade reunion of 1884, Rufus Dawes scratched the old scab when he said that "tributes to the [brigade's] valor and bravery are more pointed in the reports of Stonewall Jackson than in Genl Pope's, where the battle of Brawner Farm was characterized as a 'skirmish.'"[36]

Jerome Watrous, who had served with the 6th and later on the 4th Brigade staff and after the war would edit the *Milwaukee Sunday Telegraph*, which featured regular articles about the war and about veterans' activities, recalled the 6th's first battle on its twenty-fourth anniversary. He told the familiar story of the long marches and lack of real action that preceded the battle. The regiment "had been in the service more than a year, and had devoted most of the time to preparation for the hard work before it." Although they fought in many more battles, "it never had a sharper or bloodier work in the same length of time than it had at the battle of Brawner Farm." Watrous believed the battle brought the Wisconsin regiments into closer fellowship; prior to the fight, the 2nd had "felt rather above the 6th and 7th." Likewise, the 6th, having been mustered in two months before the 7th, felt superior to the junior regiment. "After the battle of Brawner Farm, however, regimental lines disappeared, as far as friendships were concerned."[37]

Frank Haskell, who had started the war as a lieutenant in the 6th, had by Gettysburg risen to be one of the best staff officers in the army. His account of the great battle, published as a pamphlet after his death at Cold Harbor, described the Army of the Potomac in a way that could also describe the Iron Brigade and the 6th Wisconsin: They were

> no band of school girls. They were not the men likely to be crushed or utterly discouraged by any new circumstances in which they might find themselves placed. They had lost some battles, they had gained some. They knew what defeat was, and what was victory. But here is the greatest praise I can bestow upon them, or upon any army: With the elation of victory, or the depression of defeat, amidst the hardest toils of the campaign, under unwelcome leadership, at all times, and under all circumstances, they were a reliable army still. The Army of the Potomac would do as it was told, always.

Similarly, in his recollections, published long after his death, John Gibbon ended his account of Gainesville by paying his men the highest compliment a professional soldier could give a volunteer: "My command exhibited in the highest degree the effects of discipline and drill, officers and men standing up to their work like old soldiers."[38]

Although perhaps irrelevant by a strategic standpoint, Brawner Farm loomed large to the men who fought it—both in the moment and forever afterward—its relevance an embodiment of the evolution of the Union army. Although the 6th Wisconsin was just one unit, and this was just one small if extraordinarily bloody fight, its performance on that late afternoon and evening not only proved the mettle of this particular outfit on this particular battlefield but also demonstrated how the much-maligned, often poorly led, and frequently defeated Army of the Potomac managed to retain the sense of élan and professionalism that allowed it to grind out its eventual victory over the Army of Northern Virginia. The Iron Brigade would not survive the war, but the 6th Wisconsin—reinforced in 1864 by hundreds of draftees and a few survivors of the 2nd Wisconsin—would be part of the hard-fought salvation of the Union, and the handful of men who had fought at Brawner Farm and also witnessed the surrender at Appomattox no doubt harkened back to the gun-flash-lit evening on that ridge in Virginia.

Notes

1. William J. K. Beaudot and Lance J. Herdegen, *An Irishman in the Iron Brigade: The Civil War Memoirs of James P. Sullivan, Sergt., Company K, 6th Wisconsin Volunteers* (New York: Fordham University Press, 1993), 165. Usually called Gainesville by Union participants, and sometimes Groveton by Confederates, Alan Nolan settled the name as Brawner Farm in his 1961 book *The Iron Brigade.* Alan D. Gaff, *Brave Men's Tears: The Iron Brigade at Brawner Farm*, 2nd ed., rev. (Dayton, OH: Morningside, 1988), 179–80.

2. Andrew S. Bledsoe, *Citizen-Officers: The Union and Confederate Volunteer Junior Officer Corps in the American Civil War* (Baton Rouge: Louisiana State University Press, 2015), esp. 62–101.

3. Alan T. Nolan, *The Iron Brigade: A Military History* (1961; repr., Bloomington: Indiana University Press, 1991), 28, 98.

4. Edward Bragg to Cornelia Bragg, July 10, 1861, Edward Bragg Papers, Wisconsin Historical Society, Madison; Edwin Brown to Ruth Brown, October 22, 1861, Brown Papers, Civil War Museum, Kenosha, WI; Peter S. Carmichael, *The War for the Common Soldier: How Men Thought, Fought, and Survived in Civil War Armies* (Chapel Hill: University of North Carolina Press, 2018), for instance, 44–45, 81–82, 117–19.

5. Henry Matrau to his parents, August 15, 1861, in *Letters Home: Henry Matrau of the Iron Brigade*, ed. Marcia Reid-Green (Lincoln: University of Nebraska Press, 1998), 13; Ezra Hewitt to Lucy P. Hewitt, September 14, 1861, Ezra P. Hewitt Pension File, WC14922, "Case Files of Approved Pension Applications of Widows and Other Dependents of Civil War Veterans, ca. 1861–ca. 1910," Fold 3.com, accessed July 6, 2021, https://www.fold3.com/publication/24/us-civil-war-widows-pensions-1861-1910.

6. Edwin Brown to Ruth Brown, October 28, 1861, Brown Papers.

7. Edwin Brown to Ruth Brown, June 22, 1862, and to his father, July 16, 1862, Brown Papers.

8. Charles Royster, *A Revolutionary People at War: The Continental Army and American Character, 1775–1783* (Chapel Hill: University of North Carolina Press, 1979); Andrew F. Lang, *In the Wake of War: Military Occupation, Emancipation, and Civil War America* (Baton Rouge: Louisiana State University Press, 2017).

9. *Roster of Wisconsin Volunteers, War of the Rebellion, 1861–1865*, vol. 1 (Madison: Democrat Printing Co., 1886), 494–537; *Baraboo (WI) Republic*, June 25, 1862.

10. Much has been written about the Iron Brigade, and my narrative of the role played by the 6th Wisconsin in the campaign and battle of Brawner Farm/Second Bull Run draws heavily on Gaff, *Brave Men's Tears*; Lance J. Herdegen, *The Iron Brigade in Civil War and Memory: The Black Hats from Bull Run to Appomattox and Thereafter* (El Dorado Hills, CA: Savas Beatie, 2012), 161–213; and John J. Hennessy, *Return to Bull Run: The Campaign and Battle of Second Manassas* (Norman: University of Oklahoma Press, 1999).

11. *Rufus Dawes of the Iron Brigade: Service with the Sixth Wisconsin Volunteers during the American Civil War* (London: Leonaur, 2012), 60; Philip Cheek and Mair Pointon, *History of the Sauk County Riflemen, Known as Company "A" 6th Wisconsin Veteran Volunteer Infantry, 1861–1865* (N.p.: Philip Cheek, 1909), 31; Beaudot and Herdegen, *Irishman in the Iron Brigade*, 43.

12. Cheek and Pointon, *Sauk County*, 32; *Rufus Dawes*, 61–62.

13. Graff, *Brave Men's Tears*, 56, 59; *Rufus Dawes*, 63; Cheek and Pointon, *Sauk County*, 36.

14. US War Department, *The War of the Rebellion: A Compilation of the Official Records of the Union and Confederate Armies*, 128 vols., index and atlas (Washington, DC: Government Printing Office, 1880–1901), ser. 1, 12(2): 380–82 (hereafter cited as *OR*).

15. *OR* 12(2): 380–82.

16. Cheek and Pointon, *Sauk County*, 37; Beaudot and Herdegen, *Irishman in the Iron Brigade*, 44.

17. Cheek and Pointon, *Sauk County*, 38; Henry Matrau to his parents, September 13, 1862, in *Letters Home*, 33.

18. Rufus Dawes Diary, vol. 1, p. 19, Wisconsin Historical Society, Madison. Although called a "diary," this section is actually a summary of the battles in which Dawes and the 6th took part. He drew heavily on this sketch in writing his memoirs years later.

19. Dawes Diary, 19–20.

20. Beaudot and Herdegen, *Irishman in the Iron Brigade*, 45; *Rufus Dawes*, 65.

21. Cheek and Pointon, *Sauk County*, 38–39; George Fairfield Diary, August 28, 1862, Wisconsin Historical Society.

22. *Rufus Dawes*, 11, 12. For quote, see Sir Walter Scott, "Marmion," 1808, in *Smaller Specimens of English Literature; Selected from the Chief English Writers and Arranged Chronologically*, ed. William Smith (London: John Murray, 1869), 272.

23. *Rufus Dawes*, 66–67; Cheek and Pointon, *Sauk County*, 39.

24. *Rufus Dawes*, 67.

25. *Rufus Dawes*, 68; Fairfield Diary, August 28, 1862; John Gibbon, *Personal Recollections of the Civil War* (New York: G. P. Putnam's Sons, 1928), 58; Fairfield Diary, August 29, 1862.

26. Hennessy, *Return to Bull Run*, 191–92.

27. Gaff, *Brave Men's Tears*, 95.

28. *Rufus Dawes*, 75.

29. *Rufus Dawes*, 73; Edwin Brown to Ruth Brown, ca. September 1, 1862, Brown Papers.

30. *Rufus Dawes*, 74; Murray's September 6, 1862, letter is printed in *The Blackhat*, no. 6, p. 11, no date. The *Blackhat* was a newsletter published occasionally in the 1980s for members of the 6th Wisconsin reenactment and competitive black powder rifle team.

31. Bragg to Cordelia Bragg, September 13, 1862, Bragg Papers.

32. *Baraboo Republic*, September 3 and 10, 1862.

33. *Appleton (WI) Crescent*, September 6, 1862; *Baraboo Republic*, September 17, 1862.

34. *Baraboo Republic*, September 24, 1862.

35. *Appleton Crescent*, August 23 and September 20, 1862.

36. Brig. Gen. John Gibbon to Adjutant General, US Army, December 4, 1863, *OR* 12(2): 380–82; *Lancaster (WI) Teller*, September 4, 1884.

37. *Weekly Wisconsin* (Milwaukee), September 4, 1886.

38. Frank Haskell, *The Battle of Gettysburg* (n.p., ca. 1881), 2; Gibbon, *Personal Recollections*, 54. The 6th and their fellow westerners were a product of the reorganization and retraining of the Army of the Potomac described in Albert Z. Conner Jr. and Chris Mackowski's *Seizing Destiny: The Army of the Potomac's "Valley Forge" and the Civil War Winter That Saved the Union* (El Dorado Hills, CA: Savas Beatie, 2016). For the regiment's heroics at Gettysburg, see Lance J. Herdegen, *In the Bloody Railroad Cut at Gettysburg* (Dayton: Morningside, 1990).

AS AMBITIOUS AS HE WAS BRAVE AND DARING

General John Bell Hood at the Battle of Second Manassas

KEITH S. BOHANNON

On September 13, 1862, an article titled "The Texas Brigade" appeared in the *Richmond Daily Enquirer*. The writer, who identified himself as "Eyewitness," wrote glowingly of the actions at the battle of Second Manassas of the Texas Brigade and its commander, Brig. Gen. John Bell Hood. Hood's "courage and genius" were unfailing, crowed "Eyewitness," and on the plains at Manassas he "found a field for exercise." Several weeks later, Thomas J. Goree, an officer on the staff of Hood's immediate superior, Lt. Gen. James Longstreet, wrote his mother that "it is very probable that Genl. Hood will be promoted to Major Genl. for his gallantry in these various contests. No man deserves it more. He is one of the finest young officers I ever saw." These quotes and others attest to Hood's status in the fall of 1862 as one of the rising stars in Robert E. Lee's army.[1]

Second Manassas was John B. Hood's first time commanding an infantry division, and by all accounts the hard fighting of his men contributed greatly to Confederate victory in that battle. Hood had been "inexperienced as an administrator and strategist" prior to this time, Douglas S. Freeman rightfully points out, but at Second Manassas Hood showed in multiple instances his fitness for high command. On the evening of August 29, 1862, Hood participated, possibly for the first time, in discussions with the army's leadership about tactical dispositions and planning for the following day's battle. Later that night, Hood informed Gen. Richard Anderson, another Confederate division commander, of his men's dangerous proximity to Union artillery, resulting in the withdrawal of that division before dawn on August 30. During the decisive advance of General Longstreet's wing of Lee's army on the thirtieth, Hood coordinated the movement of multiple brigades on Chinn Ridge, including several outside of his own division.[2]

Hood's performance, however, was not spotless. Several field officers in the Texas Brigade particularly complained about a leadership decision Hood made at a critical phase of the engagement on August 30, in which he temporarily assigned his assistant adjutant general, Capt. William Harvey Sellers, to command the Texas Brigade, resulting in a fragmented advance and less decisive blow to the enemy. Yet several of these critics, along with Hood's superiors, praised Hood's overall role in the battle of August 30, exonerating him of culpability. Hood, for his part, evinced no regrets, recommending Sellers for promotion.

John Bell Hood, a native of the Bluegrass region of Kentucky, graduated from the US Military Academy in the class of 1853 with a mediocre academic record. In almost every subject area, including infantry tactics and artillery, he ranked near the bottom of his class. Despite this, the general milieu of West Point markedly influenced the young Kentuckian. Like most cadets, Hood internalized the military ethos of the academy and saw its administrators and officers, especially Superintendent Robert E. Lee, as models of professional conduct. Hood hoped upon graduating from West Point to receive a commission in the cavalry, but his low class ranking resulted in him entering the army as a second lieutenant in the 4th US Infantry. He remained in this command briefly before receiving an assignment in 1856 to the newly created 2nd US Cavalry. For the next five years, Hood served on the Texas frontier, a life that consisted mainly of duty at small, isolated posts and occasional patrols.

Hood was two months shy of his thirtieth birthday when he resigned his commission as first lieutenant in the US Army in April 1861 to cast his lot with the Confederacy. He entered Confederate service from Texas, and after brief duty as a cavalry instructor on the Peninsula in Virginia, Hood accepted the colonelcy of the 4th Texas Infantry in October 1861. His background as a professional soldier, antebellum association with Texas, and skill with commanding volunteer soldiers made him an effective and popular regimental commander. During the war's first winter, Hood told his men "that no regiment . . . should ever be allowed to go forth upon the battle-field and return with more trophies of war than the Fourth Texas, that the number of colors and guns captured, and prisoners taken, constituted the true test of the work done by any command in an engagement." Similar statements appear in other wartime and postbellum writings by Hood, indicating the measures by which he gauged success on the battlefield.[3]

In mid-March 1862, Hood took command of the Texas Brigade, composed of the 1st, 4th, and 5th Texas Regiments, the 18th Georgia Regiment, and the Hampton Legion of South Carolina. Hood and his brigade won praise that spring in a small fight at Eltham's Landing on May 7, 1862. Hood's immediate superior, Brig. Gen. Chase Whiting, singled out the Texas Brigade commander's "conspicuous gallantry" on the field.[4]

Like most professional army officers during the Civil War, Hood saw the conflict as an opportunity to serve his nation while also gaining distinction and promotion. Col. Evander M. Law commented on Hood's ambitious nature in an 1887 article in the *Southern Bivouac*. As Law recalled, on June 10, 1862, he received orders to report to his immediate superior, General Whiting. When Law arrived at Whiting's headquarters, a meeting between Whiting and Hood had just ended. Whiting had wanted Hood's brigade to reinforce the troops of Gen. Thomas J. "Stonewall" Jackson in the Shenandoah Valley, but Hood strongly opposed sending his Texans there. Whiting suggested to Law that Hood believed that "as the great battles of the [summer] campaign would be fought around Richmond, he would have a better opportunity of winning distinction there than in an outlying district in the Valley, the military operations of which must be regarded as accessories only to the great drama to be enacted about the Confederate capital."[5] In Law's view, Hood longed to be in the main action.

Although the Texas Brigade did travel to the Shenandoah Valley, its stay there was brief. Hood's men returned with the balance of Jackson's command to Robert E. Lee's army in time to earn fame in the Seven Days' campaign, particularly in the battle of Gaines's Mill. There Hood personally led the 4th Texas into battle. Hood was "exceedingly popular with the brigade," assessed Lt. Col. Walter B. Botts of the 5th Texas not long after Gaines's Mill. Botts noted that Hood claimed "to be a Texian, having spent most of his life" in the state and having his home there. Hood also requested that his name be registered with the War Department as being from Texas.[6]

Several weeks after the Seven Days' campaign, Hood's division commander, General Whiting, received a medical furlough and never returned to his old command. Whiting's performance during the Seven Days' campaign, writes Douglas S. Freeman, had been relatively undistinguished, although he had done nothing to discredit himself. As senior general in the division, Hood took command of Whiting's two brigades. In addition to the Texas Brigade, the division included Colonel Law's "Old Third Brigade." The "Old Third" consisted of the 2nd and 11th Mississippi, 4th Alabama, and 6th North Carolina and had received its nickname in 1861 upon being designated the Third Brigade of the Army of the Shenandoah.

The "Old Third" fought at First Manassas and, in the words of Robert E. Lee in late July 1862, had been "distinguished for good service from the beginning of the war in Virginia." Hood thought highly of Law and his men, writing the Confederate secretary of war a month prior to Second Manassas that he knew of "no officer more worthy of promotion" than Law and "no troops in better condition than those under his command." A visitor to Law's camps in the fall of 1862 claimed that the men in the Old Third were "very much attached" to Hood and believed that Colonel Law "possessed the entire confidence of almost every officer and man" in the brigade.[7]

Law's Old Third and the Texas Brigade spent the days immediately prior to the battle of Second Manassas engaged in an exhausting forced march through heat and dust as part of an effort by Longstreet's wing of the Army of Northern Virginia to join Jackson's wing. On the afternoon of August 28, 1862, Law's men and skirmishers from the Texas Brigade engaged in movements that contributed to Federals retiring eastward from a position in Thoroughfare Gap in the Bull Run Mountains. That evening at sunset, Hood's men bivouacked a short distance east of Thoroughfare Gap.[8]

Before daylight on August 29, 1862, Hood's division marched as the vanguard of Longstreet's wing, hoping to connect with Jackson's divisions close to Manassas Junction. Jackson's men had fought the Federals to a bloody standstill the previous day at Brawner Farm. In accordance with instructions from Longstreet, Hood placed in front of his brigades an advance guard of approximately 150 picked Texas riflemen commanded by Lt. Col. John C. Upton of the 5th Texas. Upton, according to Hood, was "preeminent in his sphere as an outpost officer." Hood impressed upon Upton the importance of hastening to support Jackson's embattled men, assuring the lieutenant

Brig. Gen. John Bell Hood's introduction to division command at Second Manassas added to his reputation as a rising star in the Army of Northern Virginia. (Carte de visite with "J. A. Sheldon, photographer, 101 Canal Street, New Orleans" on the back. Library of Congress Prints and Photographs Division, reproduction number LC-DIG-ppmsca-78086)

colonel that the rest of Hood's division would be available to provide assistance if needed. Upton pushed ahead so rapidly that on two or three occasions Lee sent orders for him to halt since the main column was unable to keep within supporting distance. By the time Upton's men finally stopped, the Texans had advanced about eight miles.[9]

After marching for hours toward the sound of gunfire where Union attacks tested Stonewall Jackson's men, Hood's division arrived on the Manassas battlefield midmorning on August 29. Around 10:30 a.m., Hood met Jackson on the Warrenton Turnpike. Jackson extended a "hearty welcome" to Hood as the latter's division formed facing eastward astride the turnpike. Jackson sent Henry Kyd Douglas of his staff to assist the Texas Brigade in deploying with its left flank resting on the Warrenton Turnpike. At noon, wrote Andrew N. Erskine of the 4th Texas, Lee passed the Texans "and very soon we were ordered to double quick in the direction of the heavy firing of artillery" being "soon placed in line of battle."

Evander Law's regiments, accompanied by Longstreet and Hood, deployed north of the Warrenton Turnpike and advanced eastward. When Law's men halted on a low ridge, a gap of several hundred yards existed between a ridge to their left rear and the right of Jackson's line deployed along an unfinished railroad cut. In the early afternoon, the Confederates filled the high ground in this gap with a concentration of nineteen cannon that, according to Law, "opened fire with marked effect upon the enemy."[10]

Companies of skirmishers deployed in front of Hood's division kept up a continual fire at their opponents while the majority of men spent the afternoon resting, the soldiers of Law's brigade enduring occasional enemy artillery fire. Around 4:00 p.m., as Union troops assaulted the right flank of Jackson's position, Law's troops advanced eastward as far as Groveton, where they halted.[11]

That evening at approximately five o'clock, Lee "became anxious" to attack the Federals along and south of the Warrenton Turnpike. Longstreet suggested that as the day was far from spent, the Confederates instead launch a reconnaissance in force to get troops into a favorable position to attack at daylight the next morning. In an 1887 article in *Battles and Leaders,* Longstreet claimed that Lee "reluctantly gave consent" to the reconnaissance in force, although Longstreet wrote years later in his memoirs that Lee had only a "moment's hesitation" before ordering Brig. Gen. Cadmus Wilcox's three brigades and a brigade under Brig. Gen. Nathan "Shanks" Evans to support Hood's division in a forced reconnaissance at dusk to develop the enemy's main position.[12]

Lee stated in an 1870 conversation with William Allan that he ordered Longstreet's advance on the afternoon of August 29 to relieve the pressure being placed on Jackson's command by Federal attacks. Hood, Lee stated, "did not like the place and said so," an unclear statement that seems to refer to the division commander's position astride the Warrenton Turnpike. Lee remembered telling the division commander "he must attack any how and relieve Jackson."[13]

According to Hood's official report and Chaplain Nicholas Davis of the Texas Brigade, a courier from Longstreet gave Hood the order to advance just before sunset on the twenty-ninth. The Texas Brigade's jumping off point was inside an extension of Brawner's Woods south of the Warrenton Turnpike and about a half mile west of the Groveton crossroads. A 5th Texas private on the skirmish line recalled hearing "the clarion voice of Hood ringing out 'Fix bayonet' 'F-o-r-w-a-r-d,' and with a yell we set out for the Yanks." At the same time, a Union division under Brig. Gen. John Hatch with orders to pursue supposedly retreating Rebels advanced westward astride the turnpike toward Hood's men.[14]

North of the Warrenton Turnpike, Law's regiments marched eastward around the buildings and over the fences of Groveton before coming under the fire of Capt. George A. Gerrish's battery and a large body of infantry 400 yards away. "Delivering volley after volley," wrote Law, "my men continued a rapid and uninterrupted advance upon the battery and its supports." As the Confederates charged up the slope where the battery stood, Union artillerists limbered up three of their cannon and retreated with their infantry supports. The crew of the fourth Federal howitzer continued firing until Confederates overwhelmed the artillerists, members of the 4th Alabama wresting a sponge rammer from the hands of a cannoneer as he attempted to drive his last charge home.[15]

On the south side of the Warrenton Turnpike, the Texas Brigade advanced eastward from the cover of Brawner's Woods. Hood's line likely stretched some 700 yards south of the turnpike and overlapped the left of the opposing Federal line by quite some distance, but the darkness made it almost impossible for the Southerners to realize their advantage. Two attacking Federal brigades became intermingled and eventually retreated eastward after trading several volleys with the Confederates. The Confederates charged up a ridge where they engaged in a confused struggle at close quarters with Federals. A Georgian in the Texas Brigade, writing a few days later, said that a hand-to-hand fight "amid pitch darkness . . . is absolutely diabolical. Bayonets, butts of muskets, and even fists were used freely. The yells of the victors, the shriek of the wounded, and the groans of the dying, together with the rattle and flash of musketry in the darkness, and the unusual confusion of men running to and fro, made up a scene that beggars all description."[16]

By 8:00 p.m. the fighting had ended, it being in the words of Lt. Col. Philip A. Work of the 1st Texas "too dark to distinguish friend from foe at a distance of 20 paces." The Texas Brigade advanced a short distance farther, crossing Young's Branch and stopping on the shoulder of Chinn Ridge. While Law's brigade moved into place on the left of the Texans, the Confederate commands of Generals Wilcox and Evans stood by in support. Thousands of Confederates were in a seemingly advantageous location near the center of the Union position, ready to attack on the morning of the thirtieth.[17]

Despite the close-quarters fighting and dramatic flashes of gunfire during the evening engagement on August 29, the casualties on both sides were low. The Texas Brigade likely suffered no more than sixty casualties. Hood's Division captured a piece of artillery, six stands of colors, and around 150 prisoners.[18]

While Hood's exact movements prior to and during the night attack are unknown, Chaplain Davis of the 4th Texas wrote that the general was in the charge of his division and that he "received and sent forward three or four other brigades." These additional troops were likely from the command of General Wilcox, which arrived at Hood's position after the musketry had died down. When the fighting ended, Hood and Wilcox received orders from Longstreet to examine the enemy's position in their front and report on the feasibility of launching a dawn attack. Hood believed that the inability to distinguish friend from foe in the darkness made it impossible "to select a position and form upon it for action next morning." Hood likely also realized what Evander Law told Wilcox that evening after the fighting had diminished: that the Confederates had engaged only a single division of Federals thrown out in front of their main line, and that if Hood's division advanced farther in front of the Confederate main line, it would expose both its flanks to attack.

In his memoir, *Advance and Retreat*, Hood related riding to the rear about two miles after the night attack on the twenty-ninth to find Longstreet and Lee in an open field. Hood recommended that his division retire to the main Confederate line. "After a brief interview," Hood received orders to withdraw his division. In an 1870 interview, Lee made an apparent reference to this meeting, claiming that Hood returned to the army commander after dark "delighted and excited," claiming that the enemy dead were lying thick "like a bed of roses."[19]

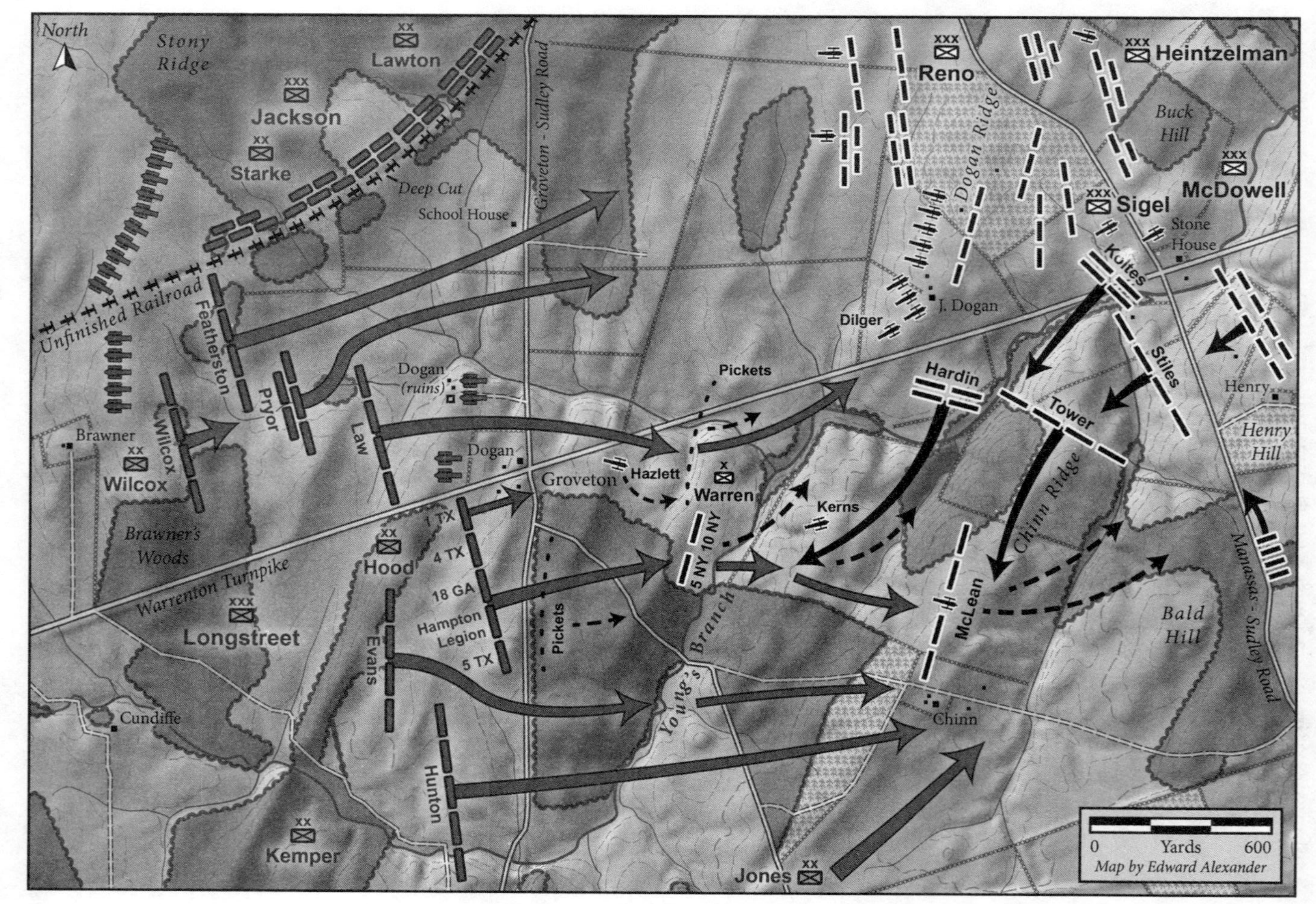

Hood's attack at Second Manassas, August 30, 1862

Unfortunately, neither Hood's official report of Second Manassas nor his memoir offer substantial details about the meeting he held with Lee and Longstreet, but postbellum notes by Wilcox provide an alternate version of events with more particulars. According to Wilcox, he and Hood conferred after the fighting on the night of August 29 and agreed that they should withdraw. Between 10:00 and 10:30 p.m., Hood made this suggestion to Lee, but the army commander objected, replying that he did not want to abandon the ground taken. When Hood rode back and told Wilcox of the meeting, Wilcox rode to Longstreet and persuaded the wing commander to order a withdrawal. Longstreet claimed in his official report of Second Manassas and in a postbellum article that he told Lee that "none of the reports received of the Federal positions favored attack," and the army commander subsequently ordered the men back to the positions from which they had started the evening attack.[20]

Despite orders to withdraw, multiple sources suggest that some of the Texans remained in close proximity to the enemy until near dawn. Col. John M. Stone of the 2nd Mississippi encountered Col. Jerome B. Robertson of the 5th Texas after receiving the orders to withdraw. Robertson declined to join Stone in retreating, "saying his men were broken down and asleep, and, without orders from General Hood, he preferred remaining there." Pvt. Robert Campbell of Robertson's 5th Texas remembered things differently, claiming that Captain Sellers of Hood's staff told Robertson that while the line would fall back to its original position, a company of the 5th Texas and a company from the Hampton Legion would remain in an advanced position "as a precautionary step." At least two members of the 1st Texas, including Colonel Work, wrote of spending the night within 150 to 200 yards of the enemy until near dawn.[21]

Just as Hood prepared to lie down to rest before dawn on August 30, a staff officer informed him that Gen. Richard H. Anderson's division had bivouacked for the night along the Warrenton Turnpike between Hood's division and the enemy. Knowing that Anderson's men would be exposed to massed Union artillery fire in the morning, Hood mounted his horse and rode to find Anderson. After hearing Hood's warning, Anderson roused his exhausted men shortly before daybreak and moved them to the rear, approximately a mile to the base of Stuart's Hill.[22]

On the morning of August 30, Hood made one of his most valuable contributions to the Confederate victory at Second Manassas. When Col. Stephen D. Lee arrived on the field with his artillery battalion, he consulted with Hood and followed the general's suggestion to deploy the batteries on a commanding ridge immediately to the left and rear of Law's brigade. Hood had not been the first person to recognize the importance of this position, it having been occupied by Southern batteries under Col. James B. Walton the day before, but Hood's suggestion that Colonel Lee post his cannon there proved fortuitous for the Confederates on the thirtieth.[23]

That same morning, General Evans assumed command of the Confederate troops to the immediate right and left of the Warrenton Turnpike. According to Evans's report of Second Manassas, these troops included the two brigades of Hood's division and Evans's own brigade of South Carolinians. Although Evans outranked Hood and might have technically commanded Hood's division on August 30, no official or unofficial evidence indicates that he exercised control that day over any unit other than his own brigade. (Douglas S. Freeman suggests that Evans had only "titular authority" over Hood's troops.) The command arrangement likely existed at the insistence of Evans, whom Longstreet staff officer Moxley Sorrel dubbed "difficult to manage" and "unruly." Evans's well-known fondness for alcohol likely contributed to the erratic and unmanageable behavior noted by Sorrel and many others.[24]

While the skirmishers of Hood's division engaged the enemy throughout the morning and early afternoon of August 30, most of his men rested and watched the Federal assault against Stonewall Jackson's position to the north, "a saddening and magnificent spectacle," according to one Texan. At some point between 1:30 and 2:00 p.m., Longstreet rode to his front at the request of Hood and Evans, who indicated an attack being made on Jackson. Longstreet, realizing that the Federal column would be vulnerable to enfilading and reverse artillery fire, ordered up batteries, including Cap. James Reilly's, as rapidly as possible.[25]

When attacking lines of Union infantry north of the Warrenton Turnpike under Maj. Gen. Fitz John Porter broke and began moving to the rear as a "confused mass of fugitives," Longstreet turned to Hood and ordered him to move his brigades forward. Hood subsequently galloped up in front of the Texas Brigade, while his assistant adjutant general, Captain Sellers, rode out to the Texans' skirmish line. Sellers ordered the skirmishers to advance and draw the fire of Union skirmishers before the main Confederate battle line got into a belt of woods. In a few moments, the men heard Hood shout, "Attention Texas Brigade, forward march." A 5th Texas private remembered that "men were never more frenzied in their passions as our boys were."[26]

The Texans' advance was part of a massive assault ordered by Lee and Longstreet that afternoon to envelop and drive back the left of the Union army, seize Henry Hill, and gain control of the Federal line of retreat.

Execution of the Confederate attack would be difficult, given the limited amount of daylight left (approximately three hours) and the need to coordinate the movements of five Southern divisions covering an initial front of more than a mile and a half. The Texas Brigade, which had to advance just over a mile and a half to reach Henry Hill, was the column of direction for the assault. The ground between the Texans and Henry Hill consisted of rolling hills cut by Young's Branch and several smaller streams.[27]

A few minutes after the Texas Brigade began its advance, a messenger told Hood to ride back and report to Longstreet. Hood rode at full speed and found the wing commander between a quarter and a half mile in the rear. Hood claimed that Longstreet "instructed me not to allow my division to move so far forward as to throw itself beyond the prompt support of the troops he had ordered to the front." While Hood met with Longstreet, Hood's troops did exactly what Longstreet feared.[28]

Before leaving the Texans to report to Longstreet, Hood gave command of the Texas Brigade to his assistant adjutant general, Captain Sellers. Sellers, a Texan since boyhood, had participated as a youth in the 1842 Mier expedition, an ill-fated raid by Texans against Mexican settlements. Sellers and most of the other Texans captured in the debacle spent twenty-one months as prisoners in Mexico before being released. A few years after returning from Mexican prisons, Sellers served as a lieutenant in the Mexican War. In July 1861, Sellers enlisted in the 5th Texas Infantry, achieving the rank of regimental adjutant before joining Hood's staff in March 1862 as a captain and assistant adjutant general. Hood had specifically requested Sellers for the promotion and appointment, noting that he was "an able, energetic and efficient officer, and well qualified for the position."[29]

As Hood's assistant adjutant general, Sellers exercised considerable authority both off and on the battlefield. "Officers and men considered the AAG an extension of the general," writes Robert E. L. Krick in *Staff Officers in Gray,* accepting orders from him as if they came from the commander himself. Official reports of the fighting on the evening of August 29 reveal that Sellers had ordered forward several regiments of the Texas Brigade and assisted them in reforming after dusk.[30]

Hood probably had not turned the Texas Brigade over to its senior field officer, Col. William T. Wofford of the 18th Georgia, on August 30 because Wofford was a Georgian. "The Texians," Hood told Wofford later that fall, "would not be satisfied with any person but a Texian" to command them. At the same time, Hood admitted to Wofford that the 18th Georgia "had done as much to give character to the Brigade as any Regt. in it."[31]

Hood's absence from his division during its initial advance on August 30 likely contributed to its disjointed movement and the subsequent piecemeal attacks made by individual regiments. In the case of the Texas Brigade, although Captain Sellers passed along orders and provided direction to regimental commanders, he had no experience in brigade command and could not keep the regiments together. Sellers also had his horse shot while Hood rode to the rear to meet Longstreet, a situation that undoubtedly limited Sellers's mobility for a time.[32]

In a Texas Brigade history published in 1910, Joseph B. Polley claimed that there was "so little concert of action between the regiments of the Texas Brigade on August 30th, 1862 that any attempt to describe their movements . . . would be confusing to writer and reader." On the brigade's left, Lt. Col. Philip A. Work of the 1st Texas moved forward with the regiment's left resting on the Warrenton Turnpike. The 1st marched only about 125 yards when Work realized his men were detached from the rest of the brigade. Work continued advancing the 1st along the turnpike and came under artillery fire. Later, when attempting to advance to support the rest of the Texas Brigade on Chinn Ridge, Work received orders in person from Sellers to retire to the ravine where Young's Branch flowed. Work's regiment saw no appreciable action on August 30.[33]

On the right of the Texas Brigade, the 18th Georgia, Hampton Legion, and 5th Texas drove a line of Federal skirmishers and their reserves from the 10th New York Regiment through a strip of woods before emerging into an open field. At this point the yelling Confederates encountered, in the words of Col. Jerome Robertson of the 5th Texas, "the . . . Fifth New York, who, after permitting the fleeing regiment to pass its lines, presented a solid front for a short time." The Texans recognized the colorful Zouave uniforms of the New Yorkers as the men had traded taunts across the Potomac River the previous winter. Animosities ran high between the Texas Brigade and the Zouaves, as revealed by Lt. James Lemon of the 18th Georgia, who referred in his memoir to the "much-hated" 5th New York "in their gaudy red & blue outfits."[34]

Pvt. Robert Campbell of the 5th Texas remembered that the "Zouaves were at a charge bayonet—and when we were within 20 paces of them they fired upon us." This initial volley caused little damage in the 5th Texas but knocked forty men out of the ranks of the 18th Georgia. The Confederates then received orders to fix bayonets, fire, and charge. Their volley sent dozens of Zouaves to the ground and the survivors began to break for the rear in small groups, running down a long, open slope to Young's Branch and up a rise on the other side. "Then it was that the Enfielders proved destruction," wrote a member of the 5th Texas. "Every man took deliberate aim, and each shot went home." Within minutes, the Georgians, Texans, and South Carolinians had killed or wounded several hundred Zouaves, leaving the grassy slopes along Young's Branch covered with bodies.[35]

When the Confederates subsequently entered the wooded ravine through which Young's Branch flowed, the 18th Georgia halted "to take breath" under orders of its colonel, William Wofford. Harvey Sellers ordered Col. Benjamin F. Carter of the 4th Texas and Colonel Robertson of the 5th Texas to halt their regiments and reform the ranks. Some men in the right wing of the 5th Texas didn't receive the order to halt due to the death of Colonel Upton earlier in the assault and instead advanced out of the ravine toward a Union battery and its infantry supports posted on an open knoll. While the 5th Texas provided an enfilade fire against the Federal infantry, the 4th Texas and 18th Georgia launched a costly charge against the battery through a hail of shot and shell. After shooting down thirty of the Federal battery's horses and several of its artillerists, the Georgians and Texans claimed the four Parrott rifles of Capt. Mark Kerns's battery.

Despite capturing the Union cannon, the Texas Brigade was in a dangerous situation. The men had advanced nearly three-quarters of a mile and were well in front of any other Confederates of Longstreet's wing. They had also suffered extensive casualties, and their ranks were in disarray. Facing another Federal battery and its infantry support on Chinn Ridge, Hood's men pushed forward to the cover of a ravine. At this point the 4th Texas retired westward to Young's Branch where, under orders from Sellers, it joined the 1st Texas. Both regiments spent the remainder of the battle unengaged. The 18th Georgia, 5th Texas, and Hampton Legion prepared to advance farther.[36]

After Hood's meeting in the Confederate rear with Longstreet, Hood "rode at as rapid a course" as his favorite horse could go to rejoin the Texas Brigade. After passing the dead and wounded along Young's Branch, Hood eventually found his regiments. "Being a long distance in advance of our troops," Hood ordered his men to hold their ground. On Chinn Ridge, a short distance to the east, Hood rode into a gap between the 5th Texas and other Confederates, dismounted, and spied a Union battery and supporting lines of infantry.

When the South Carolina regiments of General Evans's brigade arrived on Chinn Ridge, Hood ordered Col. John H. Means of the 17th South Carolina to "take the Federal battery which was then within sixty yards." Later, when Confederate Maj. Gen. David R. Jones arrived with his division, Hood assisted in coordinating attacks that ultimately drove Union troops off Chinn

Ridge and eastward across the Sudley Road. Colonel Robertson of the 5th Texas, whose regiment lost heavily in the fighting on Chinn Ridge, claimed with some exaggeration that Hood "put in every brigade on our right" during this phase of the fighting "and in doing it showed superior judgment and skill." Hood's presence undoubtedly inspired numbers of Jones's men; a Georgian remembered seeing Hood riding down the lines at a full gallop exclaiming, "Go it boys, we'll give them more than they can attend to!"[37]

Despite Hood's staffer Harvey Sellers's errors, he also displayed notable bravery on August 30. J. Mark Smither, a member of the 5th Texas, recalled how Sellers rode in front of Confederate lines to the crest of a ridge at one point to reconnoiter. Amid heavy fire, Sellers "coolly surveyed the situation in his front" with his field glasses. Another officer, witnessing Sellers's ride up the hill, later claimed that he said to himself, "Right here is where Old Harvey is going up."[38]

Evander Law's brigade also saw action on August 30. Law's men initially supported around two dozen Confederate cannon in a position northwest of Groveton. After remaining there for roughly half an hour, Law received orders from Hood to move across the Warrenton Turnpike and connect with the Texas Brigade. Being unable to locate the Texas Brigade, Law ordered three of his regiments to a tree line in the ravine formed by Young's Branch at the base of Dogan's Ridge south of the Turnpike.

Some of Law's men began to ascend Dogan Ridge, but fire from two Federal batteries drove them back down. When a Federal regiment countercharged down the ridge, Law's men repulsed it and ascended the slope in pursuit. Upon entering the Dogan orchard, Law's regiments encountered elements of the Union Iron Brigade supported by Capt. Hubert Dilger's 1st Ohio Battery. Following a brief fight in the orchard and a failed attempt to capture Dilger's cannon, Law continued advancing until ordered after dark to halt by Longstreet. A member of the 6th North Carolina, evincing no modesty in a letter published on September 10, 1862, in the *Raleigh Standard*, claimed that the fighting of Law's brigade at Second Manassas "is pronounced by the Generals as the brightest thing of the war, and probably unsurpassed in history."[39]

Hood's two brigades captured four cannon, eight colors, and numerous prisoners at Second Manassas. Hood boasted in his official report that as to his men's "gallantry and unflinching courage they stand unsurpassed within the history of the world." Longstreet's report of the battle mentioned Hood, Law, and Wofford as being "most prominently distinguished" on both August 29 and 30.[40]

The considerable contribution that Hood's division made to Confederate victory came at a steep price. Law's regiments suffered 320 casualties in both days of fighting, while the Texas Brigade lost 610 men. The 5th Texas, the hardest hit of Hood's regiments, sustained 257 casualties out of 521 officers and men taken into action. Seven color bearers fell carrying the 5th's Lone Star banner, which Federal bullets pierced twenty-eight times in the fighting.[41]

On the whole, Hood's performance at Second Manassas displayed considerable skill as a division commander. On the night of August 29, he exercised prudence in insisting that his men withdraw from their isolated position in front of Confederate lines and later informing General Anderson of the same danger. The next morning, Hood's suggestion to Col. Stephen D. Lee to place guns on the high ground between Longstreet's and Jackson's lines contributed to what was one of the great days of the Civil War for the artillery of the Army of Northern Virginia.

The choice of Hood's division as the column of direction for Longstreet's assault on August 30 reveals the confidence that Lee and Longstreet placed in Hood and his brigades. Lee claimed several weeks later that he relied on the Texans "in all the tight places." Longstreet's summons to the rear prevented Hood from leading his division in the initial phases of its attack on August 30, but upon Hood's return to the firing line on Chinn Ridge he assisted in sending forward and motivating Southern brigades as they reached the front.[42]

Hood's biggest error at Second Manassas was his failure to designate a field officer to command the Texas Brigade. Sensitivity to the state pride of the Texans was not a sufficient reason to send them into battle under a staff officer who was a captain, even if that staff officer held the rank of assistant adjutant general. Hood, however, clearly felt that he had not made a mistake in giving Sellers temporary brigade command on August 30. Hood's official report of the battle of Sharpsburg, fought only a few weeks after Second Manassas, claimed that Sellers "has proven himself competent to command a brigade under all circumstances." At Second Manassas, Hood noted, Sellers had his horse shot and acted gallantly while "pushing forward the troops and transmitting orders."[43]

Scott Patchan's fine book *Second Manassas: Longstreet's Attack and the Struggle for Chinn Ridge* offers two specific criticisms of Sellers's performance on August 30. In the first case, Patchan points out that Sellers ordered the 1st Texas to retire to Young's Branch and rest as it tried to move forward to join the rest of the brigade. Colonel Work of the 1st regretted his regiment's inaction on that day and stated that he "received no notice and did not discover the movements of the other regiments of the brigade" in time to participate in the assaults. Patchan's criticism of Sellers in this instance seems justified, especially since his orders resulted in an entire regiment of the Texas Brigade being kept out of action on August 30.[44]

Patchan's second criticism is that Sellers attempted to halt several regiments of the Texas Brigade in the ravine of Young's Branch instead of having them advance against the Pennsylvania Reserves and Kerns's battery. While reports confirm that Sellers ordered the 4th and 5th Texas to halt, Colonel Wofford of the 18th Georgia suggests that he made the decision to halt his regiment in the ravine to rest the men before maneuvering them to get within a very close distance (forty yards) of the Federals. Colonel Robertson of the 5th Texas states that the halt provided his men an opportunity to reform their disordered ranks. Furthermore, Robertson wrote that the halt had lasted "scarcely a minute" before he discovered that the right of the 5th had continued advancing and he ordered the rest of the regiment forward. Wofford's and Robertson's reports suggest that the halts of their regiments in Young's Branch were brief, helpful in allowing the men to rest and reform ranks, and likely had little impact on their successful attempts to drive off the Pennsylvania Reserves and capture Kerns's cannon.[45]

On October 24, 1862, Hood wrote Confederate adjutant and inspector general Samuel Cooper recommending that Capt. Harvey Sellers and Lt. Col. Benjamin F. Carter of the 4th Texas receive promotions to the rank of brigadier general. Hood said that both officers had "distinguished themselves upon many hotly contested fields, and I regard them as the best qualified Officers for the position of Brigadier General that I have met with during the War coming from civilian life." Twelve days later, Hood wrote Cooper again, but this time recommended that Sellers receive a promotion only to the rank of major and remain on Hood's staff as assistant adjutant general.[46]

Despite Hood's personal confidence in Sellers's leadership, evidence of resentment at the staff officer's temporary appointment to brigade command on August 30 appears in several sources. Col. Jerome Robertson, who might have been angry that he had not been chosen to lead the brigade at Second Manassas, wrote in his official report that "the separation of regiments of the brigade during the battle probably increased the casualties in my regiment, interfering to some extent with its efficiency, and demonstrated the absolute necessity of having a brigade commander present with brigades at all times during the engagement." In a letter published in the *Houston Tri-Weekly Telegraph,* Robertson claimed that the Texas Brigade had gotten scattered at Second Manassas "for the want of a Brigadier General" but seemingly exonerated Hood by claiming that he was "off putting in other brigades."[47]

Officers of the 18th Georgia complained to the Confederate secretary of war that at Second Manassas "the Brigade was sent into action without a Brigade commander [and] under the direction of a staff officer . . . for no other reason as we could see than because our Col [William T. Wofford] was the senior officer present and was not a Texan." Hood rectified the situation several days after Second Manassas, and Colonel Wofford commanded the Texas Brigade throughout the Maryland campaign. The permanent solution to the problem involved transferring out the non-Texas units and promoting Colonel Robertson to brigadier general and command of the Texas Brigade.[48]

Hood's pride in the performance of his division at Second Manassas was warranted, especially when measured against his belief "that the number of colors and guns captured, and prisoners taken, constituted the true test of the work done by any command in an engagement." At the same time, the lack of coordination among his attacking regiments on August 30 clearly prevented Hood's command from delivering a heavier blow against the enemy that afternoon, especially south of the Warrenton Turnpike. While the disjointed and halting nature of the advances was due in part to difficult terrain and the heroic resistance mounted by several lines of outnumbered Federals, the lack of experience of Hood's assistant adjutant general, Captain Sellers, was also a contributing factor.

The criticisms of Hood by subordinates for placing Harvey Sellers in command during a critical juncture on August 30 detracted little if any from Hood's rising reputation as an officer whose aggressive proclivities and leadership on the battlefield helped Lee's army achieve decisive victories in the summer and fall of 1862. At the same time, Hood won accolades from his superiors and a promotion to major general in the fall of 1862. Stonewall Jackson echoed the sentiments of many when he wrote the Confederate secretary of war at the end of September that Hood had fought "with such ability and zeal as to command my admiration. I regard him as one of the most promising officers in the army."[49]

Notes

I would like to acknowledge the following individuals for their assistance with this essay: James Burgess, Rick Eiserman, Caroline E. Janney, Robert E. L. Krick, Robert K. Krick, James Ogden III, Kathryn Shively, Jeffrey Stocker, O. Lee Sturkey, Jeffry Wert, and Dana Wooley.

1. "Eyewitness," "The Texas Brigade," *Richmond Daily Enquirer*, September 13, 1862; Thomas W. Cutrer, ed., *Longstreet's Aide: The Civil War Letters of Major Thomas J. Goree* (Charlottesville: University Press of Virginia, 1995), 100.

2. Douglas Southall Freeman, *Lee's Lieutenants: A Study in Command*, 3 vols. (New York: Charles Scribner's Sons, 1943), 1:lii.

3. Brian Craig Miller makes the significant point that average academic performances at West Point did not always hinder successful military service during the Civil War. This was certainly the case with Hood during his tenure in brigade and division command. Richard McMurry, *John Bell Hood and the War for Southern Independence* (Lexington: University Press of Kentucky, 1982), 3–28; Brian Craig Miller, *John Bell Hood and the Fight for Civil War Memory* (Knoxville: University of Tennessee Press, 2019), 22–25; John B. Hood, *Advance and Retreat* (1880; repr., New York: Da Capo, 1993), 19; US War Department, *The War of the Rebellion: A Compilation of the Official Records of the Union and Confederate Armies*, 128 vols., index and atlas (Washington, DC: Government Printing Office, 1880–1901), ser. 1, 12(1): 37 (hereafter cited as *OR*, with all citations from series 1 unless otherwise noted); Susannah J. Ural, *Hood's Texas Brigade* (Baton Rouge: Louisiana State University Press, 2017), 80.

4. Hood, *Advance and Retreat*, 21l; McMurry, *John Bell Hood*, 35–40.

5. Evander Law, "The Fight for Richmond in 1862," in *Southern Bivouac*, 6 vols. and index (1882–87; repr., Wilmington, NC: Broadfoot, 1993), 6:652.

6. Hood, *Advance and Retreat*, 21–22; Robert E. L. Krick, "The Men Who Carried This Position Were Soldiers Indeed: The Decisive Charge of Whiting's Division at Gaines' Mill," in *The Richmond Campaign of 1862: The Peninsula and the Seven Days*, ed. Gary W. Gallagher (Chapel Hill: University of North Carolina Press, 2000), 181–216; "Lieut. Col. Botts—Army Intelligence," *Houston Tri-Weekly Telegraph*, August 11, 1862. For more on Hood's strong identity as a Texan, see Gary W. Gallagher and Joseph T. Glatthaar, eds., *Leaders of the Lost Cause: New Perspectives on the Confederate High Command* (Mechanicsburg: Stackpole Books, 2004), 252.

7. Freeman, *Lee's Lieutenants*, 1:621; *OR* 11(3): 654; John B. Hood to G. W. Randolph, July 30, 1862, Compiled Service Record of Evander M. Law, M331, National Archives and Records Administration, Washington, DC; "Visitor," "The Old Third," *Raleigh Standard*, November 5, 1862.

8. J. B. Polley, *Hood's Texas Brigade* (1910; repr., Dayton: Morningside, 1976), 72–78; Hood, *Advance and Retreat*, 32.

9. *OR* 12(2): 605; Hood, *Advance and Retreat*, 33; Donald E. Everett, ed., *Chaplain Davis and Hood's Texas Brigade* (1962; repr., Baton Rouge: Louisiana State University Press, 1999), 110.

10. In an 1874 letter to Union general Fitz John Porter, Hood said that his division had been "prepared to meet yours any time after 11 o'clock" in the morning on August 29. Hood, *Advance and Retreat*, 33; *OR* 12(2): 622; John Cussons, *The Passage of Thoroughfare Gap and the Assembling of Lee's Army for the Second Battle of Manassas* (York, PA: Gazette Print, 1906), 12; Andrew N. Erskine, "Letter from Virginia," *Galveston Weekly News*, October 8, 1862; John B. Hood to Fitz John Porter, February 9, 1874, Fitz John Porter Papers, microfilm reel 4, frame 336, Library of Congress, Washington, DC.

11. *OR* 12(2): 622; John M. Stone, "Reminiscences of the Second Battle of Manassas," in *Camp Fires of the Confederacy*, ed. Ben Labree (Louisville: Courier-Journal Job Printing

Company, 1898), 298; Jeffrey D. Stocker, ed., *From Huntsville to Appomattox* (Knoxville: University of Tennessee Press, 1996), 54–55.

12. Lee's staff officer Charles Marshall remembered in 1878 that Lee had been "anxious to attack" on the afternoon of the twenty-ninth but that Longstreet "advised against it." Longstreet claimed in an article published in 1878 in the *Atlantic Monthly* that he ordered the reconnaissance at dark on August 29 "in order to assure myself that there was, or that there was not, a point in my front that would justify an attack." The reconnaissance, Longstreet claimed, revealed that the Federal position was too strong to warrant an attack. James Longstreet, "Our March against Pope," in *Battles and Leaders of the Civil War*, ed. Robert Underwood Johnson and Clarence Clough Buel, 4 vols. (New York: Century, 1884–88), 2:519; James Longstreet, *From Manassas to Appomattox* (Philadelphia: J. B. Lippincott Co., 1896), 183; *Proceedings and Report of the Board of Army Officers, Convened by Special Orders No. 78, Headquarters of the Army, Adjutant General's Office, Washington, April 12, 1878, in the Case of Fitz-John Porter*, 3 pts. (Washington, DC: Government Printing Office, 1879), 2:211–12; James Longstreet, "Pope's Virginia Campaign," *Atlantic Monthly*, September 1878, 360; John J. Hennessy, *Return to Bull Run: The Campaign and Battle of Second Manassas* (New York: Simon and Schuster, 1993), 288–89.

13. Quoted in Gary W. Gallagher, ed., *Lee the Soldier* (Lincoln: University of Nebraska Press, 1996), 17.

14. *OR* 12(2): 605; Everett, *Chaplain Davis*, 112; Hennessy, *Return to Bull Run*, 289; George Skoch and Mark Perkins, eds., *Lone Star Confederate: A Gallant and Good Soldier of the Fifth Texas Infantry* (College Station: Texas A&M University Press, 2003), 67.

15. *OR* 12(2): 623; Evander Law, "The Virginia Campaign of 1862," *Philadelphia Weekly Press*, November 2, 1887; Stocker, *From Huntsville to Appomattox*, 55.

16. Hennessy, *Return to Bull Run*, 294–99; "Potomac," "Correspondence of the Southern Confederacy," *Atlanta Southern Confederacy*, October 11, 1862.

17. *OR* 12(2): 612; Hennessy, *Return to Bull Run*, 299.

18. *OR* 12(2): 605, 608, 612, 623; "Casualties among the South Carolina Troops," *Charleston Mercury*, September 12, 1862.

19. Lee claimed that the dead Yankees described by Hood as lying thick "like a bed of roses" after dark on August 29 were Zouaves. Although Hood's men did encounter a Zouave regiment on the evening of August 29, the description Lee offers is more likely from August 30, when the Texas Brigade inflicted heavy losses on another Zouave regiment, the 5th New York. Everett, *Chaplain Davis*, 113; *OR* 12(2): 598: Longstreet, *From Manassas to Appomattox*, 184; Hood, *Advance and Retreat*, 32; Law, "Virginia Campaign of 1862"; Gallagher, *Lee the Soldier*, 17.

20. Evander Law claimed that he told Wilcox after the evening attack on August 29 that the main Union line was intact and that attacking it in the morning would not be a good idea. Law claimed that Wilcox then went to Longstreet to get him to recall an order to attack the next morning. Cadmus Wilcox to Maj. G. M. Sorrel, October 14, 1862, Cadmus Wilcox Papers, Library of Congress; *Proceedings and Report of the Board of Army Officers*, 2:269; Longstreet, "Our March against Pope," 520; *OR* 12(2): 565, 605; Jeffry Wert, *General James Longstreet* (New York: Simon and Schuster, 1994), 171; Hennessy, *Return to Bull Run*, 303–4; Law, "Virginia Campaign of 1862."

21. Stone, "Reminiscences of the Second Battle of Manassas," 298; *OR* 12(2): 611; Skoch and Perkins, *Lone Star Confederate*, 69–70; Watters Berryman to mother, September 4, 1862, Berryman Collection, Historical Research Center, Texas Heritage Museum, Hill College, Hillsboro, TX; Andrew Erskine to wife, September 2, 1862, original in private possession, typescript copy provided by Rick Eiserman.

22. Hood, *Advance and Retreat*, 35; Hennessy, *Return to Bull Run*, 309–10.

23. *OR* 12 (2): 577; Hennessy, *Return to Bull Run*, 315–16.

24. During the second week of September 1862, Evans had Hood arrested over a disagreement regarding whose brigade should have possession of Federal ambulances captured by Hood's brigades at Second Manassas on August 30. *OR* 12(2): 628; Freeman, *Lee's Lieutenants*, 2:147; G. Moxley Sorrel, *Recollections of a Confederate Staff Officer* (1905; repr., Wilmington, NC: Broadfoot, 1991), 93. On Evans's drunkenness, see W. Eric Emerson and Karen Stokes, eds., *Faith, Valor and Devotion: The Civil War Letters of William Porcher DuBose* (Columbia: University of South Carolina Press, 2010), 114–15; on Hood's arrest by Evans, see Hood, *Advance and Retreat*, 38–39; and Everett, *Chaplain Davis*, 124–25. For Evans's claim that he continued during the 1862 Maryland campaign to command not only his own brigade but also the Texas and 3rd (Law's) Brigades, see *Proceedings of a General Court Martial in the Trial of Col. F. W. McMaster, 17th Regiment, S.C.V. Held at Wilmington, N.C., March 30th, 1863* (Columbia: South Carolinian Steam Press, 1863), 11, 76.

25. Polley, *Hood's Texas Brigade*, 83; *Proceedings and Report of the Board of Army Officers*, 2:122; Hood, *Advance and Retreat*, 36.

26. Law, "Virginia Campaign of 1862"; M. V. Smith, *Reminiscences of the Civil War* (n.p., n.d.), 16; Skoch and Perkins, *Lone Star Confederate*, 73; R. H. Leonard, "The Texians at Manassas," *Houston Tri-Weekly Telegraph*, November 28, 1862.

27. Hennessy, *Return to Bull Run*, 362–64.

28. Hood, *Advance and Retreat*, 36.

29. Robert E. L. Krick, *Staff Officers in Gray* (Chapel Hill: University of North Carolina Press, 2003), 262; Herman Leonard to Francis Wilshin, October 27, 1966, 5th Texas Regiment file, Historical Research Center, Texas Heritage Museum; "One of Hood's Staff," *New Orleans Daily Picayune*, November 2, 1879; John B. Hood to Gen. Samuel Cooper, March 14, 1862, Compiled Service Record of William Harvey Sellers, M331, National Archives.

30. Krick, *Staff Officers in Gray*, 8; *OR* 12(2), 608, 614; Skoch and Perkins, *Lone Star Confederate*, 69. For more on the role of assistant adjutant generals on the staff of generals, see J. Boone Bartholomes Jr., *Buff Facings and Gilt Buttons: Staff and Headquarters Operations in the Army of Northern Virginia, 1862–1865* (Columbia: University of South Carolina Press, 1998), 17–18, 26–27.

31. William T. Wofford to Hon. G. W. Randolph, Manassas, Bartow County, GA, November 12, 1862, Letters Received by the C.S. Secretary of War, 2220-W-1862, M474, National Archives.

32. *OR* 19(1): 924.

33. Agent Arthur H. Edey of the 5th Texas, writing from Richmond on September 8, 1862, claimed that Hood ordered a halt "for some wise reason" during the early stages of the attack on August 30 and that the 1st and 4th Texas "heard the order and stopped in a ravine." Polley, *Hood's Texas Brigade*, 84; *OR* 12 (2):613–14; A. H. Edey, Agency, 5th Texas Vol., Richmond, September 8, 1862, *Houston Tri-Weekly Telegraph*, October 3, 1862.

34. *OR* 1 (2): 617; Polley, *Hood's Texas Brigade*, 16–17; Mark Lemon, ed., *Feed Them the Steel! Being the Wartime Recollections of Capt. James Lile Lemon, Co. A, 18th Georgia Infantry, C.S.A.* (n.p., 2013), 31.

35. Skoch and Perkins, *Lone Star Confederate*, 74; "Potomac," "Correspondence of the Southern Confederacy" ; [unidentified member of Co. A, 5th Texas], Special Correspondence, Gordonsville, September 10, 1862, *Houston Tri-Weekly Telegraph*, September 29, 1862.

36. Hennessy, *Return to Bull Run*, 375–78; *OR* 12(2): 609, 615–16, 618. For an excellent tactical history of the battle on August 30, 1862, see Scott C. Patchan, *Second Manassas: Longstreet's Attack and the Struggle for Chinn Ridge* (Washington, DC: Potomac Books, 2011).

37. Hood, *Advance and Retreat*, 37; Harold B. Simpson, ed., *Touched with Valor: Civil War Papers and Casualty Reports of Hood's Texas Brigade* (Hillsboro, TX: Hill Junior College Press, 1964), 29; Harold B. Simpson, *Hood's Texas Brigade in Reunion and Memory* (Hillsboro, TX: Hill Junior College Press, 1974), 330; Berrien M. Zettler, *War Stories and School-Day Incidents for the Children* (New York: Neale, 1912), 107.

38. Herman Leonard to Francis Wilshin, October 27, 1966, Sellers file, Manassas National Battlefield Park Library, Manassas, VA.

39. Patchan, *Second Manassas*, 80–83; John J. Hennessy, *Historical Report of the Troop Movements for the Second Battle of Manassas, August 28 through August 30, 1862* (Denver: US Department of the Interior, National Park Service, Denver Service Center, 1985), 386, 419, 454, 497; *OR* 12 (2): 624; Stocker, *From Huntsville to Appomattox*, 58; [unidentified member of the 6th North Carolina Infantry], "The Late Battles," *Raleigh Standard*, September 10, 1862.

40. *OR* 12(2): 565, 606.

41. The 11th Mississippi Regiment suffered thirty-five total casualties on August 29 and fifty total casualties on August 30. *OR* 12(2): 606, 610, 618–19, 625; "The Battles of Manassas Plains," *Houston Tri-Weekly Telegraph*, September 29, 1862; "List of Killed and Wounded in Hampton Legion," *Charleston Daily Courier*, September 11, 1862; "Casualties" [11th Mississippi], *Richmond Semi-Weekly Enquirer*, September 12, 1862.

42. Polley, *Hood's Texas Brigade*, 135.

43. *OR* 19(1): 924.

44. Patchan, *Second Manassas*, 119; *OR* 12(2): 613–14.

45. Patchan, *Second Manassas*, 27, 28, 119; *OR* 1(2): 609, 615.

46. Ellsworth Marshall Rust, *Rust of Virginia* (Baltimore: Waverly Press, 1940), 206–7; John B. Hood to Samuel Cooper, Div. Head Quarters, November 5, 1862, Letters Received by the C.S. Adjutant and Inspector General, RG 109, 1998-H, National Archives.

47. *OR* 12(2): 618; Jerome Robertson, "Letter from Col. Robertson, Five Miles from Fairfax C.H., September 3, 1862," *Houston Tri-Weekly Telegraph*, September 29, 1862.

48. Lt. Col. Solon Z. Ruff et al., Winchester, VA, October 24, 1862, enclosure with letter from William T. Wofford to Hon. G. W. Randolph, Manassas, Bartow County, GA, November 12, 1862, Letters Received by the C.S. Secretary of War, 2220-W-1862, M474, National Archives.

49. Patchan, *Second Manassas*, 119–120; Quoted in Hood, *Advance and Retreat*, 19, 45–46.

A CARNIVAL OF HYPOCRISY

The Ordeal of Fitz John Porter

WILLIAM MARVEL

It was an uncomfortable hour at the White House on Wednesday afternoon, September 3, 1862, as Maj. Gen. John Pope told President Abraham Lincoln what he thought had gone wrong on the Bull Run battlefield. Even for someone more honest with himself than Pope was, it would have been difficult to accept responsibility for a defeat as humiliating as Pope had just suffered. Instead, as such men will, he ascribed it to the failures of others.

In Pope's self-serving narrative, Maj. Gen. Fitz John Porter had deliberately disobeyed Pope's order to attack Maj. Gen. Stonewall Jackson's retreating forces on August 29. He further alleged that Porter, as a surrogate of Maj. Gen. George B. McClellan, had passed up that golden opportunity solely to prevent Pope from succeeding where McClellan had not. As a result, Pope's army had been badly thrashed and driven from the field, retreating all the way to the defenses of Washington in disarray.

As he listened to Pope, the president worried as much about his political position as he did about the military situation. He had chosen Pope to command a new army composed of troops whom McClellan had expected for his operation against Richmond, and much of the Northern public held Lincoln responsible for forcing McClellan to abandon his campaign and transfer his army to Pope. At the same time, most of his cabinet members mistrusted McClellan enough to petition for his dismissal, and on September 2 Lincoln had exasperated them by naming McClellan to command all the forces defending Washington. He deemed McClellan the only man who could restore the fighting spirit of Pope's battered army, but he shared the suspicion of some cabinet members that McClellan had hesitated to help Pope at a critical moment. Frustrated by his squabbling generals, Lincoln invited Pope to take a criminal view of Porter's performance by introducing him to Porter's telegrams to Maj. Gen. Ambrose E. Burnside, which mocked Pope's arrogant orders and tactical confusion.[1]

Those telegrams gave Pope evidence, and Lincoln's willingness to share them gave him encouragement. The next morning, he read the president and Secretary of the Navy Gideon Welles a defensive report that Welles described as a "manifesto," throwing the responsibility for Bull Run on those Pope said undermined him. He demanded "immediate publication" of the report, accusing numerous generals of a determination to see him fail at whatever the cost to the country—with McClellan, Porter, and Maj. Gen. William B. Franklin foremost among them. On September 5 the cabinet discussed Pope's report, and all agreed that it should not be published, but in apparent concession to his disgruntled cabinet members the president ordered a court of inquiry into the conduct of Porter, Franklin, and one of Porter's brigade commanders, Brig. Gen. Charles Griffin. Lincoln wrote the entire order himself, charging the court with determining whether those three and their commands were "in the battle," and if not, why.[2]

The focus fell on Porter, a career soldier from a family in which, for three generations, the men had always chosen military service as the path out of poverty and obscurity. He graduated eighth in the West Point class of 1845, winning brevets in Mexico and plaudits everywhere. He and McClellan had been close before the war and almost inseparable from the moment McClellan took command of the Army of the Potomac. When the clamor for emancipation began to color military operations in political tones, McClellan came to represent the conservative element, which made him the particular target of Radical Republican animosity. Because of their close association, Porter provided an excellent proxy for those who wanted to "get" McClellan.

To deflect blame for the loss at Second Bull Run, Maj. Gen. John Pope insisted that Maj. Gen. Fitz John Porter had deliberately disobeyed orders on August 29, 1862. (Library of Congress Prints and Photographs Division, reproduction number LC-DIG-ppmsca-32300)

Lincoln needed McClellan at that juncture, so he ordered no inquiry into his conduct. As McClellan prepared to pursue the Confederates invading Maryland, he asked the president to temporarily suspend the proceedings against Porter, Franklin, and Griffin, and they were returned to duty. The court of inquiry was quietly adjourned, and the question subsided for all but Porter. Charges were resurrected against him when the military crisis had passed and when prosecuting him presented more political advantage than liability.[3]

The administration had fared badly in the state elections of 1862, which ran from March through early November. The preliminary emancipation proclamation, the suspension of habeas corpus, and government repression of the ensuing dissent had led to a conservative backlash against Republican candidates for Congress and the state legislatures. Disaffection also afflicted the army, where many felt tricked into fighting a war of abolition under the guise of preserving the Union. Officers were already leaving the service over it, often expressing their dissatisfaction in their letters of resignation.[4]

Even an indirect assault on the conservative McClellan clique would have worsened damage at the polls, if launched prematurely. Prosecuting Porter might pin the Bull Run disaster on something besides Lincoln's interference in military operations in Virginia and could disguise the incompetence of the president's apparent pet, Pope. Creating the impression that Porter had acted from treasonable motives—a common Radical Republican strategy for discrediting Democratic generals—would help discredit the conservative element generally and signal the inauguration of a crackdown on officers critical of government policy. It simply had to wait until after the last state election, in New York, on November 4.[5]

Lincoln removed McClellan from command of the Army of the Potomac on November 5, replacing him with Burnside. In the same order he relieved Porter of command of the Fifth Corps and ordered him to Washington, where newspapers speculated that he had finally come to answer charges of failing to support Pope at Bull Run. A legally questionable military commission was directed to determine whether charges against him were warranted, but it was quickly dissolved in favor of a court-martial appointed to try him on specific charges.[6] General-in-Chief Henry Halleck's signature appeared on the order, but a War Department insider deduced that Secretary of War Edwin Stanton had selected the generals to sit on the court—and with the aim of securing a conviction.[7]

In its final configuration, the court consisted entirely of men with personal or political reasons to vote for conviction. Maj. Gen. David Hunter, who would preside, had proven himself Radical to the core. Brig. Gen. James A. Garfield, a disciple and house guest of Treasury secretary Salmon P. Chase, had imbibed Chase's antipathy for the McClellan faction and had accepted Maj. Gen. Irvin McDowell's assurances of Porter's guilt, but he disguised his prejudice instead of recusing himself.[8] Brig. Gen. Silas Casey resented Porter for having him removed from command of a division in Porter's corps—a grievance both Stanton and the president knew about.[9]

The court included two old generals whom Stanton knew well. Halleck dutifully prejudiced one of them, and Secretary Chase worked on the other.[10] Glaring conflicts of interest should have disqualified another pair of generals from the court, because both had played dubious roles at Second Bull Run, and Porter's conviction would distract from their shortcomings. One of them, who was accused by two officers of drinking heavily during the battle, would also serve as a prosecution witness.[11]

The eighth court member was reliably Republican.[12] When the ninth member raised a legal question about his appointment, he was promptly replaced by Brig. Gen. John P. Slough, whom a schoolmate described as "a warm personal friend of Secretary Stanton."[13]

The government prosecutor would be Joseph Holt, a crony of Stanton's from James Buchanan's administration whose appointment Stanton had secured for the new position of judge advocate general. It was probably no coincidence that Holt was installed on the very day Pope first complained about McClellan and Porter.[14]

The court convened on November 27, 1862, in rooms over a restaurant on Fourteenth Street, near the corner of Pennsylvania Avenue. The prosecution waited for Pope to reach the capital from his new post west of the Mississippi and didn't provide Porter with a copy of the charges against him until December 1. The trial began December 3, and at the outset Porter was asked if he had any objection to any member of the court. The court had not yet shown its unanimous hostility, and Porter did not yet have McClellan's opinion that Hunter was hostile. Nor did he know anything about the influence that cabinet members had exerted on three other members, or Slough's friendship with Stanton. He may have considered it imprudent to admit having spurned General Casey as a subordinate. The order establishing the court also hinted broadly that objections would be frowned upon, carrying the unusual (and patently false) assertion that "no other officers than those named can be assembled without manifest injury to the service." Porter's attorneys, the nationally renowned defense lawyer Reverdy Johnson and Harvard-trained Charles Eames, probably advised against any challenges, and he made none.[15]

Still, Porter must have recognized enough political and personal hostility on the court to suspect an engineered verdict. He asked that the trial be open to the public, ostensibly to counteract prejudicial newspaper speculation but actually to avoid the absolute secrecy of the star-chamber proceeding he anticipated. Hunter cleared the room for secret "deliberation" when any question arose, including this simple request, yet Holt finally announced that the court would remain open "in accordance with the custom of the service."[16]

Holt's charges included a surprise. All official correspondence thus far had indicated that Porter was the subject of accusations made by Pope, but the court-martial charges were signed by Brig. Gen. Benjamin S. Roberts, of Pope's staff. Holt, or Stanton, must have detected late in the game that the Articles of War required the president to appoint the members of any court-martial if the accusations against an officer were made by the commander of his army. If the charges were Pope's, Porter could have challenged the legality of the court.[17]

Roberts was not known for his probity, having resigned from the army in 1839 to avoid a court-martial over thousands of dollars in missing federal funds in his custody. Reappointed during the Mexican War, he was later court-martialed and dismissed for negligence of duty and assorted frauds and fabrications, only to be immediately reinstated through political connections.[18] Along with Lt. Col. Thomas C. H. Smith, one of Pope's aides, Roberts was surreptitiously acting as Pope's prosecutorial assistant in the action against Porter. The composition of Stanton's court provided the best assurance of a conviction, so Roberts had assumed the role of accuser to save Holt from trying the case before a new court that might show a semblance of impartiality. Ten weeks before, Pope had vowed to push the charges if he could, and in testimony before Congress three years later he took full credit for bringing Porter "to justice," but under oath at the trial he denied any connection to the prosecution. Clearly, Holt, Pope, and Roberts had colluded on this deceit, which would prove typical of the prosecutorial cabal.[19]

Fixing the blame for Bull Run on Porter would relieve everyone from Pope to the president of responsibility, and Holt relied heavily on the tacit bias of these particular generals to win a conviction. Porter's attorneys objected that charges filed by a member of Pope's personal staff amounted to Pope's own action, but Holt avoided that point, simply noting that Pope was not mentioned anywhere in the order for the court-martial. That was enough for the court, and after another secret discussion the nine generals overruled the objection—just as they would overrule every single defense objection over the next five weeks, and often with flagrantly contradictory reasoning. Reverdy Johnson later characterized the court's evidentiary rulings as "so superlatively absurd as to almost destroy every hope of justice." That he qualified such hopelessness at all, after witnessing the court's manifest determination to hobble the defense and aid the prosecution, may have implied a hope for an objective review of the proceedings by Lincoln.[20]

Holt employed an early example of the prosecutorial trick of "charge stacking," or piling on multiple charges for a single alleged transgression, in hopes of finding guilt somewhere. He alleged that Porter had violated two separate Articles of War, enumerating nine separate specifications, and a conviction on any of the specifications warranted a death sentence under military law. Porter was not insensible to that peril.[21]

First, Holt charged Porter with violating the Ninth Article of War by disobeying an order in the face of the enemy. The first specification involved the technically true allegation that Porter had not marched to Bristoe Station on August 28 at the precise hour Pope had specified: because of the fatigue of his men and the darkness of the night, Porter had delayed his departure by two hours, with no practical impact on operations. The second and third specifications alleged disobedience of Pope's notorious "Joint Order" for Porter and McDowell to march to Gainesville on August 29 and block the imagined retreat of Stonewall Jackson—which the presence of Maj. Gen. James Longstreet's corps prevented, although Pope and his apologists obstinately denied it. McDowell had failed to comply with that order, too, yet no charges were preferred against him, and he was going to testify for the prosecution. The fourth and fifth specifications were improvised from a single incident in which two of Porter's brigades lost their way on an early morning march on August 30 and missed that day's fighting. Each brigade was listed in a separate charge of disobeying Pope's order for Porter to appear on the field with "your command."

The second charge, under the Fifty-Second Article of War, was the more distressing to Porter, because it was the article commonly applied to officers who showed cowardice on the battlefield. Once again, Holt contrived multiple specifications from the single charge that Porter failed to undertake an assault on the Gainesville Road called for by Pope in a 4:30 p.m. order on August 29. The first specification merely noted that the attack had been ordered and that Porter had not made it. The second added the false allegation that instead of attacking when ordered, Porter had retreated. The third specification simply inflated the inaccuracy of the second, charging that Porter had "shamefully" retreated all the way to Manassas Junction.

Holt had composed an even more ludicrous fourth specification under the second charge, claiming that Porter's August 30 assault on Jackson's line at the Deep Cut had failed because he waited too long and wielded too little force. Continuing an insinuation of deliberate negligence in favor of the enemy, Holt also suggested that Porter had made little effort to rally his troops after they were repulsed. The casualties from Porter's assault and the part his troops played in blunting Longstreet's flank attack belied every word of the specification, for which Holt announced that he would offer no proof. He had apparently composed it solely for newspaper regurgitation, and by the sly trick of calling no witnesses to prove it, he deprived the defense of any chance for rebuttal.[22]

Pope took the stand on December 4. He did well enough responding to friendly questions from Holt, but in cross-examination Reverdy Johnson began tripping him up almost immediately. Johnson focused on whether Porter had offered explanations for his digressions from orders and whether Pope had expressed his satisfaction with them. Pope declared that it was "quite impossible that I could have been satisfied," yet he could not categorically deny that he had told Porter he was satisfied. He did recall talking with Porter at Fairfax Court House on September 2, during the retreat to Washington, after Porter had received an odd telegram from McClellan, asking him to give Pope all the support he would give McClellan. Correctly assuming that such a superfluous appeal must have resulted from some defensive communication of Pope's, Porter confronted Pope over it at his headquarters, asking what insinuations Pope had made to suggest he was not already offering his full support. After initial denials, Pope conceded that he was unhappy with Porter for disregarding his attack order of 4:30 p.m. on August 29. He was also aggravated that Griffin's brigade had not come to the battlefield with Porter on August 30; he made no reference to another much smaller brigade, which also went astray.[23]

Sometime during the meeting, Pope revealed that he knew Porter thought poorly of him. That raised the question of whether his dislike had moved Porter to deliberately undermine Pope's success. In July, Porter had written disparagingly about Pope to one Joseph Kennedy, in Washington, and Pope had seen it. Porter expressed regret at Kennedy's violation of his confidentiality but did not disavow the sentiments in the letter, which ridiculed Pope's arrogant orders and his disdain for military precautions (besides calling him "an ass"). Porter explained that he diverged from Pope's 4:30 order because the enemy outflanked him that evening, instead of the other way around, and the order had arrived just before dark. Griffin, meanwhile, had simply lost his way. According to Pope's chief of staff, Col. George Ruggles, who happened to be in the room, the conversation lasted about twenty minutes, and at its conclusion Pope said Porter's explanations were satisfactory except about Griffin's brigade.[24]

Ruggles did not hear all the details of their talk, but a few days later Pope confirmed much of it. He asked Ruggles to act as his principal witness against

Porter on a charge of disobedience of orders, admitting that he did not wish to appear in such a trial. Ruggles declined, reminding Pope of his earlier assurance that he accepted Porter's explanations.[25]

In his testimony to the court, Pope contradicted both Porter and Ruggles, insisting that he was entirely dissatisfied. When asked about his overtures to Ruggles on the subject of charges against Porter and Ruggles's reminder of his purported satisfaction, Pope professed to recall no such discussion. The mention of Ruggles did seem to stir some nervous reflection, however, and finally Pope conceded that he probably told Porter he would take no action against him. Johnson pounced on that, asking how Pope could possibly have hesitated to press charges if he believed that his army had suffered a terrible defeat and the national capital had been exposed to capture because Porter had disobeyed his orders. Recognizing that Johnson had just trapped him into admitting either that he had pressed the charges or that he had not considered Porter's conduct criminal, Pope refused to answer. Hunter came to his aid, ejecting everyone but Holt and the court members, and when the doors reopened Holt announced that the question had been disallowed as irrelevant. The defense had already prepared a written objection, pointing out that the question was directly relevant to Pope's credibility: if he was as dissatisfied on September 2 as he claimed, he was criminally negligent in not filing charges against Porter then and there. On receipt of that objection Hunter cleared the courtroom again; after another closed-door huddle, everyone went home with Holt's promise of a decision on the objection in the morning.[26]

That evening Pope sent Holt a note urging him to bring Benny Roberts to the stand so he could assist Holt through the rest of the trial, but Holt's immediate concern was the contradiction that had been left hanging that afternoon. Before court on December 5, he and Pope developed a plausible rationale for his failure to immediately file charges for Porter's supposedly destructive disobedience.[27]

As the trial resumed, Pope asked permission to answer the question the court had ruled irrelevant. That apparent challenge to the court's judgment immediately precipitated another secret conference. Behind closed doors Holt may have summarized the answer, which would reduce the force of the defense's point, and the question was allowed.[28]

Porter's dispatches to Burnside now came into play. In a long soliloquy based on what "I now remember," Pope maintained that they were the disparaging correspondence he had mentioned to Porter at Fairfax Court House, rather than the Kennedy letter, which he had seen in July. Perhaps to avoid naming the cabinet officer who showed him Kennedy's letter, Pope claimed he knew about the Burnside dispatches by September 2, before he could have seen them. It was clearly a conscious substitution, rather than a lapse of memory, for he spoke of the correspondence in the plural except for one accidental allusion to it as "a letter." Porter apologized for it, said Pope, adding that the apology was what he was "satisfied" with. He had no intention of letting Porter's disobedience go unreported, at least insofar as giving the government the information it needed to pursue a case against him, and he had accomplished that in his report.

"I have not preferred charges against him," Pope mendaciously insisted. "I have merely set forth the facts in my official reports." Moments later he changed his story again, testifying that it was after his return to Washington that the president apprised him of the Burnside dispatches—which, Lincoln remarked, had left him fearing that Porter "would fail to do his duty." The dispatches themselves "opened my eyes," Pope said, and persuaded him that Porter's failures on the field had been deliberate. At Fairfax Court House he had not suspected calculated sabotage and for that reason had told Porter he would take no action against him.[29]

Notwithstanding the inconsistency about when Pope first saw the dispatches, the defense went on to other subjects. Johnson's inquiries revealed that Pope knew almost nothing of Porter's position on the battlefield, which he could not pinpoint on a map. Several times Johnson asked Pope to say whether Porter would have been disobedient if the tactical situation had been different from what Pope supposed and had made it imprudent to carry out an order to attack. Would it have constituted disobedience if some of Porter's troops went astray without his knowledge when he was ordered to the field with his corps? Each time, a member of the court objected, initiating another secret deliberation, but the questions were always disallowed because they required an opinion. Yet Holt had been allowed to ask Pope what he thought would have happened had Porter obeyed the August 29 attack order, and despite his ignorance of that part of the battlefield Pope had insisted "we should have destroyed the army of Jackson." This began a carnival of hypocrisy in which opinions likely to be detrimental to Porter were always relevant and admissible, while those that might help his case never were. Before the end of the trial, the defense attorneys found it so fruitless to point out the inconsistency that they ceased to even offer objections.[30]

The undisguised prejudice of the court's decisions might have caught the public eye had newspapers covered the case more closely, but most included only summaries or disconnected excerpts, selected or edited for the desired political slant. Stanton had also handpicked a military commission to look for dirt on Maj. Gen. Don Carlos Buell, another McClellan associate and suspected conservative, and the concurrent proceedings competed for editorial attention.[31]

Benny Roberts took the stand the day after Pope was excused. Like Pope, he conceded that he knew nothing about the ground or the resistance Porter had faced on August 29. Despite that admitted ignorance, Holt asked Roberts what he thought would have happened if Porter had attacked as Pope desired in his 4:30 p.m. order. Not yet comprehending the unmitigated audacity of the court's bias, Porter's lawyers jumped to object, to no avail. Hunter cleared the room again, and when he reopened the proceedings Holt decreed that the question would be answered, offering no explanation for that extraordinary contradiction of the previous day's ruling on opinions.

"I do not doubt at all," Roberts obligingly responded, "that it would have resulted in the defeat, if not in the capture, of the main army of the Confederates that were on the field at the time." Soon afterward, he also insisted that Porter should have launched an assault long before he received the 4:30 order. Eames pointed out that the joint order remained in effect until the 4:30 order was received and required Porter to hold himself ready throughout the afternoon of August 29 to withdraw across Bull Run. Did that not explain his failure to attack earlier in the afternoon? Eames asked. A member of the court objected, and that question, which undermined Roberts's last accusative assertion, was not allowed. Eames rephrased it, but that raised an objection as well.[32]

Most of the objections probably came from Garfield—who, in Porter's estimation, "played the part of Judge Advocate." Garfield surely understood that his own prominence in the effort to convict Porter would reflect badly on him if it became known, and he spent the next fifteen years blocking all Porter's attempts at vindication. When the case was finally reviewed and Porter was exonerated, Garfield led a crusade to deny him even token restoration.[33]

Capt. Douglass Pope, the general's nephew and aide, was called to show that he delivered the 4:30 attack order early enough that Porter had plenty of daylight for the operation, and he testified that he put it in Porter's hands "by 5 o'clock." One of Porter's division commanders and two staff officers all concurred that the order arrived a good hour and a half later than Captain Pope insisted. Four weeks later, after the defense rested, Holt introduced Charles Duffee, who said he had ridden with Captain Pope to deliver the order, and he estimated that it took them "about an hour" to reach Porter with the order, or at least as late as 5:30. Duffee turned out to have served under Pope's other agent in the prosecution, Smith, who later approached other former subordinates, asking them to offer similar corroboration on this point.[34]

Smith himself presented the most ridiculous testimony in the trial. His principal contribution at this stage of Porter's ordeal was to recount his first and only interview with Porter and to share the incredible powers of intuition he claimed, by which he instantly concluded that Porter was a traitor. According to Smith, he met Porter near Bristoe Station on August 28 to discuss ammunition Porter had requested. Testifying to a comment that sounded suspiciously similar to one of Porter's sarcastic telegrams to Burnside, Smith implied that Porter ridiculed Pope's frantically fluctuating orders. Porter's "sneering manner" persisted in an aside about Pope taking care of his wounded from the Bristoe fight, Smith added, and it instantly persuaded him that Porter would "fail" Pope.

"I had one of those clear convictions," Smith said, "that a man has a few times, perhaps, in his life, as to the character and purposes of a person whom he sees for the first time." He said he told Pope that evening, "I was so certain that Fitz John Porter was a traitor, that I would shoot him that night, so far as any crime before God was concerned, if the law would allow me to do it."[35]

Holt solicited further clairvoyance from Smith when he asked what would have happened had Porter attacked the enemy between five and six o'clock on the afternoon of August 29. Given the court's previous rejections of opinions, the defense tried once again to object, but despite his lack of military training and minimal experience, Smith was allowed to respond. He acknowledged his ignorance of conditions and troop dispositions on Porter's front, prompting another objection on grounds of admitted incompetence, but the court insisted on an answer. Smith said an attack by Porter would have routed the enemy.[36]

The defense questioned Smith closely on his professed ability to deduce Porter's thoughts by his speech. Smith painted Porter's attitude as a "general indifference in regard to the success of General Pope in that campaign." Yet they never discussed Pope or the campaign itself, so how could Smith recognize the sneering if Porter's manner was consistently courteous? Smith offered no explanation except to repeat his observation that Porter evinced "a sneering, indifferent manner and tone," but later he retracted even that, somewhat. "As for the sneering," he added finally, "it was somewhat suppressed." That, with Porter's probable sarcasm about Pope's frenetic movements, led Smith to conclude that "General Porter was determined so far not to cooperate as to force us back to Washington." Before leaving the stand, Smith added that Porter's facial expression also identified him as a traitor, lending him the appearance of "a man with a crime on his mind."[37]

Neither John Pope nor Benny Roberts enjoyed a reputation for veracity among fellow officers in the old army, and Smith would later engage in active deception on Pope's behalf, to help deter Porter from restoring his reputation. All their predictions of Porter's treachery and testimony about his inscrutably incriminating manner sustained a scheme to manufacture a case around the disparaging Burnside dispatches. Certainly, Porter held Pope in contempt as an arrogant incompetent, as did many others, but Holt meant to bend that disdain into proof that Porter sacrificed a battle to deny Pope victory.

McDowell, whose court of inquiry was meeting in the same building, testified primarily to his encounter with Porter near noon on August 29, as Porter was deploying to attack what turned out to be Longstreet's advance. Porter quickly deduced that McDowell intended to veil his own mistakes by withholding the exculpatory testimony Porter had expected. Although defense witnesses described McDowell discouraging Porter from that attack, McDowell portrayed Porter as reluctant to fight. His memory served him conveniently, and one of Porter's staff officers found McDowell's testimony "directly opposite to what he said to General Porter at the time." McDowell could not "recollect" telling Porter he was too far out for an independent attack, instead contending that he expected him to make one.[38]

Holt asked McDowell the now-routine question of what would have happened if Porter "had thrown himself upon the right wing of the enemy" as Pope wished, and by now the defense knew it was pointless to object. "I think it would have been decisive in our favor," McDowell replied, cautioning that it was "a mere opinion."[39]

While McDowell was on the stand, the Army of the Potomac took a severe beating under Burnside at Fredericksburg. As Northerners gradually became conscious of how thorough the defeat was and how lopsided the losses were for the Union army, the Lincoln administration again began to feel the pressure of public disapproval. By New Year's, even friendlier newspapers were growing critical of what seemed like bungling interference by the administration. It appeared that withdrawing McClellan from before Richmond and sending his army to Pope had precipitated disaster and that replacing McClellan with Burnside had consigned the army to seemingly useless slaughter. The January 3 issue of *Harper's Weekly* bore a savage back-page cartoon of Columbia pointing an accusing finger at Lincoln, a cringing Stanton, and a befuddled Halleck, demanding, "Where are my 15,000

Sons—murdered at Fredericksburg?" Burnside had told Lincoln and Stanton that he would write a letter taking the blame on himself, and Stanton badgered him to hurry up and get it published.[40]

Stanton also goaded Hunter's court to haste for the same reason: he and the president needed news that would shift the responsibility for military failures from their own shoulders. Two days after the *Harper's Weekly* cartoon appeared, Stanton sent Hunter a note complaining that the trial had lasted more than four weeks, insisting that he hurry it to a conclusion "without any unnecessary delay." McDowell's court of inquiry was then in its seventh week and would continue for six more weeks without any prodding from Stanton, but Stanton declared that "the state of the service" demanded a speedy conclusion to Porter's trial.[41]

Five days later, Porter's attorneys read their 25,000-word defense summary to the court. So superfluous did that formality seem to General Garfield that he wrote his mother a letter while it was being read, without being reprimanded. Holt knew the court was with him, as the biased evidentiary rulings revealed: so certain was he that he declined to submit a prosecutorial summation, ostensibly to avoid delay.

That afternoon, when the reading of the defense was done, the generals and Holt sequestered themselves and decided the nine specifications, finding Porter guilty of everything but losing the two errant brigades; they edited a couple of specifications so they could still find him guilty of those, although in one instance the editing eliminated any criminality. Despite later blustering, they probably never seriously considered a sentence of death, which might have aroused sympathy and outrage without advancing the political goals of the trial. Except for Holt and Hunter, the court members also may have shied from what many of them must have recognized, at least subliminally, as judicial murder. Conviction alone served the purposes of the prosecution, but conviction on such serious charges did require at least peremptory dismissal for the sake of credibility. One court member suggested adding a prohibition against ever "holding any office of trust or profit under the Government of the United States," and his colleagues agreed. Those recommendations went to the White House with some 900 manuscript pages of trial transcript. A printed copy of the prosecution testimony may have accompanied it: Pope's confederates had published it for prejudicial distribution before the defense ever called a witness, and Holt would use it in the future to sway doubters and stymie Porter's petitions for reconsideration.[42]

There was no appeal process for courts-martial. A defendant's only hope for redress lay with the judge advocate general and the president, each of whom was supposed to review the case after trial for factual, logical, or legal flaws and bias. Lincoln therefore directed Holt to "revise" the record, by which he obviously meant for him to "review" it and provide a summary. Even if Holt had not been so committed to obtaining a conviction, his competency for reviewing the case was already compromised because he had abdicated his role as judge advocate general to serve as prosecutor. Rather than examining a subordinate's conduct for errors and improprieties, he would be judging his own, and Joseph Holt never admitted a mistake unless the only alternative explanation was outright corruption. Instead of a summary, he finally composed what amounted to the prosecution argument he had deemed unnecessary for the court.[43]

Focusing intently on the assertions of the government witnesses and belittling the contradictions exposed by the defense, Holt presented Lincoln with the most damning indictment possible. Knowing the president's annoyance at Porter's disdainful dispatches to Burnside, he focused on the "animus" against Pope contained in those messages and on the affinity for McClellan that they confirmed. Turning next to the putative predictions by Roberts and Smith that Porter would fail Pope, he paid particular attention to Smith's alleged intuition that Porter was a traitor. Praising that sixth sense as an "intercommunication of spirits," Holt begged the president to credit Smith's description of the defendant as "a man having a crime on his mind." McDowell had only an "impression" that he had not told Lt. Col. Frederick T. Locke, Porter's chief of staff, that Porter should remain where he was, but Holt inflated that to a positive denial. He included all the solicited opinions that an attack by Porter would have crushed the enemy. Complimenting the court for dismissing the specifications over the two brigades that went astray, he congratulated the generals (and himself, by implication) for dismissing the preposterous final specification, which he had fabricated from whole cloth. That, he contended, showed that the court was determined to find Porter guilty only of charges for which there was "the clearest and most convincing proof."[44]

Holt knew that the president suffered from a broad streak of gullibility, and he had it from a good source. Barely a year before, Lincoln's old friend Joshua Speed had apprised Holt privately that Lincoln was "so honest himself that he is slow to believe that others are not equally so." Holt therefore sent his jaundiced condensation of the case to the White House with confidence that it would be accepted as a good-faith summary of the proceedings.[45]

Lincoln himself carried some prejudice into the case. He had given Pope the evidence to aid his plea of treachery and had ordered the first investigation. The trial had barely begun and no charges were yet defined when the president let it slip that he considered Porter guilty, yet he held the final responsibility for making certain the court-martial had been fair. So trusting a man might have found it difficult to imagine his war minister and judge advocate general manipulating the process, or that they could find nine generals sufficiently biased to partake in a judicial travesty. The discriminatory rulings on evidence would have stood out had he read the trial transcript; the emphasis on Smith's mind reading should have caught the eye of a lawyer as experienced as Lincoln anyway, but the president's incentive for scrutinizing the decision was not enhanced by the political cover it gave him. If it were established that Pope had been betrayed, that would absolve him of responsibility for his defeat, which in turn would relieve Lincoln of blame for scuttling McClellan's campaign in favor of Pope's. Insinuating double-dealing by Porter would also provoke suspicion about McClellan's own loyalty, lending an air of prudence to his removal, even if Burnside had failed miserably. With the Army of the Potomac engaged in its infamous Mud March, and another controversial change in commanders looming only four days away, Lincoln scrawled his approval of the proceedings, verdict, and sentence. With that, Porter's career was ruined.[46]

With Porter's conviction, McClellan and those around him had been stained with treason, at least in the eyes of those who did not doubt the honesty of their government. The trial provided the administration with an excuse for Bull Run and a measure of absolution for Fredericksburg, and it gave the Republican Party enough political ammunition to survive every election for the rest of the war.

Without income and in debt for his lawyers' fees, Porter went to New York to live in the home of his wife's aunt. While many Democrats doubted his guilt, he was scorned as a traitor by much of the public and many of his old friends. Pope's coterie and his Radical Republican allies colluded to cultivate that impression, distributing the 131-page booklet of prosecution testimony to congressmen and discouraging them from publishing a complete transcript. Partisan interest in associating Porter with disloyalty increased as McClellan's popularity among Democrats rose, so the editorial assaults on him escalated with the beginning of the annual state election cycle in March 1863. Those attacks continued unabated through the New York election in November, subsided through the winter, and resumed with renewed ferocity the next year, when McClellan became the Democratic candidate for president.[47]

Not until 1866 did Porter begin actively compiling evidence to support a request for a rehearing. That spring, William Swinton's history of the Army of the Potomac appeared. Swinton, a war correspondent for the *New York Times*, had written a hatchet job on McClellan for the 1864 presidential campaign, but his book used new information in a fairly objective review of battles he had covered during the war. His chapter on Second Bull Run dismantled the crux of the government case against Porter, confirming his assertion that Longstreet's corps had stood squarely before him when Pope ordered him to attack Jackson's supposedly vulnerable flank. Maps, drawn by one of Pope's own former staff officers, contradicted the claims of Pope, Roberts, Smith, and McDowell that Porter could have fallen on the Rebel flank and rear all day on August 29. Footnoted references to newly available Confederate reports of the battle corroborated defense testimony that enemy forces "covered Porter's whole front."[48]

Swinton's book drew immediate journalistic attention for the vindication this afforded Porter. Longstreet and Robert E. Lee both confirmed for Porter that plenty of Confederate troops faced him all afternoon on August 29 and that his smaller force should have been "destroyed" had he attacked. The book also drew criticism from the Radical press, which dubbed Swinton a "Copperhead Historian."[49]

Porter began seeking evidence about the more conspicuous mendacity in the prosecution testimony and collecting information about enemy dispositions at Bull Run from former Confederates he had known in the old army, such as Lee. With the publication of flattering, exculpatory articles on his conduct at Bull Run, he gathered recommendations from several sympathetic Republicans and sent President Andrew Johnson a petition for a rehearing. It sat unanswered for months. After the president suspended Stanton from the war office and appointed Ulysses Grant interim secretary, Porter pressed for an answer, asking Grant for an impartial commission of army officers. Holt learned of it immediately, alerting Pope, but he managed to quash the appeal by himself. Disingenuously asserting that the Confederate testimony proved nothing, Holt presented Grant with a long argument characterizing any reconsideration or retrial as "improper." Holt's vitriolic literary style was also evident in a derogatory article on Porter's appeal that appeared simultaneously in the Republican organ the *Washington Chronicle*.[50]

Porter's first gambit at a rehearing only made his road to restoration more difficult. It afforded his political enemies in Congress another opportunity for malicious grandstanding, and it moved James Garfield to interpose another impediment. As a congressman from Ohio, Garfield introduced a bill requiring Senate approval for any cashiered officer reappointed to the army, which he brazenly denied having aimed at Porter. The bill passed.[51]

Porter's appeal was lost in the chaos of Edwin Stanton's restoration to the War Department, his dismissal, and Johnson's impeachment. Not until Grant assumed the presidency did Porter try again, forwarding the request to him through the new general-in-chief of the army, William T. Sherman. Pope learned of this petition, too, and compiled a rebuttal he called his "Brief Statement of the Case of Fitz John Porter." Illustrated with a map drawn by Thomas C. H. Smith that depicted his own fantasy of Confederate troop positions at Bull Run on August 29, it included distorted excerpts from the report of Stonewall Jackson to "prove" Pope's case. Using Jackson's account of the fierce pressure he faced while he was under attack by Porter on August 30, Pope mispresented it as Jackson's situation on the afternoon of August 29, when Porter had disregarded Pope's order to attack. Lest some careful eye detect that fairly obvious manipulation of the evidence, he gave it only to Grant, his secretary of war, and Sherman. Had he not also sent a copy to Garfield, who shared it with a newspaper, its fraudulence might never have been exposed.[52]

Not many years before, Holt had shown a decided readiness to suborn perjury in an effort to connect the Confederate government to Lincoln's assassination, and he returned to that practice to sink Porter's latest appeal. In a subtle hint to William Blair Lord, who had acted as his recorder at Porter's court-martial, Holt wrote to ask whether Lord remembered telling him during the trial that Porter had admitted his guilt to Lord in a private moment. Holt explained that it would be wonderful if Lord had a written record of that recollection and if he could supply a witness to the admission. Lord provided both, with a copy of a letter to his wife and a former *New York Times* reporter's corroboration of a story that later disintegrated under cross-examination. During a break in the trial, Lord and the reporter had ostensibly accompanied Porter to his quarters (which neither of them was able to locate or describe accurately), where he supposedly admitted to them, "I warn't loyal to Pope." Holt kept their identities secret for the moment, but he revealed the anonymous allegation to Porter's stubborn and malicious political enemy Sen. Zachariah Chandler, who publicized it on the Senate floor.[53]

That first petition to Grant also went unanswered. Two years into Grant's second term, Porter submitted another, and Grant gave it to his secretary of war, who in turn inevitably asked the opinion of Holt. On Pope's behalf, Thomas C. H. Smith came to the capital to help prepare a report that predictably discouraged any action, and Grant decided to do nothing with the appeal.[54]

Not until fifteen years after his dismissal did Porter realize a glimmer of hope. His friend and neighbor Theodore Randolph, Democratic senator from New Jersey, presented another petition and a growing file of documentation to President Rutherford B. Hayes in the last days of 1877. Hayes warned that he, too, was biased against Porter from his own experience with the Army of the Potomac in 1862, but he came to a decision that may have evinced an effort to ease the animosities of the war years. On his orders, the War Department created a board of officers in April 1878 to review the Porter case.[55]

Most of the testimony would be taken at West Point. The superintendent, Maj. Gen. John M. Schofield, would chair the board, which would include Brig. Gen. Alfred H. Terry and Col. George W. Getty. Getty was the only one Porter really knew: both had served in the 4th Artillery together, and, as a subordinate of Porter's, Getty had earned complimentary remarks from him on the Peninsula. Terry would have been a stranger, but his wartime correspondence revealed that he had been no friend to the McClellan clique, although he admitted that recent articles had caused him to question his early bias against Porter. Porter may have known Schofield as a cadet, and Schofield remembered Porter—perhaps mistakenly—for having treated him harshly in a cadet court-martial.[56]

Although the board lacked judicial authority, testimony was taken under oath and was subject to cross-examination. The government was represented by Judge Advocate Asa Bird Gardner, a Tammany Hall creature whom Theodore Roosevelt would later fire for apparent corruption as New York City's district attorney. Porter could ill afford it, but he hired three lawyers to conduct his side of the examinations, and they demolished much of the original trial testimony as well as discredited new testimony supplied on behalf of Pope. Pope resisted appearing as a government witness, which would have subjected his inconsistent narrative to the perils of cross-examination, and Gardner strove to preserve Pope's version of events. With his help, Pope avoided having to take the stand.[57]

Despite hosts of new witnesses, the government's original case gradually collapsed under the weight of manifestly false testimony on even the most minor details. Porter had claimed that one reason he failed to march from Bristoe Station at 1:00 a.m. on August 28 was the intense darkness, which was proved by the testimony of Porter's witness and by exposing the perjury of Gardner's. Smith showed up with a new story to dispute that point, recounting a reconnaissance he made that night that he had never previously mentioned, on which he said he had no trouble finding his way. Gardner seated numerous other witnesses who swore they remembered adequate light that night, but none of whom could recall how light any other night had been or satisfactorily explain why they remembered that particular one.[58]

Joseph Choate, one of Porter's lawyers, began breaking Smith down on his claim to have seen a crime in Porter's eyes, but Schofield asked why he bothered. Choate said that Holt and President Lincoln had evidently credited Smith's telepathic talent, and he had to assume the board would, too. Schofield, who obviously concurred in the absurdity of Smith's claim, simply replied that Choate's inquiry was unnecessary.[59]

In a break between sessions, Smith took Douglass Pope and his courier Duffee back to the Bull Run battlefield to look for a route they could have ridden that would have brought them to Porter's position as early as they claimed. Their changing tale about their route cost them still more credibility, especially when they remembered landmark buildings that had not existed during the battle. In another attempt to prove timely delivery of the attack order, Smith convinced another member of his old regiment to say that he had accompanied Pope and Duffee, but telltale blunders betrayed him: he said they found Porter in his headquarters tent by Bethlehem Church, which he recognized by its steeple, but Porter had no tents on that campaign, and Bethlehem Church was then a tumbledown ruin that had never had a steeple. Porter hired an Ohio lawyer who found other members of Smith's regiment whom Smith had solicited to say they, too, had ridden with Captain Pope, and one of them doubted that even Duffee had accompanied him. Duffee admitted lying when interviewed by that lawyer, but he refused to change his story.[60]

Lord and Ormsby took the stand, finally revealing themselves as the source of the anonymous accusations Senator Chandler had broadcast seven years before, but their tale did not wear well under cross-examination. A cavalry sergeant produced by Gardner claimed to have spotted Porter at Manassas Junction after the alleged retreat there, with a slouch hat instead of a forage cap, without his beard, and wearing a major general's uniform, although Porter had none until after the Bull Run campaign. Capt. George Dobson, another of Smith's recruited witnesses, related a fabulous story of leading a reconnaissance on August 29 into the territory Longstreet occupied and finding no enemy there; Porter's lawyers demonstrated that the reconnaissance had been imaginary. A former Confederate chaplain said he had watched Porter's approach from a private home, long before Rebel infantry arrived; he adorned his testimony with an anecdote about the white man who owned the house, but the man he named did not move to that vicinity until after the war, during which the house belonged to a free Black woman. The chaplain, Dobson, the sergeant, Lord, and Ormsby typified those whose testimony Porter's lawyers characterized as "ridiculous," and the board seemed to concur.[61]

General McDowell arrived from his California post in October. His staff had scoured his papers and found three "lost" dispatches from Porter that he had received on August 29, 1862, which he had forwarded to the board without realizing their exculpatory significance. The most important of them was headed with the hour of 6:00 p.m., and it demonstrated that Porter had still not received Pope's 4:30 attack order by then. Collectively, the messages also illustrated that Porter considered himself under McDowell's immediate authority and that he was anxious for information. Finally, they showed that the uncommunicative McDowell had received dispatches from Porter that he had never acknowledged, much less answered.[62]

Choate grilled McDowell mercilessly about the dispatches, leaving the impression that he had deliberately suppressed them. Choate also belabored the hapless general for helping Pope with his deceptive "Brief Statement." McDowell had provided Pope with the excerpt from Stonewall Jackson's report that misrepresented the battlefield situation on August 29, and Choate forced him to acknowledge that the excerpt instead referred to August 30. Porter's chief of staff, Colonel Locke, had testified that McDowell gave him instructions for Porter to hold fast until McDowell got into position for a joint attack, and Locke's courier corroborated that meeting, but McDowell did not "recollect" it. To the contrary, McDowell insisted that he had told Porter to attack from where he was. Longstreet had already testified that his corps was on the field by midday of August 29, and Choate asked whether McDowell thought Porter should have attacked Longstreet's 25,000-man corps with the 9,000 men he had left after McDowell took one division away. McDowell objected to the question because it called for an opinion, but Choate reminded him of the opinion he had given in the court-martial. McDowell dodged the question but could not elude the implication that his interference had diverted Porter from a potentially successful assault early in the day, while his failure to communicate had left Porter idle the rest of the afternoon.[63]

Not until the spring of 1879 did the board conclude its deliberations, reporting that Holt's charges and specifications had "no discernible resemblance to the facts of the case as now established." Focusing on the "errors" of the court-martial and the "erroneous" evidence that led to Porter's conviction, the three officers overlooked glaring indications of perjury, collusion, and corruption. They criticized Porter only for his unkind remarks about Pope, reasoning that the Burnside dispatches led to the "misinterpretation of his motives and his conduct." Justice, they concluded, required restoring Porter to his old rank, from the date of his original appointment.[64]

It was an astounding triumph for Porter, after more than sixteen years of degradation, but his ordeal was not over. By 1879 President Hayes was facing a Democratic Congress and needed the strongest possible support of the House minority leader—who happened to be James Garfield. Instead of reinstating Porter, Hayes handed the board's report to Congress without recommendation.[65]

Senator Randolph entered a bill for Porter's reinstatement as a colonel in the regular army, and it won committee recommendation, but it lingered throughout the Forty-Sixth Congress. Presidential hopeful Garfield characterized it as the work of "Confederate brigadiers" then sitting in Congress. To Porter's surprise, Sen. Ambrose Burnside raised his voice against it. Burnside had always supported him in earlier appeals, but Garfield got to him through former general and congressman Jacob D. Cox, who was their common friend. Cox had produced a biased assessment of the Schofield board's report that seemed to sway Burnside, whose failure as commander of the Army of the Potomac had involved the same unsupportive subordinates Pope claimed he had faced. Sen. John A. Logan, another Republican and former general who regarded himself as the foremost public representative of all Union veterans, made political hay out of bashing Porter in long screeds notable for their venom and inaccuracy. Just before the second session ended, Porter's bill was scrubbed from the schedule. The *National Republican* crowed that Porter had no hope of persuading the next Congress, either, and with James Garfield in the White House it wouldn't have mattered.[66]

Porter's prospects improved somewhat with the assassination of Garfield—the second member of his court-martial to be murdered (after Brig. Gen. John P. Slough, in 1867). He gained even more sympathy when General Grant gave the case closer scrutiny than he had had time for while serving as president and came away convinced of Porter's innocence. Senator Logan nevertheless refused to consider Grant's analysis and attacked Porter's next attempt at restoration with even greater ferocity. After enduring more denunciatory bombast than when he was first dismissed, Porter saw his bill die without attention early in 1883.[67]

Late that year he submitted yet another bill, and it passed the House with more than a two-thirds majority. Despite relentlessly fervent opposition from Logan, whose own presidential aspirations peaked that election year, it also passed handily in the Senate. President Chester Arthur vetoed it in July 1884 on the sentimental grounds that it had been "approved by Abraham Lincoln," whose son—a fervent opponent of Porter's reinstatement—was sitting in

Arthur's cabinet as secretary of war. Grant commiserated with Porter, calling Arthur's veto "the merest sophistry."[68]

In December 1885, with the era of reconciliation under way, a former Confederate general entered a new bill on Porter's behalf. For many Americans, the passions of the 1860s were abating, as was evident from the number of Republicans who came to regard Porter's case as a matter of simple justice rather than partisan loyalty. Porter's bill was warmly endorsed in the Democratic-majority House by a Republican who was a Union veteran of Second Bull Run, and it passed in February. Logan leveled his customary abuse in the Republican-controlled Senate, but it passed by a wide margin there, too. Six days later, Democratic president Grover Cleveland signed it. Shortly afterward he sent Porter's nomination as colonel to the Senate, where it was confirmed on August 3, backdated to August 5, 1861. Porter immediately asked to go on the retired list.[69]

Having given up any claim to retroactive compensation early in the process, to make it easier for congressmen to vote for him, Porter never received back pay or retirement. The campaign to reclaim even nominal status as an army officer had cost him a small fortune for lawyers, printing, postage, and travel, besides occupying most of his spare time for twenty years. He was already growing old and sick by the time he realized his goal, and his economic situation gradually deteriorated. Two years later he applied for an eight-dollar-per-month service pension as a Mexican War veteran, and the year after that he sold his home, living out the last dozen years of his life in rented houses.[70]

He believed he had rescued his reputation, so it all seemed worthwhile to him. John Pope had planted a seed of doubt, however, and a host of accomplices high and low had helped it to germinate. When Porter's line died out, a century and a half after his birth, historians had not finished blaming him for the disaster at Bull Run on the grounds that he defied the orders of a man he detested and wished to see fail.[71]

Notes

1. *The Salmon P. Chase Papers*, ed. John Niven, 5 vols. (Kent: Kent State University Press, 1993–98), 1:368–70; *Diary of Gideon Welles*, ed. Howard K. Beale, 3 vols. (New York: W. W. Norton, 1960), 1:104–5; US War Department, *The War of the Rebellion: A Compilation of the Official Records of the Union and Confederate Armies*, 128 vols., index and atlas (Washington, DC: Government Printing Office, 1880–1901), ser. 1, 12(2): 840 (hereafter cited as *OR*, with all citations from series 1 unless otherwise noted).

2. *Diary of Gideon Welles*, 1:109–11; Pope to Lincoln, September 5, 1862, Abraham Lincoln Papers, Library of Congress, Washington, DC (hereafter cited as LC); Special Orders No. 222, September 5, 1862, Court Martial Case File MM-51, RG 153, National Archives and Records Administration, Washington, DC; *OR* 12(3): 811.

3. *The Civil War Papers of George B. McClellan: Selected Correspondence, 1860–1865*, ed. Stephen W. Sears (New York: Ticknor and Fields, 1989), 436–37. The court of inquiry for Porter, Franklin, and Griffin met without a quorum on September 6 and 8, 1862, but interest in the inquiry seemed to languish when the three would-be defendants were returned to duty. One of the court members was appointed to command a corps, and on September 15 Maj. Gen. Henry Halleck ordered the court to adjourn indefinitely. Record of Proceedings, Court Martial Case File MM-51, RG 153, National Archives.

4. On soldier dissent, especially over emancipation, see William Marvel, *Lincoln's Darkest Year: The War in 1862* (Boston: Houghton Mifflin, 2008), 241–45.

5. On summary dismissals and courts-martial of dissident officers, including for expressing disagreement in their letters of resignations, see Marvel, *Lincoln's Darkest Year*, 244; and Jonathan W. White, *Emancipation, the Union Army, and the Reelection of Abraham Lincoln* (Baton Rouge: Louisiana State University Press, 2014), 41–53. For the Radical strategy of smearing Democratic generals as disloyal, see William A. Blair, *With Malice toward Some: Treason and Loyalty in the Civil War Era* (Chapel Hill: University of North Carolina Press, 2014), 164–66.

6. *War Diary and Letters of Stephen Minot Weld, 1861–1865* (Cambridge: Massachusetts Historical Society, 1927), 150; *Evening Star* (Washington, DC), November 12, 1862; *Daily National Republican* (Washington, DC), November 13, 1862; Special Orders No. 350, November 17, 1862, reel 2, Fitz John Porter Papers, LC (hereafter cited as FJPP).

7. *OR* 12(2): 821. In a typescript memoir of trial incidents, Porter identified Assistant Secretary John Tucker as the War Department official who had remarked that the court was "made to convict" (reel 25, FJPP). James B. Fry, who spent most of his army career on staff duty at army headquarters, corroborated that Stanton made a practice of selecting reliable or pliable officers for commissions in which he desired a particular outcome. See Fry's *Operations of the Army under Buell from June 10th to October 30th, 1862, and the "Buell Commission"* (New York: D. Van Nostrand, 1884), 110.

8. *OR* 14:341, ser. 3, 2:42–43; *Chase Papers*, 1:420–21; Frederick D. Williams, ed., *The Wild Life of the Army: Civil War Letters of James A. Garfield* (East Lansing: Michigan State University Press, 1964), 141, 148.

9. *OR* 51(1): 714–15; Porter to "My dear Mac," undated, reel 29, FJPP; *The Collected Works of Abraham Lincoln*, ed. Roy P. Basler, 9 vols. (New Brunswick, NJ: Rutgers University Press, 1953–55), 5:361, 446.

10. These were Maj. Gen. Ethan Allen Hitchcock and Brig. Gen. Napoleon Buford—both obscure, long-retired officers whom Stanton invited to his house for Thanksgiving dinner just after the trial opened. Chase had also lobbied Buford to vote for conviction. See Ethan Allen Hitchcock Diary, November 26–28, 1862, Gilcrease Museum, Tulsa, OK; and Porter's notes on John Buford's warning about Chase's prejudicial comments to Napoleon Buford, handwritten chronology (reel 2) and typescript memoir of trial incidents (reel 25), FJPP.

11. *Diary of Gideon Welles,* 1:110; transcript of William H. Paine Journal, August 29, 1862, reel 2, FJPP; John P. Hatch to Porter, September 6, 1866, reel 3, FJPP; *OR* 12(2): 1035–37.

12. Brig. Gen. Benjamin Prentiss's public utterances showed him sufficiently hostile to conservative thinking to judge Porter antagonistically, and years later he said he never doubted Porter's guilt (Prentiss to John A. Logan, March 19, 1880, Bound Volume 753, Logan Papers, Abraham Lincoln Presidential Library, Springfield, IL).

13. *OR* 12(2): 822; *Evening Star,* November 28, 1862; US Congress, Committee on the Judiciary, *Impeachment Investigation: Testimony Taken before the Judiciary Committee of the House of Representatives in the Investigation of the Charges against Andrew Johnson* (Washington, DC: Government Printing Office, 1867), 665.

14. The post of judge advocate general was created as a promotion for Maj. John F. Lee, who had been judge advocate of the army since 1849, but Stanton called the unemployed Holt into his office on the day Congress authorized it; the position remained vacant until Holt was appointed on September 3, and Major Lee resigned his commission on September 4. C. P. Wolcott to Holt, July 9, 18, 1862, box 34, Joseph Holt Papers, LC; *OR,* ser. 3, 2:957; John F. Lee to Abraham Lincoln, September 4, 1862, reel 113, Letters Received by the Adjutant General, 1861–1870, M619, Records of the Adjutant General, RG 94, National Archives.

15. *OR* 12(2): 821, 824; *Civil War Papers of George B. McClellan,* 532.

16. *OR* 12(2): 824.

17. *Revised Regulations for the Army of the United States, 1861* (Washington, DC: Government Printing Office, 1861), 509; *OR* 12(2): 827, 828.

18. James W. Schaumburg to Porter, September 23, 1867, and printed proceedings of Roberts's 1849 court-martial, both reel 3, FJPP.

19. Pope to Richard Yates, September 21, 1862, and to William Butler, September 26, 1862, Pope Papers, Chicago History Center; *Supplemental Report of the Joint Committee on the Conduct of the War,* 2 vols. (Washington, DC: Government Printing Office, 1866), 2:190; *OR* 12(2): 840.

20. *OR* 12(2): 828; Johnson to Henry Halleck, December 14, 1863, reel 3, FJPP.

21. In his typescript memoir of trial incidents (reel 25), FJPP, Porter mentioned his apprehension of the possibility of execution while listening to some of the more incriminating perjury offered to the court.

22. *OR* 12(2): 824–27.

23. *OR* 12(2): 82–83, 829–36, 976, and 12(3):787–88; undated memo on the September 2 interview, reel 30, George B. McClellan Papers, LC.

24. Undated memo on the September 2 interview, reel 30, George B. McClellan Papers; *OR* 12(2): 976.

25. *OR* 12(2): 976–77.

26. *OR* 12(2): 837–39.

27. Pope to Holt, December 4, 1862, box 35, Holt Papers.

28. *OR* 12(2): 839–40.

29. *OR* 12(2): 840–41.

30. *OR* 12(2): 834, 841–60.

31. *National Republican* (Washington, DC), December 10, 15, 1862; *New York Herald,* December 10, 14, 1864; *OR* 16(1): 6–7; Fry, *Operations of the Army under Buell,* 109–11. For details on the calculated bias of the officers on Buell's commission, see Stephen D. Engle,

Don Carlos Buell: Most Promising of All (Chapel Hill: University of North Carolina Press, 1999), 323–27.

32. *OR* 12(2): 866–69.

33. Porter to Stephen M. Weld Jr., January 16, 1863, Fitz John Porter Papers, Massachusetts Historical Society, Boston.

34. *OR* 12(2): 875, 947, 957, 972, 1031.

35. *OR* 12(2): 889–90.

36. *OR* 12(2): 891.

37. *OR* 12(2): 894–95, 899.

38. *OR* 12(2): 906–11; *War Diary and Letters of Stephen Minot Weld,* 153.

39. *OR* 12(2): 906.

40. *Harper's Weekly,* January 3, 1863, 16; "Extracts from the Journal of Henry J. Raymond," *Scribner's Monthly,* January 1880, 424.

41. *OR* 12(2): 1053.

42. *OR* 12(2): 1049–51, 1075–112; *Proceedings of a General Court Martial, for the Trial of Maj. Gen. Fitz John Porter, U.S. Vols* (Washington, DC: n.p., 1862); Prentiss to Logan, March 19, 1880, Bound Volume 753, Logan Papers (on adding the prohibition against holding office).

43. *OR* 12(2): 1134.

44. *OR* 12(2): 1112–33.

45. Speed to Holt, December 31, 1861, box 31, Holt Papers.

46. *The Diary of Orville Hickman Browning,* ed. Theodore Calvin Pease and James G. Randall, 2 vols. (Springfield: Illinois State Historical Library, 1925, 1933), 1:589; *OR* 12 (2, supplement): 1052.

47. *The Diary of George Templeton Strong,* ed. Allan Nevins and Milton Halsey Thomas, 4 vols. (New York: Macmillan, 1952), 3:289. During the 1864 presidential campaign, the *Chicago Tribune* alone ran nine separate articles disparaging Porter and associating him with McClellan.

48. William Swinton, *The Times Review of McClellan: His Military Career Reviewed and Exposed* (New York: New York Times, 1864), and *Campaigns of the Army of the Potomac* (New York: Charles B. Richardson, 1866), 5, 186–87.

49. *Evening Star,* May 9, 1866; *Nashville Daily Union,* May 9, 1866; *Memphis Public Ledger,* May 10, 1866; Longstreet to Porter, September 23, 1866, reel 3, October 7, 1867, reel 22, and Lee to Porter, October 31, 1867, reel 22, FJPP; *Chicago Tribune,* May 11, 1866; *New York Tribune,* May 31, 1866.

50. Porter to Andrew Johnson, January 14, 1867, reel 12, and to William Prime, January 29, reel 3, FJPP; *The Papers of Ulysses S. Grant,* ed. John Y. Simon, 30 vols. (Carbondale: Southern Illinois University Press, 1967–2008), 17:329–36; *Washington Chronicle,* September 16, 1867.

51. *Congressional Globe,* 40th Cong., 2nd Sess., 132–24, 1500–1501 (1868); *Journal of the Senate,* 40th Cong., 2nd Sess., 635 (1868).

52. The extended process of uncovering the deception behind Pope's "Brief Statement" is illuminated by assorted documents within Porter's appeal, file R574, roll 581, Letters Received by the Adjutant General, 1861–1870, M619, Records of the Adjutant General, RG 94, National Archives.

53. Holt to Lord, May 27, 1871, Lord to Holt, May 30, 1871, and Waterman Ormsby to Lord, "May 22, 1870" (obviously misdated, and probably deliberately antedated), all in container

64, Holt Papers; *Congressional Globe*, 41st Cong., 2nd Sess., 1444–48 (1870). On Holt's frequent solicitation of perjury, see Joseph George Jr., "Subornation of Perjury in the Lincoln Conspiracy Trial? Joseph Holt, Robert Purdy, and the Lon Letter," *Civil War History* 38, no. 3 (September 1992): 232–41; Seymour J. Frank, "The Conspiracy to Implicate Confederate Leaders in Lincoln's Assassination," *Mississippi Valley Historical Review* 40, no. 4 (March 1954): 629–36; and William Marvel, *Lincoln's Autocrat: The Life of Edwin Stanton* (Chapel Hill: University of North Carolina Press, 2015), 378, 408–9, 425, 426, 538n65, 548n65.

54. *West-Jersey Pioneer* (Bridgeton, NJ), April 1, 1875; Pope to "My dear Smith," April 12, 1875, box 1, Thomas C. H. Smith Papers, Ohio History Connection, Columbus; confidential memorandum of Secretary of War W. W. Belknap, May 31, 1875, file R574, roll 581, Letters Received by the Adjutant General, 1861–1870, M619, Records of the Adjutant General, RG 94, National Archives.

55. Randolph to Porter, December 29, 30, 1877, reel 5, FJPP; *Evening Star* and *National Republican*, both April 13, 1878.

56. Terry to "Dear Sissy," November 16, 1862, Terry Family Papers, Sterling Library, Yale University; George Ruggles to Porter, April 26, 1878, reel 5, FJPP; John M. Schofield, *Forty-Six Years in the Army* (New York: Century, 1897), 241–42. While serving as secretary of war, Schofield pulled his cadet court-martial record, in which a petition for clemency contained the signatures of all court members except Porter and George Thomas, who may have been absent for that day's proceedings; that disordered box of records also includes numerous cases besides Schofield's, and he may have confused the various petitions. Proceedings in the trials of Schofield, Nelson Bowman Sweitzer, Samuel Kinsey, et al., Case File HH-215, RG 153, National Archives.

57. *New York Tribune*, December 25, 1900, October 21, 1901. Gardner spelled his name "Gardiner" from 1884 onward.

58. *Proceedings and Report of the Board of Army Officers, Convened by Special Orders No. 78, Headquarters of the Army, Adjutant General's Office, Washington, April 12, 1878, in the Case of Fitz-John Porter*, 3 pts. (Washington, DC: Government Printing Office, 1879), 2:223, 358–59, 370, 586–88, 590, 695 (hereafter cited as *PRBAO*).

59. *PRBAO*, 2:380–81.

60. *PRBAO*, 2:576–78, 609–13, 616–19, 625–26, 628, 3:1095–116, 1253; Porter to Peter Getz, July 7, 1880, and to Henry S. Limes, August 7, 1880, reel 23, FJPP.

61. *PRBAO*, 2:837–41, 3:1057–63, 996–1007, 1119, 1260, 1675.

62. *PRBAO*, 2:771–74, 776–777.

63. *PRBAO*, 2:722–25, 735–40, 765–67, 774–77, 779–82, 786–87.

64. *PRBAO*, 3:1717–20.

65. *Evening Star*, May 26, 1879.

66. *Evening Star*, January 20, 27, February 9, 17, December 14, 1880; *National Republican*, February 28, April 1, 1880, January 25, 1881; Cox to Garfield, February 14, 1880 (copy), Fitz John Porter Papers, American Antiquarian Society, Worcester, MA; Burnside to Garfield, March 2, 1880, reel 51, James A. Garfield Papers, LC.

67. Grant, "An Undeserved Stigma," *North American Review* 135, no. 313 (December 1882): 536–46; Grant to Logan, December 30, 1881, reel 12, FJPP; *Evening Star*, January 14, February 28, June 24, December 11, 1882, January 2, 1883.

68. *Rock Island (IL) Argus*, February 15, 1884; *Washington Bee*, March 15, 1884; *Congressional Record*, 48th Cong., 1st Sess., 98, 318, 482, 839–40, 1825–65 (1884); *A Compilation of Messages and Papers of the Presidents*, 11 vols. (Washington, DC: Bureau of National Literature, 1913), 6:4808–10; Grant to Porter, July 4, 1884, reel 15, FJPP.

69. *National Tribune* (Washington, DC), December 31, 1886; *Evening Star*, January 19, February 11–13, 15–19, July 2, 26, 27, August 3, 1886; *Alexandria (VA) Gazette*, August 7, 1886.

70. *Congressional Record*, 46th Cong., 3rd Sess., 124 (1880); original application, September 18, 1888, Certificate 12861, Mexican War Pension Files, RG 15, National Archives.

71. Wallace J. Schutz and Walter N. Trenerry, *Abandoned by Lincoln: A Military Biography of General John Pope* (Urbana: University of Illinois Press, 1990), 126, 168. Porter's last surviving grandchild died in 1985, and his only great-grandchild appears to have died in childhood.

A NATIONAL DISGRACE

The Battle to Protect the Bull Run Monuments

CAROLINE E. JANNEY

At 6:00 a.m. on Sunday, June 11, 1865, a specially commissioned train rolled out of Washington headed south toward the old battlefields at Manassas. After picking up more passengers in Alexandria, the train continued southwest toward Fairfax Station. There the party was met by cavalry general William Gamble, who had arranged fifty ambulances and army wagons for the remaining eighteen miles of the journey. As the caravan continued west, the physical evidence of four years of war became ever more apparent. Earthworks and denuded hills stretched out before the travelers. Scrub oak and pine sprung up in fields that had once teemed with wheat and corn. Scattered here and there stood little log huts, most tottering on the verge of collapse, the last remnants of winter camps. The scarred landscape offered a solemn reminder of the day's purpose: the dedication of two monuments.[1]

Planned and erected by troops from the 16th Massachusetts Battery and the 5th Pennsylvania Heavy Artillery stationed at nearby Fairfax Court

House, the Bull Run monument on Henry Hill was unimposing by later standards. In the center stood an obelisk about twenty-seven feet high composed of red sandstone hewn into square blocks. At the four corners of the base, the soldiers had placed conical 200-pound shells, with a fifth shell capping the shaft. An identical monument had been built at Groveton, the site of the August 1862 battle. Only two months after the surrender of Lee's army, on the fields where US forces had twice been defeated by rebel armies, Union veterans and civilians reclaimed the space. Dedicated to the battles' Union dead, the monuments and their ceremonies honored the Union cause in no uncertain terms. The soldiers left no doubt that they were the ultimate victors, and that the loyal patriots had not given their lives in vain. In death they had bravely ensured that the Union would be preserved and that slavery would never again tear the nation asunder.

The soldiers who erected the monuments presumed the memorials to their fallen comrades would remain undisturbed on the hallowed fields, their meaning and form unchallenged and unchanged for perpetuity. Acting in the moment, they had not thought about the long-term fate of the monuments. They had not sought to purchase the land on which the sandstone obelisks stood nor made efforts to maintain or protect them. Moreover, the War Department's decision not to create a national cemetery at Bull Run meant the monuments would receive no federal protection or funding. In the decades that followed, the plains of Manassas would recede in prominence as a site for Union memorials. Throughout the 1880s and into the early 1900s, Union veterans from every loyal state erected thousands of regimental and state monuments at Gettysburg, Antietam, Chickamauga, Vicksburg, and Shiloh, even as Congress worked to designate the sites as national battlefields.

Yet by the early 1900s, some denied that the Manassas monuments had ever existed. Efforts by a handful of Union veterans to create a national park on the site focused the nation's attention on the stone sentinels. But Congress refused to appropriate any funds to protect them. Ironically, it took the determination of Confederate veterans and their female allies to preserve the field as a Southern memorial to ensure that the monuments to Union patriots would be protected for future generations. Most important, the story of their rise—and almost fall—offers an important reminder that memory has always been intimately entwined with contemporary politics and culture.

On May 23 and 24, 1865, the victorious Union soldiers representing the Army of the Potomac and Maj. Gen. William T. Sherman's western troops marched through Washington, DC, in the "Grand Review of the

Armies. But not all units would participate in the celebration, including those of Bvt. Brig. Gen. William Gamble's 1st Separate Brigade of the Twenty-Second Corps, Department of Washington, who remained on duty near Fairfax Court House. As their comrades in arms gathered in the capital for the review, Gamble informed the War Department that the skeletons of men who had fallen in the two Bull Run battles dotted the landscape. If his men could not participate in the review, perhaps they might undertake an effort to gather and bury the bones of their Union comrades who had died on the field and erect some sort of memorial in their memory.[2]

Permission granted, on May 28, General Gamble ordered Lt. James M. McCallum of the 16th Massachusetts Light Battery, a railroad conductor prior to the war, detached from his command to oversee the construction of the memorial. McCallum would supervise some 100 mechanics and laborers detailed from the 5th Pennsylvania Heavy Artillery, none of whom had fought at either Bull Run battle, having been mustered into the army in the fall of 1864. With no attempt to condemn the land or otherwise acquire title to it, the detail first selected a site at Groveton on the Dogan farm near the Deep Cut of the unfinished railroad, where some 1,500 soldiers' remains now reposed. Using wood axes and stone hammers provided by the War Department to quarry the red sandstone from the unfinished railroad cut, they placed a tin box containing a history of the battle and other relics picked up from the field into the cornerstone before stacking the stone into a sixteen-foot obelisk. They planted four cedar trees, one at each corner of the monument's earthen terrace, and then enclosed the entire area with a cedar fence. Next, they moved to Henry Hill, the center of fighting for the 1861 battle, where they repeated the process (minus the cornerstone box). When both shafts had been completed, the soldiers traversed the battlefield collecting shells to adorn the monuments. Col. J. H. Taylor, a staff officer to Maj. Gen. Christopher Augur, commander of the Department of Washington, suggested the text for the cement plaques. On Henry Hill, one side of the obelisk was inscribed "To the memory of the patriots who fell at Bull Run, July 21, 1865." The Groveton monument was identical except for the name and dates. The reverse side of both the plaques read "Erected June 10, 1865."[3]

Despite later claims, the Bull Run and Groveton monuments were not the only monuments built and dedicated by active-duty soldiers during the war. Nor were they the first at Manassas. Only six weeks after the first battle of Bull Run, members of the 8th Georgia Infantry dedicated a marker on Henry Hill where their colonel, Francis S. Bartow, fell. Returning to the field in late August 1862 during the Second Manassas campaign, members of the

On June 11, 1865, dignitaries and soldiers gathered on the fields at Bull Run to dedicate two monuments to those who fell for the Union cause, including this one positioned on Henry Hill. (Library of Congress Prints and Photographs Division, reproduction number LC-DIG-cwpb-04028)

8th Georgia discovered that the monument to Bartow had been torn down and assumed that Yankee vandals had been the culprits. While the Bartow monument proved the lone Confederate monument erected to multiple soldiers during the war, at least three Union monuments were dedicated on battlefields by April 1865. In December 1861, a Union private engraved a piece of limestone with the names of his comrades from the 32nd Indiana (also known as the 1st German Regiment) who had fallen near Munfordville, Kentucky. Following the battle of Stones River at Murfreesboro, Tennessee, in late December 1863, soldiers from Col. William B. Hazen's brigade constructed a large stone cenotaph to mark the burial plots of their comrades. In a departure from the mortuary monuments, in the summer of 1864 Union troops stationed near Vicksburg dedicated a marble obelisk commemorating the city's surrender the previous year.[4]

Yet none of the other Union monuments had been located so close to the nation's capital nor received such an elaborate dedication ceremony. On June 10, General Gamble sent invitations for an impromptu ceremony to be held the next day. Among those instructed that the train would depart Washington at 6:00 a.m. were Maj. Gen. Samuel Heintzelman (wounded as a division commander at First Bull Run; commander of the Third Corps at Second

Bull Run), Maj. Gen. Orlando B. Wilcox (captured at First Bull Run while a brigade commander in Heintzelman's division), Maj. Gen. Henry W. Benham (US Corps of Engineers), Maj. Gen. Montgomery Meigs (quartermaster general), and Brig. Gen. John F. Farnsworth (wounded at Second Bull Run; congressman of Illinois), along with Judge A. B. Olin (DC Supreme Court), Professor Joseph Henry (Smithsonian Institute), and Rev. Dr. Robert McMurdy. Joined by hundreds of others along the route, the party crested Henry Hill around noon, where the 16th Massachusetts Battery, the 5th Pennsylvania Heavy Artillery, and detachments of the 13th New York and 8th Illinois Cavalries were drawn up in line on the field north of the monument. As the crowd gathered, the soldiers advanced in columns with arms reversed to form a hollow square while the band played a solemn funeral dirge.[5]

Unlike the celebratory monument dedications that would follow on battlefields in the coming decades, this occasion served as a funeral service for the soldiers denied a Christian burial during the fighting. After opening with a reading from the Psalms, Rev. Dr. McMurdy's invocation asked that God "witness the consecration of this pile to the memory of our fallen heroes." In a call and response, the reverend and crowd asked the Lord for mercy and comfort "for the years where we have suffered adversity." Dressed in the same stole he had worn at Lincoln's funeral services, McMurdy implicitly tied the soldiers' sacrifice to that of their commander in chief. Like Lincoln, they had given their lives "to the cause of the Union and liberty." In honoring the dead, the survivors honored the Union cause.[6]

Yet the services did not shy away from pointing out the reason for the collective mourning. A hymn written for the occasion by Rev. John Pierpont and sung to the tune of the Old Hundredth Psalm by the assembled congregation echoed the sermons preached on the morning following Lincoln's death. In solemn chorus, the song heralded slavery as the cause of both the war and the president's death and rejoiced that Union soldiers had secured freedom.

> Here on Virginia's sacred soil,
> Where slavery bred and drove the gangs,
> The horrid serpent lay in coil,
> Here Freedom's sons first felt her fangs

the second stanza offered. But the third stanza invoked a refrain that would become standard in Union memories of Bull Run:

> They fought—they fell; but not in vain,
> Lost they the battle of Bull Run;

The blows that broke the bondman's chains,
At last were on this ground begun.

Not content to merely recast the losses at Bull Run as battles on the way to ultimate Union victory, the hymn concluded by condemning the rebel dead who still slumbered on the same ground.

And so, upon the bloody spot,
Where now this monument is raised,
Shall rebel bones and memories rot;
But patriot names for aye be praised.[7]

After the hymn, the 5th Pennsylvania Heavy Artillery paraded past the onlookers with reversed arms in the funeral drill before the 16th Massachusetts Battery fired a salute. The crowd then beseeched Judge Olin to offer a few remarks. Observing that he was unprepared to do so, the DC Supreme Court judge quickly found his words. This sacred spot marked the "first struggle to restore the Union" and "vindicate the principles of free government," he declared. Like Pierpont's hymns, he conceded that "in the dark days that followed the battle that was fought on this field many thought that the cause was lost." But the men in blue had triumphed in the end. The crowd then called upon the generals to make brief addresses. In a seeming rebuke to Pierpont's closing stanza, Wilcox asked that all meet at the monument as brothers, not thinking of "causes or crimes." He would extend the right hand to all, he insisted, letting "justice fall on those who had deluded the people." The vociferous cheers of soldiers called next upon Heintzelman, who gave a brief narrative of the first battle before saying that he was "in favor of justice first, and mercy afterwards."[8] Too many lives had been sacrificed to forget the cause in the name of mercy.[9]

With the dedication of the Bull Run monument complete, the crowd dispersed for a midday break. Some enjoyed refreshments beneath the shade of the trees; others strolled the field searching for souvenirs such as shot and shells as well more macabre relics, including skulls and bones. Others posed for photographs. According to one New York newspaper, the "ubiquitous" Alexander Gardner and a full corps of attendants had been busy taking pictures from various vantage points throughout the event. Gardner had arrived on the field in July 1861 with his horse-drawn darkroom to document the war's first battle. It seemed only fitting that he should return to record the monument dedication as the war's closing scene, a sentiment expressed in Gardner's 1866 *Photographic Sketch Book of the War,* which closed with an image of the dedication.[10]

His lens captured the martial nature of the affair even more than the newspaper reports did. In one plate, the troops detailed from the 5th Pennsylvania Heavy Artillery to construct the monument gathered around its base, while a second featured the entire regiment. Another showcased the officers who attended the dedication, featuring the memorial's chief architect, Lt. James M. McCallum, standing just above the others. As one Union veteran later remarked, "It is impossible to look at that photograph and not be entirely convinced that these monuments were built under the authority of the United States government." A handful of others, however, bore witness to the civilians in attendance, most notably the women and children. Among them was Mrs. Kimball, widow of a Union colonel, and Mrs. Norris, who had crowned the obelisk with a wreath of red, white, and blue flowers. Yet overwhelmingly, this was an affair of the Union military. Unlike the Confederate memorial services that would commence the following spring under the direction of ladies, Union soldiers were responsible for creating and orchestrating commemorations to their dead.[11]

After lunch, most of the party departed for the Groveton battlefield, approximately two miles away near the railroad cut, to dedicate the second monument. Built by the same soldiers, the monument resembled that at Bull Run and carried a near exact inscription in memory of the "patriots who fell at Groveton Aug. 28–30, 1862." But there were several notable differences. First, the Groveton monument included a more significant number of artillery shells that adorned its base as well as a pyramid of cannonballs that crowned the obelisk. Second, the monument was enclosed by a field of several acres, which now served as a densely filled "City of the Dead." Here the remains of Union soldiers had been buried in trenches marked only by headboards indicating the number in each, ranging from 50 to 400.[12] This monument, perhaps even more so than that at Bull Run, served as a grave marker for the hundreds of nameless men who slumbered around its base. And yet the service proved far shorter, with only the singing of another hymn by Pierpont, which once more invoked slavery as a cause of the war and freedom as a fruit of Union victory. Equally as significant, it closed with a condemnation of the rebel cause:

> The traitorous captains and their hordes,
> That, glorying, left this fatal ground,
> Where are they now? The exulting lords;
> Of them no monument is found.[13]

The entire occasion offered a far cry from the reconciliationist rhetoric that would become commonplace at national battlefield dedications and Blue-Gray reunions of the 1890s and early 1900s, where the cause and consequences of the war would be ignored in the name of the American soldier.[14] The services at Manassas left no doubt who had been the ultimate victors and losers, who held the moral high ground and who did not, and what had been achieved by Union victory. Praising the dedication, the *New York Times* predicted that similar tributes would soon dot every prominent battlefield of the war: "In no better way can the deeds of the hundreds of nameless dead, who fell in defense of our liberties, be kept green in the memories of future generations." A Connecticut newspaper agreed but cautioned that such memorials might also "suggest misfortunes, humiliation and ruin, to the people in whose sight they are built."[15] Some relished this thought; others worried where the consequences of such humiliation might lead.

A week later, rumors began to circulate that local rebels had defaced the monuments. While some Northern papers hoped it was not true, they noted there was strong reason to believe the reports. Some pointed to guerrillas as the culprits, a distinct possibility in the region where John S. Mosby's Partisan Rangers had terrorized Union troops for the better part of two years. Others sneered at the hypocrisy of the rebels who flocked to take the oath of allegiance and receive their pardons. "The temper of people in that part of Virginia is not a whit more loyal than it was six months ago," observed the *New York Times*. The reports of vandalism were soon contradicted, and Union soldiers were glad to learn that was the case. Had it not been, they warned in no uncertain terms, "some of our soldiers would have taken terrible revenge for such an insult."[16]

While tempers cooled over the coming months, the potential for destruction did not. By midsummer of 1865, the Groveton monument had been defaced. Touring the field, newspaper reporter Whitelaw Reid found the inscription altered. Someone had "carefully and conspicuously interlined" the original text so that it now read "In memory of the Confederate Patriots." Reid could only surmise that returning rebels were responsible. Author John Townsend Trowbridge encountered the vandalism soon after, but his travel companion refused to let it remain, climbing onto the base and grinding the "offensive word" out of the tablet.[17]

Even more troubling was the state of the battlefield. In early March 1866, Edward B. Fowler, the late colonel of the 14th New York, reported that exposed bones on both the Bull Run and Groveton fields were being carried away by trophy hunters and the fields were about to be plowed for spring planting. Like many Unionists, he begged the government to collect the bones and properly inter them.[18]

Roused by such reports of Union grave desecration throughout the South, the Northern public soon joined the veterans in demanding that the loyal dead still slumbering in shallow or mass graves on Southern battlefields be provided proper burials. The first efforts had been undertaken in June 1865 by Capt. James M. Moore, assistant quartermaster, whose crew interred the remains of more than 700 Union soldiers near the battlefields of the Wilderness and Spotsylvania, arranging the cemeteries similar to those found in Washington and inscribing the names of the deceased on wooden headboards at each grave. By the spring of 1866, Congress had finally provided the financial support for gathering all the remains of Union soldiers still reposing in the former Confederacy. This massive reinterment project would send quartermaster crews across the South to scout for grave sites and organize cemeteries for Union soldiers similar to those that had been created during the war at Gettysburg, Arlington, Chattanooga, Knoxville, and Stones River.[19] In Virginia, burial crews fanned out across the old battlefields, recovering remains and reinterring them at new cemeteries in Culpeper, Glendale, Williamsburg, Richmond, City Point, Fredericksburg, and Winchester.[20]

In March 1866, Col. Marshall J. Ludington of the Quartermaster Department sent Lt. R. W. Tyler to survey the condition of Union burials at Bull Run as well as the prospects for establishing a national cemetery on the site. In the wake of both battles, the Union army had retreated, leaving Confederates to tend to the dead who had not been buried during the battle. As such, Tyler found few visible graves on the site of the first battle, including several on Henry Hill interred at the time of the monument construction. On the field of the 1862 battle, he found more graves of both the Union and the Confederate dead. He located thirty Union graves in the enclosed acre around the monument, some with scanty headboards indicating only that they belonged to members of the US Regular Cavalry. Other were scattered throughout the vicinity, including on Brawner Farm, near the Chinn House, and along the unfinished railroad where 200 to 300 men had been "buried in a pile and a log pen built around them." In most instances, the remains of Union soldiers seemed to have been buried where they fell by simply throwing dirt over them rather than by digging a grave. In some cases, large numbers had been gathered and covered in a common pile. Very few headboards remained, "the inhabitants having destroyed them," but among those with headboards, most names were no longer legible. Remnants of blue clothing and US buttons protruded from the earth, as did skulls and other bones. What the elements had not exposed, the rooting of hogs had uncovered. Perhaps most disturbing, Tyler had heard that locals had carted off large quantities of human bones to the bone grinder, where they would become fertilizer.[21]

Tyler recommended that the remains be gathered and placed in two small enclosures, one on each battlefield. He reported that the two monuments had been "somewhat mutilated by the ill disposed inhabitants of that vicinity" and suggested preferable sites, seeing how the land on which the monuments stood belonged to rebels who expected the United States would pay substantial sums for the title (a problem that would resurface decades later). Instead, Tyler proposed that the government reinter the remains on an eminence just north of the Stone House, which belonged to G. A. Starbuck, "a Northern man" who was willing to donate the land as a burial ground. "The remains to be removed consists of nothing but a few bones," Tyler explained. The endeavor would require little in the way of trouble or expense. But even Tyler must have recognized that differentiating between friend and foe would be difficult given the state of the remains.[22]

Despite Tyler's proposal, the fields marking the war's first battle and two of the earliest monuments would not serve as the site of a national cemetery. Quartermaster General Meigs decided instead to reinter in Arlington Cemetery the remains of the Union soldiers from Bull Run and other sites along the Orange & Alexandria Railroad. At Arlington they would be deposited in a ten-foot-deep by twenty-foot-wide underground vault over which "cairns or pyramids of stones may be erected." Excavations on the field began in May 1866 when the burial crews collected 5 remains on Dogan's land, and by the end of July, the crews located another 1,791.[23]

When Starbuck learned that the bodies were to be removed to Arlington, he immediately wrote to Meigs offering a "very pretty position for a burial place on our farm" just north of the Stone House overlooking both battlefields. He estimated that approximately 4,000 Union remains might be located in the vicinity and declared that such a site would be "as safe from depredations as at Arlington or in the vicinity of other Battle Grounds." He explained that visitors frequently arrived in search of their loved one's remains and universally preferred that they be interred in a cemetery on the field. "Here they fought & lost their lives in their endeavor to Save the Government & crush the rebellion," he observed. "Here their remains have been lain nearly 4 & 5 years & here methinks on the Field of Battle is the most appropriate final resting place for their remains since but few can be recognised by name." But his intentions were more than altruistic: a native of New York, he had purchased the property with plans to open a boardinghouse for those who wished to visit the battlefield. Removing the remains to Arlington (which did not yet carry the honor or prestige it would later assume) might reduce the number of visitors to Bull Run and, hence, the income he would derive from the property. "We are plain working people trying to get a living by industry and economy," he closed.[24]

Starbuck's pleadings would go in vain. The Bull Run and Groveton dead would be removed to Arlington, and most would never be identified. A handful whose skeletons remained intact received individual graves, but most would rest for eternity in a collective tomb for unknown Union dead adjacent to one of Mary Lee's rose gardens. There, the skeletal remains of approximately 2,111 soldiers commingled in a vault topped by a large altar tomb that soon became a centerpiece of the cemetery's memorial activities. The inscription, authored by Meigs, paid homage to the soldiers "gathered after the war from the fields of Bull Run and the route to the Rappahannock" whose names "could not be identified" but whose grateful country honored them as a "noble army of martyrs."[25]

Even as the Bull Run dead at Arlington came to symbolize the sacrifice of every Union soldier death, the lack of a national cemetery on or near the battlefield meant there would be no federal presence to watch over the ground. In establishing the national cemeteries, Congress had directed the War Department to employ a superintendent for each burial ground who would reside in a lodge constructed on cemetery property "for the purpose of guarding and protecting the cemetery and giving information to parties visiting the same." Cognizant of the fact that the new national cemeteries were to be established in the unreconstructed South, legislators ensured that the act levied stiff penalties against any person who destroyed, mutilated, defaced, or removed any tomb, monument, or gravestone. The cemetery superintendent was authorized to arrest any person engaged in such activity to bring before a federal (not state) court.[26] But the monuments at Bull Run and Groveton would be afforded no such protection.

In 1879, the Quartermaster Department ordered an inspection of the memorials—but only after Dorothea Dix, the former superintendent of army nurses, asked General Meigs about their status. That March, Oliver Cox, an agent hired by Meigs to evaluate both monuments, reported that the Bull Run monument appeared sound, excepting that the foundation had given way on one corner, causing the obelisk to lean. The Groveton monument likewise appeared in good condition other than the defaced inscription. But considering the "soft and yielding material" of which both were composed as well as their "unprotected and exposed situation," they were in a "remarkably good state of preservation." Cox proposed enclosing both with a fence (the cedar fence surrounding the Groveton monument having decayed) and replacing their cement plaques with marble ones and, for the Bull Run monument, repositioning and underpinning it. But, he observed, as the grounds did not belong to the government, the expenditure should not exceed $100. Only the bare minimum should be done to protect the memorials. Meigs agreed. Replying to Dix's inquiry, he assured her that the monuments were in "good condition for their age." He would direct "small necessary repairs" to preserve them, provided that the landowner consented. "The sites do not belong to the United States," he informed her.[27] The long-term fate of the memorials was of little concern to Meigs and the US government.

In the fifteen years following the war, the pace of Union monument construction intensified, providing both memorials to the fallen and reminders to future generations of the war's meaning. Local communities, from Maine to Minnesota and beyond, dedicated monuments to the men of their town featuring obelisks or soldiers at rest with simple inscriptions such as "In memory of our soldiers" or "To our heroic dead."[28] But Gettysburg proved to be the most popular location for regimental and state memorials for veterans of the Army of the Potomac. Since the war, the Gettysburg Battlefield Memorial Association had been working to improve the field for tourists, rebuilding Union works, placing wooden placards on key battlefield locations, and arranging several dozen condemned cannon on the landscape.[29] But in the late 1870s, veterans first proposed monuments on the field of battle (as opposed to in the cemetery). On August 1, 1878, Brig. Gen. Strong Vincent's men dedicated a tablet to their commander on the southern slope of Little Round Top, where he fell mortally wounded. The following year, veterans of the 2nd Massachusetts erected a monument to the men of their brigade who had fallen in Spangler's Meadow.[30]

Yet these mortuary memorials soon gave way to monuments that celebrated entire units—both the men who had died and the surviving veterans. And no battlefield proved more popular than Gettysburg, where veterans of the Army of the Potomac memoralized their first decisive victory of the war. After a series of humiliating defeats along the Peninsula, at Second Bull Run, in Fredericksburg, and at Chancellorsville (and a string of unsuccessful commanders), in July 1863 the largest US army had finally whipped Lee's seemingly invincible army, sending it back into Virginia. For the Army of the Potomac veterans, Gettysburg was the beginning of the inevitable victory over treason.[31] Anticipating the twenty-fifth anniversary of the battle, in 1884 the legislatures of loyal states began providing funds for each unit that had fought at Gettysburg. Within two years, more than 100 tablets and monuments had been dedicated. As one guidebook observed, the field was quickly becoming a "National Mecca." "The more the work is decorated with these works of art," the author believed, "the more powerful becomes the impulse of the traveler and patriot to visit or revisit the field of glory."[32] By the late 1880s, the marble, granite, and bronze statuary that dotted the southern Pennsylvania battlefield served as poignant reminders that Gettysburg was an exclusively Union memorial park.

All of this unfolded during the years in which the United States began moving toward a spirit of national reconciliation. In the 1880s and 1890s, Union and Confederate veterans began to participate in joint Blue-Gray reunions, while popular magazines such as *The Century* increasingly valorized the battles and leaders of the war. Northern veterans continued to espouse their allegiance to the Union cause (and in many cases emancipation) at monument dedications and Memorial Days, while Confederate veterans persisted in their tributes to the Lost Cause at Southern-only events. But when the former foes met at Blue-Gray reunions, they agreed to remain silent on the divisive political issues of the conflict. Instead, they commiserated on the severity of camp life and marches while commending each other for their bravery on the field of battle.[33]

It was a natural extension of such sentiment that led Union veterans to invite former Confederates to join their efforts for the creation of a national military park at Chickamauga in 1889.[34] President Benjamin Harrison signed the enabling legislation in August 1890, and Congress appointed the Chickamauga and Chattanooga National Military Park Commission, which was composed of two civilian veterans—a Union and a Confederate—and one veteran still on active duty in the army.[35] Not only would both sides have say over the placement of monuments on the field, but federal money had been appropriated to commemorate both the victors and losers in the war. Such was an unprecedented gesture of national reunion. Later that year, veterans from Antietam won a small victory when they gained a congressional appropriation to mark the battle lines at Sharpsburg. As the financial difficulties of the Panic of 1893 subsided, three more battlefields were authorized as national parks: Shiloh (1894), Gettysburg (1895), and Vicksburg (1899).[36] These national parks were not merely to be tourist destinations. Rather, they had been designated by Congress both as memorials to the great Civil War armies and as fields for historical and professional study by the US military.[37]

Amid this wave of national park enthusiasm, veterans north and south recommended other battlefields as potential sites throughout the 1890s. In February 1900, Rep. Peter J. Otey, a Confederate veteran from Lynchburg, Virginia, introduced a bill to establish a battle park on the site of the battle of Bull Run for the "purpose of preserving and suitably marking for historical and professional study of the most famous battle of the war." The bill, however, stalled in the Committee on Military Affairs.[38]

The following year, George Carr Round, a Manassas resident and Union veteran, attempted a different approach by calling the nation's attention to the Bull Run and Groveton monuments. Born in 1839 in eastern Pennsylvania and raised in Windsor, New York, Round had been attending Wesleyan University in Connecticut when the war erupted. Withdrawing from college, he served with the 1st Connecticut Heavy Artillery for three years before his appointment as a lieutenant with the Army Signal Corps. After the war, he returned to law school and after graduation practiced briefly in New York. But in 1869, he moved to Manassas, where he opened a law firm. A Republican, Round soon became an avid supporter of public education, securing funding to open the first free public school (for white children). He served in the Virginia legislature (1872–74) as well as on the Manassas and state normal school boards. Amid all of this, he found time for veterans' activities, including as a member of the Grand Army of the Republic (GAR) Manassas Picket Post and the president of the US Signal Corps Association.[39]

On December 1, 1901, Rep. John F. Rixey (D-VA) presented a memorial written by Round to Congress urging the federal government to protect the monuments by acquiring proper titles to the land on which they stood. But the monuments served only as pretext for his larger aim of establishing a national park. Round asked that Congress purchase not only the land surrounding the monuments but also "so much of the adjacent country as will enable the people of the United States and tourists from abroad studying our history to view the said battlefields without trespassing upon private property." Rixey's bill, however, focused only on protecting "the monuments already erected on the battlefields of Bull Run," directing the secretary of war to purchase for the United States as much land around the monuments as would be sufficient to enable citizens to visit them and to provide suitable roadways and approaches to the property from public highways. Rixey suggested an appropriation of $25,000 to complete the work.[40]

By early February, Round had turned his attention to the secretary of war, who would have final say if the bill passed. Pressing his true agenda, Round observed that if the secretary found it "possible to do more than has been indicated," he recommended installing 50 to 100 permanent tablets to replace the wooden ones erected on the fields by the GAR in 1892. "I also suggest two steel towers, one on Henry Hill and another on Douglass Hill [Stony Ridge], from which tourists could easily see" the entirety of both battlefields. But he cautioned against erecting any new memorials. "The present monuments are of course rude, but they were erected by the veterans. . . . Let them stand forever as they are."[41]

Almost immediately, Round was on the defensive, penning a letter to Washington's *Evening Star* noting that some GAR comrades feared his proposition would injure the prospects of establishing a national park at Fredericksburg. He pointed out that the Fredericksburg proposition was a vast undertaking, much like Gettysburg and Chickamauga, that would take years and a substantial budget. His insisted that his goal was to protect the monuments built by Union soldiers. "Long before any of the grand military parks were projected this beginning was made at Bull Run." He pointed out that the government had spent hundreds of thousands of dollars on the Fitz John Porter case and had paid $200,000 for Arlington. The $25,000 requested was paltry in comparison. The United States should be "forever committed" to protecting the memorials, he observed, before turning once more to the idea of a park: "Whether they should go further and erect the towers of observation I suggested to the Secretary of War is so far one to which the government is not committed."[42]

In April 1902, the Committee on Military Affairs began hearings on the proposed bill. Called to testify, Round offered newspaper clippings as well as the Gardner photographs from the 1865 dedication as evidence that the US government had created the monuments. Union veterans who had helped construct the monuments supported these claims. Albert N. Seip, a signal officer attached to General Gamble's staff, described the soldiers detailed to build the monuments and read an entry from his diary recounting the dedication. Samuel Brown and Josiah George, soldiers in Company M of the 5th Pennsylvania Heavy Artillery, recalled their work as stonemasons. Soldiers of the US Army had constructed the memorials, they all insisted, and as such, the federal government bore responsibility for preserving and maintaining them.[43]

Most of the committee's questioning, however, centered on who currently owned the land and how much it would cost to buy. Round presented a War Department map marking the monuments and the sections of the field he believed the government should purchase. He explained that the Henry heirs (the grandchildren of Judith Henry, who was killed during the 1861 battle) owned 128 acres and had agreed to sell for $15,000. As their attorney, he observed that they had not consented to the construction of the monument on their property, nor had they received any payment since. When the chairman asked whether the owners charged admission to the monument, Round explained that they leased the farmhouse to a Union veteran (Henry Steen), who charged fifty cents, giving half to the owners. During the last year alone, some 200–300 visitors had paid to visit the Bull Run monument. The Groveton monument sat on property belonging to Mollie Dogan and her children and consisted of 10 to 30 acres, but as he did not represent her, Round had never been able to determine a selling price. Unlike the Bull Run monument, which sat adjacent to the Henry house, the Groveton monument was about a half mile from the Dogan home. The family did not charge admission, yet visitors repeatedly took down fences or left gates open. When pressed on the amount of land to be purchased, Round recommended that the government acquire the entire Henry farm, staffing the home with a keeper who could watch over the property and maintain the roads, as well as the Dogan homestead. Perhaps most noteworthy, he recommended a tower constructed near the Henry house for viewing the battlefield of First Bull Run—a feature that had nothing to do with protecting the monuments. Whether unimpressed by Round's rationale or simply overwhelmed with the number of battlefield preservation bills introduced, the Bull Run monuments bill never made it out of committee.[44]

Round thus turned to the GAR. He had first introduced the topic at the 1901 national encampment prior to his memorial to Congress with no response, but in 1903 he pressed the most powerful veterans' organization to support the bill. Again, he met resistance. His staunchest opponent proved to be former GAR commander in chief Brig. Gen. Louis Wagner, a captain with the 88th Pennsylvania who was wounded and captured at Second Bull Run. Wagner emphatically declared that no such monuments existed and dismissed the bill as an "effort to manufacture sentiment, appealing to patriotism of the Grand Army to get rid of a bad real estate speculation." Another comrade concurred, deriding the Henry heirs for "trying to unload their property on the government." Round retorted that this "manufactured sentiment" arose during a GAR excursion to the field, which included several comrades from Pennsylvania. Finding that the monuments had been erected on private property, they had resolved to go home and bring the matter before their posts. Moreover, Round observed, "if there is any state that ought to take an interest in this, it is Pennsylvania." After all, it was the 5th Pennsylvania Heavy Artillery that had been detailed to build the monuments. But the matter was settled. The GAR would not throw its considerable political clout behind the bill.[45]

Attitudes began to shift in 1905 when the Society of the Army of the Potomac met at Manassas for its annual reunion. Although this was a separate veterans' organization, General Wagner and other Pennsylvania GAR comrades who had objected to the proposal in 1903 attended the two-day event, where they listened to Round recount the history of the Bull Run monument following a picnic lunch at the site. Equally noteworthy was the attendance of Confederate veterans, including now US senator John Warwick Daniel. Leveraging the reconciliationist spirit of the day, speakers gushed about the fraternal feelings evident on the field while newspaper headlines reported that the Blue and the Gray had been "Reunited at Bull Run." Most important for Round, the Confederate veterans agreed to support the legislation protecting the monuments.[46]

At the national encampment that August, the GAR finally agreed to appoint a committee on the Bull Run battlefield monuments. The following year, the committee submitted that the United States was "honor bound" to acquire title to the land on which the monuments stood and to construct roads to make them accessible. Committee members likewise endorsed the plan for a single tower on Henry Hill, "where the two battles ended." But that was the limit. There would be no push for more land or an entire military park. To those who might yet object, questioning why two Union defeats should be commemorated at all, they offered that the results of both battles had been "providential; the reverses there encountered were part of the mighty struggle which in its final outcome decided that the United States was to become a leading nation in the world." As such, the committee urged the encampment to adopt resolutions encouraging congressional action.[47]

While the GAR let the issue linger, other Confederates acted. In 1904, the United Daughters of the Confederacy (UDC) dedicated an obelisk in the Confederate cemetery at Groveton. The following year, veterans from the 7th Georgia erected seven small marble markers denoting their position during the two battles. In 1906, the first Union regimental monuments appeared when New York unveiled memorials to the 5th New York (Duryea's Zouaves), the 10th New York (National Zouaves), and the 84th New York, known as the Brooklyn 14th. Each regiment had purchased the plot of land for its respective monument, and Union general Hiram Duryea provided funds for an iron memorial gateway at the Warrenton Turnpike entrance. At the October dedication, Confederate veterans joined their former enemies for the ceremonies, where appeals for a more expansive effort to secure the battlefield found support. Calls for more regimental markers by both sides provided incentive for congressional action, and once more pleas for a national park emerged. Before departing, the Union and Confederate veterans joined forces to establish the Bull Run Battle Park Association to promote the park idea.[48]

Still, Congress had refused to move on Rixey's bill. Frustrated, in 1907 former Confederate veteran Senator Daniel introduced a bill in the Senate expanding significantly on the earlier proposal. His additions noted that "many military organizations" supported the measure and that the Commonwealth of Virginia had ceded to the United States jurisdiction over any land that might be required for said purpose. The bill observed that veterans' organizations should be entitled to erect monuments on land owned by the United States (after approval by the secretary of war). Finally, in keeping with the establishment of other national military parks, the bill designated the president to appoint a three-person commission to include both a Union and a Confederate veteran. A proposal that began with an effort to protect monuments dedicated explicitly to loyal Union patriots had now evolved into one that fully embraced reconciliation—one that would honor both sides equally. But the bill never made it out of committee. Once more, Round's efforts had been thwarted.[49]

Nearly a decade later, amid the war's semicentennial anniversary, attention once more turned to the monuments. In April 1911, just before the fiftieth anniversary of First Bull Run, dubbed the Peace Jubilee, new bills protecting the monuments were submitted in both the House and the Senate. Once more, Virginia Democrats had introduced the bills, both of whom were sons of Confederate veterans. Hearings in the Committee on Military Affairs began a year later. George Round testified once more on the monuments' origins and fielded questions on property values, while a representative from the GAR's committee detailed the association's increasing concern and commitment to protecting the memorials. Veterans from New York recounted the 1906 dedication of their regimental memorials, observing that the monuments remained "in a quasi unprotected condition." All agreed that Congress had a duty to protect the monuments already there and others that might soon be erected "for all time." And all used the occasion to ask for much more: they wanted a park designation for the battlefield.[50]

But unlike the 1902 testimony that featured only Union veterans, the 1912 hearings included that of former Confederates whose motivations had little to do with the Union monuments. While the Union veterans at least positioned their pleas for a battlefield park under the pretext of protecting the monuments, Confederate veterans couched their call for a park in the reconciliationist spirit of the day. Speaking on behalf of the Confederate veterans, Capt. D. B. Mull of Fitzgerald, Georgia, noted that "Bull Run is a sacred spot for many of our soldiers on both sides. . . . Many of our friends died there upon that battlefield defending what they thought was right and just." The land was of little agricultural use and would likely never produce anything. But "it has," he concluded, "produced heroism, and we desire both sides, that this heroism be perpetuated for time immemorial."[51]

Even more astounding was testimony from Mary L. Alexander, president of the local UDC chapter. Although she described the poor condition of the Union monument at Groveton, she explained that her principal work was in protecting the Confederate monument erected by her chapter in 1904 (which unlike the Union monuments, she pointed out, had been paid for solely by women). Her chief concern was that the state of Virginia had been unable to maintain the roads that led to the monuments. When Round observed that this was merely one of the questions under consideration, she conceded that "the United States government should take some steps, some action, looking to a protection of these monuments." But the Daughters were not interested in creating a battlefield park. That was the province of men. Her real motivation in testifying revolved solely around the Confederate monument. "While you are putting in a highway for your monuments," she quipped, "then I will get over that highway to our monument." Unlike veterans of both sides who proved capable of indulging in blue-gray gush when practical, the Daughters proved skeptical if not resistant to most reconciliationist gestures and fiercely devoted to their Confederate identity. Alexander was no exception. "If I were to stand here and say that I was not a rebel I would tell an untruth," she insisted. "I was born and raised in the cradle of the South, and stand here the daughter of a Confederate soldier; and as a woman who went through four years of the war." But now was the time to lay aside "unfriendly sentiment" and come together to care for these monuments.[52]

In March 1913, Congress passed and President Woodrow Wilson signed the bill into law directing the War Department to *inquire* into the practicability of purchasing the monuments' land. The secretary of war subsequently appointed a three-man board of officers (all active duty and none of whom were Confederate veterans) to survey the site, interview landowners, and obtain a reasonable price for the purchase of 128 acres on the Henry farm and 145 acres on the Dogan farm. Again, they interviewed Round, who insisted that $20,000 was a reasonable price to pay the Henry heirs, who had no legal obligation to protect the monuments yet had done so for nearly half a century. In December 1913 the War Department submitted its report to Congress concluding that the tracts should be purchased and placed under the charge of the Quartermaster Corps "for the protection and maintenance of any monuments or other memorials erected thereon." There was no need, the department concluded, to purchase additional land for a memorial park. The following month, Congressman Charles Carlin once more introduced a bill authorizing the purchase of land on the Bull Run battlefield. And once more, Congress failed to act. [53]

By 1917, the United States had turned its attention to Europe as a world war raged. Still, George Round persisted in his efforts to protect the Bull Run monuments. In a petition to Congress titled *Is the United States Too Poor to Own Its Own Monuments?*, he described the government's failure to act as a "national disgrace." The pamphlet recounted the monuments' origins as well as the campaign to protect them, imploring Congress to act before the Union veterans who had built them all perished. "While expending billions in preparedness for the future, I submit we ought to expend a few thousands to preserve these unique memorials as lessons of posterity," he closed.[54]

Round would not live to see the monuments or the battlefield protected. Despite his constant efforts to rally Union veterans to the monuments' defense, after Round's death in 1918 it would be white Southerners who oversaw the field and its interpretation. In 1921, the UDC and Sons of Confederate Veterans established the Manassas Battlefield Corporation, which developed a Confederate park at the Henry farm to "give a voice to the South and challenge depictions of their Confederate ancestors as enemies of [their] country." The Manassas Battlefield Corporation hoped the park would become the "supreme battlefield memorial" and lobbied state legislatures to appropriate funding for memorials and markers that would recall Confederate heroics. Fourteen years later, the Franklin D. Roosevelt administration incorporated the Confederate park into a New Deal Recreational Demonstration Area. Not until 1940 would the federal government establish the Manassas National Battlefield Park, finally taking full ownership and responsibility for the memorials established by its victorious soldiers.[55]

Although unique in many respects, the Bull Run and Groveton monuments stand today as representative of many facets of Civil War memorialization. They serve as testament to the immediate desire of Union soldiers to commemorate the human cost of war and of their devotion to the Union cause. The story of their preservation embodies the surge of reconciliationist sentiment surrounding the semicentennial of the war. And perhaps most important, the monuments function as stark reminders that memory has always been intimately connected to contemporary politics and culture. Both Unionists and Confederates failed to imagine that memorials to their respective causes might ever fall out of fashion. They assumed that what had been written in stone would endure for all time.

Notes

1. S. P. Heintzelman Journal, June 11, 1865, Bull Run Monument Files, Manassas National Battlefield Park, Manassas, VA (hereafter, MANA); *New York Times*, June 12, 1865; *Evening Star* (Washington, DC), June 12, 1865; *Richmond Daily Whig*, June 14, 1865.

2. *New York Times*, June 13, 1865; *Boston Semi-Weekly Advertiser*, June 14, 1865; James McCallum CSR, Fold3.com, accessed July 29, 2024; Bvt. Brig. Gen. William Gamble to Gen. Daniel McCallum, June 19, 1865, Bull Run Monument Files, MANA; Michael W. Panhorst, "Sacred to the Memory: Two of the Nation's Oldest Monuments Stand on the Bull Run Battlefield," *Civil War Times*, April 2010, 60–64; *Protection of Monuments on Battle Fields of Bull Run: Hearings on H.R. 1330, before the Committee on Military Affairs*, 62nd Cong., 33–36 (1912); Protection of Monuments on Battle Field of Bull Run, H.R. 481, 63rd Cong. (1913). Lt. James McCallom's name is sometimes spelled "McCallum."

3. Special Orders No. 98, Headquarters 1st Separate Brigade, Fairfax Court House, May 28, 1865, Bull Run Monument Files, MANA; Bill to Protect the Monuments Already Erected, 33–36; Unfinished Railroad Cultural Landscape Report, 1.30, MANA; Panhorst, "Sacred to the Memory."

4. *Richmond Daily Dispatch*, September 10, 1861; *New Orleans Times-Picayune*, September 13, 1861; Robert E. L. Krick, "The Civil War's First Monument: Bartow's Marker at Manassas," *Blue and Gray Magazine*, April 1991, 32–34; Michael W. Panhorst, "'The First of Our Hundred Battle Monuments': Civil War Battlefield Monuments Built by Active-Duty Soldiers during the Civil War," *Southern Cultures* 20, no. 4 (Winter 2014): 22–43.

5. Heintzelman Journal, June 11, 1865, MANA; *New York Herald*, June 13, 1865.

6. Bill to Protect the Monuments Already Erected, 33; *New York Herald*, June 13, 1865; John R. Neff, *Honoring the Civil War Dead: Commemoration and the Problem of Reconciliation* (Lawrence: University Press of Kansas, 2005), 84–85, 91; Thomas Reed Turner, *Beware the People Weeping: Public Opinion and the Assassination of Abraham Lincoln* (Baton Rouge: Louisiana State University Press, 1982), 78; Edward J. Blum, *Reforging the White Republic: Race, Religion, and American Nationalism* (Baton Rouge: Louisiana State University Press, 2005), 25–26. According to David B. Chesebrough, sermons are "reflections of current thought, emotions, problems, issues, values, practices, prejudices, and beliefs" (Chesebrough, *No Sorrow Like Our Sorrow: Northern Protestant Ministers and the Assassination of Lincoln* [Kent, OH: Kent State University Press, 1994], xx, 63).

7. *New York Times*, June 12 and 13, 1865; *New York Herald*, June 13, 1865. Pierpont wrote two separate hymns, one sung at each monument dedication, both of which specifically addressed slavery.

8. *New York Herald*, June 13, 1865; *Richmond Daily Whig*, June 14, 1865.

9. *New York Herald*, June 13, 1865; *Boston Semi-Weekly Advertiser*, June 14, 1865. Some newspapers reported that the salute followed the hymn.

10. *New York Herald*, June 13, 1865; Alexander Gardner, *Gardner's Photographic Sketch Book of the War* (1866; repr., New York: Dover Publications, 1959), "Introduction to Dover Edition," n.p., and plate 100.

11. *Daily National Intelligencer*, June 13, 1865; *Hearing before the Committee of Military Affairs on H.R. 1330, Before the Committee on Military Affairs*, 62nd Cong., 8 (1912).

12. *Boston Semi-Weekly Advertiser*, June 14, 1865; *Morning Democrat* (Davenport, IA), June 17, 1865.

13. *New York Herald*, June 13, 1865.

14. Caroline E. Janney, *Remembering the Civil War: Reunion and the Limits of Reconciliation* (Chapel Hill: University of North Carolina Press, 2013).

15. *New York Times*, June 13, 1865; *Hartford (CT) Courant*, June 14, 1865.

16. *New York Times*, June 16, 1865; *Richmond Daily Whig*, June 19, 1865; *Evening Star*, June 17, 1865; *Flag of Our Union* (Boston), July 8, 1865. This story appeared in newspapers across the country.

17. Whitelaw Reid, *After the War: A Southern Tour: May 1, 1865–May 1, 1866* (Cincinnati: Moore, Wilstach & Baldwin, 1866), 312; John Townsend Trowbridge, *The South: A Tour of Its Battle-Fields and Ruined Cities, a Journey through the Desolated States, and Talks with the People* (1867; repr., Macon, GA: Mercer University Press, 2006), 88.

18. Edward B. Fowler to Hon. James Humphrey, March 15, 1866, transcription on file in 1866 Grave Files, MANA.

19. Neff, *Honoring the Civil War Dead*, 108–11, 127, 131; *New York Observer and Chronicle*, July 13, August 31, 1865; *New York Times*, July 4, 1865. On April 13, 1866, Congress passed an act to "preserve from desecration the graves of the soldiers of the United States that fell in battle or died of disease in the field and in hospital during the war of rebellion." On February 22, 1867, Congress passed legislation that formally linked these resting places under the National Cemetery System. (Frederick Phisterer, *The Army in the Civil War: Statistical Record of the Armies of the United States* [New York: Charles Scribner's Sons, 1882], 8:77)

20. *Statement of the Disposition of Some of the Bodies of Deceased Union Soldiers . . . National Cemeteries*, vol. 1 (Washington, DC: Government Printing Office, 1868), 8–9. Some Confederate prisoners or soldiers who had died in Northern hospitals were interred in national cemeteries, but overwhelmingly, national cemeteries were reserved only for loyal US soldiers. These national cemeteries, however, were not to be for white soldiers alone. In a radical departure from the antebellum period in which racially integrated cemeteries were rare, the burial corps routinely included Black soldiers in the memorial grounds. Neff, *Honoring the Civil War Dead*, 125–67, 224; William A. Blair, *Cities of the Dead: Contesting the Memory of the Civil War in the South, 1865-1914* (Chapel Hill: University of North Carolina Press, 2004), 52–53, 179–93; *Daily Phoenix*, August 1, 1869.

21. R. W. Tyler to Col. M. J. Ludington, March 28, 1866, original from RG 92, National Archives and Records Administration (NARA), Washington, DC, transcription on file in 1866 Grave Files, MANA; *Cleveland Daily Leader*, Nov. 27, 1865.

22. R. W. Tyler to Col. M. J. Ludington, March 28, 1866, original from RG 92, NARA, transcription on file in 1866 Grave Files, MANA; "The Union Dead on the Battlefields of Virginia," *New York Times*, April 8, 1866.

23. Col. Q.M. Department to Col. M. J. Ludington, March 26, 1866, original from RG 92, NARA, transcription on file in 1866 Grave Files, MANA; *Public Ledger* (Memphis, Tenn.),

April 17, 1866; *Statement of the Disposition of Some of the Bodies of Deceased Union Soldiers*, 8–9; Micki McElya, *The Politics of Mourning: Death and Honor in Arlington National Cemetery* (Cambridge, MA: Harvard University Press, 2016), 111–12; Kathryn Allamong Jacob, *Testament to the Union: Civil War Monuments in Washington, DC* (Baltimore: Johns Hopkins University Press, 1998), 156–57.

24. G. A. Starbuck and M. A. Starbuck to Gen. Meigs, June 9, 1865, transcription on file in 1866 Grave Files, MANA. On Arlington not carrying the prestige it would attain in the twentieth century, see McElya, *Politics of Mourning*, 97.

25. McElya, *Politics of Mourning*, 151–53.

26. A Bill to Establish and to Protect National Cemeteries, H.R. 788, 39th Cong. (1866).

27. Oliver Cox to Col. A. F. Rockwell, March 12, 1879, and Montgomery C. Meigs to Miss D. L. Dix, March 15, 1879, Bull Run Monuments File, MANA. Dix had helped to raise funds for a monument to fallen Union soldiers at Fort Monroe dedicated in 1868.

28. Mildred C. Baruch and Ellen J. Beckman, *Civil War Union Monuments: A List of Union Monuments, Markers and Memorials of the American Civil War, 1861–1865* (N.p.: Daughters of Union Veterans of the Civil War, 1978), 122, 142.

29. Jim Weeks, *Gettysburg: Memory, Market, and an American Shrine* (Princeton, NJ: Princeton University Press, 2003), 21; James Marten, *Sing Not War: The Lives of Union and Confederate Veterans in Gilded Age America* (Chapel Hill: University of North Carolina Press, 2011), 133–35.

30. John M. Vanderslice, *Gettysburg: A History of the Gettysburg Battle-field Memorial Association, with an Account of the Battle, Giving Movements, Positions, and Losses of the Commands Engaged* (Philadelphia: Memorial Association, 1897), 211.

31. M. Keith Harris, "Across the Bloody Chasm: Reconciliation in the Wake of the Civil War" (PhD diss., University of Virginia, 2009),101.

32. J. Howard Wert, *A Complete Hand-book of the Monuments and Indications and Guide to the Positions on the Gettysburg Battlefield* (Harrisburg, PA: B.M. Sturgeon, 1886), 5.

33. For more on reconciliation and its limits, see Janney, *Remembering the Civil War.*

34. Timothy B. Smith, *The Golden Age of Battlefield Preservation: The Decade of the 1890s and the Establishment of America's First Five Military Parks* (Knoxville: University of Tennessee Press, 2008), xvii, 5.

35. Smith, *Golden Age*, 7, 9, 34, 55, 61.

36. Timothy B. Smith, *This Great Battlefield of Shiloh: History, Memory, and the Establishment of a Civil War National Military Park* (Knoxville: University of Tennessee Press, 2004), 18; Smith, *Golden Age*, 36–37.

37. A Bill to Establish a National Military Park at the Battlefield of Chickamauga, H.R. Rep. No. 643 (1889–90).

38. A Bill to Establish Battle Park on Bull Run, H.R. 7837, 56th Cong. (1900).

39. George Carr Round CSR, Fold3.com, accessed July 30, 2024; *Alexandria Gazette*, November 9, 1918; *Evening Star*, November 7, 1918; Joan M. Zenzen, *Battling for Manassas: The Fifty-Year Preservation Struggle at Manassas National Battlefield Park* (State College: Penn State University Press, 1997), 5–7. At the 1901 National Encampment of the GAR, C. A. E. Spamer of Baltimore filed a resolution urging protection of the monuments (*National Tribune* [Washington, DC], August 16, 1906; Protection of Monuments, 5).

40. Protection of Monuments, 28; *Baltimore Sun*, December 2, 1901; A Bill to Protect the Monuments Already Erected on the Battlefields of Bull Run, Virginia, H.R. 277, 57th Cong. (1901).

41. *Topeka Daily Herald*, February 24, 1902. Douglas Hill, also known as Douglas Heights, was part of the Brawner Farm. The misspelling "Douglass" is Round's.

42. *Evening Star*, February 19, 1902.

43. Protection of Monuments, 29–36.

44. Protection of Monuments, 29–32.

45. *Journal . . . Annual Encampment* 37 (1903): 307–8, 315–17; *Denver Rocky Mountain News*, September 6, 1905. In November 1903, Congressman Rixey reintroduced the exact same bill. The following year, the Department of Maryland reintroduced the resolution to the GAR, but again no endorsement was gained. See A Bill to Protect the Monuments Already Erected on the Battlefields of Bull Run, Virginia, H.R. 1964, 58th Cong. (1903).

46. *Evening Star*, May 10, 12, 1905; *Washington Post*, May 11, 1905.

47. *Journal . . . National Encampment* 40 (1906): 94, 207, 387–89.

48. Henry and Robinson Farm CLR, 2–62, MANA; *Journal . . . National Encampment* 41 (1907): 257–58.

49. A Bill to Protect the Monuments Already Erected on the Battlefields of Bull Run, Virginia . . . , S. 8180, 59th Cong. (1907).

50. *Evening Star*, August 13, 1909; *Protection of Monuments*, 3–12. Both bills nearly replicated the 1911 Senate bill. The House bill was introduced by Charles Carlin and the Senate bill by Claude Swanson.

51. *Protection of Monuments*, 10–11.

52. *Protection of Monuments*, 13–15. For more on the UDC as resistant to reconciliation, see Janney, *Remembering the Civil War*, chapter 8. For more on battlefields as the province of men, see chapter 7.

53. A Bill to Protect the Monuments Already Erected on the Battle Fields, H.R. Rep. No. 1479, 62nd Cong. (1913); Protection of Monuments, 1–8; Zenzen, *Battling for Manassas*, 11–12; A Bill Authorizing the Purchase of Certain Lands on the Battle Fields of Bull Run, H.R. 12466, 63rd Cong. (1914).

54. George Carr Round, *Is the United States Too Poor to Own Its Own Monuments?*, 1917, Bull Run Monuments File, MANA.

55. Zenzen, *Battling for Manassas*, 13; Henry and Robinson Farm CLR, 2–69–75, MANA. For more on the efforts to create a national battlefield park, see Zenzen, *Battling for Manassas*.

BIBLIOGRAPHIC ESSAY

Relatively few books cover the Second Manassas campaign as a discrete event. Its position between Robert E. Lee's first major campaign, the Seven Days' battles, and Lee's first invasion of the North, the Antietam campaign, has resulted in relatively thin coverage of the campaign and battle. As a result, only a handful of books describe the campaign alone, whereas many other works encompass the campaign as a part of larger movements.

A student of Second Manassas should begin with the US War Department, *The War of the Rebellion: A Compilation of the Official Records of the Union and Confederate Armies*, 128 vols., index and atlas (Washington, DC: Government Printing Office, 1880–1901), colloquially known as the *Official Records* or *OR*. To obtain a full picture of the campaign, one must turn to an unusually large number of *OR* volumes because of the lack of a unified Union command structure and because the preliminary and concluding aspects of the campaign represented, respectively, the end of the Seven Days' battles and the start of the Antietam campaign. Series 1, volume 12, parts 2 and 3, encompass the major actions of John Pope's forces and the battle of Second Manassas, while the supplement to part 2 contains Fitz John Porter's court-martial. Volume 11, parts 1, 2, and 3, trace George B. McClellan's Army of the Potomac from June through September 1862, as well as Ambrose E. Burnside's Ninth Corps, both of whose forces reinforced Pope's Army of Virginia. Series 3, volume 2, offers materials from the Union secretary of war's office that are germane. The *Supplement to the Official Records of the Union and Confederate Armies* (Wilmington, NC: Broadfoot, 1994–2001), part 1, volume 2, addendum to series 1, volumes 11–12, also contain approximately three dozen documents pertaining to the campaign.

Other standard sources provide additional postwar testimony on Second Manassas and its attendant controversies, many of which are easily accessed by the modern reader either in a library or through an online edition. *The Southern Historical Society Papers*, ed. J. William Jones and others, 52 vols. (1876–1959; repr., with 3-vol. index, Wilmington, NC: Broadfoot, 1990–92), and *Confederate Veteran*, 40 vols. (1893–1932; repr., with 3-vol. index, Wilmington, NC: Broadfoot, 1984–86), provide abundant materials written by Confederate veterans. For insight into US veteran perspectives, readers should consult the *Papers of the Military Order of the Loyal Legion of the United States*, 66 vols. and 3-vol. index (Wilmington, NC: Broadfoot, 1991–96), and the *Papers of the Military Historical Society of Massachusetts*, vol. 1, *Campaigns in Virginia, 1861–62*, ed. Theodore F. Dwight (1895; repr., Wilmington, NC: Broadfoot, 1989).

Further contemporary testimony from both sides appeared in *Century Magazine*, later published in volume 2 of *Battles and Leaders of the Civil War*, ed. Robert Underwood Johnson and Clarence Clough Buel, 4 vols. (New York: Century, 1884–88). Additional material from *Century Magazine* that went uncollected in the original four volumes appeared in *Battles and Leaders of the Civil War*, vols. 4 and 5, ed. Peter Cozzens (Urbana: University of Illinois Press, 2002 and 2004). A handful of other pertinent articles from nineteenth-century periodical literature appear in *The New Annals of the Civil War*, ed. Peter Cozzens and Robert I. Girardi (Mechanicsburg, PA: Stackpole Books, 2004).

Memoirs from Union officers provide sustained discussion of the Second Manassas campaign from the perspective of leadership. John Pope's war reminiscences, published as *The Military Memoirs of General John Pope*, ed. Peter Cozzens and Robert I. Girardi (Chapel Hill: University of North Carolina Press, 1998), offer some of the commanding general's reflections on the 1862 campaign while also yielding important context about his decision-making. David H. Strother, a skilled topographer on Pope's staff, kept detailed notes on headquarters activities, which appear in *A Virginia Yankee in the Civil War: The Diaries of David Hunter Strother*, ed. Cecil D. Eby Jr. (Chapel Hill: University of North Carolina Press, 1961). Herman Haupt offered his essential opinions on railroad logistics in *Reminiscences of General Herman Haupt* (Milwaukee: Wright and Joys, 1901). Carl Schurz, a German immigrant who played an important role in the First Corps of Pope's Army of Virginia, related his war experiences in the second volume of *The Reminiscences of Carl*

Schurz, 3 vols. (New York: McClure, 1907). Brig. Gen. George H. Gordon also penned several colorful histories of the campaign: *Brook Farm to Cedar Mountain: In the War of the Great Rebellion, 1861–62* (Cambridge, MA: Riverside Press, 1883), and *History of the Campaign of the Army of Virginia, under John Pope, Brigadier-General U.S.A.; Late Major-General U.S. Volunteers; From Cedar Mountain to Alexandria, 1862* (Boston: Houghton, Osgood and Company, 1880).

A number of more recent secondary sources render assessments of Union leaders. Peter Cozzens, *General John Pope: A Life for the Nation* (Urbana: University of Illinois Press, 2000), is a superb look at the controversial commander of the Army of Virginia and is also one of the best military histories of the US side of the campaign to date. William Marvel provides well-researched portraits of three key players on the US side of the campaign in *Radical Sacrifice: The Rise and Ruin of Fitz John Porter* (Chapel Hill: University of North Carolina Press, 2021), *Lincoln's Autocrat: The Life of Edwin Stanton* (Chapel Hill: University of North Carolina Press, 2015), and *Burnside* (Chapel Hill: University of North Carolina Press, 1991). Although it is dated and fails to connect its subject matter with the reference to French anti-Semitism in its title, Austrian chemist and immigrant Otto Eisenschiml's *The Celebrated Case of Fitz John Porter: An American Dreyfus Affair* (Indianapolis: Bobbs-Merrill, 1950) remains a spirited account of Porter's life and postwar attempts at exoneration. Both Stephen W. Sears, *George B. McClellan: The Young Napoleon* (New York: Ticknor and Fields, 1988), and Ethan S. Rafuse, *McClellan's War: The Failure of Moderation in the Struggle for the Union* (Bloomington: Indiana University Press, 2005), depict McClellan's problematic participation in the campaign. William B. Styple, in his monumental tome *Philip Kearny: A Very God of War; The Life and Letters of Major-General Philip Kearny* (Gettysburg: Bellegrove, 2022), gives an exhaustive account of the ill-fated division leader.

Firsthand testimony from Confederate leadership remains comparatively scarcer than that of Union accounts, although a number of Confederate staff officers provided evidence from headquarters. Though Lee never wrote his memoirs, *The Wartime Papers of R. E. Lee*, ed. Clifford Dowdey and Louis H. Manarin (Boston: Little, Brown, 1961), provides key documents from the Confederate commander's perspective. James Longstreet, one of Lee's chief lieutenants, offered his viewpoint in *From Manassas to Appomattox: Memoirs of the Civil War in America* (1896; repr., Bloomington: Indiana University Press, 1960). Jubal Early, a Confederate brigadier general under Richard S. Ewell who participated in important moments from Cedar Mountain to Chantilly, offered detailed accounts in the published oration *Jackson's*

Campaign against Pope, in August, 1862 (Baltimore: Foley Bros. Printers, 1883) and in his complete autobiography, *Narrative of the War between the States* (1912; repr., New York: Da Capo Press with Broadfoot, 1989); the 1989 reprint includes an introduction by Gary W. Gallagher. Lee's headquarters staff later published several accounts of great value, including Walter H. Taylor, *General Lee: His Campaigns in Virginia 1861–1865 with Personal Reminiscences* (New York: Braunworth, 1906). Charles Marshall's *An Aide-de-Camp of Lee*, ed. Frederick Maurice (Boston: Little, Brown, 1927), gives unparalleled insight into Lee's thoughts during the campaign; a paperback reprint retitled *Lee's Aide-de-Camp* comes with additional context provided in an introduction by Gary W. Gallagher (Lincoln: University of Nebraska Press, 2000). Edward Porter Alexander's memoirs, *Fighting for the Confederacy: The Personal Recollections of General Edward Porter Alexander*, ed. Gary W. Gallagher (1989; repr., Chapel Hill: University of North Carolina Press, 1998), keenly reflects on artillery in the campaign from the perspective of a staff officer. Stonewall Jackson's cartographer Jedediah Hotchkiss kept a thorough journal, published later as *Make Me a Map of the Valley: The Civil War Journals of Stonewall Jackson's Topographer*, ed. Archie P. McDonald (Dallas: Southern Methodist University Press, 1973). The recollections of Henry Kyd Douglas, which appeared as *I Rode with Stonewall: The War Experiences of the Youngest Member of Jackson's Staff* (Chapel Hill: University of North Carolina Press, 1940), provides some important information on Confederate leadership during the campaign, though, because of Douglas's propensity to exaggerate, it must be used with care.

Secondary accounts of Confederate leadership yield additional insight into the course of the campaign. Gary W. Gallagher provides a good starting point in *Lee and His Generals in War and Memory* (Baton Rouge: Louisiana State University Press, 1998), in which he offers a helpful assessment of Lee, Longstreet, and Jackson at Second Manassas while wading through some of the postwar controversies over the battle. Christian B. Keller's *The Great Partnership: Robert E. Lee, Stonewall Jackson, and the Fate of the Confederacy* (New York: Pegasus Books, 2019) considers the leadership dynamic of the Confederate high command. Many biographies provide detail on other Confederate leaders, such as Elizabeth Varon, *Longstreet: The Confederate General Who Defied the South* (New York: Simon and Schuster, 2023), and Donald C. Pfanz, *Richard S. Ewell* (Chapel Hill: University of North Carolina Press, 1998).

One early account of Second Manassas stands out: that of John Codman Ropes. A member of the Massachusetts Historical Society and the Military

Historical Society of Massachusetts, Ropes himself did not serve in the Civil War, though many of his circle in Boston did. Interested in military history and urged on by friends, Ropes turned his considerable talents to writing, resulting in *The Army under Pope* (New York: Charles Scribner's Sons, 1881), a volume in the Campaigns of the Civil War series. Even-handed, temperate in tone, and based on primary source material, the book provides an ideal starting place for studying the campaign. A modern reprint (Wilmington, NC: Broadfoot, 1989) bears an introduction from William A. Blair, which adds detail on Ropes's life and other works. Ropes also contributed an introduction to a rough Confederate analogue to his book, though one more expansive in scope. That volume, *The Army of Northern Virginia in 1862* (Cambridge, MA: Riverside Press, 1892), written by William Allan, one of Jackson's staff officers, similarly provided fair treatment of the subject combined with solid research rooted in primary sources.

Overall, modern scholarship on the Second Manassas campaign is relatively thin, considering its important military and political ramifications, its intricacy, and its controversies. The starting place for serious study remains John J. Hennessy, *Return to Bull Run: The Campaign and Battle of Second Manassas* (1993; repr., Norman: University of Oklahoma Press, 1999), which provides thorough discussion of the military dimensions of the campaign while also giving due attention to its political context. Hennessy's *Second Manassas Battlefield Map Study* (Lynchburg, VA: Howard, 1991) aids readers who hope to grasp the complicated troop movements of the campaign. The battle of Second Manassas can best be understood after treading the ground; Joseph W. A. Whitehorne, *The Battle of Second Manassas: Self-Guided Tour* (Washington, DC: Center of Military History, United States Army, 1990), and Ethan S. Rafuse, *Manassas: A Battlefield Guide* (Lincoln: University of Nebraska, 2014), both provide excellent battlefield guidebooks, while Dan Welch and Kevin R. Pawlak, *Never Such a Campaign: The Battle of Second Manassas, August 28–30, 1862* (El Dorado, CA: Savas Beatie, 2024), also offers a useful tour with superior maps.

Several books describe portions of the action during the climactic days of fighting. Alan D. Gaff, *Brave Men's Tears: The Iron Brigade at Brawner Farm* (Dayton, OH: Morningside, 1985), is a classic study of the first day's fighting at the battle of Second Bull Run, while Scott Patchan, *Second Manassas: Longstreet's Attack and the Struggle for Chinn Ridge* (Washington, DC: Potomac Books, 2011), covers the closing salvo of the main battle. A pair of modern studies depict both the prelude and coda to the campaign. Robert K. Krick, *Stonewall Jackson at Cedar Mountain* (1990; repr., Chapel Hill: University of North Carolina Press, 2000), gives a vivid portrait of Jackson's opening battle against Banks. And David A. Welker ably describes the sharp fighting that broke out when Jackson attempted to cut off Pope's retreat in his book *Tempest at Ox Hill: The Battle of Chantilly* (New York: Da Capo Press, 2001).

Other books discuss the Second Manassas campaign as part of a larger treatment of the Civil War in Virginia in 1862. Benjamin Franklin Cooling, *Counter-Thrust: From the Peninsula to the Antietam* (Lincoln: University of Nebraska Press, 2007), considers Confederate action from the Seven Days to Antietam as one large offensive. Taken together, Joseph L. Harsh's *Confederate Tide Rising: Robert E. Lee and the Making of Southern Strategy, 1861–1862* (Kent: Kent State University Press, 1998) and *Taken at the Flood: Robert E. Lee and Confederate Strategy in the Maryland Campaign of 1862* (Kent: Kent State University Press, 1999) feature the campaign in its larger military context.

A handful of scholarly works examine the armies themselves and place those who fought in a larger social context. Joseph T. Glatthaar provides a detailed study of the military and political dimension of the main Confederate army with *General Lee's Army from Victory to Collapse* (New York: Free Press, 2008). John H. Matsui, *The First Republican Army: The Army of Virginia and the Radicalization of the Civil War* (Charlottesville: University of Virginia Press, 2016), provides a similar treatment of Pope's army.

The fighting at Second Manassas features prominently in many unit histories of the regiments that fought there, both those written by survivors and those penned later. Comparing these accounts shows how writing and interpretation of the Civil War have changed over the century and a half since the war. A few examples illustrate the range of accounts available. Veteran Alfred Davenport, a former private, wrote of the heroic stand and near annihilation of the 5th New York Infantry at Chinn Ridge at Second Manassas in *Camp and Field Life of the Fifth New York Volunteer Infantry (Duryee Zouaves)* (1879; repr., Gaithersburg, MD: Butternut Press, 1984). Brian Pohanka's *Vortex of Hell: A History of the 5th New York Volunteer Infantry, Duryée's Zouaves, 1861–1863* (Lynchburg, VA: Schroeder Publications, 2012) covers the same ground with considerable aplomb and with a greater depth of research. Former Confederate sergeant J. B. Polley's *Hood's Texas Brigade: Its Marches, Its Battles, Its Achievements* (1910; repr., Dayton, OH: Morningside, 1976) remains a romanticized, if classic, account that provides the view of the 5th New York's Confederate antagonists. With colorful anecdotes, Harold B. Simpson retells the tale in *Hood's Texas Brigade: Lee's Grenadier Guard* (Waco, TX: Texian Press, 1970), while Susannah J. Ural gives a more scholarly and sober take in *Hood's Texas Brigade: The Soldiers and Families of the Confederacy's Most Celebrated Unit* (Baton Rouge: Louisiana State University Press, 2017). Jeffry D. Wert compares two famous brigades that fought at Manassas in *Brotherhood of Valor: The Common Soldiers of the Stonewall Brigade, C.S.A., and Iron Brigade, U.S.A.* (New York: Simon and Schuster, 1999). The above provide only the briefest sample of the much wider literature on Confederate and Union military units.

Readers who wish to learn more about the activities of a particular unit during the battle should consult reference works, such as Charles W. Dornbusch's *Military Bibliography of the Civil War*, 4 vols. (New York: New York Public Library, 1961–72; repr., Dayton, OH: Morningside, 1987), with a revised vol. 4 and additional volume compiled by Silas Felton (Dayton, OH: Morningside, 2003 and 2020). Garold L. Cole's thoroughly indexed books place otherwise arcane accounts close at hand. The pair of volumes are *Civil War Eyewitnesses: An Annotated Bibliography of Books and Articles, 1955–1986* (Columbia: University of South Carolina Press, 1988) and *Civil War Eyewitnesses: An Annotated Bibliography of Books and Articles, 1986–1996* (Columbia: University of South Carolina Press, 2000).

CONTRIBUTORS

KEITH S. BOHANNON is a professor of history at the University of West Georgia in Carrollton, Georgia.

GARY W. GALLAGHER has published widely about the era of the Civil War, including *The Enduring Civil War: Reflections on the Great American Crisis* (2020).

JOHN J. HENNESSY retired as the chief historian at Fredericksburg and Spotsylvania National Military Park. He is the author of dozens of articles and four books, including *Return to Bull Run: The Campaign and Battle of Second Manassas* (1993).

CAROLINE E. JANNEY is the John L. Nau III Professor of the History of the American Civil War and director of the John L. Nau Center for Civil War History at the University of Virginia. She has published eight books, including *Remembering the Civil War: Reunion and the Limits of Reconciliation* (2013) and *Ends of War: The Unfinished Fight of Lee's Army after Appomattox* (2021), winner of the 2022 Lincoln Prize.

PETER C. LUEBKE received his PhD from the University of Virginia in 2014. He has written and presented widely on American military history. He is the editor of a scholarly edition of Albion Tourgée's *The Story of a Thousand* (2011) as well as *The Autobiography of John A. Dahlgren* (2019).

JAMES MARTEN is professor emeritus of history at Marquette University and a former president of the Society of Civil War Historians. Among his books are *America's Corporal: James Tanner in War and Peace* (2014), *Sing Not War: The Lives of Union and Confederate Veterans in Gilded Age America* (2011), and a forthcoming history of the 6th Wisconsin.

WILLIAM MARVEL is an independent scholar from northern New Hampshire who has written twenty books about the Civil War era, including *Radical Sacrifice: The Rise and Ruin of Fitz John Porter* (2021).

KATHRYN J. SHIVELY is an associate professor of history at Virginia Commonwealth University and the author of *Nature's Civil War: Common Soldiers and the Environment in 1862 Virginia* (2013), winner of the Wiley-Silver Prize for best first book on the Civil War.

CECILY ZANDER is an assistant professor of history at Texas Woman's University and a senior fellow at the Center for Presidential History at Southern Methodist University. Her first book, *The Army under Fire: The Politics of Antimilitarism in the Civil War Era*, was published in 2024.

INDEX

Page numbers in italics refer to illustrations.

African Americans: as absent from Pope's general orders, 15, 29; employed by US army, 47, 48, 49, 52, 61nn36–38; intelligence brought to Union lines by, 47, 48, 61n36. *See also* enslaved people; enslavers; slavery

Alexandria, VA, 24, 25, 67, 110; and Army of Virginia Third Corps, 5; and Bull Run monuments, 218; and enslaved refugees, 23, 42, 47; Union depot at, 21, 23. *See also* Orange & Alexandria Railroad

Allan, William, 136, 137, 247; and Lee, 124, 125, 134, 138, 139, 174

Anderson, Richard, 169, 177, 183

Antietam, battle of, 71, 91n7, 248; Confederate retreat after, 70; memorialization of, 12, 219, 230; Second Manassas campaign overshadowed by, 3, 65, 90n2, 243; and 6th Wisconsin, 160, 161. *See also* Maryland campaign

Aquia Landing, 21, 22, 23, 25, 47, 61

Army of Northern Virginia, 4, *8*, 65, 71, 80, 100, 115, 164; at Cedar Mountain, 114; concerns about casualties, 90, 96n62; culture and strategy of aggression of, 10, 66, 136, 137; and epistolary descriptions of war, 68, 69, 90; and Hood, *172*, 183; hunger faced by, 5; in Lost Cause myth, 139; members' support for Lee's strategy, 72, 73, 78, 79, 90; and Peninsula campaign, 2; at Seven Days, 73, 74; in Southern press, 69, 70; and Texas Brigade, 171; vilification of Pope by, 86, 87

—units of: First Corps, 74; Second Corps, 74; 2nd Virginia Infantry, 79; 4th Texas Infantry, 91n7, 170; 5th Texas Infantry, 9, 179, 180, 181, 183; 8th Georgia Infantry, 220; 10th Alabama Infantry, 75; 12th Georgia Infantry, 78; 13th South Carolina Infantry, 88; 14th Louisiana Infantry, 86; 18th Georgia Infantry, 180; 21st Virginia Infantry, 5; 34th North Carolina Infantry, 69; 60th Georgia Infantry, 89; Hampton Legion, 180; "Old Third" Brigade, 171. *See also* Texas Brigade

Army of the Potomac, 25, 31n8, 65, 67, 73, 136, 243; African Americans in, 48; and Army of Virginia dissolution, 55; defeat at Fredericksburg, 202, 203; failure at Seven Days, 3, 4; and Halleck's failures, 21; and historiography, 243; and inter-army political discord, 18, 19, 100, 109, 111, 115; McClellan's command of, 191, 193; members' loyalties to McClellan, 38, 116; members' varied experiences, 11, 16, 146; memory and memorialization of, 219, 220, 229, 230; and Peninsula Campaign, 149; poor leadership of, 5; and Porter's court-martial, 202, 205, 208, 211; reinforcement of Pope's Army of Virginia, 5; reorganization and retraining of, 167n38; and Seven Pines battle, 133; and Society of the Army of the Potomac, 234; and subordination of ideology to pragmatism, 48; support for emancipation, 38, 55, 56; support for Pope's hard war, 38, 112; valor at Brawner Farm, 164; victory at Gettysburg, 229. *See also* McClellan, George B.

—units of: First Corps, 55; 2nd Massachusetts, 49, 54, 56, 229; 2nd Wisconsin Infantry, 147; Fifth Corps, 5, 7, 33n22, 135, 158, 193; 5th New York Infantry, 9, 180, 181, 234, 248; 7th Wisconsin Infantry, 147; Ninth Corps, 4, 16, 22, 243; 10th New York Infantry, 180; Eleventh Corps, 55; Twelfth Corps, 55; 19th Indiana Infantry, 147. *See also* 6th Wisconsin

Army of Virginia, 6, 63n58, 65, 134; defeat of, 24, 29, 55, 56; dissolution of, 55; and enslaved refugees, 29, 42, 46, 47, 59n16, 61n33; formation of, 4, 17, 38, 100; and inter-army political discord, 100; policies toward slavery and confiscation, 52, 98; Pope as commander of, 2, 4, 7, 51, 97, 98; subordination of ideology to pragmatism, 49; support for emancipation, 38; and ties between military and political aspects of war, 11, 98; vilification by Confederate civilians, 85, 88. *See also* Army of Virginia—logistical collapse of; Army of Virginia—members of; Pope, John; Pope, John—general orders of

—logistical collapse of, 9, 10, 14, 24, 29, 30n1; and Confederate civilian interference, 26, 31n3; due to divided command, 15, 19, 26, 27, 150; and Frémont's independent-mindedness, 18, 19; and Halleck's decisions, 21; and medical crises, 24, 33n24, 34n24; as out of Pope's hands, 15; and Pope's administrative failures, 20, 26, 27, 34nn28–30; and supply and communication lines, 20, 21, 22, 23, 25, 26, 34n26; and horses, 24, 34n25. *See also* Army of Virginia; Army of Virginia—members of; Pope, John

—members of: apolitical stances of, 122n62; embrace of Pope's hard war, 38, 110, 111, 112, 113; epiphanies regarding slavery, 41, 43, 45, 50, 51, 52, 53, 55, 56; hostility toward enslaved people, 58n1, 61n41; interactions with enslaved people, 10, 39, 40, 41, 43, 45, 49, 50; loyalties to McClellan, 38, 116; opposition to formal emancipation proclamation, 55, 63n59; on Pope's prospects, 111; and racist tropes, 58n1; on significance of emancipation to war effort, 55, 56; on slavery and emancipation, 36, 38, 40, 41, 43, 45, 46, 49, 50, 51, 53, 55, 59n13, 118n8; white civilian interactions with, 39, 40. *See also* Army of Virginia; Army of Virginia—logistical collapse of; Pope, John

—units of: First Corps, 6, 17, 18, 19, 20, 27, 32n13, 38, 244; Second Corps, 17, 18, 19, 27, 39; Third Corps, 5, 6, 17, 31, 33, 39, 221; 5th Connecticut Infantry, 114; 33rd Iowa Infantry, 112; 84th Pennsylvania Infantry, 50

Ball's Bluff, battle of, 102, 103, 104
Banks, Nathaniel, 32n11, 39, 48, 54, 100, 107, 111; at Cedar Mountain, 4, 114, 134, 150, 248; and tensions with Pope, 19, 26, 32n14; views on slavery, 39, 47
Bartow, Francis S., monument to, 220, 221
Blue Ridge, 5, 36, 39, 44, 48
Bragg, Edward, 148, 156, 157, 160; exemplary leadership by, 146, 147, 159, 161
Brawner Farm, battle of, 3, 6, 7, 11, 146, 151, *156*, 165n1, 165n10, 171, 241n41; casualties, 157, 158, 159, 226; in press, 161, 162; and 6th Wisconsin, 11, 146, 163, 164, 165; and Union defeat at Second Bull Run, 146, 160. *See also* Groveton, Union monument at; Iron Brigade; 6th Wisconsin
Bristoe Station, 5, 6, 24, 64n63, 196, 201, 208
Brockway, Charles, 53, 54
Bull Run campaign, First, 37, 47, 158, 221, 222, 233, 235
Bull Run campaign, Second: memory and memorialization of, 12, 145, *221*, 222–32 passim, 235, 236; and Pope's limitations as commander, 115, 117n3; scholarship of, 2, 15, 65, 90n2, 243–49; slavery and emancipation and, 3, 10, 37, 39, 40, 41, 55, 56, 119n13; summary of events, 3–9; terminology, 3, 90n1; terrain, 8, 9; and ties between military operations and politics, 3, 10–12, 17, 37, 38, 53, 55, 56, 81, 98–103, 115–17, 119n14, 146, 192, 213n3; and Union army fortunes and morale, 1, 2, 9; Union defeat at, 10, 14, 30n1; viewed through lens of slavery and emancipation, 3, 10, 37, 39, 40, 41, 55, 56, 119n13. *See also* Manassas campaign, Second
Burnside, Ambrose, 4, 16, 31n8, 243, 245; and defeat at Fredericksburg battle, 202, 203; and Lee's strategy, 134, 135; and logistical collapse of Army of Virginia, 21, 22, 23, 29, 33n19; and Porter's court-martial, 191, 193, 198, 199, 201, 202, 203, 204, 205, 210, 211
Butler, Benjamin F.,84, 85, 86
casualties, 2, 11, 76, 104, 133, 175, 184, 189n41, 197; in Army of Northern Virginia, 90, 96n62; in Brawner Farm battle, 157, 158, 159, 160, 226; in Cedar Mountain battle, 76, 93n28; in 6th Wisconsin, 155, 157, 158, 159, 160; in Texas Brigade, 175, 181, 183; in Texas 5th Infantry, 183
Catlett's Station, 5, 23, 50, 51, 78
Cedar Mountain, battle of, 2, 4, 19, 68, 70, 77, 85, 134, 135, 150, 245, 247; casualties in, 76, 93n28; and hard war, 114; and Pope, 115
Centreville, VA, 6, 7, 9
Chandler, Zachariah, 102; criticism of McClellan, 104; and Joint Committee on the Conduct of the War, 103, 120n28; opposition to slavery, 101; and Fitz John Porter, 207, 209
Chantilly, battle of, 2, 9, 76, 77, 93n28, 245
Charleston, SC, 69, 126, 127
Chase, Salmon: and politics and military strategy, 107, 115; and Porter's court-martial, 193, 194, 213n10; support for Irvin McDowell, 39; support for Pope, 17, 100, 107, 111, 31n9, 32n9
Chinn Ridge, 8, 9, 169, 175, 180, 181, 182, 183, 248
Choate, Joseph, 209, 210
civilians, Confederate: antipathy toward Pope, 89, 90, 113, 114; approval of Lee's generalship, 67, 68, 76, 80, 90; and Army of Virginia's withdrawal, 29; and bushwhacking, 16; contact with Union soldiers, 10, 39, 56, 87, 88; contempt for "Yankees," 88, 89, 90, 114; and hard war, 84, 87, 88, 112, 114; praise for Jackson, 79; sabotage by, 10, 15, 25, 26; on Second Manassas campaign, 10, 71; support of Army of Northern Virginia's aggressive posture, 66, 72, 76, 80, 89; support of slavery, 46, 88, 89; Union policies and practices toward, 3, 4, 16, 17, 23, 27, 30n2, 35n34, 35n35, 37, 38, 39, 52, 80, 98, 108, 110, 112, 118n12. *See also* hard war; home front, morale on

Committee on the Conduct of the War, Joint. *See* Joint Committee on the Conduct of the War
Confederacy: and Second Manassas campaign, 1, 2; and inevitability of Civil War's disruption of slavery, 106, 119n13; memory and memorialization of, 219, 221, 224, 225, 230, 234, 236, 237; offensive stance under Lee, 134, 139, 143n61; on Pope's general orders, 76, 82, 83, 84, 117; prospect of foreign support for, 105, 111, 125, 128, 129; strategic problem of, 128, 131, 140n7. *See also* civilians, Confederate
Confiscation Act, First, 47, 102
Confiscation Act, Second, 62n49; and front lines, 44, 52, 89; and preliminary emancipation proclamation, 111; and Union defeat at Seven Days, 81, 94n42, 102; and uncooperative commanders, 103
Congress, Confederate, 74, 79, 84
Congress, US: and Civil War memorialization, 12, 219, 226–37 passim, 239n19, 241n45; Confederate attitude toward, 66, 90; conservative resurgence in 1862 elections, 193; disillusionment with Pope, 11; and emancipation, 52, 81, 102; and Lincoln's promotion of colonization, 120n22; and Pope's tour of Washington, 11, 16, 17, 98, 101, 105–9, 111; and Porter's court-martial, 195, 205, 206, 211, 212; and Republican hope in Pope's leadership, 97, 98, 99, 101, 107; and Second Confiscation Act, 52, 111; stern confiscation policies of, 15, 27, 28, 31n9, 32n9, 35; and war policy, 37, 38, 81, 102. *See also* Joint Committee on the Conduct of War; Republicans, Radical
"contrabands." *See* African Americans; enslaved people
Culpeper, VA, 4, 22, 24, 25, 41, 43, 44, 50, 85, 135, 136; Civil War memorialization in, 226; enslaved people in, 56, 60n22
Davis, Jefferson, 71, 129; and Lee's advice, 133, 135, 136; and Lee's offensive strategy, 79, 130, 131, 132, 137, 138; as more cautious than Lee, 142n28; response to Pope's general orders, 82, 84, 114
Dawes, Rufus, 147; and charge at Brawner Farm, 155, 160; at Gettysburg, 160; and emancipatory war, 45, 46; exemplary leadership of, 146, 159; in fog of war, 153, 156, 157, 159, 160; and rebel corpses, 150; resentment toward Pope, 116, 163. *See also* 6th Wisconsin
Democrats, 120n32; in Army of Virginia, 55; and Civil War memorialization, 235; and conciliation, 55; and emancipation, 53, 55; on Joint Committee on the Conduct of the War, 103, 104, 105, 120n28; on Pope's general orders, 113; and Porter's court-martial, 205, 207, 211, 212; as responsible for failures of Union army, 106; in Union army leadership, 11, 12, 55, 98, 99, 100, 101, 193, 213
divine intervention, belief in, 67, 68, 71, 73, 78, 79, 80
Douglas, Henry Kyd, 137, 143n53, 173; recollections of, 246

Eastern Theater: hard war in, 28, 30n2, 119n12; and Lee, 65, 66, 67, 80; Lincoln on, 3; and Second Manassas campaign, 1, 2, 10, 15, 21, 98
emancipation: in Civil War memorialization, 230; and Confederate retributive war, 10, 54, 66, 84, 89; and congressional confiscation policies, 29, 52, 111; legal versus spontaneous, 53, 54; and Lincoln, 55, 81, 101, 102, 107, 111, 117n4, 119n18, 120n22, 122n57; and McClellan, 4, 54, 55, 81, 117n6, 118n6, 191; as measure against Confederate war effort, 49, 53, 56, 81, 119n14; and Pope, 31n9, 38, 52, 105, 106, 107, 108; and Radical Republicans, 101, 102, 105, 117n4; and Second Manassas campaign,

10; Union army attitudes and policy toward, 10, 36, 37–41, 50–56, 213n4; as Union war aim, 37, 38, 101, 111. *See also* Army of Virginia—members of; Confiscation Act, Second; enslaved people; enslavers; slavery
Emancipation Act, District of Columbia, 40, 42
Emancipation Proclamation, 55
emancipation proclamation, preliminary, 3, 52, 65, 107, 111, 122n57, 193
enslaved people: attitudes toward US army, 10, 40, 41; children of, 44, 50; and emancipation policy, 53; equation of war to emancipation by, 40; and First Confiscation Act, 47, 102; interactions with US soldiers, 39, 40, 41, 42, 49, 54; journeys to freedom, 29, 31n9, 32n9, 37, 38, 41, 42, 43, 44, 47, 48, 49, 56, 57, 57, 59n12, 60n22, 61n35, 62n42, 64n63, 84; myth of loyalty to enslavers, 41, 43; recapture by Confederates, 64n63, 88, 89, 96n60; and Second Confiscation Act, 52, 81, 89; sexual exploitation of, 51; US army attitudes toward, 10, 36, 45, 46, 49, 50, 58n1; violence and terror faced by, 50, 51; women, 44, 51, 60n20
enslavers: attempts to contain news of Union's advance, 42; attempts to reclaim slaves, 45; violence and terrorization by, 50
Evans, Nathan "Shanks," 173, 175, 181; erratic behavior of, 178, 188n24
Ewell, Richard, 5, 161, 245; and Jackson, 15, 18, 74, 98; memorialization of, 145; in Southern press, 78; wounding of, 6, 78, 158

5th New York Infantry, 187n19, 248; in battle against 5th Texas Infantry, 9, 180, 181; memorial to, 234
5th Texas Infantry: in battle against 5th New York Infantry, 9, 180, 181; casualties in, 183
Franklin, William B.,191, 192
Fredericksburg, VA, 113; civilian sabotage in, 15; Civil War memorialization in, 226, 232; conclusion of Peninsula campaign in, 4, 21, 36, 150; Confederate civilians in, 70, 87, 88; and Confederate forces, 134, 135, 149; and emancipatory war, 40–51, 59n14, 59n16, 60n20, 60n22; evacuation of, 29; and Porter's court-martial, 202, 203, 205; and 6th Wisconsin, 150; and troops commanded by Irving McDowell, 32n11, 39, 40; Union disciplinary problems in, 16; Union loss at, 202, 229; Union supply lines through, 23
Frémont, John C.: advancement of abolition, 16, 102; and demoralization of First Corps command, 18–19; on emancipation proclamation, 16; and formation of Army of Virginia, 17, 32n11, 38, 39, 107; Lincoln's intervention against, 102, 119n18; tensions with Pope, 18–19, 32n13, 58n5, 100

Gainesville, FL, 88, 89; Union pursuit of Confederate forces through, 5, 6, 7, 196
Gainesville, battle of. *See* Brawner Farm, battle of
Gamble, William, 218, 220, 221, 232
Garfield, James A.: assassination of, 211; and obstruction of Porter's reinstatement, 200, 203, 206, 207, 211
Gettysburg, battle of, 160, 164, 167n38; memorialization of, 219, 226, 229, 230, 232
Gibbon, John: as commander of Iron Brigade, 6, 146, 147, 151–59; opposition to emancipatory war, 50, 55; praise for by Northern press, 161; recollections of, 164; resentment toward Pope, 163
Gordonsville, VA, 4, 18, 79, 85, 134, 135
Groveton, VA, 6, 89, 151, 173, 174, 182
Groveton, battle of. *See* Brawner Farm, battle of

Groveton, Union monument at, 218, 219, 220, 228, 229, 231, 233, 236, 237; defacement of, 225; differences from Bull Run monument, 224

Halleck, Henry Wager, 95n49; and Army of Virginia's logistical collapse, 21, 22, 23, 25, 26, 33n19, 34n26; and battle of Fredericksburg, 202, 203; and Confederate retaliatory war, 83, 84, 85; criticism of Pope's hard war, 28; and Lincoln's General Orders No. 100, 80, 81, 94n41; and McClellan-Pope discord, 110, 113, 115, 118n9; and Porter's court-martial, 193, 194, 213n3; and Western operations, 18, 100, 109

hard war, 4, 10, 15, 28, 30n2; and conciliation, 15, 37, 38; Confederate unity and aggression aroused by, 66, 71, 76, 77, 80–89, 114; and home front, 25, 26, 27, 29, 30n2, 34n34, 35n34, 37, 52, 56, 67, 68, 71, 87, 88, 108, 112, 114; McClellan's resistance to, 121; political and strategic implications of, 37; as Pope's way of resolving logistical disorder, 10, 27, 114; during Pope's Western campaigns, 108; Union disillusionment with, 111, 115, 116, 117, 119n12. *See also* Pope, John; Pope, John—general orders of

Harrison's Landing, 73, 81, 108, 110, 113, 133

Heintzelman, Samuel, 5, 7, 23, 33n22, 221, 222, 223

Hennessy, John J., 247

Henry Hill, 9; and Civil War memorialization, 218–26, *221*, 232, 234; Texas Brigade's advance toward, 8, 178, 179

Hood, John Bell: ambitions of distinction, 170; as commander of Texas Brigade, 170; conference with Lee and Longstreet, 175, 177, 181, 187n19; contributions to Confederate victory, 11, 177, 178, 183; distinction during Seven Days campaign, 170; as 4th Texas Infantry colonel, 170; Evander M. Law on, 170; leadership skills of, 178, 181, 182, 183, 185; at Manassas battlefield, 173–83, *176*, 186n10; and march to join Jackson's forces, 171, 173; and orders to withdraw, 175, 187n20; promotion to major general, 185; recollections of, 175; as rising star in Lee's army, 168, *172*; and Sellers, 11, 169, 179, 180, 183, 184, 185; Texan identity of, 171, 179; and Texas Brigade advance toward Henry Hill, 9, 178, 179; at West Point, 169, 186n3

Holt, Joseph, 214n14, 216n53; and Porter's court-martial, 194–203, 204, 209, 210; and Porter's petition for rehearing, 206, 207

home front: and Davis, 131, 132, 134; and Jackson, 89; and Lee's strategy, 67, 68, 71, 72, 73, 76, 125, 126, 136, 139; and Stuart, 75; Union, 104. *See also* civilians, Confederate; hard war; press, Northern; press, Southern; women, diary accounts of

Iron Brigade, 182; commemoration of, 145, 146; courage and enthusiasm of, 147, 164; and Gibbon, 55; historiography of, 165n10, 249; impact of Brawner Farm battle on, 11, 160; postwar reunion, 163. *See also* Brawner Farm, battle of; Gibbon, John; 6th Wisconsin

Jackson, Thomas "Stonewall," 15, 18, 22, 64, 83, 86, 115, 130, 149, 155; at Brawner Farm, 6, 152, 158, 171; at Cedar Mountain, 4, 19, 114, 134, 150; correspondence with Lee, 28, 114; flanking maneuver commanded by, 76; in foreign press, 72; on Manassas battlefield, 6, 7, 8, 12, 19, 173, 174, 178, 183, 190, 196, 206, 207, 210; as part of Lee's offensive strategy, 4, 5, 74, 75, 133, 134, 135, 136, 137; as revered by Confederacy, 66, 75, 77, 78, 79, 80, 87, 89, 90, 94n37; at Seven Days, 75, 92n24, 133, 170; in

Southern press, 77, 78; at Shenandoah Valley, 1, 16, 76, 98, 131, 132
James River, 3, 21, 67, 73, 113, 135, 136
Johnson, Andrew: impeachment of, 207; on Joint Committee on the Conduct of the War, 103, 120n28; and Porter's court-martial, 206
Johnson, Reverdy, 194, 195, 197, 198, 199
Johnston, Joseph E., 93n29, 107; Confederacy's dismay with, 72; and Davis, 130; military passivity of, 10, 66, 72, 73; and retreat, 76, 77; wounded in battle, 75, 132
Joint Committee on the Conduct of the War: and Ball's Bluff incident, 103, 104; Pope's testimony before, 62n49, 108, 109, 117; and Radical Republicans, 103–9, 120n28, 121n35, 121n36

King, Rufus, 18, 151, 32n11; mistrust of information from "contrabands," 61n36; at Brawner Farm, 6, 150, 153, 158; promotion to divisional command, 147; and John Washington, 49

Law, Evander M., 178, 187n20; and advance on Union battery, 174, 175; at Dogan Ridge, 182; at Groveton, 173; Hood's praise of, 171; on Hood, 170; and regimental casualties, 183
Lee, Robert E., 158; civilian depictions of, 67, 68, 70, 71, 80; in Civil War memorialization, 219, 229; in Civil War scholarship, 245, 246; and conclusion of Second Manassas campaign, 2, 138; and Confederate strategy of unremitting aggression, 10, 11, 28, 66, 76, 83, 85, 86, 114, 124–39, *138*, 140n8, 143n61; culture of command of, 4, 5, 66, 74, 75, 76, 77, 92n22, 133, 137, 138, 142n36; and Davis, 82, 94n35; in foreign press, 72; general orders of, 139; and Halleck, 84, 85, 95n49; as head of Military Department of South Carolina, Georgia, and East Florida, 11, 126–30, 140n6, 141n26; and Henry Hill, 8; and Hood, 168, 169, 171, 173, 175, 177, 178, 183, 185, 187n19; as ineffective leader, 73; and Jackson's shadow, 66, 74, 78, 79, 80, 90, 92n25; as less cautious than Davis, 142n28; and Longstreet, 187n12; and Lost Cause myth, 139, 144n62; military education of, 125, 126, 140, 140n4, 140n5; mistakes of, 143n61; and Porter's court-martial, 206; praise from Southern press, 69, 70, 73, 77; in postwar discussion with Allan, 124, 125, 138, 139, 174; recollections of, 174; rise to command, 2; and Seven Days battles, 16, 65, 72, 133, 142n36; success at Shenandoah Valley, 4; and Union high command discord, 3; vilification of Pope by, 86, 114
Lincoln, Abraham, 28, 106; appointment of Pope as Army of Virginia commander, 4, 17, 31n8, 97, 100, 111, 133; as commander in chief, 3, 15, 16, 31n4, 37; and dedication ceremony of Bull Run and Groveton monuments, 222; and Emancipation Act, District of Columbia, 40; and emancipation as war measure, 38, 53, 54; and Emancipation Proclamation, 55; and formation of Army of Virginia, 4, 133; General Orders No. 100, 81, 94n41; and McClellan, 3, 4, 10, 28, 192, 193; in Northern press, 110, 202, 203; and political-military tensions, 102; and Pope, 5, 12, 32n10, 34n32, 94, 115; and Porter's court-martial, 190, 191, 192, 193, 196, 199, 204, 205, 209; and preliminary emancipation proclamation, 65, 122n57; reaction to emancipation policy of, 81, 102, 119n18, 120n22; removal of Pope from command, 5, 12, 115; and Second Confiscation Act, 52; in Southern press, 85, 86; support for confiscation policies in Missouri, 28, 35; tensions with Radical Republicans, 101, 102, 103, 107, 117n4, 120n20
Logan, John A., 211, 212

Longstreet, James: and Army of Virginia's logistical collapse, 6, 115, 117n3; Confederacy's approval of, 76, 78, 79; and Confederate flanking attack, 8, 9; in historiography, 246; and Hood, 168, 171, 173, 174, 175, 177, 178, 179, 180, 181, 183; and Law, 182, 187; in Lee's culture of command, 7, 66, 74, 75, 92n22, 133, 134, 135, 136, 137, 158, 187n12; and Porter's court-martial, 206, 209, 210; recollections of, 173, 177, 187n12, 245; success of during Seven Days battles, 74, 75

Lost Cause myth, 12, 86, 139, 140n7, 144n62, 230

Manassas campaign, First, 12, 171

Manassas campaign, Second, 2; memory and memorialization of, 2, 12, 145, 221, 222–26, 228, 229, 231, 232, 235, 236; and other military engagements in June–September 1862, 65–72, 79; summary of events, 3–9; terminology for, 3, 90n1; terrain of, 8, 9; as testing ground for Lee's command style, 10, 11, 66, 72–80; and ties between military operations and politics, 3, 10–12, 17, 37, 38, 53, 55, 56, 81, 98–103, 115–17, 119n14, 146, 192, 213n3; as transformative phase of Confederacy, 1, 2, 10, 65–66, 67, 68, 76; as transformative phase of Confederate style of war, 1, 9, 10, 66, 67, 80–90; scholarship of, 2, 3, 65, 243–49. *See also* Bull Run campaign, Second

Manassas Gap Railroad, 5, 6, 22

Manassas Junction, 6, 69, 88, 150, 171, 196, 209; recapture of enslaved people at, 64n63; Union supply depot at, 5, 78, 151

Maryland campaign, 185; and Civil War historiography, 90n2, 248; Confederate public's optimism about, 67, 70, 71, 77, 78, 79, 80; and Evans, 188n24; and Lee, 2, 3, 10, 11, 66; and McClellan, 192. *See also* Antietam, battle of

Massachusetts, 22, 39, 48, 49, 103

McClellan, George B., 9, 65; administrative skills of, 10, 16, 28; and Army of Potomac's pragmatism, 48; on blame for Ball's Bluff defeat, 104; in Civil War scholarship, 243; conciliatory views and tactics of, 11, 14, 28, 38, 39, 54, 55, 61n38, 63n59, 81, 98, 108, 112, 117n6, 118n6; Confederate civilian perspective on, 70, 73, 80; as Democratic presidential candidate, 205, 206, 208; failure at Seven Days, 16, 81, 97, 107, 108; and Joint Committee on the Conduct of the War, 103, 104, 108, 109, 110, 121n36; and Robert E. Lee, 73, 75, 76, 82, 133, 134, 135, 136; loyalty of soldiers to, 116; opposition to emancipatory war, 4, 54, 55, 81; and Pope, 3, 9, 18, 21, 26, 28, 32n12, 34n27, 55, 100, 107, 109, 110, 111, 113, 190, 191, 194; and Peninsula campaign, 3, 4, 16, 32n12, 67, 74, 97, 98, 102, 133; and Porter's court-martial, 12, 191, 192, 193, 194, 197, 202, 204, 205; on Republican leadership, 16, 17, 28; removal from command of Army of Potomac, 193; Republican contempt for, 17, 100, 101, 103, 104, 105, 107, 115, 116, 191, 192, 193; and Stanton, 100, 118n9

McDowell, Irvin, 9, 19, 53, 54, 148; and Army of Virginia's logistical collapse, 6, 7, 22, 23, 26; and enslaved refugees, 40, 42, 44, 47, 48, 49; and First Bull Run defeat, 102; and formation and dismantling of Army of Virginia, 17, 32n11, 55, 100, 107; personality of, 39; on Pope's narrative of defeat, 115, 193, 202; and Porter's court-martial, 193, 196, 202, 203, 204, 206, 210; and 6th Wisconsin, 148, 150, 151; support for conciliatory war, 39, 58n7

Meigs, Montgomery: and Army of Virginia's logistical collapse, 21, 25; and Civil War memorialization, 222, 227, 228, 229 memory and memorialization: and Blue-Grey reunions, 225, 230; and condemnation of rebel cause, 223, 224, 225; and Grand Army of the Republic, 231, 232, 233, 234, 235; and Grand Review of the Armies, 219, 220; and human cost of war, 237; interplay with contemporary politics, economics, and culture, 219, 230, 237, 238; and Lost Cause myth, 12, 139, 230; and reconciliationist sentiment, 225, 237, 230, 235, 236; and semicentennial, 235, 237; and United Daughters of the Confederacy, 234, 236, 237, 241n52. *See also* monuments; veterans

Missouri: Confederate portrait of Pope's savagery in, 82, 84, 85; Frémont's emancipation proclamation in, 102, 119n18; Union pacification of, 15, 16, 18, 28, 29, 30n2, 35n34, 35n35, 80, 81, 108, 118n12

monuments: Francis S. Bartow, 220, 221; Bull Run (at Henry Hill), 12, 220, *221*, 228, 229, 233; Bull Run and Groveton dedication ceremony, 218–25, 221; Chickamauga, 12, 219, 230, 232; Confederate cemetery at Groveton, 234; defacement of, 221, 225; efforts to build national park on Bull Run battlefield, 231–37; erected during war, 220, 221; at Gettysburg battlefield, 219, 226, 229, 230; and grave desecration, 225, 226, 227; Groveton (Union), 12, 218, 219, 220, 224, 225, 228, 229, 231, 233, 236, 237; and Manassas Battlefield Corporation, 237; and Manassas National Battlefield Park, 237; martial nature of, 224; neglect of, 228, 229, 235; in Northern press, 225; proposed Bull Run national cemetery, 226, 227; reinterment of Union soldier remains at Arlington Cemetery, 227–28; to Union cause, 225, 230. *See also* memory and memorialization; veterans; veterans associations

Navy, US, 126, 127, 128

New Orleans, LA, 67; Confederate portrait of Union savagery in, 84, 85

Orange & Alexandria Railroad, 5, 47, 57, 74, 78, 150, 227

Pendleton, William Nelson, 137, 138

Peninsula campaign, 11; and Army of Northern Virginia, 2; and Army of the Potomac, 149; and emancipation, 42, 59n16, 89, 107; and Fredericksburg, 4, 21, 36, 150; and McClellan, 3, 4, 16, 67, 74, 97, 98, 102, 133; and narrative of Lee's rise to command, 2; Union failures during, 37, 70, 97, 111, 229. *See also* Seven Days battles

Pennsylvania: Confederate forces in, 67; and Joint Committee on the Conduct of the War, 103, 120n128; and Lee's strategy, 133; press in, 53. *See also* Gettysburg, battle of

Piedmont, 39, 44, 48, 72, 77

Pollard, Edward A., 1, 71, 72

Pope, John: as Army of Virginia commander, 2, 4, 16, 17, 38, 97, 100, 105–10; and Banks, 19, 26, 32n14; biographies of, 117n3; on emancipation, 4, 15, 17, 29, 31n9, 32n9, 52, 62n49; in Civil War scholarship, 243, 244, 245; defeat and reassignment of, 9, 24, 55, 56, 138; disdain toward subordinates, 7, 10, 18, 20, 25, 29, 33n16, 163; and Frémont, 18–19, 32n13, 58n5, 100; and hard war, 4, 10, 15, 16, 28, 80–89, 97, 108; and Lincoln, 4, 5, 12, 17, 31n8, 32n10, 34n32, 94, 97, 100, 105, 111, 115, 133; and McClellan, 18, 21, 26, 28, 32n12, 34n27, 100, 107, 109, 110, 111, 113, 190, 191, 194; and Porter's court-martial, 12, 191, 197, 198, 207; pragmatic motives of, 15, 27, 28, 29, 35n35, 35n36, 52; as Radical Republicans' hope, 100, 101, 105–10, 115, 117; self-serving narrative of defeat of, 190, 191, *192*, 207;

Pope, John (*continued*)
shortcomings as commander, 7, 10, 19, 20, 27, 33n22, 34n28, 114, 115, 116, 118n11, 150; and Sigel, 19, 26, 27; and Stanton, 35n36, 106, 107; support for emancipatory war, 107, 108; as tool for implementing political and social change, 38; Union disillusionment with, 111, 115, 116, 117, 119n12; vilification of by Lee, 86; and West Point, 4, 15, 17, 105–6. *See also* hard war; Pope, John—general orders of
—general orders of, 81, 110; as attempt to resolve logistical disorder, 10, 27, 114; contributions to Confederate retributive war, 14, 66, 67, 84, 89; heralding shift to hard war, 30n2, 82, 111, 112, 118n12, 119n12; No. 3, 27; No. 3 (1861 Missouri), 35; No. 5, 27, 82, 88, 111, 112; No. 6, 27, 112; No. 7, 27, 82, 88, 112; No. 11, 28, 34n32, 82, 83, 87, 94n44, 112; No. 12, 31n3; No. 13, 112; No. 19, 28, 29; omission of African Americans from, 4, 15, 29
Porter, Fitz John: deferred reinstatement of, 211, 212; as Pope's scapegoat for Army of Virginia's defeat, 191, 192, 195; as proxy for McClellan, 191, 205; public scorn of, 205, 215n47; recollections of, 213n7, 214n21; at West Point, 191, 208
—court-martial of, 9, 12, 193, 194, 243; and "charge stacking," 196–97, 214n21; collapse of case in 1878, 208–11, 216n56; an court's bias for prosecution, 193–95, 198, 199, 200, 202–5, 213n7, 213n10, 214n12, 214n14; and exoneration, 9, 200; and Holt's review, 204; and inconsistencies in Pope's testimony, 198, 199; and objections from defense, 195, 196; and petitions for rehearing, 205–6, 207, 208, 215n52; and Reverdy Johnson's cross-examination of Pope, 197, 198, 199; and testimony of Thomas C. H. Smith, 201, 202. *See also* Holt, Joseph
press, Northern: and Civil War memorialization, 223, 225; on emancipation, 50, 54; hatchet job on McClellan by, 206; on military service and conscription, 162, 163; on political interference in military operations, 202, 203; and 6th Wisconsin, 160, 161, 162; and Stanton, 101; support for Pope's hard war, *83*, 84, 86, 109, 110, 112, 113
press, Southern: on Lee, 73, 77; praise for Jackson, 77, 78; praise for retaliatory Confederate war, 85; praise for Hood, 168; reproach of Pope's hard war, 84, 85, 86, 87, 114; on Second Manassas campaign, 1, 67, 69, 77

Radical Republicans. *See* Republicans, Radical
Rapidan River, 4, 5, 43, 56, 77, 136
Rappahannock River, 5, 6, 29, 68, 69, 71, 72, 86, 136, 137; and Arlington Cemetery inscription, 228; and Army of Virginia's encounters with slavery, 36, 45, 47, 48, 57; Cow Ford crossing at, 56, 57, *57*; and 6th Wisconsin, 150
Republican Party: and 1862 elections, 97, 193; and Andrew Johnson, 120n28; and Pope, 16, 17, 29, 106; and Porter's conviction, 205; and ties to Union high command, 19; and Union soldiers' voting preferences, 122n62. *See also* Republicans, Radical
Republicans, Radical: on aggression against Confederacy, 98, 121n35; and debates over government management of war, 101, 102, 117n4; on emancipatory war, 101, 102, 103, 117n4; and Joint Committee on the Conduct of the War, 103, 104, 105; opposition to McClellan, 100, 103, 104, 105, 121n36; and Pope, 100, 101, 105–10, 115, 116, 117
Richmond, VA, 70, *83*, 129, 170; and Army of the Potomac, 3, 4, 16, 18, 67; civilians in, 87; and Confederacy's aggressive posture, 68, 69, 72, 73, 74, 75, 76, 77, 79, 85, 86, 91n15, 131, 132, 133, 134, 135, 136, 137; and emancipation, 81, 94n42; McClellan's failure to capture, 100, 102,

108, 112, 191, 202; and McDowell, 39; memorial cemetery in, 226; and Pope, 98, 109, 113; and railway connections, 22, 76; and Seven Days battles, 3, 4, 65; and 6th Wisconsin, 149, 150; and slavery, 49, 59n14
Ricketts, James B., 6, 32n11, 54, 55
Roberts, Benjamin S.: and Porter's court-martial, 195, 198, 200, 204, 206; reputation for deception, 195, 202
Ropes, John Codman, 246, 247
Round, George Carr, 231–37
Ruggles, George D.: and Army of Virginia's supply line problems, 23; and Pope-Porter tensions, 197, 198; and Pope's poor administrative skills, 19

Savannah, GA, 72; and Lee, 126, 127, 141n26
Schenck, Robert C.: and poor army administration, 26; and tensions with Pope, 18, 19, 20, 32n13
Sellers, William Harvey: military service in Mexico, 179; poor performance of, 177, 183, 184, 185; praise from Hood for, 169, 179, 183; and Texas Brigade's advance toward Henry Hill, 178, 179, 180, 181, 182
Seven Days battles, 171; and historiography, 90n2, 243, 248; Hood's fame in, 170; Jackson's complicated record at, 75, 133; and Lincoln's push for emancipation, 81, 94n42, 107; Longstreet's success during, 74, 75; and rise of Lee's command, 3, 16, 65, 72, 73, 79, 133, 137, 142n36, 243; and Second Manassas campaign, 3, 65, 71, 80, 90n2, 243. *See also* Peninsula campaign
Seward, William, 81, 111, 115
Sharpsburg, battle of, 68, 69, 72, 183, 230. *See also* Antietam, battle of
Shenandoah Valley, 5, 36, 48, 68, 69; Jackson's success in, 4, 16, 39, 76, 79, 89, 98, 131, 132; in Lee's strategy, 16; and Pope's general orders, 82, 112, 114; Texas Brigade in, 170; Union commands in, 4, 15, 107; Union soldiers' encounters with enslaved people in, 39, 41, 45; and Union supply line problems, 21
Shiloh, battle of: in Civil War memorialization, 12, 219, 230; and Union high command discord, 109; Union victory at, 37, 67
Sigel, Franz, 6; antislavery views of, 38, 39, 62n49, 100; and Brawner Farm battle, 156; and Confederate guerillas, 31n3; and enslaved refugees, 47, 48; and formation of Army of Virginia, 107; and tensions with Pope, 19, 26, 27
6th Wisconsin, 11, 145, *156*; bravery of, 155, 156, 157; at Brawner Farm, 160, 163, 164; casualties in, 155, 157, 158, 159, 160; on combat, 148, 149, 151, 152; and corpses of Confederate soldiers, 150; as example of Army of Potomac's mettle, 164; formation of, 146, 147; home front of, 160–63; and incompetence of army and corps commanders, 146, 159, 163; leadership in, 159; overrun by Jackson's forces, 155; press coverage of, 160, 161, 162; and run-up to Second Bull Run, 150. *See also* Brawner Farm, battle of; Iron Brigade
slavery: as context for understanding Second Manassas campaign, 10; inevitability of war's disruption to, 40, 46, 119n13; moral opposition to, 41, 51, 53; in Second Bull Run campaign memorialization, 12, 219, 222, 224, 238n7; and Union army leadership, 101; Union government debates on, 52, 98. *See also* African Americans; Army of Virginia—members of; emancipation; enslaved people; enslavers; Pope, John
Stanton, Edward: and Army of Virginia's ruin, 15, 16, 115; and Joint Committee on the Conduct of the War, 103; in Northern press, 101, 202; and Pope's general orders, 35n36; and Porter's court-martial, 193, 194, 195, 200, 203, 213n7, 213n10, 214n14; as secretary of war, 206, 207;

Stanton, Edward (*continued*)
support for Pope as alternative to McClellan, 16, 17, 52, 100, 106, 107; and tensions with McClellan, 100, 118n9; and Union problems with railroads, 22
Stone, Charles: as anti-emancipation Democrat, 101; blamed for Ball's Bluff incident, 104
Stuart, J. E. B., 23, 92n23; and Lee's culture of command, 66, 74, 76, 134, 137; and military intelligence, 5, 7, 75, 136; in Southern press, 78
Sumner, Charles, 94n42, 101
Swinton, William, 205–6

Texas Brigade: advance toward Henry Hill, 169, 178, 179, 180; casualties in, 175, 181, 183; and fighting at close quarters, 173–75; and Hood's confidence in Sellers, 11, 169, 179, 180, 183, 184, 185; and Law's brigade, 182; and march to join Jackson's wing of Army of Northern Virginia, 171; and orders to withdraw, 177; praise for, 168, 170. *See also* Hood, John Bell
Thoroughfare Gap, 5, 6, 26, 34n29, 171
Tyler, R. W., 226, 227

Union high command, discord within, 55, 100, 103, 116; and Lee, 3; and Lincoln, 3, 115; and Pope, 15, 18, 19, 109. *See also* Pope, John: and McClellan
United Daughters of the Confederacy (UDC): and Confederate monuments, 234, 236, 237, 241n52
Upton, John C.: appointment by Hood to command advanced guard, 171, 173; death of, 181

veterans, 3; and Civil War memorialization, 12, 219, 224, 226, 229, 230, 231, 232, 235, 236, 237; and Porter's court-martial, 211, 212; recollections of, 150, 164, 170, 173, 174, 175, 177, 187n12, 213n7, 214n21, 244, 245, 246, 248. *See also* memory and memorialization: Grand Army of the Republic; monuments; veterans associations
veterans associations, 163; Grand Army of the Republic, 231, 232, 233, 234, 235, 240n39, 241n45; Society of the Army of the Potomac, 234; Sons of Confederate Veterans, 237. *See also* memory and memorialization; monuments; veterans
Virginia: and Army of Virginia's retreat, 29; civilian sabotage in, 15; and Civil War memorialization, 222, 226, 235, 236; Confederate bushwhacking in, 16; conservative political and military culture in, 52; Lee's 1861 field command in, 11; Lee's retreat to, 229; legislature of, 231; and 6th Wisconsin, 148, 149, 160, 161, 163, 165; slavery in, 39, 40, 45, 46, 47, 50, 51, 52, 56, 57. *See also specific places and battles in*

Wade, Benjamin: and Joint Committee on the Conduct of the War, 103, 120n28; opposition to slavery, 101, 102
War Department, Confederate, 134, 135; general orders of, 83, 84, 126; war strategy of, 130
War Department, US: and Civil War memorialization, 219, 220, 228, 232, 236, 237; and historiography of Second Manassas campaign, 243; and Hood, 171; poor management of, 18; and Pope, 106, 107; and Porter's court-martial, 193, 207, 208, 213n7
Warrenton Turnpike, 6, 7, 147, 151, 158, 174, 177, 178, 180, 182, 185; geography and physical relief of, 152; Hood-Jackson meeting on, 173; memorial gateway at, 234
Washington, DC: and Civil War memorialization, 219, 220, 221, 226; and December 1861 session of Congress, 102; Emancipation Act in, 40, 42; and enslaved refugees, 45, 52; and Grand Review of the Armies, 219, 220; and Lincoln's inauguration, 32n10; Military

District of, 47; Pope's retreat to, 9, 29, 70, 76, 190; Pope's tour of, 11, 16, 17, 98, 101, 105–9, 111; rumors of evacuation from, 97; slavery in, 40, 97; and transportation routes, 22, 23, 47; Union army's defense of, 4, 21, 108, 191. *See also* Congress, US; Joint Committee on the Conduct of the War
Welles, Gideon: and Lincoln's position on emancipation, 81, 111; on McClellan-Pope tensions, 111, 191; on McClellan-Stanton tensions, 100, 118n9; on West Point theory and instruction, 121n35
West Point, 103; and Hood, 169, 186n3; and King, 147; and Lee, 125, 126, 140n5; and Pope, 4, 15, 17, 105–6; and Porter, 191, 208; Republican criticism of instruction at, 105, 121n35; and Stone, 104
William, Sherman: and Grand Review of the Armies, 219, 220; and Porter's court-martial, 207
Wilson, Woodrow, 236
Winchester, VA, 20, 68, 69; enslaved people in, 41, 47, 59n16, 60n21, 89; memorial cemetery in, 226; occupation by Federal troops, 70; residents of, 70, 80, 87
Wofford, William T., 179, 181, 182, 184, 185
women, diary accounts of, 1, 2, 67, 70, 71, 79, 80, 87, 88, 89, 91n13

Zouaves. *See* 5th New York Infantry Regiment